SHAPING SEATTLE ARCHITECTURE

A Historical Guide to the Architects

SHAPING SEATTLE ARCHITECTURE

A Historical Guide to the Architects

Jeffrey Karl Ochsner, *editor*

Editorial Board

Dennis A. Andersen
Duane A. Dietz
Katheryn Hills Krafft
David A. Rash
Thomas Veith

ARCHITECTURE
BUILDING ON 100 YEARS

AIA IN WASHINGTON
1894-1994

SHAPING SEATTLE ARCHITECTURE

A Historical Guide to the Architects

Jeffrey Karl Ochsner, *editor*

University of Washington Press, Seattle and London
in association with the American Institute of Architects Seattle Chapter
and the Seattle Architectural Foundation

Publishing Partners

AIA Seattle and Seattle Architectural Foundation, with

Ralph Anderson

Anhalt Graham Properties Inc.

John Graham Associates

Loschky Marquardt & Nesholm

NBBJ

Shannon & Wilson, Inc.

The Naramore Foundation

TRA Architecture Engineering Planning Interiors

Shaping Seattle Architecture : a historical guide to the architects /
    Jeffrey Karl Ochsner, editor.
        p.   cm.
    Includes bibliographical references and index.
    ISBN 0-295-97365-X (cloth).— ISBN 0-295-97366-8 (paper)
    1. Architects—Washington (State)—Seattle—Biography.
2. Architecture—Washington (State)—Seattle—History.
3. Seattle (Wash.)—Buildings, structures, etc.   I. Ochsner, Jeffrey Karl.
NA735.S45S53   1994
720' .92 ' 2797772—dc20   94-17618
                                                 CIP

Contents

Acknowledgments

A publication of this kind is possible only because of the combined support of many individuals. No one person could have carried out the research and writing necessary to produce this collection of essays. First, of course, there would be no book without the contributions of the authors who prepared the essays that form its text. The efforts of others should be recognized as well.

The idea of preparing a publication to coincide with the celebration, in 1994, of the one hundredth anniversary of the establishment of the American Institute of Architects in Seattle and Washington State was initiated and supported beginning in 1991 by Norman J. Johnston FAIA, Professor Emeritus at the University of Washington, and Marga Rose Hancock, Executive Vice President of AIA Seattle.

The Editorial Board, which includes Dennis A. Andersen, Duane A. Dietz, Katheryn Hills Krafft, David A. Rash, and Thomas Veith, was formed in mid-1991. This group met regularly over more than two years and was responsible for determining the architects to be included, identifying potential authors, establishing guidelines, reviewing submissions, and preparing the section on additional architects. The members of the Editorial Board also carried out their own research and were responsible for a significant number of the essays. All of the essays were subject to an intensive review by members of this board and by anonymous reviewers in the fashion typical of scholarly publications.

Several members of the Editorial Board offered supplemental assistance, without which this book would not have approached its present level of accuracy, completeness, and consistency. David Rash provided additional factual information and references for many essays; Dennis Andersen provided assistance in locating photographs for some of the essays; and Duane Dietz made available his catalogue of Seattle architects and landscape architects as the basis for beginning the listing of the additional architects. Finally, the editorial and format consistency throughout is due in part to the efforts of Thomas Veith.

Others who helped in the production of this work in many important ways include Richard Engeman, Gary Menges, Kristen Kinsey, Sandra Kroupa, Susan Cunningham, and Carla Rickerson at Special Collections and Preservation Division, University of Washington Libraries; Rick Caldwell and Carolyn Marr at the Library of the Museum of History and Industry, Seattle; Joann Fenton and others at the Art and Music Department of the Seattle Public Library; and Paul Dorpat. In addition, T. William Booth took photographs of many buildings for which historical photographs could not be found.

Others who helped one or more individual authors are listed below (in alphabetical order): Leon Alpaugh, Whatcom Genealogical Society, Bellingham; Michael Andersen, Butte-Silver Bow Public Library, Butte, Montana; Ernest "Bud" Anderson; Gerald Y. Arai; Laura Arksey, Cheney Cowles Museum, Spokane; Carol Axtman; William J. Bain, Jr.; Betty Balcom; Fred Bassetti; Mary Bassetti; Herbert Bittman; Charles O. Brantigan, Denver; Christine Carr; Nick Cirelli, Engineering Department, City of Seattle; Clarence Copeland, DCLU, City of Seattle; Shirley Courtois; David Dennis, DCLU, City of Seattle; David Dilgard, Everett Public Library—Northwest Room;

Robert L. Durham; Virjean H. Edwards, Assistant Registrar for Records, University of Washington; Robert H. Egan; Thom Emrich, Mithun Partners; David Gebhard, University of California, Santa Barbara; Carolyn Giese; Carl F. Gould, Jr.; Frederick A. Graham; Loretta Zwolak Green, Sisters of Providence Archives, Seattle; Gary Griffith, State of Washington Office of Archaeology and Historic Preservation, Olympia; Jane Hastings; Yoshio Hata, Yakima Buddhist Church, Wapato; Warren Hill, University of Washington; Joseph Holmes; John C. Houghton, Oakland, California; Mr. and Mrs. Daniel R. Huntington III, Snohomish; Art Hupy, LaConner; George Iseri, Idaho-Oregon Buddhist Temple, Ontario, Oregon; Phillip L. Jacobson, University of Washington; Laura Johnson, Callison Partnership; Roderick Kirkwood, John Graham Associates; Lawrence Kreisman; Martha Lamb; Cathleen Latendresse, Ford Museum, Greenfield Village, Michigan; Alan Lathrop, Northwest Architectural Archives, University of Minnesota Libraries, St. Paul; Ruth Lea; Carol Lichtenberg, Archives, Manuscripts and Special Collections Division, Washington State University Libraries; Wendell Lovett; Garold Malcolm, McAdoo, Malcolm & Youel; Jane MacGowan; Thelma McAdoo; Richard F. McCann, Pasadena, California; Elaine Miller, Washington State Historical Society, Tacoma; Don Mumford; Ibsen Nelson; Janet Ness, Manuscripts and University Archives Division, University of Washington Libraries; Ed Nolan, Washington State Historical Society, Tacoma; Folke Nyberg, University of Washington; Marion O'Brien, DCLU, City of Seattle; Office of Urban Conservation of the City of Seattle; Michael Olson, Gallaudet University Archives, Washington, D.C.; Betty J. Pfouts, Jefferson County Historical Society, Port Townsend; Celia Porto, NBBJ; Elizabeth Walton Potter, Eugene, Oregon; Mary Randlett, Bainbridge Island; Margaret Riddle, Everett Public Library—Northwest Room; Mr. and Mrs. John Rohrer; Lisa A. Schneider, San Francisco; Lyle J. Schreiber, Rice County Historical Society, Faribault, Minnesota; Robert M. Shields; Peter Staten; Peter Steinbrueck; Todd Strand, North Dakota State Historical Society, Bismarck; David Streatfield, University of Washington; William Strong, Mahlum & Nordfors; Daniel Taylor, Bittman Vammen Taylor; Linda Thatcher, Utah State Historical Society, Salt Lake City; Gary Thomas, Gallaudet University Archives, Washington, D.C.; Mikki Tint, Oregon Historical Society, Portland, Oregon; Eleanor Toews, Archivist, Seattle School District #1; Eduardo Tolentino, DCLU, City of Seattle; Deborah Walker; Roberta T. Walker, The Bumgardner Architects; Betsy Whitesell, NBBJ; Carolyn S. Willberg, Ellensburg Public Library; Robert Winskill, Mill Valley, California; David Wright, The Bumgardner Architects; Sadie Yamasaki, Seattle Buddhist Temple Archives; Richard Youel, McAdoo, Malcolm & Youel.

The Seattle Architectural Foundation and the Naramore Foundation both provided early financial support, which made possible the acquisition of over five hundred photographs. Additional financial assistance, as recognized elsewhere in this book, made its publication possible.

Finally, this book would not have been possible without the contributions of individuals who made an effort to preserve the architectural records of previous generations. In particular, the early efforts of Victor Steinbrueck, Robert Monroe, Richard Berner, Karyl Winn, and Norman Johnston, who began assembling architectural drawings and other materials at the Special Collections and Preservation Division and the Manuscripts and University Archives Division at the University of Washington Libraries, should be recognized. Their work preserving records of the region's architectural heritage has been the basis for a substantial portion of the research that led to this book.

Jeffrey Karl Ochsner, May 1994

Seattle School District Architect's offices, ca.1908. Ink on linen architectural drawings for several brick model schools are visible within this view. *(Washington State Historical Society, Tacoma; ca. 1908; photo by Asahel Curtis, 13729.)*

Preface

JEFFREY KARL OCHSNER

The shape of the architecture of any region can be said to result from the intersection of many influences such as tradition, available technology and materials, climate, economics, and changing aesthetic considerations. It might also be said that buildings reflect the ideas and values of a variety of individuals including their patrons, builders, users, and designers. To focus exclusively on a single characteristic or group involved in the building of a city is to fail to tell the full story of how that place was created. Nonetheless, it is necessary that one's focus be narrowed in order to limit the scope of inquiry and make possible a fruitful investigation.

This book is a historical introduction to some of Seattle's architects, offering a set of profiles of some of the most important architects in the city's history. Such a guide seemed an appropriate publication to mark the one hundredth anniversary, in 1994, of the presence of the American Institute of Architects, the largest and oldest national organization for architectural professionals, in Seattle and Washington State. While not a guide to Seattle buildings, nor a history of Seattle architecture, this book can provide an introductory perspective on the architecture of the city because of the role that architects have played in the design of its built environment.

Architects and Architecture

The practice of architecture is based on the concept that architects, like other professionals, provide services. Architects develop ideas for the design of three-dimensional form and convey these through two-dimensional drawings and written specifications. The architect is more than a drafter. Drawings and specifications are not considered products; rather, they are referred to as "instruments of service," because they embody ideas.

Design has always been central to the contribution of the architect to the built environment, and in profiling the architects of Seattle, this book can begin to offer an introduction to some of the ideas these architects have applied in shaping the city.

The architectural design process is sufficiently complex that the architect's role has come to be recognized as twofold. First, the architect is almost always responsible for the form of the project. Indeed, it has often been customary to speak of the architect as the "form-giver." Of course, the form of any building is not a result simply of the architect's decisions, but is affected by a broad range of factors such as client demands, functional requirements, site constraints, available technology, budget, zoning and building codes, and the like. However, two architects given the same project with exactly the same constraints are unlikely to come up with identical designs. Thus the design role is critical.

The architect also usually plays a second role—that of leader of the design team—and although it is customary to speak of a building as being "by" a particular architect or firm, very few buildings are designed and built by a single individual or even a single firm. Collaboration is a part of every project—between individuals in the architect's office, between an architect and consultants, such as engineers and landscape architects, between the architect and the contractor who actually constructs the project. Nonetheless, the architect is most often responsible for the direction or coordination of the effort that results in the design.

Throughout most of the nineteenth and twentieth centuries, historians' evaluations of architectural works have tended to place the greatest emphasis on visual character and artistic innovation. Creative approaches to economic feasibility, functionality, and technology have sometimes been recognized, but artistry has been the primary value on which works have been judged. Thus, the size of an architect's office or the number or size of the works the architect produced are not usually determining factors.

Fame in architecture can be fleeting and an architect who is recognized as a leader in one generation may be forgotten by later generations. Until recently there was often a tendency to make retroactive judgments in architectural history—that is, to determine the worthiness of past design efforts according to current design preferences and directions and to rewite historical narratives to fit new preferences. In the last two decades, however, the judgment of architecture exclusively according to contemporary visual standards has been challenged. Recently historians have begun to argue that works must be "contextualized": they should be judged according to the context in which they were created, not according to current standards retroactively applied. Further, judgments of significance inevitably lead to the question "Significant to whom?"

Judgments of significance must be recognized as being relative and subject to the influence of temporal factors. The reexamination of previous periods of history and the critique of earlier judgments are parts of the process of constructing a historical narrative. In architecture, for example, many architects and historians of the post–World War II period, influenced by Modernism, attacked much of the architecture of the earlier decades of the twentieth century. Today, with a new recognition of a plurality of approaches, a reassessment of the architecture of that period is taking place. Clearly such revisions mean that the determination of any list of significant architects must be subject to review and possible future change. Some of the architects included in this book may be viewed less favorably in the future while others not included might be seen to have been more important.

Architects in Seattle

Of the forty-eight illustrated essays in this book, forty-five describe the careers and designs of individual architects or, in several cases, partnerships, that are recognized as significant in Seattle's history. The selection of individuals for inclusion was difficult because, as noted, significance in architecture is so difficult to judge.

Architects currently actively practicing are not included in the essays. Difficult as it was to determine who among past practitioners should be included, it would have been impossible to make judgments about currently practicing architects. From the beginning it was decided that this would be a "historical" guide and that active practitioners would not be addressed in the text.

The architects who are included were selected for a variety of reasons. Most important, they all practiced in Seattle. Some may have practiced elsewhere, either before or after their Seattle careers, but in almost every case these practitioners maintained a Seattle office for a number of years. This is not to indicate that all of their designs were necessarily executed in Seattle. For example, in the late nineteenth century, Willis Ritchie designed courthouses and other major institutional buildings for cities and towns across western Washington from his Seattle office. In the early twentieth century, the Beezer Brothers designed buildings across the Far West for the Roman Catholic Church. And, after World War II, John Graham, Jr., created the paradigm for the regional shopping center at Northgate and then, over a number of years, designed similar projects all over the United States.

The term "architect" was construed broadly in making selections. While most of the individuals who are profiled practiced as professional architects—that is designers of buildings—a few had careers that were not strictly architectural. For example, Mother Joseph was a Catholic nun, whose career led her to become involved in the design of buildings for her order. Fred Anhalt was a Seattle designer-builder whose design contributions to Seattle are recognized but who never practiced as an architect. Similarly, although E. O. Schwagerl did design a few structures, he is primarily recognized for park design and subdivision design—indeed, he might today be characterized as an urban designer. And Butler Sturtevant was primarily a landscape architect. All of these individuals were included because it seemed appropriate to represent a range of design contributions to the shaping of Seattle.

Only a few of the architects profiled here could be considered well known locally. The most familiar may include Elmer Fisher, who is widely recognized for his contribution to Seattle in the years immediately after the 1889 fire, Ellsworth Storey, who is known for his simple, well-crafted houses of the first decades of this century, and Paul Thiry, who was one of the first architects to bring Modernism to Seattle. But even the essays on these individuals may offer surprises: few may know that Fisher gave up the practice of architecture in 1891 to become a hotel proprietor, that Ellsworth Storey was also responsible for a number of eclectic works, and that Thiry was a nationally recognized figure. Paul Hayden Kirk, Carl F. Gould, and B. Marcus Pritceca may also be known to many readers.

Many others will not be generally recognized. Yet architects such as William Boone, James Stephen, Henry Bittman, E. F. Champney, and J. Lister Holmes, and firms such as Saunders & Houghton, Somervell & Coté, Albertson, Wilson & Richardson, Bebb & Mendel, and others played key roles in shaping the architecture of Seattle. They may not all have been innovators, but they did refined work within the architectural

traditions of their times and they contributed structures that have since become key elements of the city and the region.

Others who are included may be recognized primarily for contributions in areas other than design. Victor Steinbrueck, of course, is widely known for his civic activism and his role in preserving Pioneer Square and the Pike Place Market. Lionel "Spike" Pries is probably best known as a teacher and only secondarily as a practitioner. Still others changed the character of the profession itself, beginning a process of opening doors and creating new opportunities. Elizabeth Ayer was the first woman to become a registered architect in Washington State, Kichio Allen Arai was the first American-born Asian American to have an independent practice in Seattle, Benjamin F. McAdoo, Jr., was the first African American architect to have a successful long-term practice in the city, and Olof Hanson was deaf.

Three essays focus on particular building traditions or directions rather than on individual architects or firms. An essay on Native American architecture describes structures typically built by the Coast Salish people who inhabited Puget Sound prior to Euro-American settlement. Another essay addresses the impact of pattern books, plan books, and periodicals and shows how these publications often had a direct influence on the form of building in Seattle. Finally, a third essay addresses the broad range of architecture termed "vernacular" and "popular," those ordinary buildings that make up a substantial portion of the built fabric of the city, but are often built without the participation of professional architectural designers.

One group of architects who have influenced the shape of Seattle—those from out of town—are not discussed in this volume, even though they have clearly played a critical role in the design of the city for over a century. From early skyscrapers such as the Alaska Building by Eames & Young of St.

View south from Pine Street, 1878. Seattle's early economic development was based on extractive industries that required a large capital investment in transportation facilities for exporting coal and lumber. The tideflat area beyond the wharves was later filled and became the site of railroad yards, industrial concerns, and, in recent years, the Kingdome. *(University of Washington Libraries, Special Collections Division; 1878; photo by Peterson Brothers.)*

Introduction

A Historical Overview of Architecture in Seattle

JEFFREY KARL OCHSNER

In just over a century, Seattle has become a noted urban center in the midst of a region whose buildings provide places of work, shelter, interaction, and recreation for almost three million people. In the 1980s, Seattle was popularly recognized for its "livability," a characteristic determined by rating a variety of economic and environmental factors, and it was hailed as a city that "works." While these accolades are undoubtedly in good part due to Seattle's spectacular natural setting, benign climate, and comparatively stable economy, at least some portion of the acclaim represents a recognition of the relatively high overall quality of Seattle's built urban form. Although the city has few individual structures that have achieved national fame, the generally uniform quality of its built fabric, as well as its success in creating and maintaining unique urban places and natural settings, has won national recognition.

Early Years

The earliest architecture in the Puget Sound region predates Euro-American settlement by several thousand years. Long before the mid-nineteenth century, the Coast Salish people had developed a complex culture based on fishing, hunting, and gathering. The Salish lived in villages of one or more large wood plank houses usually located on the coast or along other waterways (see the essay on Native American architecture), but their buildings have not survived. This disappearance reflects the displacement of the Native culture and the ravages of a damp climate. Today, the forms of Salish buildings in the Seattle area are known largely from photographs and other documentation.

The history of Euro-American settlement in the Northwest begins in the late eighteenth century with early voyages of exploration undertaken by various European powers. In 1792, Captain George Vancouver initiated the exploration of Puget Sound, which he named for his lieutenant, Peter Puget. When Lewis and Clark, following the Columbia River, reached the Pacific Coast in the fall of 1805, they established the basis for American claims to the Oregon Territory, including the land north of the Columbia River that was to become Washington State. However, American settlement prior to 1846 was centered in the Willamette Valley, south of the Columbia. Only after the settlement of the U.S.-Canadian boundary dispute in 1846 was the Puget Sound basin opened to American settlement.

By the 1850s a network of small towns had been established north of the Columbia extending into the Puget Sound region. Settlers were generally attracted by the ready availability of timber, which could be exported south to California. In mid-November 1851, a party led by David Denny established a new settlement at Alki (now West Seattle). The location, however, lacked a protected deep-water anchorage, so the community relocated to the opposite side of Elliott Bay in March 1852. Later that year the new town was named Seattle, after the the leader of one of the Coast Salish tribes.

The initial economic base of the community was reinforced in March 1853 when Henry Yesler agreed to build the first steam sawmill on Puget Sound in Seattle. Thereafter, the community became a center of nascent industries, but its future proved more commercial than industrial. The early construction of wharves and other improvements on the waterfront, the growth of a network of small supply ships on the Sound, and Seattle business leaders' primary focus on supply and trade led to the city's early commercial dominance in the region.

Still, the city grew more slowly than its early leaders had hoped. Indeed, the center of initial Euro-American settlement in Washington was in the southeastern corner of the state because of the available farmland and the natural transportation link provided by the Columbia River. As late as 1880, the three most populous counties in the territory were Walla Walla, Whitman, and Columbia, all in southeastern Washington. Puget Sound's remoteness and the Indian Wars of 1855-56 (and continuing fear of attack) inhibited Seattle's growth. In 1862 the population was only 182, and the nation's focus was preoccupied by Civil War, not western settlement. Slow growth led to the incorporation of the town in 1869 and a population of 1,107 by 1870.

In this period, Seattle's buildings were all made of wood, taking advantage of the local abundance of this resource. They were generally one- and two-story structures with gabled roofs. Along Front Street (now First Avenue), the commercial center of the town, the predominant form was the false front, typical of many western communities. All of these buildings were constructed by local contractors or by itinerant contractor-builders. The design was straightforward and utilitarian; embellishments were generally the simpler forms of details commonly found in pattern books and builders' guides (see the essay on Pattern Books, Plan Books, Periodicals). The one early exception was Washington's Territorial University, erected in 1861. This two-story rectangular building, in a Classical Revival style with four Ionic columns, remained the town's most impressive structure for over two decades.

The completion in 1869 of the first transcontinental railroad increased the momentum of western settlement, and the residents of the region began to plan for the arrival of the Northern Pacific, which had been chartered in 1864 to extend from the Great Lakes to Puget Sound. Seattle, as the largest community on the Sound, expected to be the terminus, but the railroad, seeking greater opportunities for land speculation, selected Tacoma in 1873. Although the city did initiate its own line, optimistically called the Seattle and Walla Walla (Walla Walla was the largest city in the territory at the time), it was three years before this line was extended just sixteen miles to the coal fields south and east of Lake Washington. Still, by the late 1870s Seattle was a major exporter of coal, via coastal steamer, to San Francisco. The city's economy continued to diversify, supporting steady growth through 1880, when the population reached 3,553.

The national depression after 1873 halted construction on the Northern Pacific, and it was not until the early 1880s that the project resumed. In 1883, Seattle finally achieved a connection to the national rail network. The anticipation of this connection precipitated the city's first real estate boom, and attracted the city's first practicing architects. The early 1880s saw rapid growth for Seattle, with the construction of new institutional and commercial structures and the expansion of residential areas. The city's coastal trade was primarily with California; the transcontinental rail connection, completed in 1883, reached the city by way of Portland (and Tacoma). It is thus not surprising that the primary models for the city's architecture in the early 1880s were the Victorian buildings of San Francisco and Portland, and that many of the earliest professional architects in the city came north from Oregon or California.

The growth of institutions in the Northwest was well represented by an expanding network of facilities, including schools, hospitals, and orphanages run by the Sisters of Providence, who had their headquarters in Vancouver, Washington. Their success was due in large part to the energy and capabili-

Downtown Seattle after the fire, June 6, 1889. Despite the increasing prevalence of commercial buildings with exterior masonry bearing walls, only one such building survived. The fire convinced city officials to initiate a building permit process and to make improvements to local building ordinances, but significantly greater fire-resistant construction methods did not appear until the twentieth century. *(University of Washington Libraries, Special Collections Division; 1889; photo by Asahel Curtis, 36930.)*

ties of Mother Joseph (see essay), who is also credited with the design of many of her order's buildings.

Seattle's first practicing professional architect, Arthur Doyle, came from Denver. He was followed in 1881 by William Boone (see essay), a successful contractor in the San Francisco Bay area before coming to Seattle. Donald MacKay (see essay), who arrived in 1882 from Portland, also apparently began his career in the building trades, a common path to the practice of architecture at the time.

The boom of the early 1880s died out after 1883 with the collapse of Henry Villard's transportation network, of which the Northern Pacific Railroad was the centerpiece. Building construction did not pick up again until 1886-87 when the Northern Pacific line through Stampede Pass in the Cascades was completed. Although Northern Pacific policy favored Tacoma, and the rail connection to Seattle was intermittently disrupted, the city boomed nonetheless, and by the 1890 census Seattle's population was 42,837.

The physical growth of the city in the late 1880s was both outward and upward. By the end of the decade, residential neighborhoods extending north to Green Lake, east to Lake Washington, south to Beacon Hill, and across Elliott Bay to West Seattle were connected to downtown Seattle by a network of streetcar and cable car lines. The initial horsecar lines were built in 1884. Construction of the city's first cable car line on Mill Street (now Yesler Way) began in 1887, and service from downtown to Lake Washington was first offered on September 27, 1888. The conversion of the horsecar lines to electric streetcars began the following year. New residential neighborhoods, providing homes for the expanding population, were developed along all of these lines, and close-in Seattle neighborhoods began to take the built form that many retain today.

The Seattle Fire and Its Aftermath

At the same time, the scale of new construction in downtown Seattle reached unprecedented heights. Although the boom of the early 1880s had seen the Frye Opera House, designed by John Nestor, built to a height of five stories, most of the city's commercial buildings were two or three stories tall. The rebuilding of downtown Seattle after the disastrous fire of 1889 brought a new metropolitan scale to the city's core.

At about 2:30 p.m., on June 6, a glue pot boiled over in a downtown cabinet shop, and by the time the fire was contained, at about sunset, the city's commercial district lay in ruins. As Chicago proved after its 1870 conflagration, a disaster of this scale need not destroy a community whose economy was healthy. Within a few days, Seattle newspapers were trumpeting plans to rebuild. The fire was seen as an opportunity to modernize: downtown streets were widened and regraded, the water and sewer system was improved, a fire department was created, and a building code was established requiring that new construction be fire-resistive (sometimes called "slow-burning" at the time). Business was carried on in a tent city while building took place. Within eighteen months much of the downtown area was rebuilt, although some construction continued thereafter. In place of the two- and three-story central city of wood, a four- to six-story city was created in brick, stone, and heavy timber, with terra-cotta and cast-iron detail.

While the growth of Seattle in the late 1880s had attracted a new generation of architects, the fire drew still more to the city. Although William Boone, the most successful prefire architect, continued to practice, Elmer Fisher (see essay) emerged as the leading architect in the years immediately after the fire, with works including the Pioneer Building, the Burke Building, and other major downtown commercial blocks. Significant contributions were also made by John Parkinson, Charles Saunders, and Edwin Houghton (see essays). Like their predecessors, Fisher and Parkinson emerged from the building trades, but they brought a new professionalism. Others, including

Saunders, Houghton, Willis Ritchie (see essay), Warren Skillings, and A. B. Chamberlin, had worked in professional offices in the East or in Europe before coming to the Seattle. The architects of this period turned eastward seeking sources for design, a direction fostered by the economic connections made possible by the transcontinental railroad. This new sophistication is evident in their widespread application of the Romanesque Revival, which emerged as a national style following the death of H. H. Richardson in 1886. The new professionalism of Seattle architects was also supported by the emergence of the national architectural press. In the early 1890s the work of Seattle architects first received national recognition when Seattle buildings were published in architectural periodicals based in Minnesota, Boston, and Chicago.

Seattle also became an exporter of architectural services. Fisher designed commercial buildings in Ellensburg and Whatcom (now Bellingham); Parkinson was responsible for school buildings in several school districts in the region; and Ritchie designed schools and county courthouses throughout western Washington. The best-known non-Seattle architectural firm to win a commission in the city during this period was Adler & Sullivan of Chicago, whose Opera House project never proceeded beyond the foundation.

The panic of 1893 and the subsequent collapse of the national economy brought this early building boom to an end. Seattle could never have maintained the pace of construction that marked the first year after the fire, but the downturn after 1893 was severe as eastern banks withdrew funds from the West. The value of building permits issued in the city had exceeded $6 million in 1889, but was barely $200,000 in 1896. Many architects who had been attracted by the prosperity of the early 1890s left the region, and some who remained were forced to turn to other fields to make a living.

One response to this difficult time was an

Denny Hotel (Washington Hotel), Seattle, 1888-93, 1903 (destroyed); A. B. Jennings, with Albert Wickersham (superintending). Begun during the boom years of the late 1880s, the Denny Hotel remained incomplete for a decade as a result of financial difficulties. The building opened as the Washington Hotel in 1903, but stood only a few years before it was demolished during the regrading of Denny Hill. *(University of Washington Libraries, Special Collections Division; 1907; photo by Asahel Curtis, 8437.)*

effort to organize the practice of architecture on a more professional basis. In 1894, architects in Seattle, Tacoma, and Spokane joined to found the Washington Society of Architects, which soon became the Washington State Chapter of the American Institute of Architects.

Years of Rapid Growth

The July 17, 1897, arrival of the steamer *Portland* from Alaska, reportedly with a "ton of gold," initiated the Klondike gold rush. The Seattle economy rebounded as the city became the primary point of embarkation, where propectors were outfitted before departing for the Yukon. Growth resumed, and Seattle's population reached 80,761 in 1900. By 1910 the census would count 237,194 residents in the city.

The early years of the new century were marked by major engineering enterprises aimed at transforming the city's topography. Filling the tideflats south of the city's center

had begun in 1895, but due to the depressed economy, progress was slow and the project was not completed until the early 1900s. The new land was used for railroad yards, warehouses, and industrial expansion. By 1910, dredging had begun to transform the Duwamish River from a meandering stream to an industrial waterway; by the end of the next decade, its course had been straightened, its banks stabilized, and Harbor Island created at its mouth. In addition, between 1911 and 1917 the Lake Washington Ship Canal linking Lake Union and Lake Washington to Puget Sound, a project first envisioned in the 1880s, was completed. But the most dramatic transformation was the regrading of the city's steep hills and deep ravines. In 1897, City Engineer R. H. Thomson initiated a massive campaign to reduce the steepest slopes and cut down the highest hills. The most significant regrading was the removal of Denny Hill, which stood just north of downtown. This project, which lowered elevations in some places more than one hundred feet, was not fully completed until the early 1930s.

With the return of prosperity after 1897, construction increased and the demand for architectural services in Seattle was renewed. Like the boom of the late 1880s, Seattle's growth between 1900 and 1914 attracted a new generation of architectural professionals. In contrast to the earlier period, the new architects rarely came from the ranks of the building trades. Many brought extensive experience in architectural offices in the East or Midwest, and an increasing number had received training in an academic program, although it can be argued that the arrival of academically trained architects in Seattle was relatively late. Practitioners who had attended the École des Beaux-Arts in Paris could be found in San Francisco and Portland as early as 1890, and they soon became leaders of their profession in those cities. But architects with academic training did not arrive in Seattle until after 1900. An apparent consequence of this difference was the dominance of architects trained in England or Germany in the Seattle professional community in the early years of the twentieth century. This may account for the relatively strong local influence during this period of the Tudor Revival and the Arts and Crafts movement and the comparative weakness of the Classical modes of design.

The early decades of the twentieth century witnessed the first applications of broad-scale planning to Seattle. Proposals for a citywide park and boulevard system had been advanced in the early 1890s by E. O. Schwagerl (see essay), but lack of funds delayed implementation. In 1903, when the project proceeded under the impetus of the City Beautiful movement, Seattle turned to the nationally recognized Olmsted Brothers of Brookline, Massachusetts, for the park and boulevard plan. Substantial portions of their plan, which echoed many of Schwagerl's earlier ideas, were put in place over the next decade. The park and boulevard plan initiated the Olmsted firm's involvement in Seattle, which continued for the next three decades, with over one hundred public and private projects in the region.

The second major citywide planning effort, the comprehensive plan published in 1911 as the *Plan of Seattle,* did not fare as well. A proposal for a plan had been initiated in 1908 by members of the Washington State Chapter of the AIA, who fostered the creation of the Municipal Plans League in 1909 and the passage of a city charter amendment supporting planning in 1910. The Bogue Plan, as the proposal came to be called (after its author, consultant Virgil G. Bogue), covered an area of more than 150 square miles. It addressed harbor and port facilities, railroads, streetcar lines, highways, roads and streets, parks, and other recreational facilities, and proposed a new civic center in the regraded area just north of downtown. But Bogue's proposal proved infeasible politically. The costs appeared overwhelming and the enabling legislation, which failed to allow for future flexibility, seemed too constraining. In addition, the location of the proposed civic center in the Denny Regrade alienated property owners in the south end of downtown, who believed their property values would fall if the plan was implemented. Thus, after a bitter campaign, it was overwhelmingly defeated at the polls. Although some parts of the Bogue Plan were implemented subsequently in a piecemeal fashion, and Seattle proceeded with much of the Olmsted-designed park and boulevard system, the civic center proposal died.

Just as technology influenced the shaping of Seattle topography in these decades, the application of new technology to building dramatically affected the form of the city's structures. The confluence of steel frame and curtainwall construction with improved fireproofing and elevator technology had led to the emergence of the skyscraper in Chicago in the late 1880s and early 1890s. By 1903 these innovations had been brought to

Alaska Building, Seattle, 1903-4, Eames & Young, with Saunders & Lawton (superintending). The first of the city's steel-framed high-rise office buildings rose fourteen stories to tower over surrounding construction. (*University of Washington Libraries, Special Collections Division; 1905; photo by Asahel Curtis, 11747.*)

Seattle in the city's first steel-framed highrise, the Alaska Building, designed by the St. Louis firm of Eames & Young. Over the following decade, locally designed high-rises by A. Warren Gould and Bebb & Mendel (see essays) were constructed. In 1914, however, new heights were reached with the 42-story, 522-foot-tall Smith Tower, designed by Gaggin & Gaggin of Syracuse, New York, for typewriter magnate L. C. Smith of Albany. When completed it was the fourth tallest building in the world and the tallest outside New York City. It remained the tallest in Seattle until 1969.

The construction of these commercial buildings also began to define the limits of downtown Seattle. An element in the controversy over the Bogue Plan had been the question of the location of the center of downtown Seattle. The Alaska Building, Hoge Building, and Smith Tower were all in or adjacent to the historical commercial center of Seattle, the area now known as Pioneer Square. In 1907, however, the regents of the University of Washington resolved the lease of the old university grounds occupying parts of several contiguous blocks at the intersection of Fourth Avenue and University Street downtown, eight blocks north of Pioneer Square. Early in 1908, a master plan for the proposed development of the Metropolitan Tract (as the site became known), designed by Howells & Stokes of New York, was announced with great fanfare. This proposal for a densely developed "city within a city" of ten-story business blocks suggested that the center of downtown might move considerably northward. New office buildings, notably the Northern Bank & Trust Company (now the Seaboard Building), by W. D. Van Siclen, completed in 1909, and the Securities Building by John Graham, Sr. (see essay), with Frank P. Allen, completed in 1913, were even farther north of the Pioneer Square area. After the failure of the Bogue Plan, however, northward expansion of the downtown core proceeded no farther than Olive Way. But by 1910 the shift of new downtown development to the north of Yesler Way (and the consequent commercial development of the city's oldest residential district) had been decisively established.

Growth outside downtown was marked by the creation of networks of institutional facilities that frequently became identified with the new neighborhoods in which they were built. Chief among these were public schools, as the Seattle School Board chose to build a system of many relatively small school buildings across the city. School buildings after 1901 usually followed the "model" plans created by James Stephen (see essay), who served as the official schools architect until late 1909, when he was succeeded by Edgar Blair. Other firms and individuals emerged as leaders in the profession with a variety of projects including significant local institutional designs. For example, Somervell & Coté and Harlan Thomas (see essays) were involved in the design of the city's early Carnegie branch libraries between 1908 and 1915. Daniel Huntington (see essay) later served as city architect and was responsible for the design of fire stations, power plants, and other municipal facilities between 1912 and 1921. And firms such as Breitung & Buchinger (see essay) built their reputations serving private institutional clients who sought designs for churches, meeting halls, and similar facilities.

Seattle architects continued to build their practices by exporting architectural services. Stephen designed schools for other communities throughout Washington State. Edwin Houghton emerged as a major designer of theaters in the Northwest after 1900. About 1911, Olof Hanson (see essay) was responsible for facilities for the deaf and blind at the state institutions in Vancouver, Washington. The Beezer Brothers (see essay) developed their multifaceted Seattle-based practice in considerable part by providing facilities for Catholic Church, including churches, schools, and hospitals in at least six western states.

The rapid growth of Seattle after 1900 was marked by equally dramatic residential development, and residential design commissions were accepted and carried out by virtually all architects practicing in Seattle. This work reflects the variety of directions found in the profession at the time, but the predominance of English and German/Swiss influence is particularly evident in Seattle residential design. As early as the mid-1890s, the leading Spokane architect, Kirtland Cutter (see essay), was responsible for Shingle Style work in the city and his later Seattle projects were knowledgeable

adaptations of Tudor and Swiss precedents. After 1900, English and Swiss eclectic work was clearly connected to the broad development of the American branch of the Arts and Crafts movement and more narrowly to the Craftsman mode of Gustav Stickley. Ellsworth Storey (see essay), who graduated from the architecture program at the University of Illinois in 1903 (and who may therefore have been the first academically trained architect to establish a Seattle practice), executed a body of work including residences, clubs, small churches, and similar modestly scaled buildings that reflected all of these tendencies over the next two decades. Some have compared his body of work to that of California architect Bernard Maybeck.

An abundance of pattern and plan books promoting bungalow designs and illustrating Craftsman homes and furnishings (see the Pattern Books, Plan Books, Periodicals essay) were widely influential in Seattle. In particular, *Bungalow Magazine,* published in Seattle from 1912 to 1918, often included and influenced Seattle projects. Architects, builders, and prospective homeowners received direct guidance from these books and magazines, and their influence is evident throughout the residential fabric of the city's older neighborhoods.

Frank Lloyd Wright and the Prairie School were introduced in Seattle in 1908 by Andrew Willatsen (see essay), who had worked in Wright's studio in Oak Park, Illinois. Willatsen was initially responsible for supervising projects for Kirtland Cutter, but in January 1909 he formed the partnership Willatsen & Byrne, which designed a series of houses in the Prairie Style in Seattle and the surrounding areas. After the firm dissolved in 1913, Willatsen continued designing buildings in the Prairie Style until the 1920s. Wright and the Prairie School may also have influenced some of the work of W. R. B. Willcox (see essay), although his projects, before his departure from Seattle in 1922, to head the Department of Architec-

Alaska-Yukon-Pacific (AYP) Exposition, Seattle, 1906-09 (destroyed), Olmsted Brothers (master planners and landscape architects) and Howard & Galloway (supervising architects). The AYP was intended to demonstrate the resources of Alaska and the importance of Seattle as Alaska's major port-of-entry. Held on the grounds of the University of Washington, the exposition was planned around a central axis focused on distant Mount Rainier. That axis was later incorporated into the plan of the University and remains a feature of the campus. *(University of Washington Libraries, Special Collections Division; 1909; UW 1478.)*

ture at the University of Oregon, seemed to encompass many of the diverse tendencies of the period.

A Maturing City

The Alaska-Yukon-Pacific (AYP) Exposition opened in Seattle on June 1, 1909. One of a series of Pacific Coast exhibitions modeled on the World's Columbian Exposition held in Chicago in 1893, the AYP was conceived in 1905 as a way to call attention to the wealth of resources in Alaska, to focus on

Second Avenue near intersection of Madison Street in downtown Seattle, about 1910. This view gives some sense of the urban scale of the heart of the city in the first decade of the twentieth century. The buildings at the left are the Leary Building (1906-8, destroyed) designed by the Beezer Brothers after Alfred Bodley, and the American Savings Bank/Empire Building (1904-6, destroyed) designed by A. W. Gould. *(University of Washington Libraries, Special Collections Division; ca. 1910; UW 14336.)*

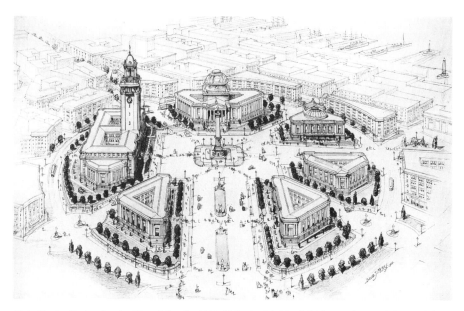

Civic Center Project for the City of Seattle, 1910-12 (unbuilt), Virgil G. Bogue. A central focus of the Bogue Plan was this City Beautiful civic center complex intended to be located in the Denny Regrade. (*University of Washington Libaries, Special Collections Division; UW 15082.*)

Seattle as its major port of entry, and to celebrate the city's achievements. The undeveloped grounds of the University of Washington were leased as the site, and the exposition plan was developed by the Olmsted Brothers, who were also responsible for landscape design. Although the main buildings were designed by Howard & Galloway of San Francisco, who sent Édouard Frère Champney (see essay) to Seattle to supervise the work, the AYP offered many opportunities for Seattle architects. The exposition ran 138 days, attracting 3.7 million visitors; and after it closed, the landscaped site was returned to the University along with several buildings that were then adapted to serve educational purposes.

In 1912 an assessment of Seattle's progress was offered by the essayist and critic Herbert Croly in the July issue of *Architectural Record*. His discussion, "The Building of Seattle: A City of Great Architectural Promise," was the first general recognition given to Seattle's architecture by a national publication. Croly noted the city's growth, its physical setting, its relationship to Alaska, and offered a favorable review of its prospects and potential. A number of Seattle's business and institutional buildings were illustrated and received favorable comments, but the city's residences were characterized as "disappointing." A particular focus of the article was the progress of the Metropolitan Tract, where the White, Henry, and Cobb buildings and the Metropolitan Theater by Howells & Stokes had already been completed. Overall, Croly characterized Seattle as a city of "most considerable promise."

The Northwest economy slowed after 1912. A lessening demand for timber was followed by a national recession in 1915, and Seattle's growth reflected this slump. The population, which had grown by almost 160,000 between 1900 and 1910, increased by only 90,000 in the next decade, for a total of 327,194 residents in 1920. Still, although the pace of growth slowed, the city did not experience anything like the decline of the mid-1890s. This is reflected in the relative stability of the architectural profession: the offices of John Graham, Sr., James Schack, Arrigo Young, and David Myers (see Schack, Young & Myers essay) generated practices whose successors continue in the profession in Seattle today.

By 1910 an increasing number of Seattle architects could boast significant academic training. Champney had attended the École des Beaux-Arts and apprenticed at leading East Coast firms; W. Marbury Somervell, who had studied architecture at Cornell, was sent to Seattle in December 1904 by Heins & LaFarge of New York in connection with their work on Saint James Cathedral; A. H. Albertson (see Albertson, Wilson & Richardson essay), a graduate of Columbia University's architecture school, was sent to the city by Howells & Stokes in 1907.

Also among this number was Carl F. Gould (see Bebb & Gould essay), a graduate of Harvard who had attended the École des Beaux-Arts and then apprenticed with McKim, Mead & White and George B. Post in New York and D. H. Burnham & Company in Chicago. He arrived in Seattle in 1908. Gould was the among the most influential Seattle architects of his generation. From 1914 to 1939 he was associated with Charles Bebb in the firm Bebb & Gould, whose practice encompassed a wide range of commercial, governmental, educational, medical, and institutional projects. In 1914, Bebb & Gould were selected to develop the revised master plan for the University of Washington. Their work required incorporation of existing campus structures as well as the general organizational scheme for the university grounds that the Olmsted Brothers had developed and implemented for the AYP. Approved by the University regents in 1915, and thereafter known as the Regents Plan, Bebb & Gould's proposal provided the basis for the organization of the central core of the campus that remains in place today. During the next thirteen years, Bebb & Gould designed a series of buildings on the campus called for in their plan. In 1914

Smith Tower, Seattle, 1910-14, Gaggin & Gaggin. The steel framing for the Smith Tower was topped out in February 1913 and installation of the terra cotta began immediately thereafter. When completed, this structure was the fourth tallest building in the world and the tallest outside New York City. *(University of Washington Libraries, Special Collections Division; 1913; UW 388.)*

Gould was also responsible for initiating the architecture program at the University of Washington—a program he chaired until 1926, when he was succeeded by Harlan Thomas.

Seattle in the 1920s

The 1920s were marked by continued slow growth in Seattle, the population reaching 365,583 in 1930. The First World War had generated a brief economic flurry, but the postwar economy remained sluggish. Automobile ownership started to have an impact on the development of Seattle in the 1920s; indeed, urban planners began to concern themselves with the efficient movement of

Olympic Hotel, Seattle, 1922-24, George B. Post & Sons with Bebb & Gould (superintending architects). When the Olympic Hotel opened in 1924, only the wings on Fourth Avenue and Seneca Street
were complete; the Fifth Avenue wing was completed in 1928-29 to the design of Robert Reamer, who
was also responsible for the penthouse added in 1930. Today, only this hotel and the nearby Cobb
Building recall the original brick and terra-cotta architecture planned by Howells & Stokes for the
entire Metropolitan Tract. *(University of Washington Libaries, Special Collections Division; 1925; UW
4077.)*

private vehicles and the problem of parking.

Even with slow growth, there was evidence of an increasing level of cultural
achievement in Seattle. The Cornish School
for the Arts, founded in 1915, moved in
1921 into its new building, designed by A. H.
Albertson. Thereafter it served as a cultural
catalyst for the city, its faculty including figures such as Mark Tobey and Martha Graham over the course of the next decade. The
Seattle Fine Arts Society, founded in 1906,
moved to increasingly larger quarters during the 1920s, changed its name to the Seattle Art Institute in 1931, and in 1933
finally moved into its own museum building
in Volunteer Park, designed by Bebb &
Gould. The University of Washington continued to grow as well, with substantial
progress toward completion of the liberal
arts quadrangle, the initiation of construction of the science quadrangle, and the
completion in 1927 of the first phase of the
Suzzallo Library.

Although financially pressed through
much of the decade, the Seattle school district embarked on a renewed construction
program. After the First World War the state
had passed a compulsory attendance law,
and high school enrollments increased dramatically. More specialized educational programs, including vocational training, were
also introduced. The Seattle school district
nonetheless continued to prefer relatively
small, neighborhood-oriented schools.

Floyd Naramore (see essay), who served as schools architect from 1919 to 1932, designed most of his school buildings in revival styles (primarily those of English derivation), although internally these schools reflected recent developments in educational planning.

Seattle architecture in the 1920s was initially dominated by academic eclecticism and the application of historical revival styles. By 1920, residential projects, in particular, reflected the waning of the residual influence of the Arts and Crafts movement and the Craftsman mode (along with the related half-timbered Tudor Revival and the Prairie School), and the ascendancy of the eclectic approach. Skilled architects in the period were able to work in a variety of historical styles as appropriate to the particular client, site, and project. As a result, Classical Revival work increasingly appeared, although English Revival styles remained most popular. The leading Seattle residential architects were probably Edwin Ivey and Arthur Loveless (see essay). Loveless, who had attended Columbia University and apprenticed with leading country house architects Delano & Aldrich in New York, successfully adapted reduced versions of the English country house model for his clients in Seattle neighborhoods. The preference for English revival styles most likely reflects the historical weakness of the Classical modes in the region, but it may also have been fostered by the surprising number of University of Pennsylvania graduates who came to Seattle. Graduates of the Penn program such as Ivey, Alban Shay, J. Lister Holmes (see essay), William J. Bain, Sr. (see essay), and, after 1928, Lionel H. Pries (see essay), brought not only professional academic training but also a familiarity with the work of eclectic residential designers in Philadelphia such as Wilson Eyre, who in turn were influenced by the prominent English architect Edwin Lutyens. Eclecticism was also evident in Seattle residential apartment construction. A variety of modes were applied not only by architects but also by contractor-builders, some of whom, such as Frederick Anhalt (see essay), became involved in all phases—development, design, construction, and management—of their own projects.

Commercial buildings over the course of the 1920s showed a dramatic stylistic change. Classical Revival motifs were typical initially, but by the end of the decade they had been supplanted by Art Deco. After 1918 the most prolific commercial architect in Seattle was the English born and trained John Graham, Sr. Although he produced buildings of all types in the course of his career, Graham is best remembered for the series of terra-cotta clad downtown commercial office buildings and department stores his firm designed in the 1920s. Initially in this work he applied Classical Revival motifs, but by the end of the decade many of his projects, including the Roosevelt Hotel and the Exchange Building, were executed in the Art Deco style. Henry Bittman (see essay), who was responsible for a series of downtown buildings in the 1920s, showed a similar transformation in his work. However, the most highly regarded example of Art Deco design in Seattle is the Northern Life Tower (now Seattle Tower), designed by A. H. Albertson, with his associates Joseph W. Wilson and Paul Richardson, and completed in 1929.

Seattle continued to be an exporter of architectural services during this period. Leading firms such as Bebb & Gould, Schack, Young & Myers, and Albertson, Wilson & Richardson all did significant work outside Seattle. The reach of the Seattle profession in this period is best exemplified in the work of B. Marcus Priteca (see essay), who was responsible for theater designs along the entire West Coast. Priteca's theaters from 1910 to the mid-1920s were generally classical in style, but after the mid-1920s he was a pioneer in the application of the Art Deco in designs for motion picture theaters.

Perhaps the architect whose career best summarizes the many tendencies of the first decades of the twentieth century is Robert C. Reamer (see essay). In his early work at Yellowstone Park and in Montana, Reamer created the rustic architecture for which he is best known. In Seattle he incorporated classical influences in the Skinner Building of the mid-1920s, and by the late 1920s he was designing Art Deco office buildings and other commercial structures. In the early 1930s his Edmond Meany Hotel (now Meany Tower Hotel), near the University of Washington campus, demonstrated technological innovation in its continuously poured slip-formed concrete structure.

The 1920s also saw the emergence of landscape architecture as an independent, professionally practiced design discipline in Seattle. Early practitioners had either been public employees, as exemplified by E. O. Schwagerl, or had combined nursery ownership and design, as exemplified by Peder Sandved in the years after 1908. However, with the opening in the city of the professional landscape design offices of Otto Holmdahl in 1919, Butler Sturtevant (see essay) in 1928, and Noble Hoggson in 1932, landscape architecture achieved a firm professional footing in the region.

Depression and War

The slow but steady growth of Seattle in the 1920s was followed by stagnation in the depression years of the 1930s. In 1940, the census indicated that the population had grown by only 2,719 people over the previous decade. The Depression brought building construction to a virtual halt. Investment in building construction in Seattle had remained fairly steady through the 1920s, with the total value of permits (including both residential and nonresidential construction) peaking at nearly $35 million in 1928. Investment declined slightly in 1929 and 1930, but collapsed to just over $4 million in 1932 and less than $2 million in 1933, at the depth of the Depression. Building activity re-

mained slow until the last years of the decade when federal funding for new public housing first became available. Only in 1940 did the value of construction, spurred by spending on war-related industry, approach the level of the pre-Depression peak.

With very little work, the architectural profession suffered through the early years of the Depression. Many of the older generation of Seattle's practitioners retired, while younger architects survived on the commissions they could obtain, primarily residential work of various scales. Architects such as Edwin Ivey (by then in practice with his associate Elizabeth Ayer; see essay), William J. Bain, Sr., and J. Lister Holmes began moving away from strict adherence to historical precedent and dependence on academically correct detail and toward more informal compositional approaches.

New Deal public works programs began to employ Seattle architects in the mid-1930s. For example, Ellsworth Storey was selected to design several projects at Moran State Park on Orcas Island, producing some of his best-known works. In 1939 the City of Seattle created the Seattle Housing Authority as the local agency to carry out the New Deal's federally funded public housing programs. The first Seattle housing complex, Yesler Terrace, was approved in 1939, and the 690-unit project was completed in the following years by a team of architects and landscape architects. This project was a precursor to the many housing projects and related facilities designed and erected over the next several years to meet the demand generated by the many new residents who came to the military bases and war-related manufacturing plants in the Puget Sound region. Indeed, between 1941 and 1945, Seattle's population swelled from 360,000 to 480,000.

During the Second World War, architects often formed temporary partnerships and joint ventures to carry out massive projects on the short wartime schedules demanded by governmental agencies. Although most of these arrangements lasted no more than two or three years, the Naramore, Bain, Brady & Johanson partnership, formed in 1943, emerged intact at the end of the war and went on to become one of the city's largest and most influential architectural firms.

Not all Seattle architects benefited from the boom of war-related construction. The Japanese American architect K. A. Arai (see essay), a graduate of the University of Washington and Harvard University, had struggled as the first Asian American to establish an independent architectural practice in the city. But in 1942, as a result of wartime hysteria, he was among those subjected to forced relocation. Though he returned to Seattle in 1947, his career never recovered.

Three significant postwar developments had their roots in the prewar period: the ascendancy of Modernism in Northwest architecture, the influence of graduates from the University of Washington in the local architectural profession, and the transformation of Seattle's urban form in response to the automobile.

Architect Paul Thiry (see essay) is widely recognized as the individual who first brought International Style architecture to the Puget Sound region. A 1928 graduate of the University of Washington, Thiry applied traditional styles in his early work, but after travel in Europe, Asia, and Central America, and after meeting Antonin Raymond and Le Corbusier in the early 1930s, Thiry returned to Seattle and, in 1935, designed his own house in the style of the European Modernists. Thereafter he became the leader in the development of Modern architecture in Seattle; and by the late 1930s, others, including John R. Sproule and J. Lister Holmes, were designing Modernist structures as well.

Thiry was only the first of many University of Washington graduates to achieve professional distinction beginning in the 1930s. The program at the university had benefited from the addition to the faculty of Lancelot Gowen in 1924 and Lionel H. Pries in 1928. Pries is remembered as the preeminent architectural faculty member of those years, later to be recalled as a legendary teacher, whose influence and example shaped and inspired a majority of the leading Seattle architects of the postwar period.

Urban Transformations

Seattle residents acquired automobiles in significant numbers in the 1920s, producing the first substantial evidence of suburban development and strip commercial construction, but the full impact of the automobile was delayed first by the Depression and then by the World War II. But as early as 1908 the nationally based "good roads" movement had lobbied for a state highway system in Washington. By the 1930s their efforts had led to the construction of a statewide network of roads. Combined federal, state, and local funding made possible the construction of the first floating bridge extending east from Seattle across Lake Washington. Opened in 1940, it provided a direct link to Mercer Island and small communities such as Bellevue on the east side of the lake, and fostered their postwar development as "bedroom suburbs."

At the same time, 1939 also saw the demise of Seattle's cable car and streetcar system. In 1919 the city had paid an inflated price to acquire the privately owned urban rail network. Over the next two decades the system was continuously embroiled in financial difficulties, which limited maintenance and improvements. Increasing automobile ownership drew many patrons away and resulted in traffic congestion. In 1939 the city converted the system to electric buses (trackless trolleys) and gasoline buses in outlying areas. Thereafter nothing would impede the growth of automobile-generated suburban sprawl in Seattle and the surrounding region.

Industrial development during World War II transformed the economy of the region. Investment during the Depression and war years provided the infrastructure to support continued development of the

Lacy V. Murrow Memorial Bridge, Seattle, 1939-40 (destroyed), Washington State Highway Department engineers with Lloyd Lovegren. The level of demand for access across Lake Washington is reflected in this photograph of the opening ceremonies, July 2, 1940. The full impact of the bridge, which allowed the development of east-side communities as bedroom suburbs, was not felt until after the Second World War. *(University of Washington Libraries, Special Collections Division; 1940; photo by Asahel Curtis, 65146.)*

region's industrial base. Boeing, a relatively small company in the 1920s and 1930s, emerged from the war an aerospace giant and a dominant force in Seattle's economy. Its use of sophisticated technology and production methods called for a better educated work force, emphasizing technical and managerial skills, and these attitudes percolated throughout the region's culture, including the architectural community.

In the late 1940s and 1950s suburban development in the last undeveloped areas within the city limits and across the Puget Sound region was the primary focus of new construction. Population growth resumed, reflecting the impact of the "baby boom," and the city's numbers increased to 467,591 in 1950 and 557,087 in 1960. For the first time, substantial increases were recorded in the metropolitan area outside the city limits, so that King County population increased from 504,980 in 1940 to 935,014 in 1960.

Depression and war had created a pent-up demand for new housing. The postwar ideal, the single family house on a large suburban lot, was supported by the new highway and road networks, the availability of low-interest mortgages, and the application of mass-production techniques to housing development. The "ranch house" became the preferred builder type in Seattle. It was publicized in regional periodicals such as *Sunset Magazine* and a new group of plan and pattern books that offered design variations and promoted a corresponding suburbanized lifestyle. Suburban tracts in outlying areas of Seattle such as View Ridge and Olympic Manor and new suburbs like Lynnwood and Lake Forest Park were made up of these long, one-story houses with shallow roofs and large "picture" windows.

Modernism and Regionalism

Suburban projects were also the dominant focus of most of the region's architects after the war. Of the leading designers who emerged in this period a majority were graduates of the University of Washington, including Paul Hayden Kirk (see essay), Roland Terry (see essay), Benjamin F. McAdoo, Jr. (see essay), Victor Steinbrueck (see essay), John Sproule, Robert Dietz, Fred Bassetti, and Wendell Lovett. Many of them initiated their careers with suburban residential projects and other suburban building types such as churches, libraries, schools, and clinics. The same was true of new arrivals Ibsen Nelsen, A. O. Bumgardner, Omer Mithun, and others. Paul Kirk, possibly influenced by the work of Portland architect Pietro Belluschi, was a particular leader in developing a clear, structurally revealing design language that appeared to draw in almost equal measure from the work of Mies van der Rohe and from the traditional architecture of Japan. He was able to apply this approach not only to residences but also to a series of institutional and medical buildings. Paul Thiry was a leader in transforming International Style modernism to fit the Northwest context in the immediate postwar years. Similar transformations took place in the work of virtually all Seattle architects, as a regional variant of Modernism, sometimes called Northwest Contemporary, gradually developed in Seattle and Portland.

By the early 1950s, awareness of the coherent character of Northwest architecture was inspiring discussion of "regionalism" as a valid concern for local architects. Regionalism had been a topic in the national periodical *Pencil Points* (now *Progressive Architecture*) in the late 1930s and early 1940s in connection with work in California and Texas, but a developed discussion of such an approach to Northwest architecture did not appear until after the war. In this, the Northwest was not unique; regionalism as a valid direction within Modern architecture only began to be discussed in articles in the architectural press—by Walter Gropius, Sigfried Giedion, and Pietro Belluschi—in 1954 and 1955. The new architecture in Seattle and the Northwest had already received received widespread attention in 1953, when the national meeting of the American Institute of Architects was held in Seattle and *Architectural Record* devoted its April 1953 issue to the region's architectural production. The same issue featured short pro and con essays by Seattle architects on the question, "Have We an Indigenous Northwest Architecture?"

The developing sense that there was a coherence to much of the city's architectural production, evidenced in these discussions, appears to reflect a growing consciousness of Seattle as a unique place that could offer its own contribution to an American architecture. This sense was also fostered by the publication for the 1953 AIA meeting of Victor Steinbrueck's *Guide to Seattle Architecture, 1850-1953*, the first attempt to present a history of the city's architectural heritage.

But regionalism was not a dominant consideration in all of the city's architectural production. As residential suburbs spread, suburban retailing followed. A decisive step was made in 1947 by Seattle architect John Graham, Jr. (see essay), who had taken over the firm founded by his father, when he created the design for Northgate, the nation's first built large scale regional shopping center with an internally focused organization. Northgate's success made it a model for many similar shopping centers across the United States over the next several decades designed by the Graham firm, which grew to become one of Seattle's largest corporate architectural practices—and its successor continues to practice in the 1990s.

Compared with suburban development, relatively few new buildings were erected in downtown Seattle in the immediate postwar period, and those that were built responded more to national trends than regional influences. Seattle city government commis-

Norton Building, Seattle, 1956-59, Skidmore, Owings & Merrill, with Bindon & Wright (superintending). Myron Goldsmith of SOM was the primary designer of this office block. Its form reflects the influence of Mies van der Rohe. The building was technologically innovative in its composite structural system and its curtainwall, which was assembled from pre-glazed units. (*University of Washington Libraries, Special Collections Division; 1959; UW 15083.*)

sioned the earliest Modern buildings downtown: the Public Safety Building (completed in 1951), the new Seattle Public Library (1956-59), and the Municipal Building (1959-61). The influence of Mies van der Rohe was evident in several of the new downtown office towers. The first Seattle office tower with an advanced aluminum and glass curtainwall, the 16-story Norton Building, was completed in 1959. Designed by Myron Goldsmith of Skidmore, Owings & Merrill's San Francisco office (with Bindon & Wright of Seattle), the building reflected the direct influence of Mies in its crisp rectilinear form set on a horizontal plaza atop a plinth. In 1969, the Seattle First National Bank headqarters (now the 1001 Fourth Avenue Plaza), by Naramore, Bain, Brady & Johanson, a four-square office tower also influenced by the Miesian tradi-

tion, finally topped the Smith Tower, which had reigned as the tallest building in Seattle since 1914. Mies's own KING Broadcasting Company building (1967), intended for a site outside downtown (on Portage Bay), was never built. That downtown buildings in the 1960s and 1970s reflected national design tendencies suggests that regionalism was less applicable to office buildings in the city's central business district. Perhaps the closest approach to regional expression in a downtown building was found in the crafted wood interiors of the Federal Office Building by Fred Bassetti & Company (with John Graham & Company and Richard Haag), completed in 1971.

Century 21, the 1962 Seattle World's Fair, was proposed in 1955 as a way of celebrating the city's growth and attracting national attention to its achievements. Planned under the direction of Paul Thiry, who was appointed its principal architect in 1957, the fair opened in 1962 and drew 9.5 million visitors. The planning and the buildings reflected the continuing powerful influence of Modernism. The fairgrounds, about one mile north of the downtown business district, occupied parts of approximately thirty city blocks, which were combined to form a unified pedestrian precinct. A monorail was built to link the fair to the downtown commercial center and was envisioned by some as the harbinger of a regional mass transit system. Thiry's Coliseum exhibited his interest in innovative applications of concrete technology. Minoru Yamasaki, a University of Washington graduate whose Detroit-based practice had achieved national stature, was responsible for the design of the U.S. Science Pavilion (with Naramore, Bain, Brady & Johanson), and its attenuated linear detailing paralleled tendencies in his other work. The most famous structure at the fair—one that became the symbol of Seattle—was the Space Needle. The project combined the talents of John Graham, Jr., who conceived the idea, and Victor Steinbrueck, who was a key participant in its

Seattle First National Bank headquarters (1001 Fourth Avenue Plaza), Seattle, 1966-69, Naramore, Bain, Brady & Johanson, with Pietro Belluschi (consulting architect). Standing in an open plaza (altered) atop a granite base, the straightforward formal expression of this office tower responds directly to its unusual structural system; each exterior curtainwall was designed as a vierendiel truss tying together the massive corner columns. *(NBBJ collection; 1969; photo by Morley Baer.)*

tural center by Richard Haag, who had emerged as one of the region's leading landscape architects after arriving from San Francisco in 1958. Reopened in 1964, Seattle Center (as it has since been named) is the site of the city's opera house, two theaters, a science museum, an outdoor stadium, and an indoor sports arena, along with other facilities.

The postwar period also saw significant growth at the University of Washington. The passage of the G.I. Bill and growing demand for access to higher education led to a rapid expansion of enrollment and a building boom on campus. In 1948 the campus first expanded beyond its historical boundaries with the creation of West Campus Parkway, a link first envisioned in 1923 by Bebb & Gould. New construction in the historical core of the campus proceeded rapidly, initially in the Collegiate Gothic mode of the older buildings, but after 1950 buildings became increasingly Modern. While the entire university expanded, the growth of the medical school was particularly astonishing as the University began its climb toward preeminence in biomedical research. In 1957 the regents created an architectural design commission to guide campus growth, a group that continues to function. In the early 1970s the central quadrangle, initially proposed in the Bebb & Gould plan of 1915, was finally completed (and became known thereafter as Red Square). Since then most of the university's growth has been at its periphery, particularly in the newer areas of the west and southwest campus.

The growing demand for architectural services in the postwar period prompted the rapid expansion of the University of Washington architectural program after 1945. New faculty who joined the program, including John Sproule, Robert Dietz, Victor Steinbrueck, Omer Mithun, Daniel Streissguth, Keith Kolb, Wendell Lovett, Norman Johnston, Gordon Varey, and others, as well as visiting and part-time faculty such as Fred Bassetti and Ibsen Nelsen, were

formal development. The Space Needle was featured several times on the cover of *Time* magazine in 1962, and seemed to embody that era's faith in technology and progress. For Seattle residents, Century 21 took on significance as the symbol of the city's "coming of age." After the fair closed, the grounds were redesigned as an urban park and cul-

Century 21 Exposition (Seattle Center), 1957-62 (altered), Paul Thiry (principal architect). The 1962 World's Fair focused on modern technology and brought worldwide attention to Seattle. *(University of Washington Libraries, Special Collections Division; 1962; UW 1728).*

firmly committed to Modernism. In 1958 the School of Architecture became the College of Architecture and Urban Planning, with long-time faculty member Arthur Herrman as the first dean. The Department of Urban Planning (later renamed Urban Design and Planning) was formed in 1962 under the chairmanship of Myer Wolfe. In 1964 the Department of Landscape Architecture was formed, chaired by Richard Haag. A program in building technology and administration, founded in the early 1960s, became the Department of Building Construction in 1968.

Public Investment and Preservation

By the early 1970s, many assumptions of the postwar period were challenged. In the years after the Second World War, Modernism had become closely associated with modernization, particularly with massive programs of freeway building and urban renewal. Modernism had endorsed a program of cataclysmic change to address the

problems of the city, and federal housing, highway, and urban renewal programs provided the funding to undertake massive projects. Seattle was fortunate in that it sometimes lagged in implementing such programs, and in the interval the adverse impacts happening in other cities often became apparent. Although Seattle had pioneered public housing developments, building Yesler Terrace and Holly Park in the early 1940s, the city never attempted the mass programs of high-rise public housing that so scarred other cities. A massive freeway building program was proposed, but after the Alaskan Way viaduct was built along the waterfront in the late 1940s and Interstate 5 was cut through the city in the early 1960s, residents fought the construction of other freeway projects. Proposals such as the R. H. Thomson Expressway along Lake Washington, which would have cut through the Arboretum and tunneled under the Montlake Cut, and a Vashon Island suspension bridge, which would have spanned Puget Sound from West Seattle, were halted by citizen opposition.

Freeway Park, Seattle, 1974-76, Lawrence Halprin & Associates (Angela Danadjieva, project designer), with Sakuma James Peterson Landscape Architects (local landscape architects). Financed as part of Forward Thrust, the 5.4-acre Freeway Park was the first project to attempt to reconnect downtown to First Hill and to repair some of the damage resulting from the construction of the interstate highway in the 1960s. The park was subsequently extended to connect to the Washington State Convention and Trade Center, which also spans the freeway. *(City of Seattle Engineering Department; 1979; 32728-37.)*

An awareness of the impacts of continuing growth and modernization in the Puget Sound region first appeared in the late 1950s and developed more rapidly in the 1960s. In 1957, citizens in Seattle and the surrounding areas had approved a regional governmental agency, Metro, to address the multijurisdictional problem of sewage that had severely polluted Lake Washington. A decade later voters approved a package of bond issues, called Forward Thrust, which provided funds for local and regional needs such as parks, highways, and sewers, as well as a new indoor athletic stadium. A regional rail mass transit system, also included on the ballot, received 57 percent of the vote, but failed due to a constitutional requirement for a 60 percent majority. It was placed on the ballot again in 1970, but by then a regional recession, often called the Boeing Bust because of the cancellation of the SST by the federal government and a sharp decline in airplane orders, made passage of any new bond issues impossible. Still, the passage of most of Forward Thrust, like the creation of Metro a decade before, represented a commitment to the future of the region.

At least one project that grew out of the Forward Thrust program was a direct attempt to rectify some of the mistakes of the 1960s. Although Paul Thiry had proposed in 1960 that twelve blocks of Interstate 5 passing through Seattle should be constructed below grade and lidded with park space to maintain the connection between downtown and First Hill, the idea remained a dream until the 1970s. Initially proposed as a small park adjacent to the freeway, Freeway Park grew into a 5.4-acre park spanning the freeway and reestablishing the link from downtown to First Hill. Designed by Angela Danadjieva of the office of Lawrence Halprin in San Francisco, the project opened in 1976 to national acclaim. Freeway Park became an oasis in downtown, with its central waterfall and extensive planting creating the illusion of an urban forest. In the 1980s, Danadjieva designed the extension of the park to connect with the new Washington State Convention and Trade Center designed by TRA, the present-day successors to Schack, Young & Myers.

Forward Thrust also provided funds for a park and aquarium on the central waterfront. During the 1950s Seattle's port had gone into a decline, but in the 1960s a bond issue was voted to fund modernization. The Port of Seattle built a new grain terminal and was among the first American ports to respond to the containerization of ocean-going shipping. As a result, the finger piers along the central waterfront became obsolete. Redevelopment was primarily incremental, giving the area its mixed collection of tourist-oriented restaurants and shops. The area between Piers 57 and 59 was rebuilt as a public park, designed by the Bumgardner Partnership, opening in 1974, and Pier 59, redesigned by Fred Bassetti & Company, opened as the Seattle Aquarium in 1976. Waterfront redevelopment has continued to the present day, with ambitious plans for the future including possible aquarium expansion as well as new construction by the Port of Seattle.

The transformation of attitudes that began in the 1960s, moving toward a commitment to protect Seattle's unique urban places, reached fruition in the early 1970s with the recognition and protection of the city's historic resources. The city's first designated historic district was created in Pioneer Square, the city's historic center. This area had been seen in the 1950s and 1960s as a site for clearance and new construction. Because the center of downtown development had gradually moved north after 1900, most of the buildings erected after the 1889

fire remained intact, although many were deteriorated or derelict, and several had been demolished for parking lots. In the early 1960s a group of local citizens, including Alan Black, Gordon White, and architect Ralph Anderson, recognizing the significance of buildings in the district, began to lease and renovate or restore some of the properties. Their efforts, and the loss of the Occidental Hotel (Seattle Hotel), which was demolished in 1963 for a parking garage, attracted the attention of the community and the city. In 1968 and 1969 a team led by Victor Steinbrueck inventoried buildings in the district in order to prepare a nomination for the National Register of Historic Places. In 1970, after a year of debate, the area became the city's first locally designated historic district with preservation guidelines for alterations and a review board to regulate demolition, rehabilitation, and new construction. Renewal in Pioneer Square followed, largely by private initiative, although fostered by federal incentive programs for rehabilitation. The Pioneer Square and Occidental parks were designed by the Seattle firm Jones & Jones. Now this district is a vital mixed-use community as well as one of the best-preserved collections of late nineteenth-century commercial architecture to be found in the United States.

In 1971 Pike Place Market became the city's second historic district as a result of the passage of a public initiative to preserve the market and to protect it from proposed demolition and urban redevelopment. The Pike Place Market had been established in 1907 as a public market where the area's farmers could sell their produce directly to local residents. A success from the day it opened, the market grew rapidly and soon included numerous buildings housing fish, meat, and related food and farming enterprises. The main market building was constructed within a year, and was followed within the next decade by the Economy Market, Corner Market, and Sanitary Market buildings. The market flour-

Pike Place Market, Seattle, 1907-present. This early view, dating from about 1908, shows the early interaction of farmers selling directly to customers on Pike Street. This direct producer-to-consumer relationship became the basis for the development of the market into one of the city's most important institutions. (*University of Washington Libraries, Special Collections Division; ca. 1908; UW 1155*).

ished through the Depression until the 1940s, when wartime internment devastated the large Japanese farming community and the market suffered. In the postwar period, deterioration of the market buildings and the focus on suburban development led downtown interests to suggest that the area was blighted and should be considered for clearance. In a 1963 plan for downtown, consultant Donald Monsen proposed that the area could be redeveloped with office towers and parking garages. Numerous clearance and renewal proposals were made throughout the 1960s. These led the City of Seattle in 1969 to adopt an ordinance providing for a 22-acre federally funded urban renewal project including a 4,000-car parking garage, office towers, hotels, and condominiums designed by Kirk, Wallace,

McKinley & Associates. This incited a vigorous citizen outcry led by the activist organization Allied Arts of Seattle and its offshoot, Friends of the Market. Victor Steinbrueck was the leader of the initiative effort to rehabilitate and preserve the market, which was strongly approved by Seattle voters on November 2, 1971. The vote provided for the designation of the market area as a local historic district. Although some portions of the market district were substantially reconstructed over the next decade by a public redevelopment authority created for this purpose, the Pike Place Market Preservation and Development Authority (after 1974, under the direction of George Rolfe, its first executive director), this renewal effort took place within the context of the preservation guidelines and under the supervision of a review board. Today, Pike Place Market is again a thriving part of the city, one that many feel represents "the best of Seattle."

With Pioneer Square and Pike Place Market already designated as historic districts, the city passed a broad preservation ordinance in 1973 and created the Office of Urban Conservation in 1975, one of the first American city governments with such an office. By 1980 four additional historic districts had been created and numerous individual buildings had been designated as landmarks worthy of protection. By the early 1980s these efforts earned Seattle national recognition and the city was characterized by some as the leading center of historic preservation in the western United States.

Still, growth and associated development pressure meant that many historic structures, particularly in downtown, were demolished. Theaters, for which Seattle was once well known, proved particularly vulnerable, as demonstrated by the loss of the Majestic, Liberty, Pantages (Palomar), and Orpheum, in the 1960s and 1970s, and, after a protracted struggle, the loss of the Mayflower (Music Hall), in 1991-92. Similarly, the White-Henry-Stuart buildings on the University's Metropolitan Tract were unfortunately demolished between 1974 and 1977, over the protests of preservationists and many in the community, to make way for the unusually shaped Rainier Bank Tower and the Commerce House (now Rainier Square) by Minoru Yamasaki (in association with NBBJ), which applied the internal organization of a suburban shopping center to a downtown block. Thereafter, however, the regents endorsed the preservation and rehabilitation of other older Metropolitan Tract buildings, including the Olympic Hotel (restored and rehabilitated by NBBJ) and the Skinner Building with its Fifth Avenue Theater.

Other facilities, although obsolete, were recycled in innovative ways. A good example

is Gas Works Park, designed by Richard Haag. Completed in 1978, this project reclaimed the site of a coal gasification plant for use as a high-density urban park. The cracking towers and other relics of the site's industrial use were incorporated as elements in the design, thereby recalling the history of the site.

At the same time that citizen activists were addressing Seattle's particular historic districts and individual landmarks, a broad effort to assess the entirety of the city's built fabric was undertaken in the mid-1970s. Victor Steinbrueck's attention to the cityscape had already led to publication of books of his Seattle sketches in 1962 and 1973, but the *Visual Inventory of Buildings and Urban Design Resources for Seattle, Washington,* prepared by Folke Nyberg and Steinbrueck between 1975 and 1977 (published by Historic Seattle), was the first attempt to survey the city's entire built environment. This recognition of the importance to the city not only of its landmark buildings but also of its vernacular and popular architecture (see essay) has grown steadily since that time.

Recent Years

The architectural history of Seattle in the last two decades is much more difficult to assess, both because the region has grown so large and so complex and because sufficient time has not passed for recent achievements to be placed in perspective. In addition, the coherence within the architectural profession that appears to have existed before the 1930s in the period of academic eclecticism, as well as in the 1950s and 1960s when Modernism was the dominant design direction, seems now to have disappeared.

The regional variant of Modernism that emphasized use of natural materials, particularly wood, and large areas of glass, and frequently featured sloped roofs and exposed structure, remained the dominant tendency among Seattle architects until the early 1970s. The challenges to Modernism that began to be mounted in the 1960s, marked, for example, by Robert Venturi's publication of *Complexity and Contradiction in Architecture* in 1966, initially had a limited effect in the Northwest. However, the national energy shortages beginning in October 1973 prompted questions about the continued availability of cheap and abundant energy resources. This, in turn, challenged an architectural tradition that had celebrated relatively lightweight structure, walls detailed as thin membranes, and expansive use of glass. With the subsequent passage of state legislation and city building code provisions limiting heat loss from buildings, architects were forced to consider other approaches to design.

Although the shared vision of Modernism began to be questioned in the late 1970s and 1980s, Seattle architects never fully endorsed the directions of postmodernism that absorbed much of the American architectural profession during the period. In place of the earlier shared vision, recent work by Seattle professionals demonstrates a multiplicity of architectural directions. Indeed, in place of a dominant view, the term "pluralism" probably best describes the local profession in the last decade.

Just as there no longer seems to be a shared design orthodoxy, the ways in which local firms approach the practice of architecture have diversified rapidly in the last two decades. By the 1990s, Seattle was home to some of the nation's largest corporate practices, several with multiple offices across the United States and a few with offices overseas. While many of the larger firms continued to seek commissions of many types, they frequently became best known for individual specialties. To name just two examples, Jones & Jones, a landscape and architecture design firm, became known for innovative work in zoological design, and TRA, which designed a variety of large public and institutional projects, became known for their work as airport designers. At the same time, in Seattle and the Puget Sound region it has remained possible to practice successfully as a sole proprietor, custom designing individual residences, remodelings and other small structures.

Nonetheless, technological developments have affected Seattle architectural firms both large and small in recent years. In particular, modern communications systems and computer technology have changed the way many Seattle architects practice their profession. These advances have allowed Seattle practitioners to expand their geographic reach far beyond the region. At the same time, competition by architects from outside Puget Sound for commissions in the region has increased dramatically as a result of these same advances.

Since the postwar period those practicing the profession have been drawn from increasingly diverse cultural and ethnic backgrounds. Early Asian American and African American practitioners such as Kichio Allen Arai and Benjamin F. McAdoo, Jr., were followed by many others. The career of Elizabeth Ayer (and others such as L. Jane Hastings, who graduated from the University of Washington in 1952, opened her own architectural practice in 1959, became a Fellow in the American Institute of Architects in 1980, and served as Chancellor of the AIA College of Fellows in 1992), proved an inspiration for succeeding generations of women architects. Indeed, by the 1990s over a third of those graduating from the professional program at the University of Washington were women.

If there is, at present in the region, no clearly shared vision of the form architecture should take, it can still be said that most local practitioners today probably share certain values. First is a concern for the particular characteristics that have given Seattle its individuality. Although local designers may disagree on what these characteristics are, most seem to be attempting to respond through design to their own understanding of the city and region as a specific place.

There is also a recognition of the importance of the natural environment and a concern that it be respected and conserved, both at the level of individual project design and in relation to regional resources. Simultaneously, the profession can probably be said to share a commitment to the city and to the values inherent in urban living. And many in the profession likely share a concern for social equity and could be considered supporters of recent Seattle efforts to provide low-income housing and social services. Finally, while there may be disagreements regarding individual buildings, most in the profession share a concern for the architectural heritage of the city and the preservation of its essential cultural resources.

In December 1986, *Progressive Architecture* published the results of a nationwide survey of 325 architects. They were asked to list their favorite places in various American cities. For Seattle, the architects selected urban places, including Pike Place Market, Pioneer Square, Freeway Park, and the downtown waterfront. Notably, these are all public places, and most were built incrementally over time. All reflect local initiative and, other than Freeway Park, all were the work of local designers across several generations. This list is clearly incomplete, but it shows the value Seattle professionals and others have placed on their architectural heritage and on working together to create urban places that work and that sustain the people who use them.

Nonetheless, the city and region face a challenging future. In 1970 the population of the city was 530,831, a decline from 1960; this decline continued over the next decade, and in 1980 there were only 493,846 residents in Seattle. The city rebounded in 1990 to 516,259, but this was still below the peak of 1960. King County population by 1970 reached 1,159,369; thus over half the county's residents were living outside Seattle. The population of the region has continued to grow as the state's recreational resources and the region's livability became nationally recognized. By 1990 the population of the greater metropolitan Seattle area (including King, Snohomish, and Pierce counties) had reached almost three million. The resulting growth, every year extending farther in all directions, is generally seen as threatening the very qualities that make the region so attractive. Whether this growth can be controlled and directed has been a frequent subject of discussion in the last two decades and will continue to occupy architects and other design professionals well into the next century. Plans including regional growth management, urban development around several higher density urban centers, and a regional rail network to address growing travel demand were all under consideration by the early 1990s. What parts of these plans will be adopted, how they will be carried forward, and what other solutions to similar problems will be discovered or designed remain uncertain. The future of Seattle and the Puget Sound region is as indistinct as the future of any other vital city in this period of change. Whatever directions do emerge, architects and other design professionals will undoubtedly continue to play a key role in giving form to the city and the region.

Note: For bibliographic information and source materials for the architectural history of Seattle, see appendix "Researching Seattle's Architectural Past," by David A. Rash.

SHAPING SEATTLE ARCHITECTURE

A Historical Guide to the Architects

Native American Architecture on Puget Sound

WAYNE SUTTLES

It is not known how long the Coast Salish tribes of the Puget Sound region have been here or by what route they came. The Northwest Coast was settled at least 9,000 years ago, and by 4,000 years ago its peoples were developing the economic and technological basis of Northwest Coast culture. The ancestors of the Coast Salish probably participated in this development. Until the mid-nineteenth century, they lived, as they no doubt had for millennia, in villages of one or more plank houses built along a shore or riverbank. Each house was the

1. Model of wall construction (photographed on the Lummi Indian Reservation, about 1930). The "wall boards" are small and rough, but the method of attachment is authentic. This was one of several displays illustrating former practices. (*University of Washington Libraries, Special Collections Division; photo by Eugene Field, ca. 1930; NA-1818.*)

home base of a group of families, who went out to different sites for fishing, hunting, and gathering, and returned with foods collected to spend the winter season together. The plank house was dwelling, food-processing and storage plant, and theater.

The most common type was the shed-roof house, consisting of a permanent frame and removable roof and wall planks, all made of western red cedar. For the frame, slablike posts were set into the ground in pairs of unequal height to form two rows parallel to the shore, the taller on the side nearest the water—the front of the house. The number of pairs determined the length of the house, the distance between them the width, and the difference in height the pitch of the roof, which was generally not great. The pairs of posts supported crossbeams, which in turn supported purlins on which the roof planks were laid. These had lipped edges and interlocked like tiles. The walls were quite separate from the frame that held the roof. They were of wider flat wall planks slung horizontally between pairs of vertical poles to which the wall planks were bound by cedar-withe ropes. The tops of the walls were secured to the ends of the roof planks, the outer set of poles extending upward beyond the roof. Some houses had doors in front, others at the ends.

Inside, the walls were lined with mats of cattail or tule rushes. Floors were bare earth, usually at the level of the ground outside, but sometimes excavated. Sleeping platforms were built out from the walls, and storage shelves hung over them. In a smaller house a section between adjacent pairs of posts was occupied by one family with its fire in the center; in a wider house this space could be occupied by two families, one on each side. Sections were often separated by low partitions. Posts might be painted or carved with symbols of the vision powers of their owners. For ceremonies, partitions were removed, fires were consolidated in the center, and a roof plank was raised to provide a new smokehole. Often the frame

2.   "Ruins of the old potlatch house of Chief Chow-its-hoot," Lummi Indian Reservation. Although the length of the house was estimated at 252 feet, Edmond S. Meany noted that it may have been longer before it was abandoned. (*University of Washington Libraries, Special Collections Division; photo by E. S. Meany, ca. 1905; NA-1237.*)

belonged to a wealthy leader who had mobilized the labor to erect it, while the planks and mats of each section of the house belonged to the family who occupied it.

The planks, split from a cedar tree trunk with wedges and carefully worked with a stone- or shell-bladed adz and dogfish-skin sandpaper, were especially valuable. The largest were three to four feet wide and over twenty feet long. They were often removed when the house was unoccupied and laid across pairs of canoes to make catamarans for transporting goods to and from other sites. At some sites there were permanent frames that people covered temporarily with planks, as in the winter village; at others, they simply erected frames of poles and leaned planks against them or laid mats over them.

The shed-roof house could be shortened by eliminating sections or extended by adding more as far as the terrain allowed. Some were huge. The frame of Old Man House, still standing on Agate Pass in 1855, measured 520 feet long, 60 feet wide, 15 feet high in front and 10 feet high in back. This house was reportedly built around 1815 by a Suquamish leader, the brother of the man for whom the city of Seattle is named. Clallam and Skagit leaders had similar houses. Perhaps around 1850, the Lummi leader Chowitsoot built a house, the frame of which was partly standing in 1905, which consisted of pairs of posts set about 24 feet apart, the front posts 12 feet high and the rear 9 feet, holding crossbeams 40 feet long and 18 inches thick at their larger ends. Edmond S. Meany estimated the length of the house at 252 feet, saying it could have been longer, as additional posts and beams could have, by then, disappeared. The rear posts bore a carved symbol of one of Chowitsoot's vision powers—the sun carrying two bags of wealth.

Larger structures have been called "potlatch houses" because they were built for the display of wealth and generosity called the potlatch, but they were also lived in. Exploring the Fraser River in 1808, Simon Fraser saw a Coast Salish village of about two hundred people all in one shed-roof house 640 feet long, 60 feet wide, and 18 feet high at the front.

Two other types of plank houses were built in this region. The gable-roof house had a central frame consisting of pairs of posts of equal height, supporting crossbeams. King posts carried by the cross beams held up the ridgepole. Rafters rested on the ridgepole, the beams, and a set of wall posts standing well outside the central frame. The roof was like that of the shed-roof house, but wall planks were sometimes set vertically into the ground. The gambrel-roof house seems to have consisted of a central frame holding a nearly flat roof plus a lean-to on each side.

From the mid-nineteenth century on, the Coast Salish began building gable-roof houses with frames of posts and beams in the old style, but with roofs and walls of shakes and milled lumber nailed to the

3. Gambrel-roof house on Penn Cove, Whidbey Island. The posts and beam at the left of the gambrel-roof structure, which appear to match those supporting its roof, suggest that it was originally part of a longer shed-roof house, now rebuilt with nailed shakes and timber to expand its interior. The three smokestacks thrust through the roof were probably for cookstoves, and the tents, mats, and planks around the structure suggest people had gathered for a potlatch. (*University of Washington Libraries, Special Collections Division; photographer unknown, ca. 1890-1905; NA-826.*) (A later view of this house, NA-694, appears in Nabokov and Easton, on page 238—see Sources of Information appendix.)

4. "Old potlatch house on Swinomish Reservation." This was probably a late-nineteenth-century dwelling used for the winter dance. *(University of Washington Libraries, Special Collections Division; photo by E. S. Meany, ca. 1905; NA-1229.)*

frame. By 1900 these were being abandoned as residences in favor of single-family houses like those of Euro-American settlers, but some of the old "smokehouses" continued to be used for winter dances. Since the resurgence of winter dances in the 1950s, a number of native communities have built new "longhouses" in modified versions of the late-nineteenth-century dwelling.

There are few illustrations of the older houses within the Puget Sound region. The shed-roof house is best seen in illustrations from adjacent regions to the north and west where this type was also used, as in sketches made by Paul Kane at Victoria in 1847, and in early photographs taken on Vancouver Island and around Neah Bay.

Other house types were used elsewhere on the Northwest Coast. To the south, the usual type was a gable-roof house with central posts supporting the ridgepole, roof planks running parallel to it, and vertical wall planks set into the ground. On the northern coast, gable-roof houses with the wall planks carefully fitted into the frames and usually with a painted facade or a "totem pole" as a doorway were typical. These were masterpieces of craftsmanship and artistry, but they could not be easily stripped of planks for seasonal moves or altered in length in response to changes in the number of occupants, and the largest of them were no bigger than one section of the biggest Coast Salish house.

Mother Joseph of the Sacred Heart (Esther Pariseau)

CHERYL SJOBLOM

In early Northwest history, Mother Joseph of the Sacred Heart (1823-1902) was among the first to care for orphans and the aged, and the first to establish a hospital. Mother Joseph also played a role as architect, a role for which she was later honored by the American Institute of Architects and the West Coast Lumbermen's Association.

The daughter of a French Canadian carriage maker, Esther Pariseau (Mother Joseph's birth name) was born April 16, 1823, in St. Elzear, Quebec. She learned carpentry at an early age, and when she joined

Mother Joseph of the Sacred Heart, 1823-1902. *(Sisters of Providence Archives, Seattle; 13, Mother Joseph Collection; photo by Hofsteater, Portland, Oregon, April 1900.)*

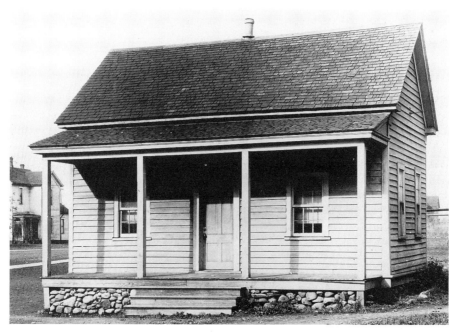

1. Sisters of Providence, Multipurpose Building, Vancouver, Washington, 1856 (destroyed), Mother Joseph of the Sacred Heart. *(Sisters of Providence Archives, Seattle; photo by Wescott Studio, Vancouver, Washington, ca. 1930; 22, Providence Academy, Vancouver, Building #1, 22.)*

2. Providence Academy, Vancouver, Washington, 1867-73 (with addition, 1891), Mother Joseph of the Sacred Heart. The size of this structure reflects the expanding mission of the Sisters of Providence in the Northwest. Providence Academy still stands and has been listed on the National Register of Historic Places since 1978. *(Sisters of Providence Archives, Seattle; 1963; Providence Academy, Vancouver, Building #2, 22.)*

the Sisters of Providence in 1843 she brought her skills as a builder to that religious community.

In 1856, Sister Joseph and four other sisters were sent to Vancouver, Washington Territory, at the request of Bishop A. M. A. Blanchet, who sought the establishment of a religious community on the frontier to provide for the social and religious needs of early settlers and Native peoples.

Mother Joseph's background in carpentry and building soon proved useful, as she was responsible for remodeling a small room for use by the sisters as a dormitory, refectory, classroom, and community room. However, her skills were soon applied to larger projects. Her first new building was a cabin large enough for four beds, four tables, and four chairs; in 1858, this became Saint Joseph Hospital (destroyed), the religious community's first hospital in the Northwest.

Tradition credits Mother Joseph with de-

signing and supervising construction of an extensive network of facilities across the Northwest, while she continued to direct the increasingly widespread activities of the Sisters of Providence. Thus, for example, she is credited with the design and construction of the House of Providence, later Providence Academy, Vancouver (1867-73; enlarged 1891). She is also known to have been involved in the design of several orphanages, hospitals, and schools in the region.

In the absence of clear records, however, the full extent of Mother Joseph's role as architect and builder remains uncertain. As the Sisters of Providence developed a far-reaching network of facilities, Mother Joseph did work with local architectural professionals on some projects. For example, the design of Saint Vincent Hospital, Portland (1874-75; destroyed), is generally credited to her, and records in the Archives of the Sisters of Providence, written in 1892, describe the building as "the masterpiece of

3. Saint Vincent Hospital, Portland, Oregon, 1874-75 (destroyed), Mother Joseph of the Sacred Heart (later additions by Warren H. Williams, architect). This first Saint Vincent Hospital was located at 12th and Marshall until 1895. Saint Vincent's was the first hospital in Oregon. *(Sisters of Providence Archives, Seattle; ca. 1875; Saint Vincent Hospital, Portland, Building #1, 53.)*

4. Providence Hospital, Seattle, 1882-83 (destroyed), Mother Joseph of the Sacred Heart with Donald MacKay. This, the third building for Providence Hospital, was located at Fifth and Madison until 1911. A brass plaque marks its location at the site of the current Federal Courthouse. *(Sisters of Providence Archives, Seattle; ca. 1893; Providence Hospital, Seattle, Building #3, 56.)*

5. Saint Peter Hospital, Olympia, Washington, 1887 (destroyed), Mother Joseph of the Sacred Heart. This first Saint Peter Hospital was located until 1924 on what is today Washington State Capitol grounds. *(Sisters of Providence Archives, Seattle, ca. 1887; Saint Peter Hospital, Olympia, Building #1, 72.)*

Mother Joseph's architectural skill." But when additions to this building were constructed in 1880 and 1882, local newspaper accounts identified Warren H. Williams as the architect of record. Whether Williams had any earlier involvement remains unknown. At Saint Mary Hospital (1879-80, later Saint Vincent Academy, destroyed) in Walla Walla, Mother Joseph was described as the "director and superintendent of the building" during the laying of the cornerstone on July 30, 1879, while O. F. Wegener, a local architect and civil engineer, was identified as the architect of record. When a larger building was later planned in 1883 to replace the original building, the local architectural firm of Allen & Whittemore was the architect of record. In contrast, Portland newspapers do indicate Mother Joseph's direct involvement in the design and construction of the Sisters of Providence hospital in Astoria in 1880.

In 1877, Mother Joseph sent three Sisters of Providence north to Seattle to provide health care and other services in the community. They eventually purchased a house at Fifth and Madison, which became their residence and first hospital. Admissions rose from 25 in 1877 to 215 in the first ten months of 1882, and the increased demand led Mother Joseph to plan a new hospital for the city.

Accounts in local newspapers identified the architect for Providence Hospital as Donald MacKay (see MacKay essay), who arrived in Seattle from Portland with plans on April 18, 1882. Bids were accepted on April 26, and construction was completed in mid-January 1883. However, tradition has credited Mother Joseph with a part in the design. In the absence of definitive evidence or contemporary records, it is difficult to sort out responsibilities for the project. Clearly, Mother Joseph had had extensive experience as a carpenter, designer-builder, and administrator of hospitals, schools, and similar institutions. No architect then in the Northwest could have matched that experi-

ence. MacKay apparently had some experience with buildings of this scale, but the program and design requirements of the Sisters of Providence could have been identified only by Mother Joseph, and although MacKay is credited with production of the drawings and supervision of construction, Mother Joseph clearly was a collaborator and possibly a co-equal participant in the design. She most likely played a similar role in the expansion of the facility in 1887, 1888, and 1893, and possibly the expansion of 1901 as well.

Mother Joseph directed the construction of facilities in other Northwest cities, including Sacred Heart Hospital, Spokane (1886; destroyed); Saint Mary Hospital, New Westminster, British Columbia (1886; destroyed); and Saint Peter Hospital, Olympia (1887; destroyed).

After Mother Joseph's death on January 19, 1902, the Portland *Catholic Sentinel* wrote: "She was adept in nearly all the arts and trades . . . but her genius found its strongest expression in architecture. The numerous buildings planned and superintended by her bear testimony to this fact. . . . From the date of the foundation of the Washington Province of the Sisterhood, Mother Joseph established no less than eleven hos–pitals, seven academies, five Indian Schools and two orphanages."

The full extent of Mother Joseph's role in the realization of Providence Hospital may never be exactly defined. However, she made a significant contribution to the development of Seattle as the leading city on Puget Sound and in the state. She was likely the first architect in Washington Territory, although she was not, as some have claimed, the first architect in the Pacific Northwest; that honor probably belongs to Absalom B. Hallock (1827-92), who arrived in Portland in 1850 and established an architectural practice in 1851. Nonetheless, Mother Joseph's contributions were significant in the development of architectural practice in the Northwest.

Donald MacKay

DAVID A. RASH

The brief architectural career of Donald MacKay in Seattle is somewhat perplexing. He can be placed as an architect in Seattle from April 1882 to March 1884, in Tacoma from March 1884 to July 1884, and in Vancouver, British Columbia, during part of 1887. Circumstantial evidence suggests that the Donald MacKay (1841-1926), who resided in Portland, Oregon, almost continuously from 1866 until his death on April 24, 1926, was this architect.

Donald MacKay was born December 25, 1841, near Woodstock, Ontario, to Scottish immigrants. After serving an apprenticeship, he entered the contracting business near his home until 1865, when he moved to San Francisco. He remained there a scant eight months before moving to Portland, where he continued to work as a contractor. MacKay had a continuous listing in the Portland city directories from 1866 to 1882.

Donald MacKay. (*Oregon Historical Society, from* Oregon Legislative Album, *1899; CN 024097.*)

1. Catholic Church of Our Lady of Good Help, Seattle, 1882 (destroyed), Donald MacKay. The existing building was turned ninety degrees to form the transept of a much enlarged church with new Gothic Revival entrances. (*University of Washington Libraries, Special Collections Division; photo by Asahel Curtis, 1247.*)

2. Providence Hospital, Seattle, 1882-83 (with additions 1887, 1888, 1893; destroyed), Donald MacKay with Mother Joseph. The original portion of this Second Empire style edifice extended only to the central tower, although the building eventually grew to a block in length. *(Museum of History and Industry, Seattle; ca. 1893; Seattle Historical Society Collection 10,952.)*

On April 18, 1882, Donald MacKay, the architect, arrived in Seattle from Portland, with drawings for a new building to house Providence Hospital (1882-83; destroyed) and for a major enlargement of the existing Church of Our Lady of Good Help (1882; destroyed) for the local Roman Catholic parish. The plans for Providence Hospital may have been provided by Esther Pariseau (better known today as Mother Joseph, see essay); however, as with his other work in Washington State, MacKay did not provide any construction-related services beyond architectural supervision.

Besides Providence Hospital and the Church of Our Lady of Good Help, MacKay designed several other major buildings in Seattle. Most of these contained suggestions of the then fashionable Second Empire style. These new buildings included the new Occidental Hotel (1882-84; destroyed), Seattle Engine House No. 1 (1883-84; destroyed),

and the Academy of the Holy Names (1883-84; destroyed). MacKay's design work in other localities included the First Presbyterian Church, Vancouver, Washington (1883-85; destroyed), Saint James Catholic Cathedral (1883-85), also at Vancouver, and an apparently unexecuted scheme in 1883 for what is now Gonzaga University in Spokane.

During the construction of the Academy of the Holy Names, an acrimonious dispute arose between MacKay and Father Francis Xavier Prefontaine, of the Seattle parish, over responsibility for directing the construction work. The specifics of the dispute are not completely known; however, MacKay clearly felt that Prefontaine had attacked his "personal and professional character" and was attempting to force him "down to the starvation terms offered me [MacKay] for my work." This dispute, in conjunction with Tacoma work already in hand, apparently prompted MacKay to remove his ar-

3. Occidental Hotel, Seattle, 1882-84 (destroyed), Donald MacKay. This structure was the most sophisticated rendition in brick construction of the Second Empire in Seattle. It provided the only creditable competition to the Tacoma Hotel in the Puget Sound area prior to 1889. (*University of Washington Libraries, Special Collections Division; photo by Dorsatz and Schwerin, ca. 1885; UW12326.*)

4. Seattle Engine House No. 1, Seattle, 1883-84 (destroyed), Donald MacKay. MacKay's only civic commission was ironically destroyed during the great fire of June 6, 1889. (*Museum History and Industry, Seattle; ca. 1885; Seattle Historical Society Collection 2516.*)

chitectural office to the City of Destiny. None of the several projected commercial works in Tacoma went beyond MacKay's drawing board, although one residence, the Edward S. "Skookum" Smith house (1884-86; destroyed), was constructed in a version of the Stick Style.

Donald MacKay's listing in the Portland city directories resumed in 1884, but, curiously, he served one term on the Portland City Council in 1883—the one year that he is missing from the directories. In 1900, while president of the North Pacific Lumber Company (a company that he helped to organize in 1882), MacKay, a prominent Republican, was accused of graft by the *Democratic Daily Times* in connection with purchases by the City of Portland and the County of Multnomah: "Not a single item enters into the consumption of the two governments that has not paid its portion in tribute." However, criminal charges were never brought against him.

During the nineteenth century, the mi-

gration of construction contractors into the profession of architecture was not uncommon, and MacKay's work in Seattle suggests a first-hand knowledge of the work by the prominent Portland architects Warren H. Williams and Joseph Sherwin. This, in conjunction with the coincidental dating obtained from the Portland city directories, does suggest that MacKay the contractor and MacKay the architect were one and the same; however, a Donald McKay in 1881 was an unsuccessful contractor bidding on the completion of the Walla Walla County Courthouse. Providence Hospital, Occidental Hotel, Seattle Engine House No. 1, and the Academy of the Holy Names were significant buildings that allowed Seattle to maintain its tenuous lead over Tacoma as the leading "metropolis" on Puget Sound during the 1880s. Another architect could have provided equivalent design services, but no other architect residing in Seattle, at the time, could have given these buildings the same design sophistication.

5. Academy of the Holy Names, Seattle, 1883-84 (destroyed), Donald MacKay. Stylistically, this was MacKay's most eclectic design, combining elements of the Italianate, Gothic Revival, and Second Empire styles. *(University of Washington Libraries, Special Collections Division; photo by Charles H. Morford, ca. 1885; UW14336.)*

6. Saint James Catholic Cathedral (now Church), Vancouver, Washington, 1883-85, Donald MacKay. Built as the original seat of the Diocese of Nesqually (now the Archdiocese of Seattle), at that time located in Vancouver. The Diocesan See was transferred in 1903 to Seattle, and Saint James in Vancouver was demoted to parish status. *(Photo by David A. Rash, 1993.)*

7. Edward S. Smith house, Tacoma, Washington, 1884-86 (destroyed), Donald MacKay. This Stick Style house was one of MacKay's few residential designs to be constructed. *(University of Washington Libraries, Special Collections Division; ca. 1925; UW14338.)*

William E. Boone

JEFFREY KARL OCHSNER

William E. Boone (1830-1921) is generally recognized as the most important architect in Seattle for the period before the fire of June 6, 1889. He is also virtually the only prefire Seattle architect who continued to practice at a significant level through the 1890s and into the twentieth century.

Boone was born in Pennsylvania September 3, 1830. Raised in Pennsylvania, he worked for several years in Chicago, then moved about 1853 to Minneapolis, where he became involved in design and construction. In 1859, he moved to California and was for many years a designer-builder in Oakland and the surrounding East Bay communities. He first came to the Puget Sound area in 1872, and in 1873 he served as con-

William E. Boone, ca. 1893. From Julian Hawthorne, *History of Washington, the Evergreen State* (New York, 1893), opposite page 114. *(University of Washington Libraries, Special Collections Division; UW14575.)*

1. Yesler-Leary Building, Seattle, 1882-83 (destroyed), Boone & Meeker. The early preeminence of Boone & Meeker in Seattle architecture is reflected in this business block, which was destroyed by the 1889 fire. Its design shows the direct influence of contemporary work in San Francisco. *(University of Washington Libraries, Special Collections Division; photo by Asahel Curtis, 6235.)*

struction superintendent for the federal prison at McNeil Island, but returned thereafter to California. He came permanently to the Northwest in 1881, and over the next few years practiced in both Seattle and Tacoma. From 1882 to 1889, Boone was in partnership with George C. Meeker in the firm of Boone & Meeker. Meeker probably remained in California for much of this time, although he may have come to Washington in the mid-1880s.

Boone & Meeker's work in the 1880s reflected prevailing Victorian conventions and frequently echoed work in California. Their Yesler-Leary Building (1882-83; destroyed) was based on the Phelan Block in San Francisco; and their Henry Yesler house (1884; destroyed) had the thin, angular, and highly agitated forms typical of the time. Outside Seattle, Boone & Meeker's projects included the Annie Wright Seminary, Tacoma (1883-84; destroyed) and the Territorial Insane Asylum, Steilacoom (1886-87; destroyed). By the late 1880s, however, the firm's work was centered in Seattle, where the partnership was responsible for several commercial blocks such as the Toklas & Singerman Building (1887; destroyed) that were consumed by the fire of 1889. Boone & Meeker's

2. Henry Yesler house, Seattle, 1884 (destroyed), Boone & Meeker. The high angularity, irregular bays, picturesque profile, and varied details of the Yesler house are typical of American High Victorian architecture. *(University of Washington Libraries, Special Collections Division; UW2503.)*

preeminence in the city was reflected in the selection of their designs from among multiple proposals for Seattle's South School and Central School in 1888. Completed in 1889, these were the Seattle School District's first brick school buildings.

Boone, practicing alone, received numerous commissions after the fire, but his leadership position in the city was chal-

3. Territorial Insane Asylum, Steilacoom, Washington, 1886-87 (destroyed), Boone & Meeker. This massive institutional structure may reflect Meeker's previous experience with this building type. John C. Proctor, of Daniels & Proctor, a Tacoma firm, replaced Boone & Meeker as supervising architect in September 1886, during construction. *(Washington State Historical Society, Tacoma; ca. 1888.)*

4. Toklas & Singerman Building, Seattle, 1887 (destroyed), Boone & Meeker. The vertical bays with tall narrow proportions and the use of constructive detail reveal the Victorian sources for the design of this commercial building. (*University of Washington Libraries, Special Collections Division; photo by A. C. Warner, ca. 1888.*)

lenged by younger architects. His initial postfire Seattle projects, including the Dexter Horton Building (1889; destroyed), the Carleton Block (1889; destroyed), and the Wah Chong Building (1889; destroyed), continued to reflect Victorian design conventions. Boone's gradual adoption of motifs derived from the Romanesque Revival mode was first evident in the four-story Marshall-Walker Block (1890-91), where he employed round arched windows. Romanesque motifs also appeared in his unbuilt project for the YMCA (1890).

Boone's major project at this time was the New York Block (1890-92; destroyed), a splendid example of the Romanesque Revival mode applied to a seven-story brick and stone commercial business block. Here Boone clearly appears to have learned from the example of Chicago architects such as Burnham & Root and to have transcended the limits of Victorian convention.

In December 1890, Boone formed the partnership of Boone & Willcox, with William H. Willcox (1832-1929), who had previously practiced in New York, Chicago,

Nebraska, and Minneapolis–St. Paul. Willcox brought considerable experience in the design of churches and may have been the primary designer of the Plymouth Congregational Church (1890-92; destroyed), a massive Gothic Revival design. The firm's proposed Trinity Methodist Episcopal Church (1891), intended for West Seattle, was never built.

In 1891, Boone & Willcox were selected to plan the new University of Washington campus. Their scheme, which included proposed designs for sixteen buildings, was the basis for the initiation of construction in October 1891. However, as a result of flaws in the legislation that created the University, the project was halted after ten days. When work on the University began again in 1893, it followed an entirely different design.

5. Central School, Seattle, 1888-89 (destroyed), Boone & Meeker. This monumental edifice was one of the city's first two brick school buildings. (*University of Washington Libraries, Special Collections Division; photo by Asahel Curtis, 2611.*)

6. Wah Chong Building, Seattle, 1889 (destroyed), William Boone. Boone's first buildings after the fire continued to follow the Victorian conventions of his prefire work. *(Museum of History and Industry, Seattle; PEMCO Webster & Stephens Collection, 83.10.8470.)*

7. Marshall-Walker Block, Seattle, 1890-91 (altered), William Boone. The rusticated stonework and round arches of this structure, also know as the Globe Hotel, are evidence of Boone's first use of Romanesque Revival motifs. It has since lost its cornice. *(University of Washington Libraries, Special Collections Division; photo by Asahel Curtis, 1064.)*

8. New York Block, Seattle, 1890-92 (destroyed), Boone & Willcox. Regarded as one of the finest business blocks in postfire Seattle, the New York Block shows the influence of the Romanesque Revival as reinterpreted by Chicago School architects such as Burnham & Root. *(University of Washington Libraries, Special Collections Division.)*

In mid-1892, Boone & Willcox dissolved their partnership and Boone again practiced on his own. His work from this period was limited to a few commercial buildings, such as the one-story Leary-Walker Block (1893; destroyed), and a few small residential projects. During the economic depression of the mid-1890s, Boone appears to have had little work.

From 1900 to 1905, Boone joined with James M. Corner (1862-1919), who had come to Seattle from Boston and had previously been in partnership with Warren P. Skillings. The new firm, Boone & Corner, was responsible for the first Seattle High School (1902-3; destroyed), built of massive masonry with Romanesque Revival and French Renaissance motifs. The firm's Walker Block (1903; destroyed) was Boone's last significant commission.

Although William Boone had begun his career as a carpenter and contractor, he was a leader in the effort to place the practice of architecture in Washington on a professional basis. He was a founding member of the Washington State Chapter of the AIA in 1894, and served as its first president. Boone apparently retired from architectural practice some time after 1910. He died in Seattle on October 29, 1921.

9. Plymouth Congregational Church, Seattle, 1890-92 (destroyed), Boone & Willcox. This Gothic Revival structure shows the influence of Boone's partner, William H. Willcox, who had considerable experience designing churches in the Midwest. (*University of Washington Libraries, Special Collections Division; photo by Asahel Curtis, 2619.*)

10. Seattle High School, Seattle, 1902-3 (destroyed), Boone & Corner. Briefly known as Washington High School and subsequently as Broadway High School, this was Seattle's first school building designed specifically to serve as a high school. The only portion now remaining on the site is the auditorium addition (1909-11) by Edgar Blair. (*University of Washington Libraries, Special Collections Division; UW5040.*)

Elmer H. Fisher

JEFFREY KARL OCHSNER
& DENNIS A. ANDERSEN

Elmer H. Fisher (ca. 1840-1905) is closely identified with the rebuilding of Seattle's commercial core after the 1889 fire. He was the most prolific of the postfire generation of Seattle architects, yet he died in obscurity a decade later and remains an enigmatic figure.

Elmer Fisher was born in Edinburgh, Scotland, about 1840. It appears that he came to the United States at age seventeen, but no definitive information on his life prior to 1880 has been discovered. Between 1880 and 1886 he lived in Minneapolis, Denver, and Butte and worked in businesses associated with hardware, farm implements, construction, and mining.

Elmer Fisher about 1890. From *A General Historical and Descriptive Review of the City of Seattle, Washington* (San Francisco, 1890). (*University of Washington Libraries, Special Collections Division.*)

By February 1886, Fisher had moved to Victoria, British Columbia, where he initiated his practice as an architect. Fisher was responsible for the design of commercial buildings and residences in Victoria, Vancouver, Nanaimo, and Goldstream.

Fisher's practice in Washington began with his design of the McCurdy Block, Port Townsend (1887), and this was followed by designs for other Port Townsend business blocks, including the the James & Hastings Building (1888-89), the N. D. Hill Building (1889), and the Hastings Building (1889-90).

By November 1887, Fisher had opened an office in Seattle. His early Seattle commissions included the unbuilt Colman Building (1887-88), the first Korn Building (1887-89; destroyed), the Gilmore and Kirkman Building (sometimes called the Bay Building; 1889-90; destroyed), and the Austin A. Bell Building (1889-90), as ,well as terrace houses, residences, an armory, and other commercial blocks. In 1888, Fisher entered a short-lived partnership with

1. Gilmore and Kirkman Building (also known as Bay Building), Seattle, 1889-90 (destroyed), Fisher & Clark. This business block reflected Victorian design conventions and showed Fisher's typical approach to facade composition. (*University of Washington Libraries, Special Collections Division; UW4664.*)

2. Austin A. Bell Building, Seattle, 1889-90 (altered), Elmer Fisher. Located in the center of the area now called Belltown, the Bell Building shows Fisher's adaptation of the Victorian Gothic to a commercial block. Portions of the original cornice are missing and the interior has apparently been damaged by fire. The building is currently unoccupied. From *Washington Magazine*, Volume 1, October 1889. *(University of Washington Libraries, Special Collections Division; UW12611.)*

3. Pioneer Building, Seattle, 1889-91, Elmer Fisher. Fisher's best known building shows his adaptation of Romanesque Revival motifs within a Victorian compositional framework. (*University of Washington Libraries, Special Collections Division; UW8813.*)

George Clark, but by mid-January 1889 Fisher was again in practice as a sole proprietor.

In January 1889, Fisher was selected by Seattle business leader Henry Yesler to design the Pioneer Building (1889-91), intended by Yesler to be the equal of any building on the Pacific Coast. Fisher designed a $250,000 six-story block for the heart of the city's business core. Fisher's next major business block, the six-story Burke

Building (1889-91; destroyed), was commissioned by Seattle civic leader Judge Thomas Burke in March 1889. With these two commissions, Fisher emerged as the leading architect in Seattle just before the 1889 fire.

As the city rebuilt after the fire, Fisher was besieged with commissions for new business blocks. Among Fisher's Seattle commercial projects were the second Korn Building (1889-90; altered), the Starr-Boyd Building (1889-90; destroyed), the Haller

4. Burke Building, Seattle, 1889-91 (destroyed), Elmer Fisher. Judge Thomas Burke, Fisher's client, suggested that he look to contemporary Chicago buildings, particularly The Rookery by Burnham & Root, as sources for design ideas for this building. Fragments of the Burke Building were retained as decorative elements in the plaza of the Seattle's new Federal Building. (*University of Washington Libraries, Special Collections Division; photo by Asahel Curtis, 93.*)

5. Sullivan Building, Seattle, 1889-91 (destroyed), Elmer Fisher. Fisher's penchant for drawing on a variety of stylistic sources was particularly evident in this building, which combines Classical and Romanesque motifs and details. (*University of Washington Libraries, Special Collections Division; photo by Asahel Curtis, 20595.*)

6. Starr-Boyd Building, Seattle, 1889-90 (destroyed), Elmer Fisher. Jointly commissioned by two owners who sought individual identity, the Starr-Boyd Building was one of Fisher's most irregular designs. (*University of Washington Libraries, Special Collections Division; photo by Asahel Curtis, 90.*)

7. Otto Ranke House, Seattle, 1890-91 (destroyed), Elmer Fisher. This was the largest of the very few houses designed by Elmer Fisher. From *Pacific Magazine*, Volume 4, August 1891. *(University of Washington Libraries, Special Collections Division.)*

sible for the design of fifty-one buildings in the twelve months after the fire) probably forced him to rely heavily on his draftsmen, and this may account for some of the variation in the design of these projects.

Fisher continued to receive commissions for new Seattle commercial buildings in 1890, although at a reduced pace. Among these buildings were two more commissioned by Henry Yesler, the Bank of Commerce (1890-91; altered) and the Yesler Block (1890-91; altered), which was later renamed the Mutual Life Building. Fisher's last large commission was the State Building (1890-91).

In late 1891, Fisher gave up the practice of architecture to become proprietor of the Abbott Hotel in Seattle. He had invested in Seattle real estate, and this seems to have be-

Building (1889-90; destroyed), the Sullivan Building (1889-91; destroyed), the Lebanon Building (1889-91; destroyed), and the Schwabacher Building (1889-90; altered). He also received commissions for buildings in Kent, Ellensburg, Bellingham, and Yakima, but his practice focused primarily on commercial work in Seattle. Fisher received only a small number of institutional projects and competed unsuccessfully for several school commissions. He was so busy he refused all but a few residential projects.

Fisher's buildings varied in detail, but they all showed a typically Victorian compositional framework in the gridding and layering of their facades. He frequently employed multiple stylistic vocabularies on a single building. In the designs for the Pioneer Building and the Burke Building, Fisher began to apply motifs and details characteristic of the Romanesque Revival mode then sweeping the country, but his compositional approach remained Victorian.

It cannot be determined to what extent Fisher was involved in the design of each of his buildings. The volume of work in his office (one account indicates he was respon-

8. Bank of Commerce Building, Seattle, 1890-91 (altered), Elmer Fisher. Sometimes called the Yesler Building, this was another of the commercial projects commissioned by Henry Yesler. The heavily rusticated stone echoes the rusticated pilasters of Yesler's Pioneer Building, located just across Pioneer Square. *(University of Washington Libraries, Special Collections Division; photo by Asahel Curtis, 4090.)*

9. Abbott Hotel, Seattle, 1889-90 (destroyed), Elmer Fisher. Fisher developed and designed this hotel. After he withdrew from architectural practice in 1891, he listed himself in the city directory as its proprietor. *(University of Wash-ington Libraries, Special Collections Division; UW4663.)*

10. State Building, Seattle, 1890-91, Elmer Fisher. The last of Fisher's large commercial commissions, this clearly recalls some contemporary work by Chicago architects. *(University of Washington Libraries, Special Collections Division; photo by Asahel Curtis, 1903.)*

come his primary focus and source of income. He lost everything in the economic collapse of 1893. Thereafter, he attempted, without success, to reopen his architectural office in Seattle. Eventually, Fisher moved to Los Angeles, where he again tried but failed to reestablish himself in architectural practice. His last years were spent as an architectural draftsman and carpenter. He died in 1905.

John Parkinson

JEFFREY KARL OCHSNER

Unlike most architects who achieved prominence in the aftermath of the 1889 Seattle
fire only to have their careers fade after 1893,
John Parkinson (1861-1935) emerged as a
major Seattle designer between 1889 and
1894 and went on to an even more significant career in Los Angeles in the early twentieth century.

John Parkinson was born in Scorton,
England, on December 12, 1861. After completing his formal schooling at age thirteen,
and following two years of intermittent employment, he entered a six-year apprenticeship with a contractor in the town of Bolton.
At the same time, he enrolled in classes at
Bolton's Mechanics Institute, where he
gained a technical education that included
training in building construction and design. Parkinson first came to North America

John Parkinson, about 1902. From *Men of the
Pacific Coast . . . 1902-1903* (San Francisco,
1902). *(University of Washington Libraries,
Special Collections Division; UW14394.)*

in 1883, initially to Winnipeg and then to
Minneapolis. In 1885 he moved permanently to California and secured a position
as a stair builder at a mill in Napa. In 1888,
Parkinson designed his first building, the
Bank of Napa, and thereafter he pursued an
architectural career.

Parkinson arrived in Seattle in January
1889. After failing to secure a position as a
draftsman, he opened his own architectural
office in February. He entered a partnership
with Cecil Evers in March, but this ended
little more than a year later, in June 1890.
Although inexperienced, Parkinson soon
received several significant commissions.
Some of his early projects, such as the Olympia Hotel, Olympia (1889; destroyed), and
Calkins Hotel, Mercer Island (1889-90;
destroyed), reflect his background in carpentry and his knowledge of wood construction. Others, such as his two large
downtown Seattle commercial buildings,
the Butler Block (1889-90; altered) and the
Seattle National Bank Building (1890-92),

1. Calkins Hotel, Mercer Island, 1889-90
(destroyed), Parkinson & Evers. Also known as
the Mercer Island Hotel, this richly detailed
structure shows Parkinson's expertise in design
and construction with wood. *(University of
Washington Libraries, Special Collections Division; UW4815.)*

display a remarkable level of coherence and repose in contrast to the agitated work of so many of his contemporaries.

Parkinson's projects included a wide variety of buildings from commercial blocks to residences, but he is particularly identified with the design of schools. The commission for the B. F. Day School (1891-92; altered), won in July 1891, marked his emergence as the city's leading school designer. In April 1892, the Seattle School Board hired Parkinson as Seattle's first Schools Architect and Superintendent of Construction. In the next two years, Parkinson was responsible for all Seattle school projects including the

3. Butler Block, Seattle, 1889-90 (altered), Parkinson & Evers. Parkinson's first large commercial block, this building was renamed the Butler Hotel when it was converted to hotel use in 1894. The upper floors were later removed and the remaining structure is now a parking garage. *(University of Washington Libraries, Special Collections Division; photo by Boyd and Braas, UW8297.)*

2. Frank Pontius house, Seattle, 1889 (destroyed), Parkinson & Evers. Parkinson's capabilities as a residential designer are well represented by this Queen Anne style house. *(University of Washington Libraries, Special Collections Division; photo by Asahel Curtis, 5330.)*

4. Seattle National Bank Building (now the Interurban Building), Seattle, 1890-92, John Parkinson. An exemplary Romanesque Revival design, built of red sandstone and red brick, this large commercial block displays a remarkable level of coherence. *(University of Washington Libraries, Special Collections Division; photo by LaRoche, 1082.)*

Pacific School (1892-93; destroyed) and the Cascade School (1893-94; destroyed).

Parkinson continued in private practice as well, and received school commissions in other districts. These included large schoolhouses such as the Ballard Central School, later known as Washington Irving School, Ballard (1891; destroyed), and the South Seattle School (1892; destroyed), and also one- and two-room schools in lumber towns such as Snohomish, Sedro, and Hamilton. According to his autobiography, he designed thirty-two schools in the Northwest in those years. Parkinson also designed several college buildings, including the Seattle Seminary Building, the first building at Seattle Pacific University (1891-93; now known as Alexander Hall), and the Jesuit College and Church, the first building at Seattle University (1893-94; now known as the Garrand Building; altered).

Parkinson was particularly concerned about his standing as an architect. He frequently published renderings of his work in professional journals and was a founding member of the Washington State Chapter of the AIA. He also entered many design competitions during his years in Seattle. Unfortunately, with the exception of his school projects, he never tasted success, although he did place second in the competition for Denny Hall at the University of Washington in 1893.

After 1892, as the economy slowed, Parkinson was able to maintain his practice for a time due to his continuing schools

5. B. F. Day School, Seattle, 1891-92 (altered), John Parkinson. Only the south wing of this building was erected initially, but the expansion in 1900 completed the composition following Parkinson's original design. *(University of Washington Libraries, Special Collections Division; photo by Asahel Curtis, 4314.)*

6. Pacific School, Seattle, 1892-93 (destroyed), John Parkinson. In his autobiography, Parkinson described this twelve-room building as the best designed of his Seattle school projects. *(University of Washington Libraries, Special Collections Division; photo by Asahel Curtis, 4323.)*

7. Seattle Seminary Building, Seattle, 1891-93, John Parkinson. This rendering by Parkinson's employee, A. B. Chamberlin, appeared in the Minneapolis-based *Northwestern Architect* in November 1891. The first building at Seattle Pacific University, this is now known as Alexander Hall.

commissions and a range of other projects. Parkinson also became an investor in Seattle real estate; he was both developer and designer of a remarkable group of stone town houses on First Hill in 1892 and of the Seattle Athletic Club Building (1892-93; destroyed). However, the panic of 1893 left Parkinson overextended, especially after April 1894 when the School Board, unable to finance any new construction, terminated his position. As a result of the slump and the limited opportunities available in Seattle, Parkinson moved to southern California.

Parkinson soon became a leader of the profession in Los Angeles, where his career lasted from 1894 almost to his death on December 9, 1935. After 1921, his son, Donald B. Parkinson (1895-1945), joined with him in partnership. Their best known buildings are the Los Angeles Coliseum, Los Angeles City Hall, and Bullock's Wilshire (Department Store) in Los Angeles.

8. Equitable Life Assurance Society Building project, Seattle, 1891-93, John Parkinson. This proposed office building was one of Parkinson's many unbuilt, but nonetheless published, designs. From *American Architect and Building News,* December 12, 1891.

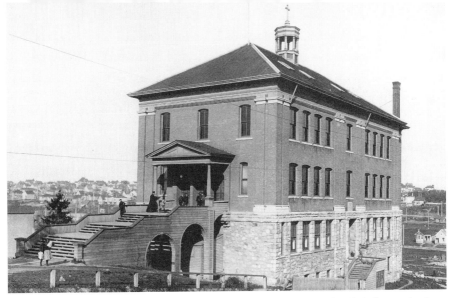

9. Jesuit College and Church, Seattle, 1893-94 (altered), John Parkinson. The relatively restrained design of this building reflects the impact of the panic of 1893. Although construction began in April 1893, it proceeded only as far as the foundation. By the time building resumed in July 1894, Parkinson had left Seattle, and construction proceeded under the direction of Father Victor Garrand, S.J. The first building at Seattle University, this is now known as the Garrand Building. *(University of Washington Libraries, Special Collections Division; photo by Asahel Curtis, 1249.)*

10. Seattle Athletic Club Building, Seattle, 1892-93 (destroyed), John Parkinson. Parkinson was both developer and designer of this building. Its character shows Parkinson's move away from the Romanesque Revival toward a classically based style. *(University of Washington, Special Collections Division; photo by Asahel Curtis, 509.)*

Charles W. Saunders

JEFFREY KARL OCHSNER

Charles Willard Saunders (1858-1935) initiated his Seattle practice just after the 1889 fire and for the next twenty years was among the leaders of the architectural profession in Seattle. He is also known for his efforts in support of early conservation legislation during his tenure in the Washington State legislature.

Saunders was born October 12, 1857, in Cambridge, Massachusetts, and was raised in the Boston area. By 1887 he had moved to Pasadena, California, where he practiced architecture in the partnership of Saunders & Saunders with his wife, Mary Channing Saunders. However, in June 1889, Saunders moved to Seattle, apparently alone, and opened his own practice.

Charles W. Saunders, about 1902. From *Men of the Pacific Coast . . . 1902-1903* (San Francisco, 1902). (*University of Washington Libraries, Special Collections Division; UW14576*)

1. Rainier Hotel, Seattle, 1889 (destroyed), Saunders & Houghton. Intended as a resort hotel, this was rushed to completion in just a few months in order to be ready to serve the anticipated influx of visitors to Seattle after the 1889 fire. (*University of Washington Libraries, Special Collections Division; photo by LaRoche, 20.*)

2. Bailey Building, Seattle, 1889-91, Saunders & Houghton. Occasionally also called the Broderick Building or the Harrisburg Block, this was the only commercial block erected after the 1889 fire to have street facades completely of stone. The design appears to show the influence of contemporary work in Chicago. *(University of Washington Libraries, Special Collections Division; photo by Asahel Curtis, 8304.)*

Saunders achieved rapid success as a result of the patronage of real estate investor and developer William Bailey. Within two months Saunders had secured a series of Seattle commissions including the Rainier Hotel (1889; destroyed), the Washington Territorial Investment Company Building (1889-90; destroyed), and the Bailey Building (1889-91), all backed by Bailey. Then, in August 1889, Saunders won the commission for a group of four eight-room schools in Seattle. The Mercer School, Minor School, and Columbia School, completed in 1890, and the Rainier School, completed in 1891, had identical floor plans, although Saunders individualized their elevations and details.

It may have been this rapidly increasing volume of work that led Saunders, in September 1889, to entered into a partnership with Edwin W. Houghton (1856-1927), an English architect who had recently arrived in Seattle (see Houghton essay). The projects completed by the Saunders & Houghton partnership varied considerably, and the roles that each partner may have

3. Mercer School, Seattle, 1889-90 (destroyed), Saunders & Houghton. Built near the base of Queen Anne Hill, this was one of four school buildings with identical plans designed for the Seattle School District. *(University of Washington Libraries, Special Collections Division; UW6019.)*

played in each of the projects cannot be determined. In addition to Saunders's backlog of commissions, the firm took on additional projects in Seattle including the Fire Department Headquarters (1889-90; destroyed), [Fire] Engine House No. 2 (1889-1890; destroyed), Terry-Denny Building (1889-91), Maud Building (1889-90), Olympic Block (1889-91; destroyed), and a few residences.

Saunders apparently returned to the East in 1891, leaving the firm's work in Houghton's hands, but by mid-1892 he had reestablished his independent Seattle practice, designing the Seattle Theater and Rainier Club (1892-93; both destroyed) for adjacent sites in downtown Seattle. Subsequently, Saunders won the commission for the University of Washington's first building, now Denny Hall (1893-94; altered), with a symmetrical chateauesque design. Saunders was also responsible for the design of the University's first gymnasium (1894-95; destroyed) and the observatory (1894-95).

4. Seattle Theater and Rainier Club, Seattle, 1892-93 (destroyed), Charles W. Saunders. The relative simplicity of this building and the restrained classicizing detail reflect a move away from the Victorian tendencies of just a few years before. Saunders positioned the theater, which had little need for natural light, to the interior of the block, allowing the Rainier Club to face the primary street. *(University of Washington Libraries, Special Collections Division; photo by Hester, 10070.)*

5. Main Building, University of Washington, Seattle, 1893-94 (altered), Charles W. Saunders. Saunders won the competition for the first building of the new University of Washington campus with this chateauesque design. It was later called the Administration Building and is now known as Denny Hall. *(University of Washington Libraries, Special Collections Division; UW6285.)*

6. Lincoln Apartments, Seattle, 1899-1900 (destroyed), Saunders & Lawton. Although built as an apartment hotel, this was soon converted to conventional hotel operation. It was known as the Lincoln Hotel until it was destroyed by a spectacular fire in 1920. *(University of Washington Libraries, Special Collections Division; photo by Asahel Curtis, 1034.)*

In 1898 Saunders and his draftsman, George Willis Lawton (1864-1928), formed the partnership Saunders & Lawton, which endured until 1915. The range of the partnership's work in Seattle is represented by the Lincoln Apartments (1899-1900; destroyed), the Bon Marché Store (1900, 1901-2; destroyed), the Lumber Exchange (1902-3; destroyed), and the Fire Department Headquarters (1902-4; destroyed), as well as numerous residences. The firm was also responsible for the Walla Walla (later Horace Mann) Elementary School (1901-2; now an alternative school), and the Beacon Hill Elementary School (1903-4; now El Centro de la Raza), although their designs were based on the model school plans prepared by James Stephen (see Stephen essay).

Saunders's work was characteristic of its period. Buildings were executed in a range of styles reflecting the options available within the framework of eclectic design. Shingle Style, Romanesque Revival, Sullivanesque, Tudor Revival, and Colonial Revival influences can all be discerned in different projects through the course of Saunders's career. Saunders & Lawton undertook an extraordinarily wide range of projects, including utilitarian structures such as warehouses and mills. They were also the designers of the first building erected specifically for the Seattle Buddhist

7. Bon Marché Store, Seattle, 1900, 1901-2 (destroyed), Saunders & Lawton. Although built to only one story initially, this appears to have been designed for vertical expansion from the beginning. The building was remarkable for its extensive use of glass, restrained detail, and clear articulation of its structural order. From *Seattle Architecturally 1902. (University of Washington Libraries, Special Collections Division; UW14574.)*

8. Lumber Exchange, Seattle, 1902-3 (destroyed), Saunders & Lawton. This office building was a simple rectangular block executed in white brick with restrained detail of classical derivation. *(Museum of History and Industry, Seattle; PEMCO Webster & Stevens Collection, 83.10.6676.)*

Church (1906-8; destroyed), a building whose roofline and panelized walls echoed Asian architecture. Their design for the Forestry Building at the Alaska-Yukon-Pacific Exposition, Seattle (1908-9; destroyed) demonstrates the inventiveness possible for such an eclectic practice. Although the forms and details of the building derived from classical sources, they were executed throughout with raw logs and unfinished wood. The firm also designed the Women's Building (1908-9; altered; now Cunningham Hall) and the Dairy Building (1908-9; destroyed) at the Exposition, but these were in much more conventional classical modes.

In 1915 the Saunders & Lawton partnership was dissolved. Saunders practiced at a reduced scale thereafter and Lawton practiced alone as well (although he later formed the partnership Lawton & Moldenhour with Herman A. Moldenhour). The Masonic

Temple (1912-16; now the Egyptian Theater), reflects this transition, as it was initally won in competition by Saunders & Lawton, but was constructed under Lawton's direction alone.

Saunders showed an early and continuing interest in the natural environment. He served as secretary of the Seattle Board of Park Commissioners from 1903 to 1905. He became involved in early state legislation supporting forest fire prevention and reforestation in 1905 and supported early conservation efforts while representing Seattle's 45th District in the legislature from 1923 to 1932. Saunders was a founding member of the Washington State Chapter of the AIA in 1894 and served as its first secretary. He retired completely from architectural practice in 1929 and died in Seattle on March 13, 1935.

9. Seattle Buddhist Church, Seattle, 1906-8 (destroyed), Saunders & Lawton. This unusual building was the first built in Seattle expressly as a Buddhist temple. The exposed basement with entrance shown in this view was not original, but resulted from the regrading of Main Street soon after the building was completed. (*Seattle Buddhist Temple Archives.*)

10. Forestry Building, Alaska-Yukon-Pacific Exposition, Seattle, 1908-9 (destroyed), Saunders & Lawton. Although executed in raw logs and unfinished timber, this building was notable for its classical forms and details. It was used by the University of Washington for educational purposes until it was demolished in 1931. (*University of Washington Libraries, Special Collections Division; photo by Nowell, X2563.*)

Willis A. Ritchie

JEFFREY KARL OCHSNER

Although Willis A. Ritchie (1864-1931) was just twenty-five when he arrived in Seattle in 1889, he quickly emerged as a leading designer of public buildings in Washington, where he is most often associated with the series of county courthouses that he designed between 1889 and 1895.

Willis Ritchie was born July 14, 1864, in Van Wert, Ohio. Raised in northwestern Ohio, Ritchie dropped out of high school just before age sixteen and was apprenticed to a carpenter and contractor. While thus employed, he studied architecture through a correspondence course. He later worked in the offices of architects in Cincinnati and Toledo, and then in Washington, D.C., at the Office of the Supervising Architect of the Treasury (at that time, the office responsible for the construction of all federal buildings in the United States).

In 1883, at the age of nineteen, Ritchie opened his own office in Lima, Ohio, but in July 1885 he moved to Winfield, Kansas, which was just beginning a building boom. There Ritchie established a practice that, over the next several years, became the leading architectural firm in the southwestern part of the state, responsible for the design of a variety of buildings including commercial blocks, schools, and county courthouses. Between 1887 and 1889, he also served as the local superintendent during construction of a federal building in Wichita.

When Ritchie arrived in Seattle in July 1889, he was without local connections, but he already had six years of architectural experience, which gave him an advantage in competing for major public projects. In September 1889, Ritchie's design was selected for the King County Courthouse (1889-91; destroyed). Although Ritchie also designed

Willis A. Ritchie, ca. 1890. From *Pacific Magazine,* Volume 3, December 1890. *(University of Washington Libraries, Special Collections Division; UW14322.)*

two fire stations and a residence in Seattle, his practice grew primarily as a result of his success in winning design competitions for public buildings located in other cities in western Washington. In his first eighteen months of practice, Ritchie won commissions for the Whatcom County Courthouse, Whatcom, now part of Bellingham (1889-91; destroyed); the Ellensburg School, Ellensburg (1890-91; destroyed); the identical Washington and Lincoln schools, Olympia (1890-91; destroyed); the Jefferson County Courthouse, Port Townsend (1890-92); and the Thurston County Courthouse, Olympia (1890-92; altered). In addition, he received commissions for two commercial blocks in Whatcom and for the Washington State Soldiers' Home, Orting (1890-91; destroyed).

Ritchie's early work in Kansas was conspicuously late Victorian in character, but after he arrived in Seattle he adopted the architectural vocabulary of the Romanesque Revival for most of his large public projects.

1. King County Courthouse, Seattle, 1889-91 (destroyed), Willis A. Ritchie. As Ritchie's first building in Washington State, this institutional structure established his reputation as a designer of large public buildings. *(University of Washington Libraries, Special Collections Division; photo by Asahel Curtis, 915.)*

2. Engine House No. 4 (Battery Street Engine House), Seattle, 1889-90 (destroyed), Willis A. Ritchie. This was one of two fire stations designed by Ritchie showing a mix of Queen Anne and Shingle Style motifs. *(Museum of History and Industry, Seattle; Seattle Historical Society Collection, 88.33.85.)*

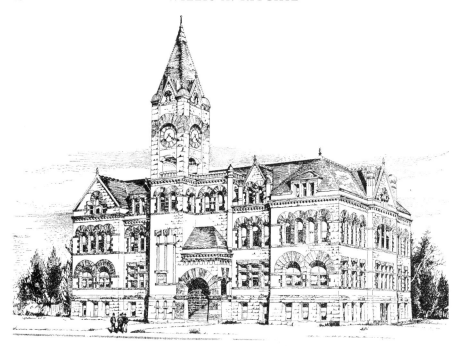

3. Whatcom County Courthouse, Whatcom (Bellingham), 1889-91 (destroyed), Willis A. Ritchie. This rendering of Ritchie's design was published in the Minneapolis-based architectural journal, *Northwestern Architect,* in May 1891.

The one exception, the King County Courthouse, was in a classical style. Ritchie's public buildings were most often characterized by asymmetrical massing and picturesque profiles with an agitated vertical emphasis. The courthouse commissions allowed greater freedom in this regard; his schools, although more simply massed, were made asymmetrical by the irregular placement of towers and smaller elements.

Ritchie's success in winning large public projects was most likely based on his previous experience, particularly his work on federal government projects. Ritchie advertised his knowledge of the latest methods of fireproofing, a critical concern in buildings which were depositories for public records.

The burst of development which offered these public building opportunities to Ritchie and sustained his Seattle practice began to slow by late 1890. Thereafter, Ritchie won only two more major commissions in western Washington, the Clark

4. Mary E. (Mrs. G. M.) Boman house, Seattle, 1890 (destroyed), Willis A. Ritchie. The only known residential design of Ritchie's Seattle years, this was a shingled structure with Queen Anne detail. From *Pacific Magazine,* Volume 4, August 1891.

5. Ellensburg School, Ellensburg, 1890-91 (destroyed), Willis A. Ritchie. Displaying Ritchie's application of Romanesque Revival motifs, this building was one of the largest schoolhouses in Washington State when opened in September 1891. *(Ellensburg Public Library.)*

6. Lincoln School, Olympia, 1890-91 (destroyed), Willis A. Ritchie. One of a pair of two identical schools, this is another example of Ritchie's application of the Romanesque Revival to public institutional structures. *(Washington State Capital Historical Museum, Olympia.)*

7. Jefferson County Courthouse, Port Townsend, 1890-92, Willis A. Ritchie. This structure, which shows Ritchie's most inventive application of the Romanesque Revival, was his largest building in western Washington. *(Jefferson County Historical Society, Port Townsend, Washington.)*

County Courthouse, Vancouver (1891-92; destroyed) and the King County Hospital, south of Seattle (1893-94; destroyed).

By late 1891, Ritchie may have seen that his opportunities in western Washington were becoming limited, as he opened an office in Spokane, to which he moved permanently when he closed his Seattle office in 1894. His Spokane career began with two major projects, the Spokane City Building (1892-94; destroyed) and the Spokane County Courthouse (1893-96). Subsequently he designed schools in Idaho and Montana, and two buildings at the University of Idaho. Although Ritchie continued in practice until his retirement in 1924, his commissions after 1905 were primarily single-family residences. He died in Spokane on January 17, 1931.

8. Thurston County Courthouse, Olympia, 1890-92 (altered), Willis A. Ritchie. The symmetrical composition of this courthouse is unusual, as Ritchie seems to have preferred more irregular designs. This building was enlarged to Ritchie's design to serve as the Washington State Capitol from 1905 to 1928. It survives today, but the original tower was destroyed by fire in 1928. *(University of Washington Libraries, Special Collections Division; ca. 1900; UW4874.)*

9. Clark County Courthouse, Vancouver, Washington, 1891-92 (destroyed), Willis A. Ritchie. This design was similar in character to that for the Whatcom County Courthouse, but was executed in brick rather than stone. (*Washington State University Libraries, Historical Photographs Collection, WSU 78-995.*)

10. Spokane County Courthouse, Spokane, 1893-96, Willis A. Ritchie. This chateauesque composition is Ritchie's largest and best known building. (*University of Washington Libraries, Special Collections Division; UW13500.*)

Edwin W. Houghton

JEFFREY KARL OCHSNER

& DENNIS A. ANDERSEN

As Seattle grew as a regional economic center in the early years of the twentieth century, it also became a center for the provision of architectural services throughout the region. One early exemplar of this development was Seattle architect Edwin Walker Houghton (1856-1927), who emerged as a leading designer of theaters in the Northwest just after the turn of the century.

Edwin W. Houghton was born August 5, 1856, in Hampshire, England, to a family of architects and quantity surveyors. He gained his architectural training in the prac-

Edwin W. Houghton, about 1909. (*University of Washington Libraries, Special Collections Division; Sayre Collection; photo by Plummer.*)

1. Olympic Block, Seattle, 1889-91 (destroyed), Saunders & Houghton. The linear classical detailing of this block shows the variety of design produced by the partnership. (*Museum of History and Industry, Seattle; ca. 1900?; Seattle Historical Society Collection, 88.33.46.*)

tices of his uncles and his brother, Thomas Marcus Houghton, apparently in the 1870s. In the mid-1880s, Houghton immigrated to western Texas, settling near El Paso, where he attempted farming for about four years. Unsuccessful in this venture, he continued west to Pasadena, California, where he first practiced architecture independently.

The exact date of Houghton's arrival in Seattle is undetermined, but in September 1889 he entered an association with Seattle architect Charles W. Saunders (1858-1935). Saunders had come to Seattle from Pasadena earlier in the year and had already won a significant number of commissions (see Saunders essay). The work of the Saunders & Houghton partnership showed considerable variation both in building types (from new commercial blocks to institutional buildings to residences) and in styles (with variants of High Victorian, Romanesque Revival, Shingle Style, and other contemporary modes). Houghton clearly became involved in projects that Saunders already had under way and the firm took on new work, so it is impossible to identify particular projects

2. Grand Opera House, Seattle, 1898-1900 (altered), Edwin W. Houghton. This was the first of Houghton's theaters for John Cort. Initially, only the basement was finished, and it was operated as a beer garden. However, within two years the building was in service as the first theater in the Cort circuit. It later burned and now serves as a parking garage. (*University of Washington Libraries, Special Collections Division; UW12936.*)

3. Charles A. Riddle house, Seattle, 1899 (altered), Edwin W. Houghton. With relatively simple volumes and continuous surfaces faced in shingles, this is one of Seattle's finest Shingle Style buildings. From *Illustrated and Descriptive Book of Buildings by E. W. Houghton, Architect* (Seattle, 1902). (*Museum of History and Industry, Seattle.*)

4. Arcade Building, Seattle, 1901-3 (destroyed), Edwin W. Houghton. This large office and retail building, filling an entire block along Second Avenue in downtown Seattle, is evidence of the scale of expansion of the downtown business district in the first decade of the twentieth century. (*University of Washington Libraries, Special Collections Division; ca. 1905; photo by Asahel Curtis, 91.*)

5. Berkshire Hotel, Seattle, 1902-3 (destroyed), Edwin W. Houghton. Houghton's preference for symmetrical compositions and classicizing detail is evident in this three-story hotel project. (*University of Washington Libraries, Special Collections Division; UW4667.*)

with each partner. Commissions in Seattle, including the Terry-Denny Building (1889-91), Maud Building (1889-90), Olympic Block (1889-91; destroyed), and two new fire stations, were all received by the firm subsequent to Houghton's arrival. When the partnership was dissolved in September 1891, Saunders temporarily left Seattle, and Houghton was responsible for finishing all of the firm's projects.

Thereafter, Houghton practiced independently. In the years after the panic of 1893, he had few commissions, but as Seattle's economy picked up after the discovery of gold in the Klondike in 1897, he emerged as a leader in the local profession. Although his practice included a variety of commercial, institutional, and residential projects, Houghton became known chiefly as a designer of theaters. He was fortunate to have been commissioned by theater proprietor and manager John Cort to design Seattle's Grand Opera House (1898-1900; altered). At the time, Cort was leading in the creation of a regional booking organization, the Northwestern Theatrical Association (sometimes called the Cort circuit), which expanded to control thirty-seven theaters in several states by 1904. While some of these were existing theaters, others were new, and several were designed by Houghton. Thus, for example, he was responsible for the Spokane Theater, Spokane (1900-1901; destroyed); Beck's Theater, New Whatcom, now Bellingham (1901-2; destroyed); and Sutton's Grand Opera, Butte, Montana (1902; destroyed). Over time, Houghton received larger commissions in Seattle, including the Moore Theater and Hotel (1903-7) and Majestic Theater (1908-9; destroyed), and theaters farther away, including the Grand Theater, Aberdeen (1905-6; destroyed); Pinney Theater Block, Boise (1907-8; destroyed); Colonial Theater, Salt Lake City (1907-8; altered); Cort Theater, Chicago (1908-9; destroyed); and Heilig Theater, Portland (1909-10; slightly altered). During his career Houghton may

have been responsible for over seventy theaters, including buildings in Los Angeles, San Francisco, and Boston, as well as Victoria and Vancouver, British Columbia.

Houghton was responsible for a range of other Seattle buildings such as the Estabrook Building (1901-2; destroyed), Arcade Building (1901-3; destroyed), Lippy Building (1901-2; altered), and Berkshire Hotel (1902-3; destroyed). Many of Houghton's larger structures show a generally symmetrical compositional approach and often feature detailing of more or less classical derivation. But he also experimented with a wide variety of styles. His Charles A. Riddle residence (1899; altered), is a fine, if late, Shingle Style composition. His unbuilt design for a downtown Seattle hotel/apartment block, the J. Hoeffler Building (1907), was described as being in the "Old German" style.

6. Moore Theater and Hotel, Seattle (1903-7), Edwin W. Houghton. This downtown Seattle theater is one of the few remaining that continue to be used in the manner for which they were designed. The white glazed brick building forms an important portion of the continuous street-wall along Second Avenue. *(University of Washington Libraries, Special Collections Division; photo by Asahel Curtis, 33604.)*

7. Imperial Building project, Tacoma, 1907 (unbuilt), Edwin W. Houghton. This visionary scheme proposed a massive building which would have included port facilities, a railroad station, warehouse space, office space, and a hotel. From *Pacific Builder and Engineer,* November 10, 1907. *(University of Washington Libraries, Special Collections Division; UW14791.)*

8. Majestic Theater, Seattle, 1908-9 (destroyed), Edwin W. Houghton. Later known as the Palace Hip Theater and then as The Empress, the Majestic was one of the the the more lavish of Houghton's theater designs. The combination of a theater and adjoining office block in one building was typical in Seattle. *(Museum of History and Industry, Seattle; PEMCO Webster & Stevens Collection, 83.10.2110.2.)*

After 1910, Houghton was eclipsed as the leading theater designer in Seattle by his onetime draftsman, B. Marcus Priteca (see Priteca essay). Nonetheless, Houghton continued to receive theater commissions such as the Clemmer Theater, Spokane (1914-15; now The Met), and the Liberty Theater, Wenatchee (1919-20).

From 1913 to 1927, Houghton's firm was known as E. W. Houghton & Son, although his son, Gordon Houghton, actually moved to Oregon about 1919. Edwin Houghton continued to practice in Seattle. Late projects included the Mrs. W. E. Gordon residence, a classicizing design in the Magnolia neighborhood in Seattle (1925), and an apartment building for B. A. Zeran in Seattle's University District (1926). He was reportedly working on a theater for the Fremont community at his death on May 16, 1927.

Houghton was one of very few Seattle architects to have a significant career extending from the 1890s into the 1920s. He was a founding member of the Washington State Chapter of the AIA in 1894. At the peak of his career, between 1900 and 1910, he was recognized as the leading theater designer in the Northwest. Unfortunately, few of his buildings survive.

9. Heilig Theater, Portland, Oregon, 1909-10 (slightly altered), Edwin W. Houghton. One of the largest of Houghton's theaters, the architecture of the Heilig was simply developed and emphasized the large volumes. Decorative detailing focused on the few openings, the street-level storefronts, and the marquee. Now the Fox Theater, the building remains but has lost its marquee, and some of the windows have been filled in. (*Oregon Historical Society; OrHi 17527.*)

10. Clemmer Theater, Spokane, 1914-15 (now The Met), E. W. Houghton & Son. This project was named for its developer, a Spokane dentist, Howard S. Clemmer. The exterior presents a somewhat severe rectilinearity which was partly mitigated by the diapered brick panels and terracotta trim. One of only a few theaters by Houghton that are still extant, this has recently been restored. (*Eastern Washington State Historical Society, Spokane, L.86-219.41.*)

Edward Otto Schwagerl

DAVID A. RASH

When one thinks about landscape architecture and city planning in Seattle during the early twentieth century, the names that invariably come to mind are the Olmsted Brothers of Brookline, Massachusetts, and Virgil Bogue of New York. While their prominence locally is understandable, it has unfortunately overshadowed the remarkable and distinguished career of Edward Otto Schwagerl (1842-1910).

Schwagerl was born on January 14, 1842, in Würzburg, Bavaria, but was raised from infancy in Paris. There he developed an appreciation for art and nature during excursions to art exhibits and to public parks and city squares, which supplemented his formal education from private tutors. At the age of twelve, he came alone to New York City, was adopted by a family there, and found employment as a sales clerk in a series of department stores. After studies at Tilton Seminary in Tilton, New Hampshire, and consideration of a vocation in the ministry, he returned to France in 1865. He worked briefly in the office of Mons Mulat, the architect laying out the grounds of the Exposition Universelle of 1867. After a year, Schwagerl returned to the United States to work for landscape architect Jacob Weidenmann in Hartford, Connecticut, where he remained for eighteen months.

During the following decade, Schwagerl continued to work in landscape design in Omaha and later in St. Louis, before settling in Cleveland. While in Cleveland, he received the commission in 1879 to design Riverview Cemetery (1879-81) near Portland, Oregon, from Henry Failing, a prominent Portland banker and real estate developer. Schwagerl traveled to Portland,

1. Riverview Cemetery, Portland, Oregon, 1879-81, Edward O. Schwagerl. Riverview Cemetery was modeled after Riverside Cemetery in Cleveland, Ohio, a design based on the "new" concept of the garden cemetery; however, Schwagerl's proposed chapel and receiving vault structure was not built. From *The West Shore*, May 1881. *(University of Washington Libraries, Special Collections Division; UW14702.)*

2. Point Defiance Park, Tacoma, 1890-92 (altered), Edward O. Schwagerl. The present Point Defiance Park is based on a plan (1902) by Hare & Hare of Kansas City, Missouri; however, portions of Schwagerl's plan were executed and survived until the 1920s. (*Tacoma Public Library.*)

3. Kinnear Park, Seattle, 1892-94, Edward O. Schwagerl. Of Schwagerl's early Seattle parks, Kinnear Park was the most highly praised by the Olmsteds and consequently was the least changed. The structures designed by Schwagerl, like this rustic trellis seat of 1892, have not survived to the present. (*University of Washington Libraries, Special Collections Division; ca. 1900; UW4797.*)

4. Kinnear Park, Seattle, 1892-94, Edward O. Schwagerl. This rustic and picturesque pavilion was built in 1894 with a workroom and storage space underneath; it was replaced by a brick comfort station in 1929. (*University of Washington Libraries, Special Collections Division; ca. 1900; UW14694.*)

but a proposal to lay out City Park (now Washington Park) failed to materialize and he returned to Cleveland.

Still, the promise of the Pacific Northwest must have held some allure for Schwagerl. By 1890, he had settled in Tacoma, where he received the commission to lay out Wright Park (1890-92; partly extant), as well as Point Defiance Park (1890-92; altered), and initiated planning for an unexecuted, but comprehensive, parks and boulevard system. Due to political considerations, his tenure lasted less than two years; Eben R. Roberts, a landscape gardener (and Schwagerl's friend), was hired to continue his work in Tacoma. By May 1892, Schwagerl was in Seattle and had accepted the position of Superintendent of Public Parks. He laid out the city's Kinnear Park (1892-94) and Denny Park (1894-95; destroyed). He

also made preliminary plans for City Park (now Volunteer Park).

In private practice in Tacoma from 1895 to 1897 and in Seattle thereafter, Schwagerl designed mostly real estate subdivisions and the residential grounds of private citizens. Of the former, the University Heights Addition to Seattle (1899) was typical of the time, while the University Place subdivision (1896-97), near Tacoma, was his largest, at 1,200 acres. Schwagerl's crowning ambition was to design a park and boulevards plan for his adopted city of Seattle, a project on which he began work while Superintendent of Public Parks. This plan was more or less complete by 1903, but when the Board of Park Commissioners sought a landscape designer for the city's official plan, they chose Olmsted Brothers, a more prestigious East Coast firm.

In a curious turn of events, some three years later, the Hunter Tract Improvement Company chose Schwagerl to work with George F. Cotterill, of the civil engineering firm of Cotterill & Whitworth, and the Sawyer Brothers, another civil engineering firm, to plan the Mount Baker Park Addition to Seattle (1906-7), instead of the Olmsted Brothers. At 200 acres, this subdivision was the largest real estate subdivision to be incorporated into the official Olmsted plan. It was also the first to include both boulevards and extensive park grounds as an integral part of the design, allowing Schwagerl one final opportunity to initiate the design of a public park—Mount Baker Park.

With Schwagerl's death on January 27, 1910, Seattle lost its most important pioneer landscape designer. None of his private residential work has been identified, and only a handful of public or semipublic landscapes in Portland, Tacoma, and Seattle remain in somewhat altered form to attest to his professional contribution to the region. Still, Seattle benefited immensely from his presence, if only for the groundwork that he prepared for others. In the case of the parks and boulevards plan, R. H. Thomson, the long-

5. Denny Park, Seattle, 1894-95 (destroyed), Edward O. Schwagerl. Although Denny Park became the first official city park in 1884, the actual work of improving the site did not occur for a decade. The park site was regraded down to its present elevation in 1930. From *Report of the Olmsted Brothers*, 1903. (*University of Washington Libraries, Special Collections Division; UW14691.*)

time City Engineer, pronounced the Olmsted plan "almost identical" to Schwagerl's plan—a testament to Schwagerl's skill and foresight.

6. University Heights Addition, Seattle, 1899, Edward O. Schwagerl. Although Schwagerl exaggerated the perspective in his presentation drawing, the relative simplicity of this eight-block real estate subdivision near the University of Washington campus is still quite evident in the center foreground. The back of Denny Hall is seen to the left. (*University of Washington Libraries, Special Collections Division; 1899; UW13426.*)

7. Mount Baker Park, Seattle, 1906-7, Edward O. Schwagerl with George F. Cotterill and Sawyer Brothers. Mount Baker Park was dedicated to the City of Seattle as part of the Mount Baker Park Addition by the Hunter Tract Improvement Company. This now-destroyed rustic bridge was part of Glenwood Drive, a promenade for carriages. *(University of Washington Libraries, Special Collections Division; ca. 1907; UW14693.)*

8. Mount Baker Boulevard, Seattle, 1906-7, Edward O. Schwagerl with George F. Cotterill and Sawyer Brothers. Another component of the Mount Baker Park Addition is its "Grand Boulevard," which runs west from Mount Baker Park to Rainier Avenue. *(University of Washington Libraries, Special Collections Division; ca. 1925; photo by Asahel Curtis, 58321.)*

9. Hunter Boulevard, Seattle, 1906-7, Edward O. Schwagerl with George F. Cotterill and Sawyer Brothers. The second boulevard in the Mount Baker Park Addition is distinctive in that the central median is not interrupted for cross traffic along its three-block length. *(Photo by David A. Rash, 1993.)*

James Stephen

KATHERYN HILLS KRAFFT

James Stephen (1858-1938) made a significant contribution to the design of public school buildings within the city of Seattle and throughout the state of Washington. However, his career also encompasses a breadth of work beyond the school buildings for which he is best known.

Stephen's father was a skilled Scottish cabinetmaker, who immigrated to Canada and eventually settled in Chicago, Illinois, where he was employed by the Pullman Car Company. Born in Ontario, Canada, on March 29, 1858, James Stephen was also trained as a cabinetmaker and worked as an organ maker at an early age. He obtained his architectural training through a correspondence course, a not uncommon method of

James Stephen, ca. 1890. *(University of Washington Libraries, Special Collections Division; UW8572.)*

1. Administration Building (now Thompson Hall), Washington Agricultural College and School of Science (now Washington State University), Pullman, 1894-95, Stephen & Josenhans. This was one of three buildings by the firm for the College. Although firm records indicate that Josenhans was the partner who had primary contact with the client (he frequently traveled to Pullman in 1894-95), the scale of these projects must have required the involvement of both principals. *(Washington State University Libraries, Historical Photographs Collection; ca. 1895; 83-048.)*

2. Green Lake School, Seattle, 1901-2 (destroyed), James Stephen. This was the initial school built according to the wood frame model plan adopted by the Seattle School Board in 1901. *(University of Washington Libraries, Special Collections Division; ca. 1902; photo by Asahel Curtis, 4315.)*

3. Interlake School (now Wallingford Center), Seattle, 1904 (addition 1908), James Stephen. Interlake School was rehabilitated and adapted into a mixed use, retail, and residential complex in 1982-83. *(University of Washington Libraries, Special Collections Division; 1904; photo by Asahel Curtis, 5413.)*

4. Summit School (now the Northwest School), Seattle, 1904-5 (additions 1914 and 1928), James Stephen. This was originally a sixteen-room grammar school, built according to a plan that varied from the model school plan. Since 1980, the old Summit School building has successfully housed a private middle and upper school. *(University of Washington Libraries, Special Collections Division; UW5051.)*

5.   YMCA Central Branch, Seattle, 1904-9 (altered 1929-31), James Stephen. The relatively simple exterior of this rectangular block encloses a variety of spaces serving a multiplicity of functions. (*University of Washington Libraries, Special Collections Division; 1909; photo by Asahel Curtis, 13423.*)

acquiring an architectural education at the time. His practice began in Hyde Park, Illinois, about 1885, although he later migrated to Pasadena, California, where he practiced for a brief period. Like many other architects, he arrived in Seattle in June 1889, immediately after the fire.

In 1894, Stephen entered into the partnership Stephen & Josenhans, with Timotheus Josenhans (1853-1929), which lasted for three years. The firm was awarded several important commissions, including the design of buildings at the Agricultural College (now Washington State University) in Pullman. Stephen left the partnership in 1897 due to the generally poor economic circumstances for building, and worked briefly constructing prefabricated Yukon River trade boats for Moran Brothers Shipbuilders in Seattle and Alaska.

Seattle School Board records indicate that, early in 1898, the Board received an application from James Stephen for appointment as a school architect. The following year he was hired to prepare plans and specifications for several schools and school additions. In 1901, the plans which Stephen developed for Green Lake School were adopted as the Model School Plan for the grammar schools the School Board anticipated building during the following decade. Shortly thereafter, Stephen was elected by the School Board to be the Official School Architect for the district, a position he held until late 1909.

Stephen was responsible for the design and supervision of over fifty school building projects undertaken by the district during this period of dramatic urban expansion. His model provided the basis for a flexible

6. John Hay School, Seattle, 1905, James Stephen. Hay School was another school designed according to the model plan adopted by the Board in 1901. The original eight-room school was designed to be expanded by adding an eight-room wing at either one or both ends of the central wing shown here, but this particular building has never been enlarged.(It is now an alternative school.) *(University of Washington Libraries, Special Collections Division; UW14784.)*

and economical approach to school construction. The wooden construction system and standard floor plan both facilitated a phased construction process in which an eight-, twelve-, or twenty-room school could be constructed and later expanded. While standard floor plans and interior finish materials were used, the exterior elevations and details of these schools varied greatly and exhibited wood detailing indicative of Stephen's background as a carpenter and cabinetmaker. Extant schools in Seattle that follow the model plan, or are variations of it, include Interlake (1904; now Wallingford Center), Summit (1904-5; now The Northwest School), John Hay (1905; now an alternative school), Seward (1905; now an alternative school), Stevens (1906), Latona (1906; altered), and Coe (1906-7; altered).

In 1907, Stephen traveled to Chicago, St. Louis, New York, and Detroit to study their schools and prepare a report on modern school building design, construction, and equipment. The following year, the School Board adopted his second model plan, which used fireproof materials (concrete, terra cotta, and brick) and included modern lavatory equipment. The brick model schools were typically executed with elements drawn from late Gothic and Jacobean styles and used an expandable floor plan similar to the earlier model plan. Extant Seattle schools that follow the brick model plan, or are variations of it, include Colman (1909), Greenwood (1909), and Emerson (1908-9). Stephen was also responsible for the design of the original portions of Seattle's oldest extant high schools, Lincoln

7. Lincoln High School (leased), Seattle, 1906-7, James Stephen. Seattle did not build a structure for use as a high school before 1900, but expansion of the city led the district to respond with several by 1910, including Lincoln and Queen Anne, both designed by Stephen. *(Seattle Public School Archives; 015-538.)*

8. Adams School, Seattle, 1908-09 (destroyed), James Stephen. Adams School was one of an early group of brick, terra-cotta, and concrete schools constructed after the adoption of a brick model plan developed by James Stephen in 1908. *(Museum of History and Industry, Seattle; ca. 1909; PEMCO Webster & Stevens Collection, 83.10.8356.)*

(1906-7; currently leased) and Queen Anne (1908-9; altered for housing).

Stephen's agreement with the school district allowed him to maintain his independent professional practice. He is known to have designed residential, ecclesiastical, and commercial buildings and fire stations during this period. These projects include the original, northernmost portion of Central Branch of the YMCA, Seattle (1904-9), and numerous schools for other school districts, including Redmond, Renton, Auburn, Olympia, Everett, Kirkland, and Bremerton.

In 1908, Stephen's son Frederick Bennett Stephen (1883-1972) returned from the University of Pennsylvania with an architectural degree and entered into partnership with his father. Stephen & Stephen is credited with the design of school buildings in districts throughout Washington, including Wenatchee, Cashmere, Richmond Beach, Vancouver, Ellensburg, Kirkland, Cle Elum, Chehalis, Fall City, and Port Townsend. William G. Brust, a former college classmate of Fred Stephen's, joined the firm in 1917. Stephen, Stephen & Brust continued to design schools as well as commercial and residential buildings.

James Stephen practiced architecture until 1928. He died in Seattle on September 27, 1938, after a long illness. He was active in several civic and professional organizations and was an avid outdoorsman, skilled photographer, and accomplished furniture maker. Stephen was a widely respected practitioner, and his skills as a builder and designer are reflected in the rich, but dwindling, legacy of his school buildings, constructed in more than fifty school districts across the state.

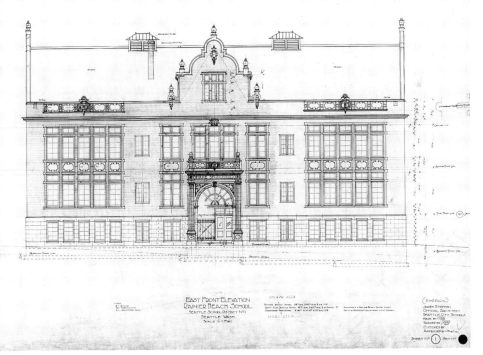

9. East Elevation of Rainier Beach (Emerson) School, Seattle, 1908-9, James Stephen. The early brick model schools were typically executed in a Jacobean style—a style popularly used for educational institutions. Although called Rainier Beach on the drawings, this school had been named Emerson by the time it opened. (*Seattle Public School Archives.*)

10. Everett High School, Everett, Washington, 1908-10 (altered), Stephen & Stephen. This brick school with terra-cotta detailing was among the firm's largest buildings outside Seattle. This is a fine example of a large institutional building executed in the Beaux-Arts Academic Classical mode typical of the period. (*Everett Public Library, Regional History Collection.*)

Pattern Books, Plan Books, Periodicals

DENNIS A. ANDERSEN &
KATHERYN HILLS KRAFFT

Seattle's earliest Euro-American settlement coincides roughly with the appearance of architectural plan and pattern books in the national American popular press. Because local contractor-builders customarily provided plans and drawings to their clients, illustrated trade literature has been of great importance and influence in the developing Puget Sound region, not only prior to the arrival of trained architects but to the present time as well. Rarely, if ever, were these sources acknowledged by their purveyors, and even trained architects frequently drew from them without giving credit.

1. Morgan J. Carkeek residence, Seattle, 1884-85 (destroyed), based on design by Palliser & Palliser architects, New York. This gaunt residence stood in just-cleared forest land on what later became First Hill. *(Museum of History and Industry, Seattle; Seattle Histrical Society Collection, 1020.)*

That plan and pattern books existed in Washington Territory is evident from the earliest catalogue of the Territorial Library in Olympia. Books were ordered by then Territorial Governor Isaac I. Stevens from East Coast publishers. Stevens was intent on building a library with a solid foundation of historical, legal, and literary works. He made sure to include Andrew Jackson Downing's *A Treatise on the Theory and Practice of Landscape Gardening* (1841) and *The Architecture of Country Houses* (1850). Stevens's own residence in Olympia, now demolished, reflected Downing's designs in spirit, if not in detail.

Detailed reportage of commercial and residential construction was a feature of most newspapers in the territory and, after 1889, in the early state. The descriptive stylistic terms which appeared in newspaper accounts, such as "Russian Style" or "Gothic cottage" or "French," are clearly derived from pattern books and illustrated articles in journals such as *Godey's Lady's Book, North Pacific Rural* (Tacoma), and *The West Shore* (Portland), all of which featured articles on house construction, interior decoration, barn design, and the like. To trace designs from these journals and pattern books to the Seattle landscape is not easily accomplished, since few buildings survive from the first quarter century of Seattle's existence. Moreover, most of them were probably small structures of which no pictorial record remains.

Pattern books by Palliser & Palliser and R. W. Shoppell were advertised in the *Seattle Post-Intelligencer*, as well as newspapers of other regional cities and larger towns during the 1880s. Morgan Carkeek, a Seattle contractor, for example, secured plans from Palliser & Palliser for his First Hill house, constructed in 1884-85.

The *Scientific American Architects and Builders Edition* was similarly well known in Seattle. Architect Hermann Steinmann was less than original when he copied the January 1888 "Residence in Michigan" for the

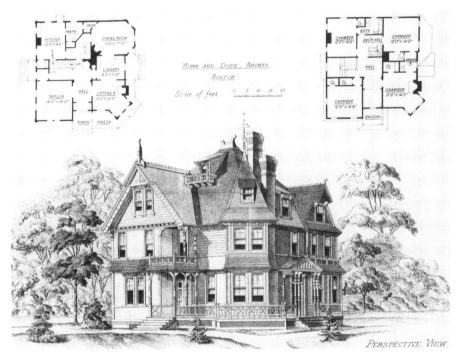

2a. Plate 41 from *Modern Architectural Designs and Details* (New York, ca. 1881) by William T. Comstock. Comstock described this design by Howe & Dodd of Boston as a "Suburban House" and provided plans, elevations, details, and perspective.

2b. C. L. Denny residence, Seattle, 1887 (destroyed), William Boone. While there are differences in the gable and to the left, this house clearly derives from the design by Howe & Dodd, as published by Comstock. *(Private collection.)*

Frederick A. Churchill house on Queen Anne Hill (1888; destroyed). David T. Denny's South Queen Anne mansion (1888; destroyed) drew its inspiration from "A Suburban Residence" in the March 1888 issue.

Not all pattern books were for residential structures, but Seattle commercial buildings that derived from pattern book sources have not yet been identified. It is easier to trace institutional structures, perhaps, because of religious or fraternal associations with particular publishers. The Benjamin D. Price Company, for example, worked under the auspices of the various Methodist denominations and, from 1875 until well into the twentieth century, published pattern books suitable for Protestant groups. Many small frame structures in older Seattle neighborhoods derive from Price's simple plan books.

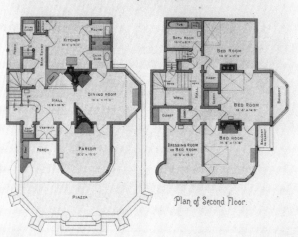

· A · Residence · Costing · Five · Thousand · Dollars ·

Plan of Second Floor.

Plan of First Floor.

3a. "A Residence Costing Five Thousand Dollars," from *Scientific American Architects and Builders Edition,* June 1887. Plates in *Scientific American* were typically in color and included plans and a perspective; specifications and a cost breakdown were sometimes provided as well. This design was based on the Mrs. W. B. Chapin house in Pomfret, Connecticut, by architect Howard Hoppin.

3b. Howard Lewis residence, Seattle, 1889 (destroyed), Elmer Fisher. Fisher not only copied the design for the house, but also duplicated the surrounding brick and rock wall. From Margaret P. Strachan, "Early Day Mansions, No. 12," *Seattle Times,* November 19, 1944. *(University of Washington Libraries, Special Collections Division; UW14814.)*

4a. "A Suburban Residence," from *Scientific American Architects and Builders Edition,* March 1888. Described as a "pleasing residence," this was estimated by *Scientific American* to cost $12,500 "without mantels and furnace."

4b. David T. Denny residence, Seattle, 1888 (destroyed). Denny named his house "Decatur Terrace" when it was completed; he was proud of the splendid views to the south and west from the foot of Queen Anne Hill. The detached kitchen of the published plan was consolidated with the main block of the house. *(University of Washington Libraries, Special Collections Division; photo by Hester, 10103.)*

Plan and pattern books were available not only through subscription or advertisement, but from public sources in Seattle as well. The published *Catalogue of the Public Library of the City of Seattle* (Seattle, 1893) listed a number of titles in the field of architecture and building under the heading "Useful Arts." Journals held at the library included *American Architect, Scientific American Architects and Builders Edition,* and *Decorator and Furnisher.* Seattle's reading public was clearly not uninformed in matters of popular architectural taste by the late 1880s and early 1890s.

The growth of Seattle from a population of just over 80,000 in 1900 to nearly 240,000 in 1910 was marked by the rapid expansion of residential neighborhoods. Clients and builders for lower and middle class housing looked increasingly toward plan books, trade periodicals, and plan services. Local architects and creative contractor-builders began to offer plans for direct sale, and they also initiated local architects' and builders' publications.

Nationally known publishers, such as the Radford Architectural Company in Chicago or the Alladin Company in Bay City, Michi-

gan, regularly published house plans, including the "Standard," a four-square house popular among builders and homeowners from the 1890s to the 1920s. Examples of four-square houses are found throughout Seattle, often embellished with ornamental windows; such houses are commonly referred to locally by the terms "Seattle box" or "classic box."

From the 1890s to the 1930s, Seattle newspapers frequently featured schematic house plans with renderings or photographs alongside plan book advertisements. The local architectural firm Robertson & Blackwell published drawings of houses from their Columbia Terrace project in the *Seattle Mail and Herald* as early as 1902. In 1907, the *Seattle Times* carried a series of advertisements by architect Clyde S. Adams, who described "A Charming Cottage for $2,000" or "A Desirable Suburban Cottage for $3,000" and

5b. House at 2330 32nd Avenue S., shown in Elmer E. Green advertisement. This was a particularly popular early Seattle bungalow side gable plan which exhibits elements of the Western Stick Style: a half-timbered front gable, bracketed roof overhangs, and gable barge boards and ornament constructed from simple "stick" lumber and decorative river rock. (City of Seattle, Urban Conservation Division of the Department of Neighborhoods; photo ca. 1979.)

5a. Advertisement for his *Practical Plan Book*, by Elmer Ellsworth Green, ca. 1912.

included rough plans for the first and second floors, a rendering, and a cost breakdown. E. Ellsworth Green advertised $25.00 plans and specifications for an eight-room bungalow in 1907. In 1912 he published a book of house plans, *Practical Plan Book*, described as an "attractive catalogue of plans" with drawings and photographs for sixty different houses costing up to $10,000. Published building permit notices indicate that Green designed dozens of houses and apartment houses in Seattle neighborhoods including Capitol Hill, the Central Area, and Mount Baker.

Victor W. Voorhees was one of the most successful Seattle architects to advertise drawings and specifications for direct sale. In 1907, he advertised plans, specifications, and details for a "Modern Bungalow" for $25.00; one was also invited to "send 50c in silver" for his book of house, cottage, and

bungalow plans. He followed this with *Western Home Builder*, a fully illustrated plan book for the potential homeowner or builder. This was heavily used in Seattle and by 1911 was in its seventh edition; many of the published designs can easily be identified in contemporary Seattle neighborhoods. Voorhees is also credited with the design of perhaps hundreds of residences, as well as commercial projects, in Seattle during the first three decades of this century.

Jud Yoho is considered to have been Seattle's most active and market-oriented bungalow entrepreneur; he was also owner of the Craftsman Bungalow Company and president of *Bungalow Magazine*. The Craftsman Bungalow Company, with offices in New York, Los Angeles, and Seattle, built and sold bungalow homes on installment purchase plans. *Bungalow Magazine*, which was modeled on Gustav Stickley's *The Craftsman*, was published initially in Los Angeles from 1909 to 1910, but moved to Seattle in 1912 where it was published until

7a. Cover, *Bungalow Magazine,* June 1916. This issue featured the J. H. Ogden house, Seattle, 1914. The design of the house appears to have been based on a California house published by the same magazine in January 1914. Such borrowing was a common practice among architects and builders. Photographs of California houses in local plan books include backgrounds apparently altered to give the impression of a Pacific Northwest landscape.

6. Advertisement for bungalow plans, from *Seattle Home Builder and Home Keeper* by W. W. DeLong and Mrs. W. W. Delong (Seattle, 1915). This volume provided technical advice for the potential home builder, written by Mr. Delong, as well as practical advice for the housewife, written by Mrs. DeLong. Mr. DeLong advised the home builder to consult with his wife: "Women spend a large part of their time in the home. It is their place of business, as well as their home, and therefore it is only right that their taste and convenience should have the largest share of consideration in building it."

7b. J. H. Ogden House, 3515 S. Mount Baker, Seattle. This photograph, taken about 1916, and published in the June 1916 issue of *Bungalow Magazine,* would very nearly match a photograph taken today.

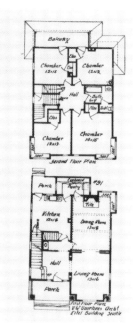

DESIGN NO. 91.

The width of this eight-room house is 28 feet; length 36 feet; height of first story 9 feet 6 inches; height of second story 8 feet 6 inches; basement 7 feet.

Approximate cost of construction, including cement basement and cement floors, $2,400.00.

Additional cost for hot air heating plant, $150.00.

Cost of one set of plans, specifications and details, $18.00.

Cost of two sets of plans, specifications and details, $22.00.

(Any plan can be reversed to suit location.)

8. Design No. 91, *Western Home Builder*, by Victor W. Voorhees (Seattle, first published ca. 1907). This popular plan book included a tremendous number of designs varying in style, size, and expense. Design No. 91, commonly referred to locally as a Classic Box, was a particular favorite with developers, builder-contractors, and homeowners. (*University of Washington Libraries, Special Collections Division; UW14785.*)

1918. The magazine featured many Seattle houses in addition to examples from southern California. Yoho used the magazine both to promote his company and to publish his own designs as well as those of his associate Edward L. Merritt (1881-?). By 1913, the Craftsman Bungalow Company had also published a plan book.

Thousands of single-family houses and small commercial structures, some designed by local architects, but the great majority constructed by contractors and builders and based on plan book designs, shaped Seattle neighborhoods during this era. Seattle contractors, builders, and tract developers clearly turned to standard house plans in order to house Seattle's growing middle class efficiently and economically. Furthermore, the range of published designs in plan books and periodicals offered homeowners the opportunity for direct participation in shaping their immediate environment.

In the 1920s, with the advent of the nationwide Architects' Small House Service Bureau, sponsored by the American Institute of Architects, additional plan services and publications became available to Seattle homeowners and builders. The Bureau helped promote small house types, such as the Cape Cod, through direct plan sales, as well as through its magazine *The Small House* (1922-32) and a series of plan books. In the post–World War II era, periodicals such as *Sunset Magazine* popularized the ranch house and minimal traditional styles through publications including *Sunset Western Ranch Houses* (1946), and *Sunset Homes for Western Living* (1947). Today, numerous homebuilding and remodeling magazines are published for a general readership and continue to influence local homeowners and builders. The publications continue to offer for sale a range of house plans and plan books as well.

THE SEATTLE BUILDING & INVESTMENT CO., INC.

Plan No. 771.

Plan No. 771 is designed for a lot of 25 ft. frontage, contains six rooms with full ceilings. There is a concrete basement half size, with cement floor, and warm air heating plant. The exterior is of rough siding and stucco. It is lighted with gas and electricity, and all rooms are tinted. Cost to build complete in Seattle, $1950.00. Price of plans and specifications in duplicate, $11.50.

9. Plan No. 771, Fred L. Fehren, from a plan book published by the Seattle Building & Investment Co., Inc. (ca. 1910). Fehren was responsible for all of the plans in this book. Plan No. 771, which fit Seattle's many narrow lots, was a particularly popular house design. Fehren also appears to have been an early promoter of the Classic Box house type. (*University of Washington Libraries, Special Collections Division; UW14786.*)

10. A view of the Capitol Hill neighborhood south of Volunteer Park, looking northwest toward housing construction on 12th Avenue, ca. 1905. This land parcel, developed by James A. Moore, a well-known Seattle developer, typifies housing development where builder-contractors and homeowners utilized standard plans from plan books and periodicals. (*University of Washington Libraries, Special Collections Division; Warner, 220.*)

Bebb & Mendel

DAVID A. RASH &

DENNIS A. ANDERSEN

Charles Herbert Bebb (1856-1942) and Louis Leonard Mendel (1867-1940) came to the Puget Sound region by separate routes during the late nineteenth century only to have the panics of 1890 and 1893 force each to seek better prospects elsewhere. Both returned before the end of the 1890s, and the firm they established became the most prominent architectural practice in Seattle during the first decade and a half of the twentieth century.

Charles H. Bebb was born at West Hall, Mortlake, Surrey, England, on April 10, 1856, to English and Irish parents. He was educated at private schools in Kensington, King's College in London, and at a prepara-

1. Diller Hotel, Seattle, 1889-90, Hetherington, Clements & Company, Louis L. Mendel, designer. The corner bay of this structure, and a similar bay on the now demolished Arlington Hotel to the west (see Fisher essay), once framed a fine view of First Avenue from University Street toward the south. (*University of Washington Libraries, Special Collections Division; photo by Asahel Curtis, 5666.*)

2. Everett Theater, Everett, Washington, 1900-1901 (altered), Charles H. Bebb. This building was already in the planning stages when Bebb and Mendel formed their partnership in February 1901. It featured a somewhat Spanish Colonial Revival stucco facade with some Sullivanesque detailing. (*Everett Public Library, Regional History Collection.*)

Charles Herbert Bebb, about 1902. From *Men of the Pacific Coast . . . 1902-1903* (San Francisco, 1902). *(University of Washington Libraries, Special Collections Division.)*

Louis Leonard Mendel, about 1902. From *Men of the Pacific Coast . . . 1902-1903* (San Francisco, 1902). *(University of Washington Libraries, Special Collections Division.)*

tory school in Switzerland before attending the University of Lausanne. He furthered his education in civil engineering at the School of Mines in London, then spent the years from 1877 to 1882 in South Africa as an engineer for the construction of the Cape Town–Kimberley Railway. He returned to London and subsequently departed for possible railroad work in the United States, but instead took a position as a construction engineer with the Illinois Terra Cotta Lumber Company, where he became involved with the development of commercial fireproofing. In 1888, this company was awarded the fireproofing contract for the Auditorium Building in Chicago by Adler & Sullivan, who hired Bebb as their chief superintending architect near the end of the project. In this capacity, Bebb came to Seattle in 1890 to superintend the construction of the Seattle Opera House, a project which did not proceed beyond site excavation. Although he returned to Adler & Sullivan's Chicago office

before the end of 1890, Bebb relocated permanently to Seattle in late 1893 as architectural engineer for the Denny Clay Company. By 1898 he had opened his own office as an architect.

Louis L. Mendel was a native of Mayen, Germany, who came to the United States in 1882 at the age of fifteen. He was first employed by the architectural firm of Lehman & Schmidt of Cleveland, Ohio, and then worked under the Schweinfurth Brothers, also in Cleveland. He may have worked briefly in the Chicago offices of Adler & Sullivan before coming to the West Coast around 1886 and locating in San Diego. After 1889, Mendel's name appears in Tacoma and Seattle directories in connection with a succession of partnerships. Projects included business, school, and public buildings in Tacoma, Seattle, Port Townsend, Sehome (now part of Bellingham), and Yakima. Between 1894 and 1898, Mendel practiced in the Los Angeles, California,

3. University Heights School, Seattle, 1902 (altered), Bebb & Mendel. This translation of the Spanish Colonial Revival into wood frame construction features animated curved parapets atop slightly projecting windows and entrances with solidly buttressed porches. The 1907-8 addition was designed by James Stephen. *(University of Washington Libraries, Special Collections Division; ca. 1905; UW14718.)*

area. About 1899, he returned to the Pacific Northwest and appears to have worked as a draftsman for Charles H. Bebb.

In February 1901, Charles H. Bebb and Louis L. Mendel formed a partnership. For the next thirteen years, the prolific firm of Bebb & Mendel designed some of Seattle's largest and finest homes, hotels, and business buildings, working in a variety of architectural styles. *The Work of Bebb and Mendel, Architects,* a large pamphlet published by the firm in 1906, contains portraits of the two men and sixty illustrations of residences and business blocks of their design. Important projects from this period included the Everett Theater, Everett (1900-1901), and several buildings in Seattle, including the Oriental Block (1902-3), University Heights School (1902), Hotel Stander (1900-1901; destroyed), and Seattle Athletic Club (1903-4; destroyed). The firm was selected in 1908 to design the Washington State Pavilion at the Alaska-Yukon-Pacific Exposition. Later work of Bebb & Mendel included civic

4. Schwabacher Hardware Company warehouse (now part of Merrill Place), Seattle, 1903-5, Bebb & Mendel. While an industrial building type like a warehouse rarely received the artistic embellishment allowed for office buildings, this structure features handsome brick facades with fine Sullivanesque detailing at the corner entrance. *(Photo by David A. Rash, 1993.)*

5. William Walker house (also known as the Walker-Ames house), Seattle, 1906-7, Bebb & Mendel. This is one of the finest examples of the manner in which Bebb & Mendel interpreted classical decorative idioms and imposed them on a large boxlike structure. It now serves as the home of the president of the University of Washington. *(University of Washington Libraries, Special Collections Division; UW2212.)*

6. Washington State Building, Alaska-Yukon-Pacific Exposition, Seattle, 1908-9 (destroyed), Bebb & Mendel. Plaster quoins, squat pediments, and decorative medallions harmonized with the Exposition's Beaux-Arts Classical style. The building, later with a fireproofed annex, housed the University of Washington Library into the 1920s. *(University of Washington Libraries, Special Collections Division; photo by Frank Howell, 1909; UW14689.)*

buildings, apartment buildings, and hotels (the Frye Hotel, Seattle, 1906-11, for example), and large office buildings (exemplified by the Hoge Building, Seattle, 1909-11). The partnership was dissolved early in 1914 when Mendel moved his offices to the Oriental Block. Bebb formed a partnership with Carl F. Gould later that same year (see Bebb & Gould essay). Bebb was a founding member of the Washington State Chapter of the AIA and his professionalism earned him the distinction along with W. R. B. Willcox (see essay) of being the first Washington State architects elected AIA Fellows in 1910.

Mendel continued his architectural practice independently or in partnerships of short duration, and was associated for a brief time with the Brown-Mendel Investment Company. He continued to design a number of large residences and some commercial work, but never again had projects on the scale he had in the course of his partnership with Charles Bebb. After his retirement, Mendel became manager of the Pine Crest Apartments in Seattle, a position he occupied until his death on June 10, 1940.

7. Fire Station No. 18, Seattle, 1910-11, Bebb & Mendel. Of the many diverse civic structures designed by Bebb & Mendel, this fire station in Ballard is one of the very few that remain. Its stepped brick gables give it a Medieval German quality. (*University of Washington Libraries, Special Collections Division; ca. 1915; UW12396.*)

8. Hoge Building, Seattle, 1909-11, Bebb & Mendel. Briefly the tallest building in Seattle, the design used the conventional formula of a sculpturally rich base, a simple shaft of ten floors, surmounted by three floors ringed with ornamental banding and a heavily ornamented cornice. (*University of Washington Libraries, Special Collections Division; photo by Asahel Curtis, 1911.*)

9. First Church of Christ Scientist, Seattle, 1908-9, 1912-14, Bebb & Mendel. Financial difficulties resulted in two separate construction campaigns for this grand cruciform building, which is surmounted by a flattened octagonal dome and ornamented with classical pilasters, elaborate stained glass, and heavy sculptural swags. *(Collection of Paul Dorpat; photo ca. 1915.)*

10. George W. Miller house, Seattle, 1921-22, Louis L. Mendel. This Capitol Hill house demonstrates Mendel's skillful use of Medieval German and Tudor elements to create notable elevations. *(Photo by David A. Rash, 1993.)*

Kirtland K. Cutter

HENRY MATTHEWS

Kirtland Kelsey Cutter (1860-1939), who practiced in Spokane from 1888 to 1923, is regarded as the leading architect of his time in eastern Washington. He was also a widely respected designer who executed projects in seven states and practiced in California from 1924 to 1939.

Cutter was born August 20, 1860, in East Rockport, Ohio; his family had played a leading role in settling the Western Reserve. Hoping to become an illustrator, he studied at the Arts Students' League in New York and subsequently in Europe. When he returned to America, he decided to become an architect, and in 1886 he traveled to Spokane. Despite his lack of architectural training, he soon received commissions, and in 1889 formed a partnership with John C.

Kirtland Kelsey Cutter. *(Eastern Washington State Historical Society, Spokane.)*

1. Harry Krutz house, Seattle, 1895 (destroyed), Cutter & Malmgren. Cutter's first work in Seattle was a quintessential Shingle Style house. From Frank Calvert, ed., *Homes and Gardens of the Pacific Coast, Volume 1: Seattle* (Beaux Arts Village, Lake Washington, 1913). *(University of Washington Libraries, Special Collections Division; UW14579.)*

Poetz (1859-1932). After the 1889 Spokane fire, Cutter & Poetz designed several ambitious downtown buildings. At the 1893 World's Columbian Exposition in Chicago, their firm gained national acclaim for the Idaho Building, a structure of massive logs on a base of rough basalt, symbolizing the mountains and forests of the state. That year Poetz departed and his place was taken by Karl Gunnar Malmgren (1862-1921), who had assisted Cutter since 1889. Cutter & Malmgren built their reputation on impressive mansions for members of Spokane's elite, and on the Davenport Hotel (1912-14). While Cutter's first houses, including examples in Bellingham and Tacoma, had been influenced by the Shingle Style, the various revival styles skillfully employed in his later residential designs established him as a quintessential eclectic. However, he never abandoned the Arts and Crafts approach he developed early in his career.

Cutter's first Seattle commission, the Harry Krutz house (1895), represents his

2. C. D. Stimson house (Stimson-Green house), Seattle, 1898-1900, Cutter & Malmgren. This Tudoresque design is given a horizontal emphasis by the inclusion of a large covered porch and a porte cochere. *(Dorothy Stimson Bullitt Collection.)*

3. C. D. Stimson house (Stimson-Green house), Seattle, 1898-1900, Cutter & Malmgren. The upper level of the library served sometimes as a stage for family theatricals. The fireplace is flanked by carved lions; the andirons represent dragons. *(Dorothy Stimson Bullitt Collection.)*

4. Rainier Club, Seattle, 1902-4 (altered), Cutter, Malmgren & Wager. The curvilinear gables of this building are said to be modeled on those of the Jacobean Aston Hall, Warwickshire, England. (*Dorothy Stimson Bullitt Collection.*)

Shingle Style phase. His half-timbered, Tudoresque mansion for the lumber baron C. D. Stimson (1898-1900) broke away from the Victorian styles that were still popular. Although its exterior is Old English in inspiration, it followed the then current American fashion of varying the character of individual rooms. The hall, dominated by a Romanesque arch supported on clustered colonnettes, led on one side to a library, finished in dark oak in a Late Medieval manner, and on the other into a light, elegant reception room in the Empire Style.

In 1902, hoping for more work in Seattle, Cutter sent an assistant, Edwin Wager, to Seattle to run the firm of Cutter, Malmgren & Wager. Their first major commission was for the prestigious Rainier Club (1902-4; altered). The design evolved from a simple rectangular block with a half-timbered upper story and a high pitched roof to a far more elaborate composition of Dutch gables executed in fire-flashed clinker brick. The arrangement of tall chimneys, irregularly

placed windows, and Gothic doorways, as well as a vast inglenook in the "grand Hall," demonstrate Cutter's romantic disposition.

After the completion of the Club in 1904, Wager started his own practice and was not replaced. However, attracted by an office building boom, Cutter reopened his Seattle branch in 1906 under two talented designers, Karl Nuese and Andrew Willatsen (see Willatsen essay). The Chicago Style Crary Building (1906-7; destroyed) on Fifth Avenue was their only office block. Most of the other projects of the firm were residential.

The picturesque asymmetry of the red brick C. J. Smith house (1906-08; altered) is typical of Cutter's Tudor architecture. The "Indian Room" for Judge Burke (1908; destroyed) shows his love of the exotic. Two other Seattle buildings illustrate his interest in the Swiss chalet: The L. B. Peeples house (1908-9) is a relatively authentic example; and the Seattle Golf and Country Club (1908-10) applies the chalet type to a building of larger scale and more complex use. In

1909 Willatsen left the firm, taking commissions with him including the Prairie Style C. H. Clarke house in The Highlands, for which Willatsen had initiated the design. Subsequently, working from Spokane, Cutter designed a new house in The Highlands for C. D. Stimson (1909-14). Very different from the turn-of-the-century mansion, this white stucco residence, opening onto generous courts and terraces, represented a step toward the Spanish Colonial Revival designs that he was to build a decade later in California. But, in his last Seattle commission, the J. T. Heffernan house (1915-17), Cutter reverted to his favorite Tudor style and produced a rambling, irregular design.

Cutter was a member of the Washington State Chapter of the AIA and served as a chapter officer in 1908 and 1911. He was elected an AIA Fellow in 1923.

In the early 1920s, soon after his last Seattle commission, Cutter closed his Spokane office and moved to southern California, where he contributed to the establishment of a regional style, particularly through the design of several award-winning houses in Palos Verdes. He died in Long Beach, California, on September 26, 1939.

5. Crary Building, Seattle, 1906-7 (destroyed), Cutter & Malmgren. Cutter's only Seattle office building, this clearly shows the influence of the Chicago School and may reflect the input of Andrew Willatsen, who was then working in Cutter & Malmgren's Seattle office. (*University of Washington Libraries, Special Collections Division; photo by Asahel Curtis, 13118.*)

6. C. J. Smith house, Seattle, 1906-8 (altered), Cutter & Malmgren. This shows Cutter's continuing command of Tudoresque design. (*Eastern Washington State Historical Society, Spokane; L84-207-4-67.*)

7. L. B. Peeples house, Seattle, 1908-9, Cutter & Malmgren. This chalet presents its gable end to the street in the traditional manner. The dominant corbels under the broad eaves and the relatively simple carved detail reflect Cutter's study in Switzerland. *(Photo by Henry Matthews, 1990.)*

8. Seattle Golf and Country Club, The Highlands, 1908-10, Cutter & Malmgren. In this design, Cutter elaborated on the chalet form and stressed fine craftsmanship. This character is particularly emphasized in this view from the rear of the structure. *(University of Washington Libraries, Special Collections Division; UW14763.)*

9. Norcliffe (C. D. Stimson house), The Highlands, Washington, 1909-14, Cutter & Malmgren. Although described at the time as "modernized Mission," this house was probably influenced by English "Free Style" architects such as Voysey and Lutyens. The house is carefully integrated with the gardens, which were designed by the Olmsted Brothers. *(Dorothy Stimson Bullitt Collection.)*

10. T. J. Heffernan house (now Bush School), Seattle, 1915-17, Cutter & Malmgren. This picturesque composition of red brick features tall chimneys, irregular stone-coped gables, and crenellated parapets. *(Photo by Henry Matthews, 1991.)*

Breitung &
Buchinger

DENNIS A. ANDERSEN

While German and Austrian schooled architects were numerous in Tacoma and Spokane, especially during the 1890s, very few Seattle architects could claim that background or training. The exceptions were German-born Carl Alfred Breitung (1868-?) and Austrian-born Theobald Buchinger (1866-1940), whose partnership lasted for only two years during this century's first decade. Each partner benefited both from the patronage of Seattle's German-American community and from the favor of the local Roman Catholic Archdiocese. During the very brief partnership, Breitung & Buchinger created several monumental projects which signaled their technical expertise as well as their knowledge of northern and central European historical styles.

Carl Alfred Breitung was born near Munich, Germany, in 1868. The brief biographical accounts available mention that he studied architecture in Munich and Rome, but at which schools is unspecified. He arrived in the United States in the late

1. Building for Capital Brewing and Malting Company (now Jackson Building), 1901-2, Carl Alfred Breitung. This corner building, Breitung's first major Seattle project, was described as "Italian Renaissance" on the outside and "German Renaissance" on the inside. The ground floor featured a saloon with lavish stucco decoration, which survives today. *(Private collection.)*

C. Alfred Breitung, about 1902. From *Men of the Pacific Coast . . . 1902-1903* (San Francisco, 1902). *(University of Washington Libraries, Special Collections Division.)*

Theobald Buchinger, about 1906. From *Seattle of To-Day* (Seattle, 1906). *(Private collection.)*

1880s, working first on the East Coast and then in Kansas City, Missouri. He opened an architectural practice in Seattle late in 1900. One of his earliest projects, a brewing house for the Capital Brewing and Malting Company (1901-2), is a handsome Renaissance Revival structure with remarkable stucco interiors (that still survive). A partnership with William Jewett was announced in 1901, but resulted in no significant commissions. Jewett died in 1905.

Theobald Buchinger, born in Vienna in 1866, had had some training at Vienna's Polytechnic University before his arrival in Washington Territory in 1887. He worked as a draftsman for several Seattle and Tacoma

2. St. Charles Hotel, Ballard (now Seattle), 1902 (altered), Theobald Buchinger. The very long, low facade with swelling bay windows was typical for small town commercial architecture at the time. From *Seattle of To-Day* (Seattle, 1906). *(Private collection.)*

architects during the late 1880s and early 1890s. In particular, Buchinger was first assistant on a number of the large courthouse and school projects under Willis A. Ritchie in the early 1890s (see Ritchie essay). Buchinger entered a partnership with Paul Bergfeld in 1899. Their early projects included small brick hotel and business blocks in Ballard and other suburban Seattle communities, as well as brewery buildings in Seattle for Hemrich Brothers (1903-4; destroyed). When Bergfeld left to practice in Alaska, Buchinger continued briefly alone.

In March 1905, Breitung and Buchinger announced their partnership and soon secured substantial work from Seattle's Roman Catholic Archdiocese. By 1906, they were preparing drawings for several Seattle projects including the House of the Good Shepherd (1906-7), the Academy of the Holy Names (1906-8), a hall for the German

3. Brew House for Hemrich Brothers, Seattle, 1903-4 (destroyed), Theobald Buchinger. This was a fairly Teutonic design typical for breweries in the late nineteenth and early twentieth centuries. Buchinger was involved in other projects for the Hemrich family who owned several breweries in the Seattle area. From *Seattle of To-Day* (Seattle, 1906). *(Private collection.)*

4. House of the Good Shepherd (now Good Shepherd Center), Seattle, 1906-7, Breitung & Buchinger. This, the first large commission of the Breitung & Buchinger partnership, and the first of a series of large commissions for Catholic institutions, is characterized by a straightforward design completed on a tight budget. *(University of Washington Libraries, Special Collections Division; photo by Asahel Curtis, 42734.)*

5. Academy of the Holy Names of Jesus and Mary, Seattle, 1906-8, Breitung & Buchinger. The Sisters of the Holy Names had maintained a fashionable girls' school which had been located in what is now the International District since 1883. Forced to relocate by the regrading of that neighborhood, they chose a location close to a heavily Catholic community and commissioned Breitung & Buchinger to create a sumptuous and appropriate monument. *(University of Washington Libraries, Special Collections Division; photo by Asahel Curtis, 11255.)*

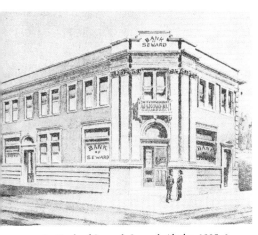

6. Bank of Seward, Seward, Alaska, 1905-6 (destroyed), Breitung & Buchinger. The monumental corner entrance of this small-town bank was marked by three pairs of classical pilasters and a balcony with a richly detailed balustrade. Decorative false quoins marked the less prominent ends of the building. From *Pacific Builder and Engineer*, Volume 2, September 1905. *(University of Washington Libraries, Special Collections Division; UW14728).*

Turnverein (1905-6; destroyed), Saint Joseph Church (1906-7; destroyed), Saint Alphonsus School, Ballard (1906-7; destroyed), and a school building for the Lourdes Academy, Ellensburg (1907-8; destroyed), as well as several residences. While some of these were rather utilitarian institutional designs, others were more pretentious: the Academy of the Holy Names is one of the few Baroque Revival buildings in Seattle, and it well reveals the partners' Bavarian and Viennese origins and training.

Their architectural exuberance and business success were not to last. Almost as suddenly as they had risen to prominence, they ceased receiving large commissions from either the German community or Catholic institutions. The partnership was dissolved for unknown reasons in May 1907. Buchinger returned to independent practice, and Breitung finished the firm's remaining large commissions under his own name. Neither partner subsequently achieved a level of ac-

7. St. Joseph Catholic Church, Seattle, 1906-7 (destroyed), Breitung & Buchinger. Although Breitung & Buchinger are primarily known for their surviving masonry structures, they were also occasionally able to apply German Baroque motifs to frame buildings such as this Seattle church. *(Museum of History and Industry, Seattle; PEMCO Webster & Stephens Collection, 83.10. 8553.)*

8. Triangle Hotel, Seattle, 1909-10, Carl Alfred Breitung. The masonry second and third floors, with projecting bays, are perched on a remarkably narrow iron-fronted ground floor. *(University of Washington Libraries, Special Collections Division; photo by James P. Lee.)*

tivity or prestige comparable to that of the partnership.

Breitung secured the commission for the large Odd Fellows Temple in Seattle (1908-10), which contains Classical and Baroque elements similar in scale to those of the Academy of the Holy Names. No other major projects can be attributed to him, although he remained in practice in Seattle until the early 1920s. In 1922, according to records in Seattle, he relocated to San Antonio, Texas; however, no record of Breitung's ever having lived or worked in San Antonio has been found.

Buchinger continued a modest practice, associating from 1924 to 1929 with Louis Leonard Mendel (see Bebb & Mendel essay), and briefly (1929) with Robert Thorne. His later work consisted primarily of small residences, commercial buildings, and remodels. Saint Mary Catholic Church, Seattle (1911-12), was an exceptional large project from this later period. The other major works cited in the obituaries following his death on December 24, 1940, all stemmed from his prolific two-year partnership with Breitung.

9. Saint Mary Catholic Church, Seattle, 1911-12, Theobald Buchinger. Buchinger freely interpreted central European architectural forms for this German-speaking Roman Catholic congregation. *(Photo by T. William Booth, 1993.)*

10. Odd Fellows Temple, Seattle, 1908-10, Carl Alfred Breitung. The brown brick and terra-cotta facades, which recall both the Good Shepherd Home and the Academy of the Holy Names, enclose a complex collection of meeting rooms, apartments, offices, and retail spaces. *(Museum of History and Industry, Seattle; PEMCO Webster & Stephens Collection, 83.10.9347.)*

John Graham, Sr.

GRANT HILDEBRAND

John Graham, Sr. (1873-1955), was a native of Liverpool, born there in 1873. He acquired his professional skills in England, by apprenticeship rather than by formal professional education. After extensive travels, which included a visit to the Puget Sound region in 1900, he moved to Seattle in 1901, where he practiced as architect from that date to the 1940s. His career embraced a great variety of building types in many styles, including a large number of Seattle's major urban commercial buildings.

An early project was the reconstruction and expansion of Trinity Episcopal Church (1902-3), originally of 1891, which had been destroyed by fire in 1901. Although Graham briefly associated with Alfred Bodley in 1904, his partnership with David J. Myers beginning the following year produced more significant Seattle work, including three apartment buildings, the Kenney Presbyterian Home, and at least two large eclec-

John Graham, Sr., about 1902. From *Men of the Pacific Coast . . . 1902-1903* (San Francisco, 1902). *(University of Washington Libraries, Special Collections Division; UW14807.)*

tic houses (see Schack, Young & Myers essay). Graham & Myers also designed several pavilions for the Alaska-Yukon-Pacific Exposition in 1909.

Graham set out on his own in 1910. One of his earliest independent Seattle works of note is the Joshua Green Building (1913), a terra-cotta clad steel frame structure of the sort done in Chicago and elsewhere before the turn of the century. In the same year he designed the Ford Assembly Plant (now the Craftsman Press) near the southeast corner of Lake Union. Ford was then putting up a number of such buildings across the country for local assembly of the Model T; Graham was a supervising architect for several of these from 1914 to 1918; he opened an office in Detroit in those years for that purpose.

The Frederick & Nelson Building (1916-19; altered) is the first of a number of finely detailed, terra-cotta clad commercial structures done by Graham over the next decade. Another is the Dexter Horton Building (1921-24), an excellent example of the large-

1. Pierre P. Ferry residence, Seattle, 1903-5, 1905-6, John Graham, Sr., and Alfred Bodley. Graham was responsible for the original design; Bodley remodeled the interior and added a new kitchen wing after the seven-month partnership ended. *(Photo by T. William Booth, 1993.)*

2. Plymouth Congregational Church, Seattle, 1910-12 (destroyed), John Graham, Sr. Graham's most prominent religious structure, this church reflects his knowledge of turn-of-the-century English classical design. *(Museum of History and Industry, Seattle; PEMCO Webster & Stephens Collection, 83.10.4627.)*

3. Ford Motor Company Assembly Building (now the Craftsman Press), Seattle, 1913 (altered), John Graham, Sr. One of a series of buildings across the country for local assembly of the Model T. Graham supervised construction of others, including one in Portland, Oregon, from his Detroit office of 1914-18. From Clarence Bagley, *History of Seattle* (Chicago, 1916), opposite page 538.

scale projects typical of Graham's career. It offers to the street an asymmetric four-story base which as a totality coheres the streetscape leading south to the Smith Tower. The entry at the north of this base leads to a Roman coffered vault; the great granite columns at center originally expressed the three-story high main banking room south of the entrance. Above are four ten-story shafts of office space separated by light wells opening to the south toward Cherry Street; such an organization was increasingly common to buildings of this size throughout the country at this date. (An example is the General Motors Building, Detroit, by Albert Kahn: finished in 1921, it was widely publicized, and Graham would have known of Kahn's career through his Ford work.)

The tiny Bank of California Building (1923-24; now a Key Bank branch) also uses a motif of classical columns of "granitex," a

4. Seattle Yacht Club, Seattle, 1919-21 (altered), John Graham, Sr. As a sailing enthusiast, a member of the Club, and a widely respected architect, Graham was an obvious choice for this commission. Graham had also designed the Yacht Club's earlier headquarters in West Seattle, completed in 1909, but whereas the earlier building was in a bracketed "Swiss" mode, this one reflected the Colonial Revival mode prevalent in the 1920s. *(Museum of History and Industry, Seattle; PEMCO Webster & Stevens Collection; 1921; 83.10.1944.)*

glazed terra-cotta cladding. The interior, recently restored, is an outstanding illustration of Graham's skill in classical detail.

Graham was particularly adept in the Art Deco style. The Roosevelt Hotel, Seattle (1928-29), is one example. Another is the Exchange Building, Seattle (1929-31), perhaps Graham's finest work. This occupies the entire street frontage from First to Second Avenue on Marion Street and abuts the Bank of California Building on Second. In overall massing, but especially in its street-level treatment and its lobby, the Exchange is an engaging play of Art Deco motifs that have remained intact over the decades. Seattle's Bon Marché Store (1928-29; altered) is less effective overall, but its extensive marquee is one of the delights of the city. Graham was also involved in one of the finest Art Deco works in the Northwest, the

U.S. Marine Hospital campus (1931-34; now Pacific Medical Center; altered), but credit must be shared with, perhaps in large measure given to, the associated office of Bebb & Gould (see essay).

From 1936 until 1942, Graham was associated with William L. Painter, in New York City. His son John Graham, Jr. (see essay), also joined the firm's New York office in the late 1930s. The firm's Coca-Cola Bottling Plant, Seattle (1939; altered), was a streamlined design, similar to other soft drink bottling plants built at this time. From 1942 until his death in Hong Kong on March 19, 1955, Graham increasingly transferred the practice to his son John Graham, Jr., who returned to Seattle by 1946. Under his direction the firm continued thereafter.

Graham's work shows no allegiance to any particular theoretical stance, nor is it de-

5. Frederick & Nelson Department Store Building, Seattle, 1916-19 (altered), John Graham, Sr. This finely detailed department store building initiated the most prolific period of Graham's career. The building was later enlarged vertically and lost its original cornice. *(Museum of History and Industry, Seattle; PEMCO Webster & Stevens Collection; ca. 1940; 83.10.9875.)*

pendent on any particular personal idiom. Rather, Graham worked eclectically, bringing to each project his skill in plan organization, a good eye for the basics and the nuances of historical styles, and a keen sense of urban scale. His work is significant not because it marks an original evolutionary or revolutionary watershed, but because, in playing a major role in the making of downtown Seattle, it was invariably executed with a sure and sensitive hand.

6. Dexter Horton Building, Seattle, 1921-24 (altered), John Graham, Sr. This large office building shows Graham's capabilities in design using terra-cotta cladding. The E-shaped plan, with four wings and deep light wells facing south, reflects the limitations of artificial illumination at the time and the necessity for natural lighting in every interior space. *(University of Washington Libraries, Special Collections Division; photo by Asahel Curtis, 32426.)*

7. Physics Hall, University of Washington, Seattle, 1927-28 (altered), John Graham, Sr. This was the first of Graham's four buildings for the University of Washington; the others are Guggenheim Hall, 1928-29; Johnson Hall, 1929-30; and the Women's Dormitory (now Hansee Hall), 1935-36 (with David J. Myers—illustrated in the Schack, Young & Myers essay). *(University of Washington Libraries, Special Collections Division; photo ca. 1927; UW14767.)*

8. The Bon Marché, Seattle, 1928-29 (altered), John Graham, Sr. As shown in this view, before subsequent enlargement and filling of the windows, the Bon Marché was designed as a relatively simple block with restrained detail focused at the entries, along the marquee, and at the cornice. The ornamental band at the cornice was lost when the building was enlarged. *(University of Washington Libraries, Special Collections Division; photo by Hamilton, 1666.)*

9. Exchange Building, 1929-31, John Graham, Sr. The form of this building, which is enhanced by the selective placement of decorative detail, reflects Graham's mastery of the Art Deco. *(University of Washington Libraries, Special Collections Division; photo by Asahel Curtis, 59425.)*

10. Coca-Cola Bottling Plant, Seattle, 1939 (altered), Graham & Painter. The streamlined form of this building reflects the design tendencies of the later 1930s and an emergent architectural form typically applied to soft drink bottling plants. *(University of Washington Libraries, Special Collections Division; Graham Collection; ca. 1940; UW14769.)*

Olof Hanson

DENNIS A. ANDERSEN,

DUANE A. DIETZ, &

JEFFREY KARL OCHSNER

There are few architects who contributed more in diverse ways to the Seattle community than Olof Hanson (1862-1933). Born in Fjelkinge, Sweden, on September 10, 1862, Hanson emigrated with his family to the United States about 1875. At the age of ten he suffered a complete loss of hearing and received the education possible at that time. He studied at the Minnesota School for the Deaf in Faribault and at Gallaudet College in Washington, D.C., where he received a B.A. in 1886 and an M.A. in 1889. A talented draftsman, he worked for a time in the architectural offices of E. Townsend Mix and I. H. Hodgson & Sons in Minneapolis.

Hanson was a special student in architecture at the École des Beaux-Arts in Paris in 1889 and 1890, and at that time traveled throughout Europe.

Olof Hanson, ca. 1914. *(Gallaudet University Archives; 14205-19.)*

1. North Dakota School for the Deaf, Devils Lake, North Dakota, 1894-96 (destroyed), Olof Hanson. Hanson's first institutional building, this Romanesque Revival structure provided classroom, administration, and dormitory space for the school. Only the central portion was built initially, but the wings were added within a few years. *(State Historical Society of North Dakota.)*

Hanson returned to the United States to work in the offices of Wilson Brothers & Company in Philadelphia on the new Pennsylvania School for the Deaf. By 1894 he had established an architectural practice in Faribault, Minnesota. He may have been responsible for over forty buildings including houses, business blocks, schools, and a church in Faribault and nearby towns. Even during the depression years of the mid-1890s, he secured significant commissions, including several institutional buildings relating to the deaf. His North Dakota School for the Deaf, at Devils Lake (1894-96; destroyed), was a large brick Romanesque Revival structure. Its large central block was ornamented by an arched entrance, which was flanked by curved multistory bay windows, showing the influence of H. H. Richardson's Romanesque Revival designs. The Boys' Dormitory for Gallaudet College (now Dawes House, Gallaudet University),

2. Boys' Dormitory, Gallaudet College (now Dawes House, Gallaudet University), Washington, D.C., 1895, Olof Hanson. This relatively straightforward brick block is enlivened by the asymmetrically placed engaged tower. (*Gallaudet University Archives; 4104-31.*)

3. McKinley Elementary School, Faribault, Minnesota, 1897-98 (destroyed), Olof Hanson. Although this institutional building has been demolished, over a dozen buildings by Hanson remain standing in Faribault. (*Gallaudet University Archives.*)

Washington D.C. (1895), was a straightforward, but elegantly detailed, brick block. His McKinley Elementary School, Faribault (1897-98; destroyed), was a variation on the Devils Lake School, a brick structure ornamented by contrasting light stone bands above the window openings.

In 1901, Hanson entered into an architectural partnership with Frank Thayer in the neighboring small city of Mankato. Together, as Thayer & Hanson, they won the competition for the Courthouse and Jail in Juneau, Alaska (1901-3; destroyed). Their Classical Revival design was prominently situated on a knoll in the city.

Thayer & Hanson moved their practice to Seattle in 1902 to be closer to the courthouse project. They soon received other commissions in Alaska and Seattle. Thayer traveled to Alaska to supervise construction of the courthouse soon after the move to Se-

4. Courthouse and Jail, Juneau, Alaska, 1901-3 (destroyed), Thayer & Hanson. Winning this prominent public building in Alaska led directly to the relocation of Thayer & Hanson from Minnesota to Seattle. A prominent site and the symmetrical composition with classical detail made this a local landmark for many years. (*University of Washington Libraries, Special Collections Division; UW14727.*)

5. Courthouse and Jail, Ketchikan, Alaska, 1903-4 (destroyed), Thayer & Hanson. Following their success in Juneau, Thayer & Hanson were awarded a second Alaska courthouse project and designed this symmetrical wood frame building with restrained classical detailing. (*Private collection.*)

attle, and he remained there for some time. Thereafter, the partnership split and Hanson continued in practice alone, primarily designing residences in the neighborhoods near the University of Washington. He may have been responsible for the design of more than twenty residences, and he undertook commercial and institutional buildings as well, including the Georgetown High School (1904-6; destroyed). Between 1906 and 1912, Hanson worked intermittently in the architectural office of James H. Schack (see Schack, Young & Myers essay) and participated in the design and construction of the Savoy Hotel (1905-6) and the First Methodist Episcopal Church (1907-10; Schack & Huntington), but he also continued to accept independent commissions such as the Snoqualmie School (1911; altered).

By 1912, Hanson's practice was focused in Vancouver, Washington, with projects in-

6. Olof Hanson residence, Seattle, 1904 (destroyed), Olof Hanson. This two-story structure, located near the University of Washington, was the first house Hanson designed for himself in Seattle. (*Gallaudet University Archives; 14224-1.*)

7. Georgetown High School, Seattle, 1904-6 (destroyed), Olof Hanson. This has also been called the Georgetown School, since high school students attended only in 1906. Thereafter the building served only elementary school children in Georgetown, and high school students took the streetcar to high schools in Seattle. (*Museum of History and Industry, Seattle; PEMCO Webster & Stevens Collection, 83.10.8455.*)

8. Snoqualmie School (now Snoqualmie Valley School District offices), Snoqualmie, Washington, 1911 (altered), Olof Hanson. Although altered for use as school district offices, this building retains its original symmetrical composition and classical detail. Its exterior has recently been restored. *(Snoqualmie Valley Historical Society, North Bend, Washington; ca. 1911; 4.96/10/B.)*

cluding the Girls' Dormitory and a classroom building for the Washington School for the Deaf (1911-12; destroyed), and dormitories for the Washington School for the Blind (1912; destroyed), although he maintained his residence and office in Seattle. He also designed an unidentified apartment house in Vancouver.

Hanson's work was not all confined to architecture and engineering, but extended to advocacy for the deaf and hearing impaired. His 1908 letter to President Theodore Roosevelt, pleading equal rights for the hearing impaired in Federal Civil Service examinations, led to a significant executive order guaranteeing protection. Hanson served in a leadership position with many organizations that advocated for the deaf, including the National Association for the Deaf (president, 1910-13), the Puget Sound Association of the Deaf, and the World Federation of the Deaf.

As an active Episcopalian, he carried out mission work on behalf of his church, conducting Sunday school services for the deaf and serving as sign lay reader for Trinity Parish in Seattle. He was ordained a deacon for particular church ministries in 1924, and in 1929 he was ordained a priest. He conducted services for the deaf in Seattle, Tacoma, Portland, and Spokane.

Hanson carried out these duties in addition to his full-time occupation as draftsman for the University of Washington Department of Buildings and Grounds, a position he held from 1919 to 1931, a time of great campus expansion.

Hanson died in Seattle on August 8, 1933. He was a recognized leader among the deaf during his life and received an honorary doctorate from Gallaudet University in 1914. As an architect, he is most widely recognized in Faribault, Minnesota, where his buildings have been nominated to the National Register of Historic Places and a street has been named in his honor. Unfortunately, few of his buildings in Washington State survive.

9.   Washington School for the Blind, Vancouver, 1912 (destroyed), Olof Hanson. This elevation shows the scale of Hanson's proposal for this state institution. *(Gallaudet University Archives, 14224-1a.)*

10.   Girls' Dormitory (Lottie Clark Hall), Washington School for the Deaf, Vancouver, 1911-12 (destroyed), Olof Hanson. This girls' dormitory was a symmetrical brick structure of Georgian inspiration. *(Gallaudet University Archives, 14224-4.)*

Ellsworth Storey

GRANT HILDEBRAND

Ellsworth Prime Storey (1879-1960) was born in Chicago on November 16, 1879, to a family of comfortable means. Like many in that city, he was enormously impressed by the Columbian Exposition of 1893, and on that basis decided to become an architect. He visited Seattle with his family three years later, and that, in turn, led him to decide that Seattle was where he would spend his life. He began in architecture at the University of Illinois in 1898, a few years behind Walter Burley Griffin, about whose work in Wright's early studio Storey seems to have been aware. During his college years, Storey and his family spent more than a year in Europe and the Middle East; he saw and recorded in photographs the great monu-

Ellsworth Storey in his office; date unknown, but obviously early. *(Photographer unknown.)*

ments, but was most strongly affected by the chalets of Switzerland.

On graduation in 1903, he came to Seattle, where he almost immediately began a house for his parents. By 1905 he had built

1. Henry C. Storey and Ellsworth Storey houses, Seattle, 1903-5, Ellsworth Storey. The Ellsworth Storey house is nearer the camera, the Henry C. Storey house in the distance, with the connecting breezeway between. These houses exemplify Storey's hallmarks: deep eaves, horizontal stretches of mullioned glazing, and above all the imaginatively straightforward use of modest local materials, in this case shingles and standard sawmill-run lumber. *(Photo by Grant Hildebrand, 1992.)*

2. Storey house. The use of dark wood to frame light plaster panels in the dining room of this house is reminiscent of Wright's houses of this period, while the simplicity of the wood trim recalls English Arts and Crafts work. *(Photo by Christian Staub, 1971.)*

an adjacent and connecting house for himself and his bride, Phoebe Mulliken. These houses, although products of his youth, are outstanding examples of the approach that remains associated with Storey's name. Their debt to the Swiss chalets is evident; they may also owe something to Wright and to the English Arts and Crafts movement as well. They also suggest the work of Bernard Maybeck and others of the Bay Area, although there is no evidence that Storey was aware of that work.

Storey did many buildings over the next two decades; they vary widely in style. A Georgian Revival dwelling for the Phiscator Estate (1907-8) and the George B. Barclay house (1907-8) were exhibited by the Portland Architectural Club in 1908. The Tudor/ Arts and Crafts Hoo-Hoo House Lumberman's Fraternity (1909; destroyed), de-

signed for the Alaska-Yukon-Pacific Exposition, served as the University of Washington Faculty Club until 1959. North of the campus, Storey did the Wrightian Sigma Nu Fraternity House (1915-16) and the Unitarian Church (now University Presbyterian Church Chapel, 1915-16; altered). The latter is a diminutive emulation of a half-timbered English parish church complete with lychgate (now moved to the corner of the site from its original position due east of the entry). Storey also designed the Elizabethan Francis G. Frink house (also known as Gray Gables, 1906-9; altered), and at least three bungalows, the George W. Trimble house (1905-6) and a pair on adjacent lots, the George A. Bruce and Edward F. Tindolph houses (1914-15). The Robert M. Evans house (1913) was executed in a style similar to that of Storey's own house.

3. Phiscator Estate dwelling (J. K. Gordon house), Seattle, 1907-8 (altered), Ellsworth Storey. Designed to promote the sale of lots and houses in the surrounding subdivision, this was an essay in the Georgian Revival. While this shows Storey's command of this eclectic style, the direction of most of his work was away from Classical Revival modes. *(Photo by T. William Booth, 1993.)*

From 1910 through 1915, Storey designed and saw built another body of work for himself, a group of speculative rental cottages adjacent to Colman Park on Lake Washington Boulevard; these are textbook examples of the elegant coordination of modest materials. These cottages, together with the Evans house and the two Storey houses, have been most influential for later designers, perhaps because, in their fresh underivative forms and their thoughtfully imaginative use of simple local materials, they have been seen as his most original interpretations of the nature of building in the Puget Sound region.

In the 1920s, Storey designed the Albert Mayer house (1920-22) and the James E. Dyer house (1922), the latter a homage to Storey's fondness for the Swiss chalet. He also designed the rectory for the Episcopal Church of the Epiphany (1921), for which he had previously designed the chapel (1910-11), in another blend of Tudor and

4. Francis G. Frink house (Gray Gables), Seattle, 1906-9 (altered), Ellsworth Storey. The Elizabethan character of the Frink house, now sadly altered, is related to English Arts and Crafts. From Frank Calvert, ed., *Homes and Gardens of the Pacific Coast, Volume 1: Seattle.* (Beaux Arts Village, Lake Washington, 1913). *(University of Washington Libraries, Special Collections Division; UW6009.)*

Arts and Crafts, and the Rainier Golf and Country Club (1922-24; altered).

During the later 1920s, Storey did markedly less work, although he did publish the Harry E. Woolley house (1924-25). In the early 1930s, of course, few architects were building anything at all. During these years Storey survived primarily on rent from the cottages.

In 1934, however, Storey was asked to design a fire-watch tower on Mount Constitution in Moran State Park on Orcas Island. For this he seems to have turned to Richardson's example, or perhaps, like Richardson, he was working largely from the suggestions offered by the material in the service of its architectural task. The tower was admired; Storey was asked to do all the subsequent work around the lake at the park. This work encompassed a bathhouse,

5. Sigma Nu Fraternity House, Seattle, 1915-16, Ellsworth Storey. The vertical masonry pylons suggest the massing of Wright's Larkin Building and Unity Temple of the prior decade. The building originally had a two-story volume behind the tall brick pylons at center. *(Photo by Grant Hildebrand, 1971.)*

6. Storey cottages, Seattle, 1910-15, Ellsworth Storey. A generous porch, and attention to simple detailing throughout, as seen here in the porch railings, give dignity to these modest buildings. *(Photo by Art Hupy.)*

7. James E. Dyer house, Seattle, 1922, Ellsworth Storey. This house is a manifestation of Storey's fondness for the Swiss chalet. *(Photo by Christian Staub, 1971)*

8. Unitarian Church (now University Presbyterian Church Chapel), Seattle, 1915-16 (altered), Ellsworth Storey. This remarkable personal interpretation of a half-timbered English parish church retains its character although its setting has been considerably built up. *(University of Washington Libraries, Special Collections Division; photo by Asahel Curtis, 39786.)*

a bridge, two picnic shelters, and the ranger's house, spaced around the perimeter of the lake. Of this work, the bathhouses adjacent to the highway, and the larger picnic shelter opposite, are representative. In each Storey used stone as substructure, logs as superstructure, both handled with a seemingly casual clarity that masks a studied sophistication. The Orcas work was completed in 1940.

Storey subsequently assisted with military construction at Sand Point Naval Air Station, and served with the FHA. In 1945 he retired; a decade later he went to live with his daughter Eunice in Ithaca, New York, where he died in 1960. In accordance with his wish, his ashes were scattered on the waters of Puget Sound.

Although Storey is hardly known nationally, few architects have engendered greater local affection. His richly developed eclectic works demonstrate his appreciation of craftsmanship and his grasp of detail. In his most original and best-known designs, he drew chalet, Arts and Crafts, and Prairie School predilections into the milieu of the region, and found in that metamorphosis a restrained but original style which still seems marvellously appropriate to the genius of the place he loved.

9. Lookout Tower, Mount Constitution, Orcas Island, 1934, Ellsworth Storey. A design dependent on a craggy massing, rough broken ashlar masonry, and the careful organization of windows with inset framing. *(Photo by Grant Hildebrand, 1970.)*

10. Bathhouses, Moran State Park, Orcas Island, 1935-40, Ellsworth Storey. Note the clear organization of materials: only rough masonry below, only dressed log timbers above. The gabled roofs at right angles are reconciled in the hipped roof of the concessions pavilion that lies between them. *(Photo by Grant Hildebrand, 1970.)*

Augustus Warren Gould

DENNIS A. ANDERSEN

Augustus Warren Gould (1872-1922) was one of the last major Seattle architects to enter the professional practice of architecture from the building and contracting trades. His background and lack of any academic training did not diminish an energetic and remarkably productive career, but it may have distanced him from his professional colleagues.

A. W. Gould was born January 15, 1872, in Salem, Nova Scotia, and received his early education in Nova Scotia and Massachusetts. One biographer describes Gould's education at Massachusetts Institute of Technology as "private studies," but the extent of academic preparation cannot be determined from school records. He moved from the contracting business to the architectural profession in the late 1890s in Boston. His projects included major institutional buildings—prisons and schools—as well as private clubs and residences. Some of these projects were accomplished in conjunction with his brother, Aaron Gould, who later practiced in Portland, Oregon.

Augustus Warren Gould arrived in 1903 to open a practice in Seattle at a time when building and construction technologies were markedly changing. High-rise steel frame business buildings with terra-cotta cladding were soon to become common among downtown structures. Gould brought to Seattle a thorough acquaintance with East Coast building techniques and a facile personal manner. A frequent speaker to civic and business organizations, he soon achieved public visibility in the construction trades. He also secured influential local patronage. The American Savings Bank and Trust Company Building (1904-6; de-

Augustus Warren Gould, about 1915. From Clarence Bagley, *History of Seattle* (Chicago, 1916). *(Private collection.)*

stroyed), which Gould designed for Judge Thomas Burke, was one of the largest construction projects in Seattle's history to that time and it introduced to the city the newest ferroconcrete construction technologies. It was followed by other downtown projects equally remarkable for Seattle at the time: the nine-story Standard Furniture Company Building (1905-7) on a site recently vacated by the initial stages of the Denny Regrade, the Seller Building (1905-6), and the Georgian Hotel Annex (1906-7; destroyed) for Puget Sound Realty Associates.

In 1909, Gould entered into a partnership with Édouard Frère Champney, which lasted for almost three years (see Champney essay). The new firm made good use of Champney's proficiency in the application of the Beaux-Arts Classical style and Gould's structural and construction expertise. Several large buildings were produced in Seattle, Aberdeen, and Vancouver, British Columbia, during the partnership.

1. Phillips Brooks School, Boston, Massachusetts, 1899-1900 (destroyed), A. W. Gould. This Boston public school from Gould's early architectural career represents his early efforts in academic Neoclassical architecture. From *Pacific Builder and Engineer,* September 23, 1906. *(University of Washington Libraries, Special Collections Division; UW14729.)*

In early 1909, A. W. Gould made proposals for the beautification of Seattle's downtown and helped to create interest in what became the Municipal Plans Commission. Although he was not a member of the Commission, he was among the architects who participated in supporting its work and paving the way for the Bogue Plan of 1911. When a multi-use county-city building with commercial rental space was proposed for the site of the present County Courthouse in 1909, A. W. Gould was one of its strongest opponents, and the project died. He retained interest in the site, however, and when, after the Bogue Plan had failed at the polls, proponents of the plan argued for a civic center site in the Regrade area, Gould undermined the project by submitting proposals for a 23-story county-city building on the Third and James site with grossly underestimated construction costs. The Regrade site proposal was turned down by the voters

in a bitterly contested election, and Gould was among those held responsible for the defeat through a misinformation campaign. For this breach of professional ethics, he was expelled from the Washington State Chapter of the AIA in extraordinary proceedings. He retained the Courthouse commission, however, although construction on the first five-story phase could not begin until 1914.

The partnership with Champney may have been another casualty of this episode. It was terminated in 1912, at the height of the controversy. Gould continued with other projects and apparently never lacked work. At impressive residences for S. J. Stillwell (1909-10) and Albert Rhodes (1914-15), Gould displayed a restrained sense of ornament, favoring instead to accent the splendor of site arrangement and visibility of structure. His Arctic Building (1913-17), designed with George Lawton, featured polychrome terra-cotta ornaments, whimsical

2. American Savings Bank/Empire Building, Seattle, 1904-6 (destroyed), A. W. Gould. Gould's first large-scale project in Seattle was designed for Judge Thomas Burke, who took a personal and excruciatingly exacting interest in all the construction and design details. The firm that erected the complicated steel framework was brought to Seattle especially for this project. This building was the first of Seattle's early "skyscrapers" to be demolished by implosion in the late 1970s. *(Private collection.)*

3. Standard Furniture Company Building (now the Broadacres Building), Seattle, 1905-7 (altered), A.W. Gould. One of the first high-rise structures to be built on land leveled by the first regrading of Denny Hill, it has since been stripped of most of its terra-cotta ornament. Its structural frame reveals Gould's engineering and technical expertise. *(University of Washington Libraries, Special Collections Division; UW14701.)*

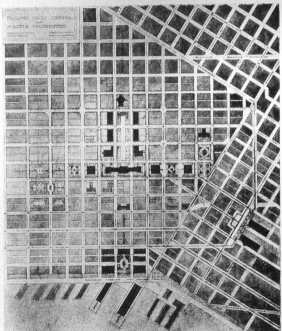

A PROPOSED PLAN FOR GROUPING THE PUBLIC BUILDINGS OF SEATTLE
Gould & Champney, Architects, Seattle

4. "A Proposed Plan for Grouping the Public Buildings of Seattle," 1909, Gould & Champney. This proposal is an example of Gould's interest in large-scale civic planning and the development of the civic center complex around the Third and James site in downtown Seattle. From Seattle Architectural Club, *Yearbook* (Seattle, 1910). *(Private collection.)*

5. Albert Rhodes house, Seattle, 1914-15, A. W. Gould. This large residence, a somewhat chilly classical villa faced with terra cotta, designed for a wealthy Seattle department store owner, enjoyed a spectacular site and garden plan. *(Private collection.)*

walrus heads (with tusks), and sumptuous classical club rooms and office interiors. Its great Dome Room remains one of the grandest interiors in downtown Seattle.

Gould was not without subsequent activity on behalf of his chosen profession. He was elected president of the Washington State Society of Architects (a local rival of the AIA) in 1917, and he was active in local and state planning and development projects, and in promotion of road building. He also served on the State Architects Examining Board.

Shortly before his death, he acquired a financial interest in a quarry near Mount Angel, Oregon, and spent much time there. He died on October 15, 1922, at the Tacoma Union Station on his way back to Seattle from a transcontinental motor tour.

6. "Proposed Motor Inn," 1907, A. W. Gould. Echoing Daniel Burnham's admonition to "make no little plans," Gould's proposal for a resort on an unidentified wooded property includes a large central hotel building flanked by vast wings of single and triple story "motor-hotel" units and announces the coming age of the automobile at a surprisingly early date. From Seattle Architectural Club, *Yearbook* (Seattle, 1910). *(University of Washington Libraries, Special Collections Division; UW14806.)*

· PROPOSED · MOTOR · INN ·
· A· WARREN · GOULD · ARCHITECT ·
· SEATTLE · WASHINGTON ·

7. Arctic Building, Seattle, 1913-17, A. W. Gould (with George Lawton). Perhaps Gould's best known building, this features an unusually witty use of polychrome and figural terra-cotta ornament. The heavy-handed opulence of the Dome Room, reminiscent of the 1890s club rooms by McKim, Mead & White, was probably somewhat old-fashioned by 1917. *(Museum of History and Industry, Seattle; PEMCO Webster & Stevens Collection, 83.10.10417.)*

8. Proposed hotel, Pioneer Square, Seattle, undocumented project ca. 1917, A. W. Gould. This photograph with a superimposed ink and wash rendering portrays a mammoth twelve-story project, clearly the stylistic kin of Gould's King County Courthouse, which would have necessitated the demolition of the Pioneer, Tremont, and Butler buildings, and is a clear indication of Gould's affinity for Pioneer Square development. *(Arthur Cole Collection.)*

9. King County Courthouse, Seattle, 1914-17 (altered), A. W. Gould. Gould violated professional ethics to secure this commission, siding with Pioneer Square property holders who fought relocation of city-county offices to the Regrade area. Later architects added upper floors long after Gould's death (see Bittman essay). *(University of Washington Libraries, Special Collections Division; photo by C. F. Todd, 12353.)*

Daniel R. Huntington

THOMAS VEITH

Daniel Riggs Huntington (1871-1962), born December 24, 1871, in Newark, New Jersey, spent his early life in New York City and was educated at Columbia Grammar School, a preparatory school for Columbia College. He began his architectural career in Denver in 1889 as an apprentice with Balcom & Rice but returned to New York in 1894 to work for six years in the office of W. Wheeler Smith. In 1900, Huntington again relocated to Denver and, with William E. Fisher, formed the firm of Fisher & Huntington which concentrated on apartments and residential work.

Huntington came to Seattle in 1904 or 1905. By 1907, he had joined James Schack

Daniel R. Huntington. *(University of Washington Libraries, Special Collections Division; UW14555.)*

in the partnership of Schack & Huntington, which designed the First Methodist Episcopal Church (1907-10), the old Arctic Club (1908-9; now the Hotel Morrison), the Delamar Apartments (1908-9), and a number of residences (see Schack, Young & Myers essay).

After this firm split, Huntington designed the Shumway Mansion, Kirkland (1909-10, relocated and altered), and the Sanitary Market (1909-10; destroyed). He shared credit for the latter structure with Carl F. Gould, who had joined him as a draftsman in 1909 (see Bebb & Gould essay). As Huntington & Gould, the two men completed a number of mixed-use buildings and several houses, although Huntington continued his independent practice with commissions such as the Johnson and Hamilton Mortuary (1909; now law offices), and the David Newbrand residence (1911). In 1912, Huntington redesigned the end of the Colman Dock (destroyed), initially designed in 1908 by the Beezer Brothers (see essay).

1. A. P. Burwell house, Seattle, 1906, D. R. Huntington. Although this structure appears to be a typical box scheme residence, it is made unique by the unusual side entrance. From Frank Calvert, ed., *Homes and Gardens of the Pacific Coast, Volume 1: Seattle* (Beaux Arts Village, Lake Washington, 1913). *(University of Washington Libraries, Special Collections Division; UW14712.)*

2. Colman Dock, Seattle, 1912 (destroyed), D. R. Huntington. The west end of the dock, badly damaged when the steamship *Alameda* rammed it in 1912, was rebuilt with this masonry building and tower, both somewhat larger and more ornate than those they replaced. *(University of Washington Libraries, Special Collections Division; photo by C. F. Todd, 121.)*

3. Wallingford Fire and Police Station, 1912-13 (altered), D. R. Huntington. This Shingle Style structure, which was also known as Fire Station No. 11, is the earliest of at least ten fire houses that Huntington designed, employing a variety of styles in an effort to blend the buildings into their respective neighborhoods. *(Collection of Paul Dorpat; photo by Webster & Stevens.)*

That same year, Huntington joined Arthur L. Loveless (see essay) in a two-year partnership responsible for several residences and apartment houses. However, this work was overshadowed by the commissions undertaken by Huntington as City Architect, a position he held from September 19, 1912, until late 1921. Among the latter were several Seattle Lighting Department structures, including the Lake Union Water Power Auxiliary Plant (1912), and the Lake Union Auxiliary Steam Electric Plant (1914), for which he designed additions in 1917-18 and 1921 (both recently remodeled for private use). He also altered the old Public Safety Building (1917) and designed the concrete piers at the University Bridge, a project for which he received an AIA Honor Award in 1927.

He completed at least ten fire houses, beginning with the Shingle Style Wallingford Fire and Police Station (Station No. 11, 1912-13) and including single-use buildings such as Station No. 33 in Lakeridge (1914; now a residence), Station No. 12 (1919; now Madrona Sally Goldmark Library), Station No. 2 in the Denny Regrade (1920), and Station No. 7 on Capitol Hill (1920; now a retail shop).

4. Lake Union Steam Plant, Seattle, 1912, 1914, 1917-18, 1921 (altered), D. R. Huntington, City Architect. The small, Mission Style, Lake Union Water Power Auxiliary Plant produced power in an emergency using the water from the Volunteer Park Reservoir. The later Lake Union Auxiliary Steam Electric Plant of 1914, with additions of 1917-18 and 1921, made the original structure technically obsolete and obscured its eclectic character with a much larger and more utilitarian, if somewhat classical, design. *(University of Washington Libraries, Special Collections Division; UW14591.)*

Among his larger projects were six fine eclectic structures at the original Firland Sanatorium (now the CRISTA campus), including the Administration Building (1913-14; now the Mike Martin Administration Building), the Detweiler Building (1913-14; now King's High School), and the crenellated Power House (1913-14). One of his best projects, and probably his last as City Architect, was the Mission Style Fremont Branch of the Seattle Public Library (1920-21).

After leaving civil service, Huntington designed a number of small commercial structures and taught briefly at the University of Washington (1923-24). He also completed his own residence (1924), the Rainier Chapter House of the Daughters of the American Revolution (1924-25), and the Northcliffe Apartments (1924-25). His West Seattle Dairy Building (1927; destroyed) was described at the time as one of the finest commercial structures in the Northwest. Fire Station No. 16, in Greenlake (1928), was a late addition to his list of municipal works.

In partnership with Arch Torbitt (ca. 1883-1958), he completed the Piedmont Apartments (later known as the Evangeline Young Women's Residence, 1928). Huntington & Torbitt also designed the Seventh Street Theater in Hoquiam (1927-28), where an "atmospheric" interior metaphorically transports patrons to an open-air evening performance space in a "Spanish village," and the Hoquiam City Hall (1928-29), both in association with Edwin St. John Griffith.

Huntington apparently left active practice after the onset of the Depression, although he was employed as an architect at Washington State University from September 1944 until August 1946. He moved to Oregon City in 1947, following retirement, but returned to the Seattle area in 1955. He died May 13, 1962.

Huntington was well regarded by his business associates and professional colleagues. He was elected president of the local

5.   Administration Building (now Mike Martin Administration Building), Firland Sanatorium (now CRISTA Ministries campus), Richmond Highlands, 1913-14, D. R. Huntington, City Architect. The Collegiate Gothic entry is complemented by the Tudor "half-timbering" of the wings. The formal symmetry of this design was abandoned in some of Huntington's later projects at Firland. *(University of Washington Libraries, Special Collections Division; UW14710.)*

6.   Detweiler Building (now King's High School), Firland Sanatorium (now CRISTA Ministries campus), Richmond Highlands, 1913-14, D. R. Huntington, City Architect. Construction of this infirmary greatly increased the capacity of the sanatorium and made it possible to move many patients out of the small cabins in which they had previously been housed. *(University of Washington Libraries, Special Collections Division; UW14711.)*

7. Fremont Branch, Seattle Public Library, Seattle, 1920-21, D. R. Huntington, City Architect. Unlike most of the branch libraries that immediately preceded it, this Mission Style building, which steps down the slope on a difficult site, does not employ a symmetrical Beaux-Arts scheme. *(Seattle Public Library; 12003.)*

8. Rainier Chapter House of the Daughters of the American Revolution, Seattle, 1924-25, D. R. Huntington. This simple, classical design is intentionally reminiscent of George Washington's home at Mount Vernon. The wood siding has been grooved to resemble stonework. Unfortunately, the railing at the edge of the low, hipped roof has been removed. *(Museum of History and Industry, Seattle; PEMCO Webster & Stevens Collection, 83.10.435.3.)*

chapter of the Amercian Institute of Architects for 1918-19 and 1925, served one term as secretary, and was a member of the board of directors.

His watercolor renderings were widely admired. His buildings were typically straightforward and elegantly detailed, characteristics perhaps attributable to his lack of a formal architectural education and his extensive portfolio of small commercial and public works commissions. Although the designs of some of his utility structures seem to anticipate the development of the Modern Movement's industrial aesthetic, his approach to these buildings more likely grew out of an innate pragmatism than a conscious search for new modes of expression. His ubiquitous city projects set a high standard for municipal work in Seattle.

9. Northcliffe Apartments, Seattle, 1924-25, D. R. Huntington. The elegant suggestion of medieval detailing at the top of this large brick structure helps to give it character and reduce its mass without obscuring its essentially pragmatic form. *(Museum of History and Industry,Seattle; PEMCO Webster & Stevens Collection, 83.10.4114.1.)*

10. Piedmont Apartments (also known as the Evangeline Young Women's Residence), Seattle, 1927, Huntington & Torbitt. This stucco structure is characterized by unusual ornaments at the "eroded" corners, Palladian windows on its east elevation which light a two-story lobby, and a continuous tile casing which wraps most of the main floor wall openings, giving the building a Moorish flavor. *(Museum of History and Industry, Seattle; PEMCO Webster & Stevens Collection, 83.10.3578.)*

Somervell & Coté

DAVID A. RASH

Prior to 1905, Seattle buildings exhibiting a Beaux-Arts Classical sensibility were invariably eastern imports, like the U.S. Post Office (1903-8; destroyed) by James Knox Taylor of Washington, D.C., the Carnegie Public Library (1903-6; destroyed) by Peter J. Weber of Chicago, or Saint James Catholic Cathedral (1903-7; altered) by Heins & LaFarge of New York. Heins & LaFarge, however, made an additional contribution to Seattle architecture by sending W. Marbury Somervell (1872-1939) to Seattle to supervise its construction. Joseph S. Coté (1874- ?), Somervell's future partner, was also dispatched to Seattle, as Somervell's assistant. Their formal partnership lasted only from 1906 to 1910, but in that time Somervell & Coté specifically sought to develop "the modern renaissance . . . along some original lines that adapt it to the Northwestern conditions."

The success of Saint James Cathedral gave Somervell & Coté instant credibility for large-scale projects. They quickly won projects from the Seattle Public Library system through the Beaux-Arts tradition of design competitions. Their first library commission was for the entrance stairs and terraces (1907-9; destroyed) for the main Carnegie building downtown, and the second was for the first three branch libraries: Green Lake, West Seattle, and University (1908-10). Their two largest private commissions, the Perry Apartments (1906-7; to be destroyed) and Providence Hospital (1907-12), were specifically intended to achieve a synthesis of Beaux-Arts Classicism and local traditions.

Somervell, who had been born on May 3, 1872, in Washington, D.C., and had studied architecture at Cornell University, apparently had a restless nature. After his partner-

ship with Coté was dissolved in 1910, he opened a very successful branch office in Vancouver, British Columbia, with a new partner, John L. Putnam, while maintaining an independent Seattle office. This allowed Somervell to design, among other works, three additional branch libraries for the Seattle system: Queen Anne (1912-14), Columbia (1912-15), and Henry L. Yesler Memorial (now Douglass-Truth) (1912-14), all with Harlan Thomas (see Thomas essay).

During World War I, Somervell served with the Corps of Engineers and the Chemical Warfare Service in France. After the armistice, he remained in Europe and was involved with the restoration of cultural

1. Saint James Catholic Cathedral, Seattle, 1903-7 (altered), Heins & LaFarge, New York City, with W. Marbury Somervell (superintending). This Italian Renaissance Revival structure was designed to acknowledge the removal of the See of the Diocese of Nesqually (now the Archdiocese of Seattle) from Vancouver, Washington. Adjacent is the original bishop's residence (1907-8; altered) by Somervell and Coté. (*University of Washington Libraries, Special Collections Division; 1908; UW14334.*)

W. Marbury Somervell. From *Pacific Builder and Engineer,* June 14, 1913. *(University of Washington Libraries, Special Collections Division; UW7250.)*

Joseph S. Coté. From *Pacific Builder and Engineer,* June 14, 1913. *(University of Washington Libraries, Special Collections Division; UW14478.)*

monuments damaged during the war. Upon his return to the United States, he and partner Putnam removed to Los Angeles, California, where they practiced together until 1929. Somervell continued working there either independently or for architect S. Tilden Norton, until 1935. By the time of his death on April 2, 1939, Somervell had retired to Cannes, France, where he had continued his lifelong avocation as an etcher.

Coté, who had been born on March 9, 1874, in the province of Quebec, Canada, and had studied architecture at Columbia University in New York City, apparently had a more reserved nature than Somervell, suggesting to some historians that he was less attuned to the business aspects of the architectural profession and consequently that Somervell had been responsible for the commercial and institutional work of the firm. Coté has been viewed as more attuned to the design aspects of the profession and consequently was thought to have been pri-

marily responsible for their residential work. Prior to World War I, however, this was hardly the case, as Coté was the principal designer of the Perry Apartments and an addition to Saint Joseph Hospital, Bellingham (1908-9); independently, he designed the Noble Hospital (1910-11; destroyed), the original building of Swedish Hospital (1911-12; destroyed), and the Sunset Club (1914-15), all in Seattle.

During World War I, Coté served as a captain in the Army Corps of Engineers until 1920, when he returned to Seattle. From 1920 until his apparent departure from Seattle after 1948, Coté's architectural practice was essentially residential in nature. These later houses were invariably in his preferred Georgian and Federal Revival styles, and ranged in scale from the large William Piggott residence (1920-21) and J. Edward Clark residence (1927-28) to the modest C. A. Sundt speculative houses (1940).

With their direct transplantation from

2. Perry Apartments, Seattle, 1906-7 (scheduled for demolition), Heins & LaFarge/Somervell & Coté. Oliver H. P. LaFarge, brother of the architect C. Grant LaFarge, was one of the investors in the building. The original entrance court was enclosed to create an enlarged lobby (1911-12) by Coté. *(University of Washington Libraries, Special Collections Division; 1912; photo by Asahel Curtis, 23959.)*

3. Providence Hospital, Seattle, 1907-12, Somervell & Coté. When the building permit was issued in 1909, this was the most expensive building to be erected in Seattle. Although the building was dedicated September 24, 1911, construction on parts of the complex continued into 1912. *(University of Washington Libraries, Special Collections Division; 1912; photo by Asahel Curtis, 25615.)*

4. Green Lake Branch, Seattle Public Library, Seattle, 1908-10, Somervell & Coté. The first of five branch libraries to be constructed with funds donated by Andrew Carnegie, this "modern French Renaissance style" design placed first of thirty-three competitors and was executed with only minor changes in detail. *(Seattle Public Libraries; 1910.)*

5. Fire Station No. 25, Seattle, 1908-9, Somervell & Coté. In addition to the work for the public library system, this Seattle landmark building and Fire Station No. 22 (1908; destroyed) were designed for the Seattle Fire Department. *(University of Washington Libraries, Special Collections Division; ca. 1910; UW12399.)*

the East Coast and formal academic training, Somervell & Coté were well suited to providing Seattle with appropriate architectural symbols for civic institutions in what was rapidly becoming the leading American metropolis in the Pacific Northwest. When *Architectural Record* published its first survey on Seattle architecture in July 1912, four of the twenty-two published buildings were wholly or partly the work of Somervell & Coté; Providence Hospital, in particular, was admired for its appropriate symbolism. At a time when American architecture was judged primarily by East Coast standards, Somervell & Coté helped Seattle come of age as "unquestionably the city of most considerable promise in these United States."

6. Clare E. Farnsworth house, Seattle, 1909-10, Somervell & Coté. This Tudor Revival house was the firm's most widely published residence. *(Photo by David A. Rash, 1992.)*

7. Yorkshire Building (now Seymour Building), Vancouver, British Columbia, 1911-12, Somervell & Putnam. The choice of the Gothic Revival style may have been inspired by the Woolworth Building (1910-13) in New York City, where John L. Putnam had worked prior to his arrival in Vancouver. *(Photo by David A. Rash, 1992.)*

8. Queen Anne Branch, Seattle Public Library, Seattle, 1912-14, W. Marbury Somervell, in association with Harlan Thomas. Somervell felt the Tudor Revival style was more in keeping with the residential nature of the Queen Anne neighborhood than the typical Classical Revival style of many Carnegie libraries. *(Museum of History and Industry, Seattle; PEMCO Webster & Stevens Collection, 83.10.10163.2.)*

9. Sunset Club, Seattle, 1914-15, Joseph S. Coté. This Georgian Revival structure was the finest of several institutional works by Coté prior to World War I. *(University of Washington Libraries, Special Collections Division; 1915; photo by Asahel Curtis, 32747.)*

10. William Piggott house, Seattle, 1920-21, Joseph S. Coté. This fine example of Coté's Georgian Revival houses, for the founder of Pacific Car and Foundry (today's PACCAR), was designed after Coté's return from military service during World War I. *(Photo by David A. Rash, 1992.)*

Harlan Thomas

NORMAN J. JOHNSTON

The career of Harlan Thomas (1870-1953) grew from mid-American roots. Thomas was born in Iowa, January 10, 1870, and was raised there and in Fort Collins and Denver after his family moved to Colorado in 1879. His early interests in drawing and mechanics, augmented by several years experience as a carpenter, led Thomas to become a draftsman in a Denver architect's office and later to attend Colorado State College, where he majored in mathematics and mechanics and earned his bachelor of science degree in 1895. That year, having previously designed a residence and two buildings for his college, Thomas opened his own architectural office in Denver. But, recently married—and with an urge that remained with him throughout his career to see the larger world and expand his skills—he soon left for his first visit to Europe, sixteen months that included architectural studies in Paris as a member of an American atelier before returning to the Denver area to resume his practice. In 1903 and 1904, he was away again, this time for fifteen months on a round-the-world adventure for further study, sketching, and painting.

It was not until 1906 that Thomas moved west and began his Seattle career. He built himself a handsome house on the west-viewing slopes of Queen Anne hill that same year. The momentum that he developed in Colorado carried him rapidly forward in Seattle as well, for in 1907 he had to his credit two major projects: the Chelsea Hotel on lower Queen Anne facing south toward Elliott Bay and the even more dramatically sited Sorrento Hotel looking westward from First Hill over the central city. The former, with its five-story stucco and brick facades, bay windows, and topping pergolas, represented a fresh standard in Seattle for apart-

Harlan Thomas, late 1930s. (*University of Washington, College of Architecture and Urban Planning archives.*)

ment/hotel living. And the seven-story Sorrento—its grand corner entrance terrace contained by the hotel's patterned brickwork and richly terra-cotta-detailed facades whose projecting framing piers, joined by flattened arches, were capped by gazebos with broad overhangs—offered Seattle its first rooftop restaurant and brought a new sophistication in residential accommodations for locals and visitors alike. In both cases, but especially at the Sorrento, Thomas accepted familiar formal *partis,* but phrased them in a versatile design vocabulary that bespoke some willingness to explore innovatively rather than accept routinely the conventions of the day.

In those years, Thomas also won several school commissions in smaller cities and towns in western Washington, including the J. M. Weatherwax High School, Aberdeen (1908-9; altered), with Russell & Rice; the Monroe High School, Monroe (1909-10; destroyed); and the Enumclaw High School, Enumclaw (1910-11; destroyed).

The bulk of Thomas's subsequent professional career was in partnership with others: Thomas, Russell & Rice; Thomas & (Clyde) Grainger (1887-1958); Thomas, Grainger & Thomas (with Harlan's son, Donald P. Tho-

1. Harlan Thomas residence, Seattle, 1906 (altered), Harlan Thomas. Although still extant, this structure has been mutilated by later alterations and additions. Its rather Mediterranean character and the round-headed arch of the principal facade were themes Thomas would employ again in his later work. From Seattle Architectural Club, *Yearbook* (Seattle, 1910). *(University of Washington, College of Architecture and Urban Planning Library.)*

mas, 1898-1970), and a number of temporary associations, producing a sequence of buildings that remain familiar in the fabric of Seattle: the Corner Market Building (1911-12) in partnership with Grainger; the

2. Chelsea Hotel, Seattle, 1907, Harlan Thomas. This building established a fresh standard for apartment/hotel living in Seattle. *(Museum of History and Industry, Seattle; PEMCO Webster & Stevens Collection, 83.10.9237.)*

Queen Anne (1912-14), Columbia (1912-15), and Henry L. Yesler (now Douglass-Truth) (1912-14) libraries with W. Marbury Somervell (see Somervell & Coté essay); the Seattle Chamber of Commerce Building (1923-25; altered) with Schack, Young & Myers (see essay); the Sales and Service Building (1925), Rhodes Department Store (1926-27, now known as the Arcade Plaza Building), and Harborview Hospital (1929-31; altered) in the partnership Thomas, Grainger & Thomas. He was also involved with projects elsewhere in Washington and Alaska. His Seattle residential work began with his own house but was versatile enough to include houses for Delta Kappa Epsilon Fraternity (1914; now Tau Kappa Epsilon) and Kappa Kappa Gamma Sorority (1930); a 500-unit World War II housing project with Smith, Carroll & Johanson in Bremerton; and, after the war, speculative housing for the developer Albert Balch in northeast Seattle.

3. Sorrento Hotel, Seattle, 1907-8, Harlan Thomas and Russell & Rice. This eclectic design was another significant contribution to the city's emerging status as an urbane center in the Pacific Northwest. *(Museum of History and Industry, Seattle; PEMCO Webster & Stevens Collection, 83.10.9468.1.)*

4. J. M. Weatherwax High School, Aberdeen, 1908-9 (altered), Harlan Thomas and Russell & Rice. This was the largest of Thomas's high school projects outside Seattle, and, like the others, was a relatively simple rectangular form with restrained, vaguely Gothic detail. From *Pacific Builder and Engineer*, November 11, 1911. *(University of Washington Libraries, Special Collections Division; UW14784.)*

5. Corner Market Building, Seattle, 1911-12, Harlan Thomas and Clyde Grainger. This occupies a key location in a picturesque center of the city's commercial downtown. *(Museum of History and Industry, Seattle; PEMCO Webster & Stevens Collection, 83.10.10020.)*

The influence of personalities and developments in American architecture in the 1920s and 1930s was clearly demonstrated in Thomas's work of those decades. Thus the refined simplicity of his Rhodes Department Store owes more than a little to Chicago School precedent, and the vertical emphasis and absence of ornament at Harborview is reminiscent of Saarinen's 1922 *Chicago Tribune* competition submittal.

Concurrently, Thomas was active in the AIA, serving as chapter president in 1924-26; he was elected a Fellow in 1928. Thomas was appointed professor of architecture and head of the Architecture Department at the University of Washington (1926-40) following the untimely departure of Carl Gould (see Bebb & Gould essay). He returned twice to Europe and became a recognized and exhibiting painter, especially after his retirement from practice in 1949. By the time of his death September 4, 1953, Thomas was

secure in his reputation as one of the more urbane and versatile members of his professional community and as a benign father figure in the memory of his former students.

6. Delta Kappa Epsilon Fraternity House (now housing Tau Kappa Epsilon), Seattle, 1914, Harlan Thomas. The Georgian Revival inspiration for this design was a nationwide enthusiasm in the those early decades of this century. From *Tyee* (Associated Students of the University of Washington, 1936). *(University of Washington Libraries, Special Collections Division; UW14535.)*

7. Seattle Chamber of Commerce Building, Seattle, 1923-25 (altered), Harlan Thomas and Schack, Young & Myers. The arched facade is an idea Thomas used earlier for his own residence but here in a more substantial Lombardic Romanesque reinterpretation. *(TRA Architects Collection; photo by Hugh Stratford.)*

9. Kappa Kappa Gamma Sorority House, Seattle, 1930 (altered), Thomas, Grainger & Thomas. Today this building retains much of its original comfortable and timeless style in spite of the awkward additions of more recent years. From *Tyee* (Associated Students of the University of Washington, 1936). *(University of Washington Libraries, Special Collections Division; UW14534.)*

8. Rhodes Department Store (now the Arcade Plaza Building), Seattle, 1926-27, Thomas, Grainger & Thomas. With a clarity of form and detail, this structure complemented the city's emerging status as the region's major commercial center. *(Museum of History and Industry, Seattle; PEMCO Webster & Stevens Collection, 83.10.3856.)*

10. Harborview Hospital, Seattle, 1929-31, Thomas, Grainger & Thomas. This large institutional structure demonstrates Thomas's ability to work successfully with emerging twentieth-century directions. *(Museum of History and Industry, Seattle; PEMCO Webster & Stevens Collection, 83.10.4371.2.)*

Édouard Frère Champney

DENNIS A. ANDERSEN

Édouard Frère Champney (1874-1929) was one of the few turn-of-the-century architects in the Pacific Northwest who possessed formal French academic architectural training. From experience with major East Coast firms, he brought to this region an unusual background in large-scale urban and landscape planning and a knowledge of elaborate Beaux-Arts eclectic styles. His talents and services were not always recognized or readily patronized by the public, and it cannot be said that his Seattle tenure was marked by great financial success. His peripatetic life and career are an interesting if sad comment on the fate of academically trained architects who struggled to live and work in the Pacific Northwest at the beginning of the twentieth century.

Édouard Frère Champney, about 1912. From *Pacific Builder and Engineer,* June 15, 1912. *(University of Washington Libraries, Special Collections Division; UW14719.)*

1. U.S. Government Pavilion, Lewis and Clark Exposition, Portland, Oregon, 1903-4 (destroyed), Office of the Supervising Architect, E. F. Champney, designer. This was an example of Champney's Beaux-Arts expertise presented in the form of a large temporary classical palace typical for the expositions which followed the World's Columbian Exposition of 1893. *(Private collection.)*

2. Statuary group including the "Spirit of the Pacific" from the Cascade Fountain of the Alaska-Yukon-Pacific Exposition, Seattle, 1909 (destroyed). Champney designed the figure on the far right, which was then modeled and executed by the sculptor Finn Frolich. *(University of Washington Libraries, Special Collections Division; 1909; photo by Frank Newell, W2576.)*

Édouard Champney was born to American parents in Écouen, France, a northern suburb of Paris, on May 4, 1874. His father, J. Wells Champney (1843-1903), was a well-known landscape and portrait painter. His mother, Elizabeth Williams Champney (1850-1922), was known in the United States as a writer of children's books, travel literature, and historical romances which often featured architectural illustrations by her husband and her son. Édouard was named after a French painter, Édouard Frère, a teacher and friend of J. Wells Champney from the family's time in France.

Édouard Frère Champney was educated in the United States and received his B.A. from Harvard University in 1896. He then attended the École des Beaux-Arts in Paris in 1899 and 1900, working in an as yet unidentified atelier. Returning to the United States, he worked in a succession of prominent East Coast firms, including those of Carrère & Hastings, E. L. Masqueray,

Hornblower & Marshall, and the Office of the Supervising Architect for the federal government in Washington, D.C. In these offices Champney was involved in large-scale projects such as mansions (in Palm Beach and Newport), public buildings, and cathedrals (including the Pro-Cathedral of the Immaculate Conception in Minneapolis, and the Cathedral of Saint Paul in St. Paul, both under Masqueray between 1904 and 1907).

Champney's French academic education had prepared him particularly well for work on several of the lavishly planned turn-of-the-century expositions. He was a draftsman for Carrère & Hastings at the Buffalo Pan American Exposition (1900). At the Louisiana Purchase Exposition in St. Louis (1904), he was involved in the design and construction of the Transportation and Agriculture Buildings, the Cascade, and the Terraces. In 1904, he worked as designer on the U.S. Government Pavilion (1903-4; de-

stroyed) for the Office of the Supervising Architect at the Lewis and Clark Exposition in Portland, Oregon.

Champney came to Seattle in 1907 as chief designer for the San Francisco firm of Howard & Galloway (headed by John Galen Howard) to supervise projects for the 1909 Alaska-Yukon-Pacific Exposition, a significant position since Howard & Galloway was responsible for design supervision for the entire Exposition. Champney was to remain in Seattle for nearly twenty years, a member of the local AIA chapter, the Architectural League of the Pacific Coast, and the Society of Beaux-Arts Architects.

He formed an architectural partnership with Augustus Warren Gould in 1909. Large commissions became a specialty of the firm

3. New Richmond Hotel, Seattle, 1909-11, Gould & Champney. Built for R. C. McCormick, this massive hotel block featured oversize classical detailing. *(University of Washington Libraries, Special Collections Division; photo by Asahel Curtis, 19271.)*

4. Seattle Electric Company Building, Seattle, 1910-11 (destroyed), Gould & Champney. Plain flat pilasters and heavily ornamented capitals, topped with overscaled brackets and cornice marked Champney's influence on this structure From Seattle Architectural Club, *Yearbook* (Seattle, 1910). *(Private collection.)*

His design for the Seattle YWCA (1912-13), begun under the Gould & Champney partnership, was completed by Champney alone, although minus an initially intended fanciful roof garden and clock tower. His design solutions for the Tacoma Elks [Club] Temple (1914-15) made imaginative use of a difficult steep site by including a spectacular public stairway on the east side of the building. Champney quite often served as associate architect on large or prestigious projects by other firms. His 1922 rendering for a Women's University Club project in conjunction with A. H. Albertson (see Albertson, Wilson & Richardson essay) shows an ornate style sadly similar only in size and general massing to what was finally built.

5. Glyn Building project, Vancouver, British Columbia, 1911, Gould & Champney. This published rendering again shows Champney's sophisticated and lively use of ornament. The proposed Glyn Building was altered and simplified to become the Rogers Building. From *Pacific Coast Architect*, May 1911. *(Seattle Public Library.)*

of Gould & Champney over the following two years. The Seattle Electric Company Building (1910-11; destroyed), the New Richmond Hotel (1909-11), the Seattle warehouse for Bekins Storage Company (partly built, 1911), and the New Farmer's Bank, Ellensburg (1911-12; with Fay Spangler) were all designed during this brief partnership. The firm also maintained a Vancouver, British Columbia, office during 1910-12.

In 1912, when his partner became embroiled in the professional ethical controversies surrounding the design competition for the King County Courthouse and the defeat of the Bogue Plan, Champney withdrew from the partnership to practice independently (see A. W. Gould essay).

6. Rogers Building, Vancouver, British Columbia, 1911-12, Gould & Champney. Champney's ornament was swept away to recall Gould's usually straightforward approach. The lions' heads which surmount the third floor medallions foreshadow the walrus heads Gould would use to decorate his Arctic Building in Seattle. *(Vancouver Public Library; 21298.)*

Champney maintained an office in Seattle until 1926, but spent much of his time in San Francisco, especially during 1912-14, when he was involved in the design and supervision of the buildings and grounds of the Pan Pacific International Exposition. After 1926, he became a permanent resident of Berkeley, California, but returned to Seattle often to supervise the initial construction phase of Saint Mark Cathedral for San Francisco architects Bakewell & Brown.

Champney died in Berkeley on June 4, 1929. An obituary in the Washington AIA *Bulletin* lamented: "Finding it difficult to adapt himself to the practical demands of the present day architectural practice, his distinguished ability failed to get due recognition in architectural accomplishment. . . . Although an agreeable companion with his vivacious personality and insight into many phases of life—his secluded habits unfortunately prevented wide acquaintanceship."

7. Young Women's Christian Association Building, Seattle, 1912-13, E. F. Champney. This little-known rendering shows the intended roof garden, penthouse, and tower which were never added. The delicately molded cornice, Italian Renaissance upper floor windows, and small pieces of polychrome terra cotta enliven an otherwise restrained brick facade. From *Pacific Coast Architect*, August 1912. *(Seattle Public Library.)*

8. Young Women's Christian Association Building, Seattle, 1912-13, E. F. Champney. As executed, the YWCA lacked the roof garden features, but otherwise added a relatively sophisticated classical composition to the Seattle cityscape. *(Museum of History and Industry, Seattle; PEMCO Webster & Stevens Collection, 83.10.9801.)*

9. French garden urns, Pan Pacific Exposition, San Francisco, 1912-14 (destroyed). Champney commuted to San Francisco to participate in this last great West Coast exposition in the Beaux-Arts style. His activities primarily involved garden planning and detailing. From Paul Elder, *Landscape and Architecture of the Exposition* (San Francisco, 1914). *(Private collection.)*

10. Elks Temple, Tacoma, 1914-15, E. F. Champney. Beaux-Arts planning and architecture here form a dramatic urban ensemble, with both building and staircase by Champney. The opulent classical decoration seems curiously at odds with the finely molded elk's head surmounting the street level entrance. *(Private collection.)*

W. R. B. Willcox

NORMAN J. JOHNSTON

Although W. R. B. (Walter Ross Baumes) Willcox (1869-1947) is chiefly remembered as an educator and the bulk of his career was centered outside Washington State, much of his early professional work as a practicing architect was completed in Seattle between 1907 and 1922. Willcox was a Vermonter, born in 1869. His interest in architecture was honed in Chicago, where he observed the late nineteenth-century work of Richardson, Root, and Sullivan. Returning to the East, he informally attended classes at Massachusetts Institute of Technology. He later moved to Philadelphia for classes in the architectural programs at the University of Pennsylvania and Drexel Institute before moving back to Vermont to begin practice

W. R. B. Willcox in 1931, taken in his office at the University of Oregon by Kenton Hamaker, a graduate of the school. *(Courtesy of Elisabeth Walton Potter.)*

1. Carnegie Public Library, Burlington, Vermont, 1901-4, Willcox & Sayward. At the 1907-8 Architectural Exhibition of the Washington State Chapter of the AIA, Willcox & Sayward exhibited several of their New England buildings; this illustration of the Burlington Library was included in the exhibition catalogue. The building is now a wing of the Fletcher Free Library. From *Architectural Exhibition of the Washington State Chapter American Institute of Architects, 1907-1908* (Seattle, 1908). *(University of Washington Libraries, Special Collectons Division; UW14827.)*

2. Dr. J. Warren Richardson residence, Seattle, 1909-10, Willcox & Sayward. The horizontal lines and overhanging roof of this house suggest the possibility of Prairie School inspiration or influence in this project. From Frank Calvert, ed., *Homes and Gardens of the Pacific Coast, Volume 1: Seattle* (Beaux Arts Village, Lake Washington, 1913). *(University of Washington Libraries, Special Collections Division.)*

in partnership with William J. Sayward (1875-1945), who had previously spent six years with McKim, Mead & White. Willcox & Sayward designed over one hundred buildings in northern New England, but the attractions that Seattle held for architects in the first decade of the new century lured the partners westward to open their Seattle office in 1907. The Willcox & Sayward partnership ended with Sayward's return to the East Coast in 1912 (although Willcox continued to use the partnership title until about 1915).

The firm's Northwest practice began with residential work but expanded to include larger private and public commissions. By the time of Willcox's departure from Seattle he had been associated with at least sixty projects in the Seattle area, the bulk of them residential but also a scattering of public, religious, and commercial work. Typical of his early residential practice is the vaguely Prairie School–inspired house for Dr. J. Warren Richardson (1909-10), chosen

for inclusion in the Seattle volume of *Homes and Gardens of the Pacific Coast,* published in 1913 by the Beaux Arts Society as "expressing the latest and best ideas in American architecture." Commercial work included the Firmin Michel Roast Beef Corporation's temporary Casino (1909; destroyed) on the grounds of the Alaska-Yukon-Pacific Exposition, the Crouley (office) Building (1909-10; later the Hotel Reynolds and currently returned to office uses), and a hotel/apartment building (1915-16; now the Pacific Hotel). Public projects, which became familiar elements in Seattle's cityscape, are the arched viaduct and footbridge over Lake Washington Boulevard in the Arboretum (1910-11) and the Queen Anne Boulevard retaining walls (1913). Both featured reinforced concrete with handsome brick inset patterning, the latter described by the 1913 *City Engineer's Annual Report* as being a "radical departure" from the monotony of typical concrete construction.

3. Casino (for the Firmin Michel Roast Beef Corporation), Alaska-Yukon-Pacific Exposition, Seattle, 1909 (destroyed), Willcox & Sayward. This small pavilion was a temporary structure where the use of stucco presaged Willcox's later frequent use of this finish material. *(University of Washington, Special Collections Division; 1909; photo by Nowell, X1818.)*

Willcox was an AIA activist. Elected a member in 1905 while still in Vermont, he joined what was then called the Washington State Chapter in 1908 and quickly assumed leadership responsibilities. A two-term chapter president (1911-13), Willcox (along with Charles H. Bebb; see Bebb & Mendel essay) was elected a Fellow in 1910, the first individuals from Washington State to be so honored. During his AIA presidency, a special committee of the chapter encouraged establishment of an architectural degree program at the University of Washington, an effort that succeeded in 1914. Willcox's involvement as a member of the chapter's committee on planning for the city led to his appointment (along with Carl F. Gould; see Bebb & Gould essay) to Seattle's Municipal Plans Commission and his enthusiastic support for Virgil Bogue's 1911 Seattle plan which the commission sponsored. (The published plan was illustrated by one of Willcox's drawings.) Its defeat at the polls in 1912 was a bitter disappointment.

No doubt his uneasiness with the conformities of historical precedent in architectural education and practice, abetted by his contacts with the innovative work of the Chicago School, led Willcox increasingly to question the design conventions of contemporary practice and its divorce, as he saw it, from any relevance to twentieth-century American life. In comments rather reminiscent of the earlier observations of Louis Sullivan and those much later of Louis Kahn, he stated that "every problem contains and suggests its own solutions." Such thinking brought him to reject the prevailing Beaux-Arts teaching techniques. Abiding, too, had been his interest in the education of future architects, as demonstrated by his initiative in founding such a program at the University of Washington. All this came to fruition after Willcox left

Seattle in 1922 and moved to Eugene, where he accepted a professorship at the University of Oregon, remaining there until his death on April 20, 1947. While he would continue his practice with work admired for its independent and unpretentious design, he gave priority to his teaching. With his leadership, Oregon's program would adopt iconoclastic directions and move away from Beaux-Arts methods. Others would follow that route—but for most not until twenty years later, following the Second World War.

4. "An Idea for a Civic Monument on Duwamish Head," Seattle, 1911, W. R. B. Willcox. This drawing, prepared by Willcox, appeared as an illustration in the City Beautiful–inspired plan for Seattle. From Virgil Bogue, *Plan of Seattle* (Seattle, 1911). (*College of Architecture and Urban Planning Library, University of Washington.*)

5. Crouley Building, Seattle, 1909-10, Willcox & Sayward. This functioned for many years as the Hotel Reynolds but has now been returned to office uses. While the design vocabulary employs traditional elements, they are used with a sufficiently free interpretation to defy any strict historical assignment. (*Museum of History and Industry, Seattle; PEMCO Webster & Stevens Collection, 83.10.2447.*)

6. North Trunk sewer viaduct and footbridge, south elevation, Washington Park, Seattle, 1910-11, Willcox & Sayward. This is an engineering project that graces rather than violates its Arboretum setting. (*Photo by Elisabeth Walton Potter, 1978.*)

7. Queen Anne boulevard retaining wall (west face), Seattle, 1913, Willcox & Sayward. This object of civic pride, appreciated by both citizenry and the City Engineering Department which sponsored it, continues to enrich Seattle's cityscape today. (*Photo by Elisabeth Walton Potter, 1978.*)

8. Leroy D. Lewis house, The Highlands, Washington, 1912-13, Willcox & Sayward. This large symmetrical house draws on American Colonial sources and shows the firm's command of eclectic design. It was featured in both *Pacific Builder and Engineer*, July 1913, and *Architectural Record*, October 1914, from which this image is reproduced.

9. Westgate Building, Eugene, Oregon, 1923 (destroyed), W. R. B. Willcox. This was long a favorite student meeting place and a comfortable University neighbor whose picturesque restraint and stucco finish were typical of Willcox's Eugene work. Its recent destruction made way for a less welcome replacement. *(University of Oregon, Knight Library, Special Collections Division.)*

Beezer Brothers

DAVID A. RASH

The Beezer Brothers arrived in Seattle from Pittsburgh, Pennsylvania, in mid-1907 and quickly established an architectural practice that became one of the most extensive regional practices headquartered in Seattle at the time. This began as early as 1909, and throughout the 1910s and 1920s they had commissions in Alaska, Montana, Idaho, Washington, Oregon, Arizona, and California. This was all the more remarkable because they acted as construction managers for their clients on many of the Seattle projects and on most of the out-of-town projects, requiring daily supervision by the firm.

The composition of the firm was possibly unique in this country, since Louis Beezer (1869-1929) and Michael J. Beezer (1869-1933) were twins. They were born July 6, 1869, at Bellefonte, Pennsylvania, to first-generation German parents. Louis, but not necessarily Michael, initially entered the construction business in Altoona, Pennsylvania, becoming a building foreman by the age of twenty-one. After a period of studying architecture in Pittsburgh, he returned to Altoona, where he began to practice architecture and was joined by his brother in 1892. By 1900 their practice was centered in Pittsburgh, where they designed primarily churches and private residences.

The variety of work in their early Seattle practice was quite wide. The year 1908 saw construction of a new steamship terminal (Colman Dock, 1908-9; destroyed), the first of many homes for the well-to-do (Homer

1. Colman Dock, Seattle, 1908-9 (destroyed), Beezer Brothers. The dome and Italianate clock tower made Colman Dock an instant waterfront landmark as the new home of the "mosquito fleet" headquartered in Seattle. (*University of Washington Libraries, Special Collections Division; photo by Webster & Stevens, ca. 1910; UW5556.*)

2.   Oliver D. Fisher residence, Seattle, 1908-9, Beezer Brothers. This excellent example of the English Arts and Crafts style is the firm's best known house. The original landscape design was by Norwegian-born Peder Sandved. From Frank Calvert, ed., *Homes and Gardens of the Pacific Coast, Volume 1: Seattle* (Beaux Arts Village, Lake Washington, 1913). *(University of Washington Libraries, Special Collections Division; UW2485.)*

L. Hillman house, 1908-9), a major office building downtown (Leary Building, later the Insurance Building, 1906-10; destroyed), and a small apartment building for Mr. and Mrs. John B. Beltinck (1908-9). During their tenure on the Pacific Coast, however, the Beezer Brothers were best known for their many banks and various structures for the Roman Catholic Church, of which they were devout members. The See of the local Roman Catholic Diocese (today's Archdiocese of Seattle) was located in Seattle after 1903, and the Beezer Brothers initially did substantial work for the Diocese locally, including Immaculate Conception School (1909-10), Cathedral School (1911-12), Immaculate Conception rectory (1910-14), and Our Lady of Mount Virgin Church (1915). They also did work for the various religious orders, with their work for the

Dominicans at Blessed Sacrament Church (1909-11, 1922-25) the most prominent in Seattle. An elaborate project (1912-22) for the Society of Jesus proposed relocating Seattle College (now Seattle University) adjacent to a rebuilt Saint Joseph Church, but this resulted in only a rectory (1919-21) and Saint Joseph School (1922-23). That their supervisory work for the Sisters of Providence during the construction of a new Saint Mary Hospital (1909-16; destroyed) at Walla Walla in 1915 and 1916 would launch their regional practice for the Church was somewhat ironic, since Robert F. Tegan of Portland, Oregon, had provided the design. Despite the wide geographic range of their work for the Catholic Church after 1915, it rarely led to commissions for non-Catholic and secular buildings. The Baker-Boyer Bank Building, Walla Walla (1909-11), pre-

3. Baker-Boyer Bank Building, Walla Walla, 1909-11, Beezer Brothers. Although the constructed building reached only seven stories, this was the first "skyscraper" in Walla Walla and is still one of the tallest buildings there. From *Up-to-the-Times Magazine,* April 1910. *(University of Washington Libraries, Special Collections Division; UW14339.)*

4. Blessed Sacrament Catholic Church, Seattle, 1909-11, 1922-25, Beezer Brothers. Despite a construction period spanning fifteen years, much of the anticipated interior finish for this English Gothic Revival church was never completed. The adjacent rectory (1913-14) is also by the firm. *(Museum of History and Industry, Seattle; PEMCO Webster & Stevens Collection; 1925; 83.10.2983.1.)*

5. Broadway State Bank (now Quality Rentals Building), Seattle, 1913, Beezer Brothers. The Beezer Brothers were best known for their many religious and bank structures. Of the latter, this Roman Classical Revival example is stylistically typical. *(Photo by David A. Rash, 1992.)*

ceded their supervisory work at Saint Mary Hospital by more than five years. Design work for the Mary Ann Larrabee Memorial Presbyterian Church, Deer Lodge, Montana (1914-16), preceded by two years work for Saint Joseph Hospital (1916-20) there.

After World War I, the Beezer Brothers worked increasingly outside of Seattle. Numerous hospitals were constructed during the early 1920s, mainly for the Sisters of Saint Joseph of Peace. Their masterpiece bank, First National Bank of Walla Walla (1919-21), was appropriately located in the city of their largest number of commissions outside Seattle. Their last major work in Seattle was O'Dea High School (1923-24).

The commission for Saint Dominic Catholic Church, San Francisco (1923-29), permanently separated the architectural offices of the twins for the first time in nearly three decades, with Louis establishing a

6. Saint Joseph Church rectory, Seattle, 1919-21, Beezer Brothers. This Italian Renaissance Revival palazzo was intended as the first phase of a larger complex to include a parochial school and church. *(Photo by David A. Rash, 1992.)*

7. First National Bank of Walla Walla (now First Federal Savings Bank), Walla Walla, 1919-21, Beezer Brothers. The stone exterior helps to give this Roman Classical Revival building a sumptuous elegance and ranks its as a masterpiece by Louis Beezer. *(Photo by David A. Rash, 1992.)*

branch office in San Francisco, where he died January 2, 1929. Work of this branch office also included the Church of the Blessed Sacrament, Hollywood (1926-29), projected to be the second largest church on the West Coast. With the departure of Louis, the Seattle office went into eclipse. Its only significant local work was the Briscoe Memorial School for Boys (1919-29?; destroyed), at Orilla (now incorporated into Kent). Michael J. Beezer retired from active practice in 1932 and died of a heart attack September 15, 1933.

Innovation and originality, in the Modern architectural sense, were not hallmarks of the designs of the Beezer Brothers; competency and functionality, as well as personal supervision, marked their practice. Their regional work for the Catholic Church provided many of the smaller cities with necessary institutional services that are often taken for granted in large cities. Their secular projects in such communities provided structures that were "metropolitan in character," a quality also taken for granted in large cities but often appreciated elsewhere.

8. Saint Anthony Hospital (now Christopher House apartments), Wenatchee, 1919-22, Beezer Brothers. This was one of several hospital buildings constructed for the Sisters of Saint Joseph of Peace in Washington, Idaho, and Montana. *(Photo by David A. Rash, 1992.)*

9. Edward J. O'Dea High School, Seattle, 1923-24, Beezer Brothers. This English Gothic Revival structure is noted for its elaborate stained glass windows, which were executed by the C. C. Belknap Glass Company. *(Photo by David A. Rash, 1992.)*

10. Saint Dominic Catholic Church, San Francisco, California, 1923-29, Beezer Brothers. At its dedication, Archbishop Hanna of San Francisco called this French Gothic Revival structure "the most beautiful Catholic church in Western America." From *The Architect and Engineer,* May 1924.

Arthur L. Loveless

THOMAS VEITH

Arthur Lamont Loveless (1873-1971), best known as an eclectic designer of houses in Seattle between 1908 and 1942, was born in Big Rapids, Michigan, on September 22, 1873. He graduated from Big Rapids High School in 1891 and then relocated to Manistee, Michigan, where he worked initially as a bookkeeper and later in various capacities at a bank. Dissatisfaction with banking eventually led him to the architecture program at Columbia University, where he was accepted in 1902. Loveless ran out of funds before he could complete his degree, and took a position with one of his teachers, William Adams Delano of Delano & Aldrich, a firm that became well known thoughout the country for the design of stately eclectic homes.

Loveless came to Seattle about 1907 and joined Clayton D. Wilson, the designer of

Arthur L. Loveless, ca. 1933. (*University of Washington Libraries, Special Collections Division; Loveless Collection.*)

1. Alexander Pantages residence, Seattle, 1909 (altered), Wilson & Loveless. Unlike most of Loveless's later houses, this structure is entered from the view side. The dormers light a third-floor ballroom. (*University of Washington Libraries, Special Collections Division; UW383.*)

2. W. T. Campbell Building, Seattle, 1911, Wilson & Loveless. This structure, on the northeast corner of California Avenue S.W. and S.W. Alaska Street, is one of several commissions completed at that intersection by Wilson & Loveless, and later by Loveless alone. *(Washington State Archives, Puget Sound Branch, King County Assessor Real Property Record, Record Group KG317/1-4.)*

Seattle's old Public Safety Building (1905-9; now the 400 Yesler Building), in the partnership of Wilson & Loveless, which was primarily involved with houses and small commercial projects. The firm's work included the William Bloch (1908), J. M. Sparkman (1909; altered), and H. B. Kennedy (1909) residences, although the best known structure from this period is the half-timbered, vaguely Norman mansion designed for theater impressario Alexander Pantages (1909; altered).

In 1912, Loveless began a brief association with Daniel R. Huntington, who was, that year, appointed city architect. The two men shared an office until 1916 or 1917, although Loveless appears to have practiced independently after 1915, completing a number of small commercial buildings and tenant improvement projects for the prominent Seattle developer Lawrence Colman. The design for Colman's residence (1922-23), and that of the John A. Porter residence (1922; altered), are early examples of Loveless's Tudor Revival work.

In 1927, Loveless won AIA Honor Awards for the designs of several buildings, including his own residence (1923-24; altered), his office (1924-25; altered), the Darrah Corbet residence (1925-26; altered), and the Zeta Psi Fraternity House (1926-28). The Corbet residence is essentially an English country house modified to fit a relatively dense suburban environment. Its placement between the street and a dramatic view is typical of Loveless's mature work. The receiving rooms and most of the bedrooms are oriented to the view rather than the sun and face away from the street, making the street side of the structure the back of the house. The bedrooms are served by a single-loaded, side-lit corridor. A processional hall separates the spacious living and dining rooms and the dining room itself functions as a hinge connecting the residential and domestic wings. While a few of his houses, such as the Paul R. Smith residence (1927-28; altered), depart in some respects from this basic scheme, most, including the Tudor Revival William E. Grimshaw (1924-

25) and H. C. Field (1930) residences, follow it closely.

Commercial work continued with alterations to the ground floor of the Colman Building for the People's Bank & Trust Company (1929; destroyed), one of a number of tenant improvement projects. Loveless also completed other types of commissions such as the Seattle Repertory Playhouse (1929-30; altered, now known as the Playhouse Theater), a project involving a significant participation by Lester P. Fey (1901-80) who joined Loveless in 1923 or 1924 and was listed as an associate in Loveless's practice after 1930.

Loveless's best known work is the Studio Building (1930-33), which incorporates the office he built for himself in 1925. The original structure was moved to the northwest

3. Lucile Eckstrom residence, Seattle, 1914 (altered), Huntington & Loveless. Later published by Loveless independently as the Canning residence, this house is one of a number of eclectic wood-clad structures he designed between 1914 and 1920. *(University of Washington Libraries, Special Collections Division; Loveless 15C.)*

4. John A. Porter Residence, Seattle, 1922 (altered), Arthur L. Loveless. The siting of this structure is typical of most of Loveless's residential projects in the 1920s and 1930s. It is entered from the street but is oriented toward the view on the opposite side, making this the back of the house. *(University of Washington Libraries, Special Collections Division; UW13396.)*

5. Arthur L. Loveless residence, Seattle, 1923-24 (altered), Arthur L. Loveless. The long entry hall of this lakefront residence allowed Loveless to use the view-dominated siting scheme he had developed for the Porter residence while maintaining a typically "English" orientation of the house to the south-facing gardens. *(University of Washington Libraries, Special Collections Division; UW13388.)*

6. Darrah Corbet residence, Seattle, 1925-26 (altered), Arthur L. Loveless. The placement of this structure at the end of Maiden Lane enhances the sense that it is a transplanted English country house. The original garage has since been made into an additional reception room, and the street-side yard has been replaced by a brick-paved forecourt. *(University of Washington Libraries, Special Collections Division; UW13399.)*

7. Zeta Psi Fraternity, Seattle, 1926-28, Arthur L. Loveless. This Tudor Revival structure is one of at least five fraternity and sorority houses designed by Loveless's firm. *(Museum of History and Industry, Seattle; PEMCO Webster & Stevens Collection, 83.10.939.1)*

8. Seattle Repertory Playhouse (now the Playhouse Theater), Seattle, 1929-30 (altered), Arthur L. Loveless. This spartan theater, its stage and auditorium situated in a remodeled warehouse, was made more gracious by the reception area courtyard, a feature lost when Nelsen, Sabin & Varey remodeled the building in 1966-67. *(University of Washington Libraries, Special Collections Division; Loveless 96A.)*

9. Studio Building, Seattle, 1930-33, Arthur L. Loveless, Architect; Lester P. Fey, Associate. The masonry used in the facade of this Seattle landmark was tinted to resemble the stone used in the buildings of the Cotswald district of England, structures Loveless greatly admired and from which he often borrowed. *(University of Washington Libraries, Special Collections Division; UW14402.)*

corner of the site and a much larger building was added to form a courtyard, which provides access to some of the ground floor shops and offices, as well as the upper floor apartments. Elegantly detailed and composed of simple materials, the structure was cited in 1961 by the AIA's Seattle Chapter as an older building of enduring quality.

With the relatively small but dramatically sited Joel McFee residence (ca. 1934; altered), the firm began regularly applying colonial detailing to the residential plan type it had developed in the 1920s. After Fey became a partner in 1935 or 1936, other such commissions were executed, including the Fritz Miller residence (1936-37) and the Delta Gamma Sorority House (1936-37; altered). The Arboretum Gatehouse (1937), an English cottage apparently designed by Fey, was an exception. Daniel Lamont (1912-87) became the third partner in 1940 and appears to have been primarily responsible for designing the Colman Pool (1940-42), another project somewhat Colonial in character.

Loveless was elected a Fellow of the AIA in 1941. However, the partnership dissolved with the onset of World War II, and Loveless retired to manage the Studio Building, which also became his residence. He trav-

10. Joel McFee residence, Seattle, ca. 1934 (altered), Arthur L. Loveless, Architect; Lester P. Fey, Associate. Although smaller than the houses Loveless designed in the 1920s, and even though no quarters were provided for domestic help, this "colonial" looking residence is still essentially an English country house. *(University of Washington Libraries, Special Collections Division; UW12636.)*

eled extensively and became an award-winning amateur photographer as well as a sophisticated collector of textiles and Chinese snuff bottles. He continued his long-standing practice of assisting students (some of whom he met in the course of his travels) with their schooling. He remained active until his death in Seattle on January 5, 1971.

Schack, Young & Myers

DAVID A. RASH

Relatively few firms that practice architecture have professional engineers on staff or as principal members. The firm of Schack, Young & Myers, founded in August 1920, was hardly the first firm to combine architecture and engineering in the United States, and locally the short-lived partnership (1906-7) of Kingsley & Bittman had combined the talents of architect William Kingsley and engineer Henry Bittman (see Bittman essay) more than a decade earlier. Still, the three-way partnership of architects James Hansen Schack (1871-1933) and David John Myers (1872-1936) with engineer Arrigo M. Young (1884-1954) proved

to be one of the most successful design firms in Seattle during the 1920s, with each principal bringing various aspects of design expertise to the firm.

James H. Schack was born October 29, 1871 in the Schleswig region of Germany and arrived in Seattle in 1901. He had received practical training in architecture from study in evening schools in Chicago and from work in various architectural offices. Although his brief partnership (1907-9) with Daniel R. Huntington (see essay) did produce the First Methodist Episcopal Church (1907-10; now the First United Methodist Church) and the first Arctic Club Building (1908-9; now the Hotel Morrison), Schack's practice was mostly in the field of commercial buildings, hotel and apartment buildings, and residences.

Arrigo M. Young was born February 19, 1884, in London. He came to Chicago at an early age and later attended the University of Michigan, where he received his bachelor of

1. First Methodist Episcopal Church (now First United Methodist Church), Seattle, 1907-10, Schack & Huntington. This Academic Eclectic melding of Byzantine form and Classical detailing was designed at a time when most Seattle churches were based on Medieval models. *(University of Washington Libraries, Special Collections Division; UW14547.)*

Left, James Hansen Schack. From *Men of the Pacific Coast . . . 1902-1903. (University of Washington Libraries, Special Collections Division; UW14581.)* Center, Arrigo M. Young. From *Pacific Builder and Engineer,* January 18, 1913. *(University of Washington Libraries, Special Collections Division; UW14584.)* Right, David John Myers. From *Pacific Builder and Engineer,* April 19, 1913. *(University of Washington Libraries, Special Collections Division; UW14585.)*

science degree in engineering. After graduation, he worked for a number of construction firms in Chicago and St. Louis as well as the architectural firm of Pond & Pond in Chicago. In August 1910 he arrived in Seattle as head of the structural department of the Moran Company, but by January 1913 he had opened an independent office as a structural engineer. Typical of his work was the Pantages Theater in Tacoma (1916-18), where Young was the structural consultant to Seattle architect B. Marcus Priteca (see essay). His independent design work was usually for industrial buildings like the power plant for Nist Brothers' Sons (1920; destroyed).

David J. Myers was born December 24, 1872, in Glasgow, Scotland. He came to Seattle with his family shortly after the fire of 1889 and worked in succession for Parkinson & Evers, John Parkinson, and Evers & Keith until 1894 (see Parkinson essay). He then left for the East Coast, where he studied architecture at the Massachusetts Institute of Technology and later worked for Clark & Thomas of Boston and McClure & Spahr of Pittsburgh. Myers returned to Seattle in 1905 as the new junior partner of John Graham, Sr. (see essay), where he re-

mained until August 1910 and was the principal designer. While in private practice, Myers worked with Virgil Bogue in 1911 on the ill-fated Municipal Plans Commission, providing most of the drawings for the proposed architectural improvements. He was also a member of the architecture faculty at the University of Washington from 1917 to 1920. Myers developed a reputation for civic, religious, and residential work, in addition to occasional commercial design.

From 1917, Schack and Myers shared office space in the Lippy Building and occasionally collaborated on design work. In August 1920, this occasional collaboration was formalized into a partnership with the addition of Young. The timing of the partnership resulted in the curious design credits for the College Club (1920-21; destroyed); Harlan Thomas was listed as principal architect, David J. Myers as associate architect, and Schack, Young & Myers as consulting engineer. Much of the firm's work was a continuation of each principal's earlier fields of work, the most notable early commission being the initial building development (1922-23)—in association with John R. Nevins—of the model city of Longview, planned by Hare & Hare of Kan-

2. Kenney Presbyterian Home, Seattle, 1907-8, Graham & Myers. The Georgian Revival style of this retirement home reflected the direct experience with contemporary Georgian Revival work and its colonial prototypes that Myers would have gained during his ten-year sojourn on the East Coast. *(Photo by David A. Rash, 1993.)*

sas City for the Long-Bell Lumber Company of Kansas City. By the mid-1920s, Schack, Young & Myers had a well-established reputation for commercial buildings, the Eldridge Buick dealership (1925-26; now a part of University Center) being perhaps their most flamboyant example. A notable late work was the Civic Auditorium (now Seattle Opera House) complex (1925-28; altered).

Shortly after the completion of the Civic Auditorium complex, Myers left the firm in May 1929 and returned to private practice until his death on May 9, 1936, by which time he was a Fellow of the AIA. Schack and Young continued in partnership until

3. W. Logan Geary residence and Roy P. Ballard residence, Seattle, 1911-12, James H. Schack. These two, similar, connected Classical Revival houses were designed and constructed simultaneously, presumably for members of the same family. *(Photo by David A. Rash, 1993.)*

4. Sunset Motor Car dealership/J. D. Lowman Building, Seattle, 1917-18 (scheduled for demolition), David J. Myers, associated with James H. Schack. This brick-clad building was designed to house an automobile dealership, acknowledged by the winged-wheel motif incorporated into the terra-cotta ornament of the gable. Myers, alone, later designed the addition (1929-30) to the north. *(Photo by David A. Rash, 1993.)*

Schack's death on March 16, 1933. By this time, Young had obtained an architectural license; he continued to practice architecture and engineering through World War II. By the time of Young's death on June 27, 1954, the firm was known as Young, Richardson, Carleton & Detlie. (Today, its successor is known as TRA.)

Contemporary proponents of International Modern architecture might have applauded the combination of architecture and engineering in one firm like Schack, Young & Myers, but decried the appearance of the actual work, since, as noted in the *Kind Words Club Yearbook* (1929): "When Schack, Young & Myers design, supervise and complete business structures along the downtown street, proletariat art isn't a problem." While the firm's Academic Eclectic output was typical of its time, its background in design, engineering, and planning made it almost uniquely suited locally for work like the initial building development of Longview and the Civic Auditorium complex.

5. Perry B. Truax residence, Seattle, 1919-20, David J. Myers. Although Myers did design other types of buildings while practicing independently, he was most noted for fine residential work like this brick Jacobethan Revival house on Capitol Hill. *(Photo by David A. Rash, 1993.)*

6. Chinese Baptist Church (now Chinese Southern Baptist Mission), Seattle, 1922-23, Schack, Young & Myers. Work for the American Baptist Mission Society of New York City included this Gothic Revival church, as well as the Japanese Baptist Church (1922-23) and the University Baptist Church (1922-26; altered), the latter in association with Frederick V. Lockman. *(Photo by David A. Rash, 1993.)*

7. Hotel Monticello, Longview, 1922-23, Schack, Young & Myers, in association with John R. Nevins. Besides this Classical Revival hotel, the Longview commission included some 320 company houses, four dormitories, and a dining hall (partly destroyed), two apartment buildings, a bank (destroyed), department store, garage, mercantile store, office building, and warehouse. *(University of Washington Libraries, Special Collections Division; 1923; UW4464.)*

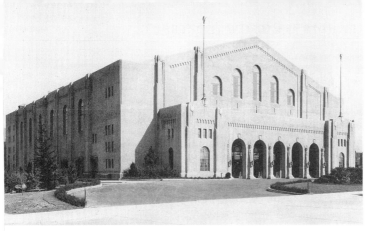

8. Civic Auditorium (now Seattle Opera House) complex, Seattle, 1925-28 (altered), Schack, Young & Myers. This complex was one of the largest commissions received by the firm and included the Civic Auditorium, Civic Arena, Veterans' Hall, and a recreational sports stadium. Today, only Veterans' Hall retains its original design. *(University of Washington Libraries, Special Collections Division; photo by Asahel Curtis, 1929; UW14600.)*

9. Baroness Apartments, Seattle, 1930-31, Schack & Young. In the late 1920s, apartment buildings became increasingly significant to the firm's practice. This restrained Art Deco style apartment building was one of Schack & Young's last executed works. *(Photo by David A. Rash, 1993.)*

10. Women's Dormitory (now Hansee Hall), University of Washington, Seattle, 1935-36, David J. Myers and John Graham, Sr., associated architects. This handsome English Gothic Revival style structure was the last work by Myers and was completed after his death in 1936. *(University of Washington Libraries, Special Collections Division; UW14566.)*

3. Mrs. Grant Smith house, Seattle, 1926-27, A. H. Albertson, architect; Joseph W. Wilson and Paul Richardson, associates. Although primarily known as designers of commercial structures and churches, the members of the firm did complete some residential commissions such as this "French Renaissance" composition on Queen Anne Hill. *(Photo by Thomas Veith, 1993.)*

4. Northern Life Tower (now Seattle Tower), Seattle, 1927-29, A. H. Albertson, architect; Joseph W. Wilson and Paul Richardson, associates. Albertson published several articles suggesting that this relatively early step-back design was inspired by local rock formations. The architects carefully controlled the color of the brickwork to achieve a subtle gradation, from dark earth tones at the base to much lighter hues at the top of the structure, accentuating the building's height and reinforcing its metaphorical relationship with the mountains. Anecdotal evidence suggests that Joseph Wilson was the actual designer. *(University of Washington Libraries, Special Collections Division; photo by Asahel Curtis, 54797.)*

ished), the South Court Apartments (1917-18), and a number of houses and school buildings. Other independent Seattle projects included the Cornish School (1920-21) and the Women's University Club (1922; designed in association with Édouard Frère Champney—see essay).

Perhaps because of Albertson's experience with medical suites at the Cobb and Stimson buildings, he was a consulting architect for the design of the Medical and Dental Building (1924-25) by John A. Creutzer. Albertson acted in this capacity with other architects as well. He was also, by this time, a member of several commissions and would soon become a national director of the AIA.

By 1924, Wilson and Richardson were generally identified as Albertson's associates on all the firm's drawings as well as in the credits accompanying the firm's published works. Early projects of the reorganized office included several additions and modifications to the old Children's Orthopedic Hospital (now Queen Anne Manor Retirement Community), as well as the Mount

Baker Park Presbyterian Church (1922-25); the Becker Building, Aberdeen (1925-26); the Security Bank Building, Olympia (1926); and the First Presbyterian Church, Yakima (1926-28).

The firm had its greatest impact with its design for the Northern Life Tower (1927-29; now Seattle Tower) which almost immediately became a Seattle landmark. Other significant projects followed, including Trinity Methodist Episcopal Church (1928-29) and the Municipal Building for the City of Everett (1928-30). With the well-integrated terra-cotta and exposed concrete facades and interiors of Saint Joseph Catholic Church (1929-30), the firm combined

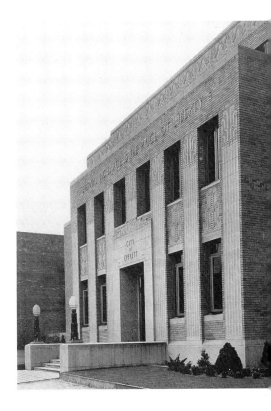

5. City of Everett Municipal Building, Everett, 1928-30, A. H. Albertson, architect; Joseph W. Wilson and Paul Richardson, associates. This Art Deco design demonstrates the facility with which the best of the firms practicing in eclectic modes adapted and developed new trends in formal expression and ornamentation. (*University of Washington Libraries, Special Collections Division; photo by Depue-Morgan; UW14634.*)

6. Young Men's Christian Association, New Central Branch, Seattle, 1929-31, A. H. Albertson, architect; Joseph W. Wilson and Paul Richardson, associates. The small, subtly arched window openings and the simple brick detailing give this building a Romanesque character belied by the Jacobean gables and hipped copper roof. (*University of Washington Libraries, Special Collections Division; photo by Asahel Curtis, 58199.*)

7. Saint Joseph Catholic Church, Seattle, 1929-30, A. H. Albertson, architect; Joseph W. Wilson and Paul Richardson, associates. An affordable design was produced by leaving the structural concrete exposed and employing simple decorative elements. The expressive concrete building which resulted was praised in the architectural press and eventually hailed as a proto-modern work. (*University of Washington Libraries, Special Collections Division; UW2488.*)

8. Law Building (now Gowan Hall), University of Washington, Seattle, 1931-33, A. H. Albertson, architect; Joseph W. Wilson and Paul Richardson, associates. This concrete frame building is a fine example of Collegiate Gothic architecture. Extensive terra-cotta work characterizes the exterior, and there is a large, generously lit library reading room on the top floor. (*University of Washington Libraries, Special Collections Division; photo by C. F. Todd, 20840.*)

eclecticism and modernity, but returned to more conventional designs for the New Central Branch of the YMCA (1929-31), Saint John Catholic Church (1930-31), and two structures at the University of Washington—the Law Building (1931-33; now known as Gowan Hall) and the New Infirmary Building (1934-35; now known as David C. Hall Health Center).

The firm became known as Albertson, Wilson & Richardson in 1935, but there was very little work. Richardson died suddenly on April 10, 1939, and that same year both Albertson and Wilson joined the state office of the FHA. Albertson retired from the FHA in 1949 as chief architect. Wilson retired about the same time, but within a few months was working again as a draftsman in the office of architect John W. Maloney. By 1953, he was employed at Boeing where he remained until 1962 or 1963. Albertson died April 18, 1964; Wilson, September 7, 1968.

Albertson, Wilson & Richardson utilized their eclectic training to produce work in a mix of styles. Their willingness to approach creatively the issues they faced in their commissions, especially after 1927, led to original buildings that engendered the development of regional sensibilities through the use of appropriate and locally significant metaphors.

9. New Infirmary Building (now David C. Hall Health Center), University of Washington, Seattle, 1934-35, Albertson, Wilson and Richardson, Architects; Bebb & Gould, Supervising Architects. This Tudor Revival structure exhibits a simplicity and restraint only partly attributable to the fact that it was built during the Depression. (*University of Washington Libraries, Special Collections Division; UW6697.*)

Andrew Willatsen

JESS M. GIESSEL &
GRANT HILDEBRAND

Andreas Christian Peter Willatzen (1876-
1974) was born in North Germany in 1876
and came to the United States in 1900. He
changed the spelling of his name to Willatsen about 1918, because of anti-German
sentiment after World War I, and thereafter
emphasized the Danish side of his heritage.

His earliest work was as a carpenter, then
draftsman. In 1902 or 1903 he began work at
Frank Lloyd Wright's Studio in Oak Park, Illinois, where he remained intermittently until 1907. Thus he was at the Studio during its
most creative period. Willatsen claimed responsibility for the Larkin Building fence of

Andrew Willatsen, date unknown. *(From slide
collection, College of Architecture and Urban
Planning, University of Washington.)*

1. Charles H. Clarke house, The Highlands, 1909, Willatsen & Byrne. This design clearly indicates the
partners' training with Wright, and especially their awareness of Wright's Hickox and Bradley houses
of 1900-1901. *(University of Washington Libraries, Special Collections Division; Willatsen Collection, ca.
1910; UW13925.)*

2. George Matzen house, Seattle, 1910, Willatsen & Byrne. The plan is a stunted cross typical of the Prairie School, confined by a narrow site. The covered terrace, now enclosed, possesses a commanding view of the Seattle skyline. *(University of Washington Libraries, Special Collections Division; ca. 1912; Willatsen Collection, UW14761.)*

3. Matzen house, interior shortly after completion. The cross axis of the plan, the typical Prairie School trim, and the custom designed glass, light fixtures, and furniture combine to make this the finest of Willatsen & Byrne's executed interiors. *(University of Washington Libraries, Special Collections Division; ca. 1912; Willatsen Collection, UW14768.)*

4. A. S. Kerry house, The Highlands, 1910-11, Willatsen & Byrne. This severely abbreviated version of an originally extensive scheme has become perhaps Willatsen & Byrne's best known work. *(Photo by Grant Hildebrand, 1982.)*

Malmgren. In 1908 that firm sent him to Seattle to supervise construction of the Seattle Golf and Country Club (see Cutter essay). There, the following year, with another Studio employee, Barry Byrne (1883-1967), he formed the partnership of Willatsen & Byrne.

In their first year, Willatsen & Byrne produced the C. H. Clarke house (1909) for a site in The Highlands north of Seattle, and soon thereafter, the Frederick Handschy house (1910); both derive from Wright's gable-roofed houses of 1900. Wright's long, low, hipped-roof schemes influenced Willatsen & Byrne's proposal for the A. S. Kerry mansion of 1910, also intended for The Highlands and built there in 1911 in much abbreviated form. The firm did many houses in the Prairie Style over the next few years; typical are the Oscar E. Maurer house (1910), the James T. McVay house (1911), the George Bellman house (1912), and the L. George Hager house (1912), all in Seattle. The firm also designed in the Craftsman

1903, and for the 1905 remodeling of the Rookery lobby; he also worked on the interiors of the Darwin Martin house in Buffalo (1904-06).

Willatsen came west to Spokane in 1907, where he found work with Cutter &

5. Carleton Huiskamp house, The Highlands, 1912 (altered), Willatsen & Byrne. This early view of Willatsen & Byrne's most important eclectic work shows the strong lines and fine detailing that demonstrate the firm's adeptness with period revival work. *(University of Washington Libraries, Special Collections Division; ca. 1912; Willatsen Collection, UW14764.)*

6. L. George Hager house, Seattle, 1912, Willatsen & Byrne. This is a good example of the firm's more modest homes: well sited, elegantly composed, finely detailed. *(Photo by Grant Hildebrand, 1987.)*

mode and in various period styles; significant examples are the Stickleyesque Albert E. Felmley house (1911), and the imposing Dutch Colonial Carleton Huiskamp house in The Highlands (1912).

The Willatsen & Byrne partnership was dissolved in the early months of 1913. Byrne went to California for a short while, then back to the Midwest, where he pursued a long career of distinction, largely in church design.

Willatsen's commissions immediately following the dissolution include the J. C. Black house in Seattle (1914), which may be his finest exterior composition. The single sweep of the central roof, and of the upper windows, is perfectly augmented by the one-story gabled projections to either end, anchored by the vaulted porch. The whole suggests one of Wright's most elegant early compositions, the gallery for Susan Lawrence Dana's house in Springfield, Illinois, completed just at the time of Willatsen's arrival at the Studio and therefore known to him. The William E. Robinson house (1913) and the Elmer E. Vogue house (1918-19), both in Seattle, are good examples of Willatsen's approach to more modest pro-

7. J. C. Black house, Seattle, 1914 (altered), Andrew Willatsen. The best known of Willatsen's work after Byrne's departure, the Black house illustrates the Prairie Style adapted to a conventional central hall plan. This was the prototype for many other Willatsen houses over the following several years. The front windows have, unfortunately, been altered. *(University of Washington Libraries, Special Collections Division; ca. 1914; Willatsen Collection, UW14760.)*

8. Frederick Hurlbut house, Seattle, 1914, Andrew Willatsen. This house draws heavily on Tudor precedents, but the horizontal bands and aligned second floor reflects the continuing influence of Willatsen's familiarity with the Prairie Style. *(University of Washington Libraries, Special Collections Division; ca. 1914; Willatsen Collection, UW 14765.)*

grams, while the Gustave E. Rasmussen house (1921-22) and Willatsen's favorite, the Orrin L. Martin house (1928), illustrate his ability with larger budgets. Traditional homes also remained in his repertoire. Two 1914 Seattle commissions reflect the Tudor style: the Frederick Hurlbut house is a personal interpretation with Prairie overtones; the Jeremiah Neterer house is a more academic work. The John H. Carter house (1916) and the Fred Burwell house (1925), both in Seattle, illustrate the Classical and Federal revivals respectively.

After the decline in popularity of the Prairie School, Willatsen worked in a wide variety of styles, designing stores, churches, and several other structures. For many years after 1915 he was responsible for general alterations to the Pike Place Market. The simplicity and common sense of his buildings won loyal clients who turned to him repeatedly for their architectural needs until his retirement in the late 1940s. The architec-

tural interest of his work, however, did not develop, and in fact rather diminished over time. A work typical of this period is Our Savior Lutheran Church (now Everett School District Performing Arts Center), Everett (1924-25). By the 1930s, Willatsen's projects were often disappointingly pedestrian, with no hint of the distinguished heritage he brought to the Northwest. There are exceptions, such as the Church and North Office (1955), and the Richard L. Desimone house (1959).

Willatsen's last years were spent in managing the apartment building he owned, studying theosophy, and producing an occasional design for a friend. He died in Seattle July 25, 1974, at the age of ninety-seven.

While Willatsen's buildings never approached Wright's level of formal and spatial sophistication, he, and Byrne as well, brought the Prairie Style to Seattle forty years before Wright's first Northwest commission.

9. Our Savior Lutheran Church (now Everett School District Performing Arts Center), Everett, 1924-25 (altered), Andrew Willatsen. This large church is evidence of Willatsen's ability to win major commissions in the 1920s. However, as represented here, his design work in those years moved almost completely away from the Prairie Style. *(University of Washington Libraries, Special Collections Division; ca. 1925; Willatsen Collection, UW14766.)*

10. Andrew Willatsen's office, Boston Block, 1915, Andrew Willatsen. The furniture and windows from this room were among the items acquired by the University of Washington shortly before Willatsen's death. The windows are in the Architecture Library in Gould Hall; a chair and the table are now in the University's Rome Center; a bookcase with leaded glass doors is in the office of the dean of the University's College of Architecture and Urban Planning. These are the only examples of Willatsen's furniture known to exist. *(University of Washington Libraries, Special Collections Division; 1915; Willatsen Collection, UW14762.)*

Bebb & Gould

T. WILLIAM BOOTH &
WILLIAM H. WILSON

Across the span of Carl F. Gould's career in Seattle, architectural design moved from eclectic adaptations of historical models to the development of nontraditional styles such as the Art Moderne. His buildings fully reflect that range of expression, and were it not for the Depression surely more works would have explored Moderne design.

Carl Freylinghausen Gould (1873-1939) was born in New York on November 24, 1873. His family's wealth allowed him a Harvard degree (1898) and five years in Paris at the École des Beaux-Arts (1898-1903). Upon his return to New York, he interned with McKim, Mead & White (1903-5), and then assisted his fellow

Carl F. Gould, ca. 1920. *(Private collection.)*

Beaux-Arts student Edward Bennett in San Francisco with the Burnham Plan for that city (1905). Gould visited Seattle while on his trip home. In 1906 he assisted his class-mate Otis Post in the George B. Post & Sons

1. Thomas Dovey residence, Seattle, 1910-11, Huntington & Gould. The front facade may be derived from an eighteenth-century Bullfinch design, but is here rendered in shingles. This is one of eight houses Gould designed along Federal Avenue from 1910 to 1928. *(Photo by T. William Booth, 1992.)*

When Gould reached Seattle in 1908, he was one of only a few local architects with extensive training in the profession. He worked as a draftsman for Everett & Baker and then for Daniel Huntington in 1909 (see Huntington essay). Huntington & Gould, as associated architects, designed six houses, a few apartments and mixed-use buildings, and (with others) entered the Washington State Capitol Campus competition (1911, fourth prize). In this same period, Gould independently designed five more houses and two commercial buildings and took an active role in promoting the Bogue Plan for Seattle published in 1911. From 1912 until he became associated with Bebb in 1914, Gould completed fifteen additional houses, became president of the Fine Arts Society (1912-16, 1926-29), began lectures at the University of Washington on domestic design, and assumed leadership in the Architectural League of the Pacific Coast.

The well-established Charles H. Bebb (see Bebb & Mendel essay) and Gould associated in mid-1914, thereby joining their complementary strengths. Their agreement acknowledged Bebb (with connections to

Charles Herbert Bebb, ca. 1917. *(Private collection.)*

firm on the winning Wisconsin State Capitol Competition. Later that year Gould and Beaux-Arts classmates Walter Blair and J. E. R. Carpenter took third place in the prestigious Union Theological Seminary Competition. A long illness (1907-8) followed these competitions, and upon recovering, Gould sought his professional fortune in Seattle.

2. F. H. Brownell residence, Seattle, 1910-12, Carl F. Gould. The use of shingles and the porte cochere recall designs by McKim, Mead & White in the 1890s. Brownell's house and garden plans owe much to the nearby Merrill house by Charles A. Platt of New York, for whom Gould was the local representative. *(Private collection; 1912.)*

3. Gould residence ("Topsfield"), Bainbridge Island, 1914-15, Carl F. Gould. For his own house Gould developed a post, beam, and panel wall system, precut and moved to the site by barge. He used the system at other remote sites, including the Merrill & Ring lumber camp at Pysht, Washington (1915-17), and the dining hall at the Friday Harbor Marine Station (1923). *(Photo by T. William Booth, 1990.)*

the political establishment) as engineer and partner in charge of management, contracts, and specifications and Gould (with connections to the arts establishment) as principal designer and planner. Both were leaders of

4. Times Square Building, Seattle, 1913-15, Bebb & Gould. Begun by Bebb & Mendel as a Gothic design, Gould transformed this into a quintessential Renaissance Revival building faced in white terra cotta. The wedge-shaped plan resembles the Flatiron Building on Times Square in New York. Upon joining Bebb, Gould also greatly modified the design of the Fisher Studio Building (1912-15), another exercise in terra cotta but in a faintly Venetian style. *(Private collection; ca. 1916.)*

the AIA locally and nationally. Gould was made a Fellow in 1926. With their combined talents Bebb & Gould designed buildings for the Government Locks at Ballard (1914-16) and acquired the commission to plan the University of Washington campus (1915), where Gould completed eighteen buildings between 1915 and 1938, including Suzzallo Library (1922-27), the grandest, and Anderson Hall (1924-25), the most suavely detailed. Bebb continued in his advisory role to Wilder & White during construction of Washington's state capitol (1916-26).

Between 1914 and 1924, Bebb & Gould flourished, designing over two hundred projects, including schools, churches, hospitals, memorials, homes, club houses, commercial structures, and monuments. These designs, created in an atelier setting, took a variety of architectural styles, depending on the wishes of the client, siting, and financial considerations.

The amiable association with Bebb also permitted Gould time to advance architectural education and the visual arts in Seattle. Gould founded the Department of Architecture (1914; now the College of Architecture and Urban Planning) at the University of Washington, and Bebb supported the curriculum and accepted Gould's absences from the firm. The University named Gould head of the department in 1915, a position in which he continued until 1926.

After 1924, Bebb's influence in the firm declined substantially, although he remained Gould's adviser on contracts, contacts with clients, and office management. In the decade after 1924, Gould completed designs for fewer than one hundred projects. Beginning in 1928 he designed five local telephone company offices in Longview, Yakima, Bremerton, Centralia, and Tacoma. His Longview Post Office (1932) and Everett Public Library (1933-34) explored variations of Art Deco. Two of the firm's Moderne projects achieved national stature with design awards from the Architectural League of New York in 1935: the U.S. Marine Hospi-

5. Administration Building, U.S. Government (Hiram Chittenden) Locks, Seattle, 1914-16, Bebb & Gould. Gould probably received this contract prior to joining Bebb. This early use of concrete as a finish material demonstrates the firm's ability to innovate with common building materials. Some areas appear to be hammered to expose the aggregate. The smooth walls, without joints, do not mimic masonry. *(Private collection; ca. 1918.)*

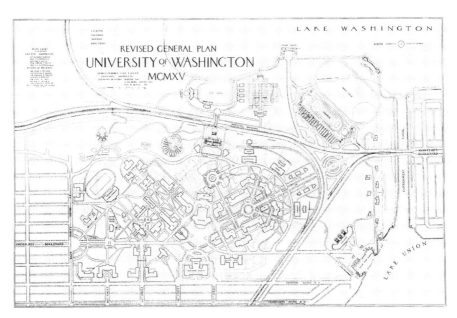

6. General Plan of the Campus, University of Washington, 1915, Bebb & Gould. The Bebb & Gould plan resolved the difficulties that arose from combining the existing campus buildings with the "Rainier Vista" axis that the Olmsted Brothers designed for the Alaska-Yukon-Pacific Exposition. The coherence of the central campus derives from Bebb & Gould's design. *(University of Washington Libraries, Special Collections Division; UW6049.)*

7. Suzzallo Library, University of Washington, 1922-27, Bebb & Gould. The western facade best shows Gould's adaption of Collegiate Gothic; it is rich in the iconography of knowledge. The great reading room on the second floor is Gould's most inspired space. The south addition (Bebb & Gould, 1933-35) is beautifully daylighted and contains frescoes of Northwest exploration by Paul Gustin and John T. ("Ted") Jacobsen. The firm also designed the library at Western Washington University, Bellingham (1924-26). (Private collection; ca. 1926.)

8. Pacific Telephone & Telegraph (now U.S. West) Company Office, Longview, 1928-29, Bebb & Gould. Gould's first work in the Moderne style reflected Pacific Telephone & Telegraph's desire to be in the vanguard of modernity. Note the Deco motifs used in the spandrels. Later Pacific Telephone buildings were less elaborately detailed. (Photo by T. William Booth, 1989.)

tal and campus (1930-32; now Pacific Medical Center; altered) and the Seattle Art Museum (1931-33).

The Depression limited the opportunities for work between 1934 and Gould's death on January 4, 1939. As technical adviser to the state of Oregon, Gould contributed to the successful outcome of the Oregon State Capitol Competition (1936). The last design in which he participated, the Penthouse Theater (1938-40; moved), a spare Moderne building on the University of Washington campus, involved collaboration with Glenn Hughes, executive director of the University's School of Drama, John Conway, the School's art director, and Sergius Sergev, professor of civil engineering at the University, to accomplish the first "theater-in-the-round." Typically, Gould's involvement with both planning and technology and his willingness to work collaboratively supported the innovative solution.

9. U.S. Marine Hospital (now Pacific Medical Center), Seattle, 1930-32 (altered), Bebb & Gould, designers, with John Graham, Sr., construction documents. Among the first hospitals designed in a high-rise configuration, this occupies a commanding site at the north end of Beacon Hill. The tower and lobby contain exemplary Art Moderne details. The firm also designed the campus and the nurses' quarters on the south and west sides. *(Photo by T. William Booth, 1990.)*

Gould's final project closed the circle of his life in the arts and architecture. On Gould's death the partnership dissolved. Thereafter, trusted draftsman John Paul Jones associated with Bebb until Bebb's death at the home of his son, J. G. Bebb, in Summit, New Jersey, June 21, 1942.

10. Art Institute of Seattle (now Seattle Art Museum), 1931-33, Bebb & Gould (in the foreground, the Thomas Burke Memorial, 1926-30, H. A. MacNeil sculptor). As the first museum in America in the Moderne style, it received nationwide acclaim. The severity of the design and the blazing light-colored stone have softened with time. For concept, scale, and mastery of materials, the interior garden court must be counted among Gould's finest spaces. *(Photo, 1933; Seattle Art Museum Collection.)*

B. Marcus Priteca

MIRIAM SUTERMEISTER

B. Marcus Priteca (1889-1971), born December 23, 1889, in Glasgow, Scotland, of east European Jewish heritage, was raised and educated in Edinburgh. His architectural training began when he was just under fifteen as an apprentice to Robert McFarlane Cameron, a Director of the Royal College of Arts in Edinburgh. During the five-year apprenticeship (1904-9), Priteca took classes in science and fine arts from Edinburgh University and the Royal College of Arts. In this way he earned his Associate of the Royal College of Arts degree by the time he was twenty. He received several medals and a traveling scholarship from the Royal Institute of Edinburgh. The scholarship, his father's need for a change of climate, and Seattle's Alaska-Yukon-Pacific Exposition served as catalysts for the Priteca family's journey to Seattle.

On arrival in 1909, Priteca secured work as a draftsman with Seattle architect E. W. Houghton (see Houghton essay). His primary interests at this time were architectural delineation and research and also music. A chance encounter with Alexander Pantages marked the beginning of his independent career as an architect, and as the exclusive architect for the Pantages theater circuit from 1910 to 1929. During the Pantages years, Priteca had branch offices in Oakland, San Francisco, and Los Angeles.

1. Seattle Pantages (Palomar) Theater, Seattle, 1913-15 (destroyed 1964), B. Marcus Priteca. An example of the combined theater–office block type frequently used by Pantages, this demonstrates Priteca's frequent extensive use of classical motifs executed in terra cotta. (*Richard F. McCann Collection; ca. 1915.*)

Priteca's Seattle Pantages (Palomar) Theater (1913-15; destroyed) and Coliseum Theater (1914-16; altered)—designed for real estate developer Joseph Gottstein and recognized as Seattle's first movie palaces—advanced the architectural sophistication of downtown Seattle. The Seattle Pantages was an example of the combined theater and office block, a type frequently done for Pantages; it was also an example of Priteca's predilection for architecture based on classical precedent. The Coliseum was designed solely as a motion picture theater; the building also included retail shops at street level. With their white glazed terra-cotta facades, the Coliseum and Seattle Pantages were architectural expressions of fantasy and delight. The success of these, and of the Pantages and Priteca collaboration, led to a large number of subsequent theaters for Pantages. Of these, the Vancouver Pantages,

B. Marcus Priteca, age seventy-two. *(Richard F. McCann Collection; photo by Joseph Scaylea, 1961.)*

2.   Seattle Pantages (Palomar) Theater, Seattle, 1913-15 (destroyed), B. Marcus Priteca. This view of the auditorium showing proscenium arch, organ screen, and boxes is representative of the elaborate detailing typical in Priteca's theater interiors. *(Richard F. McCann Collection; ca. 1915.)*

3. Coliseum Theater, Seattle, 1914-16 (altered), B. Marcus Priteca. This perspective drawing of the exterior illustrates Priteca's talents as a delineator. The original entrance canopy was later replaced. The building no longer functions as a theater, but is instead occupied by retail uses. *(Richard F. McCann Collection.)*

Vancouver, British Columbia (1916-17; destroyed), with its French Renaissance elements and its seating capacity of 1,800, was considered at the time to be the most richly embellished and efficient theater of the Pantages chain. Priteca also designed Seattle's brick and terra-cotta Orpheum Theater (1926-27; destroyed); and in association with Frederick J. Peters and the Chicago firm of Rapp & Rapp he designed the Seattle (Paramount) Theater apartment and commercial building (1927-28), for businessman L. N. Rosenbaum. The Tacoma Pantages Theater (ca. 1916-18; altered) is the earliest extant example of the collaboration between the vaudeville entrepreneur and Priteca.

Priteca's Hollywood Pantages Theater (1929-30), sited in Hollywood, California, represented a radical departure from his favored classical expression; it is a masterpiece of Art Deco design. He viewed his work on this theater as a quest for a design which would "best exemplify America of the moment. Effort centered upon motifs that were modern—never futuristic, yet based on time-tested classiccism [sic] of enduring good taste and beauty." Priteca hoped the theater would be a synthesis of comfort, pleasure, and beauty. The Hollywood Pantages, built at the apogee of Priteca's career, was the last movie palace to open in Hollywood. It stands as a memorial to the Pantages era and, in the opinion of Richard

McCann, successor to the Priteca practice, is the most architecturally influential of all Priteca's buildings.

In addition to over 150 movie theaters, including 60 of major import, Priteca's work encompassed several synagogues in the Seattle area, including Congregation Bikur Cholim (1912-15; altered, now Langston Hughes Cultural Center) and the Jewish Settlement House Educational Center

4. Vancouver Pantages Theater, Vancouver, British Columbua, 1916-17 (destroyed 1967), B. Marcus Priteca. This theater exemplifies the expansion of the Pantages Circuit into Canada. With 1,800 seats, this was among the largest of Priteca's theaters and was considered one of the most richly embellished in the Pantages Circuit. (*Vancouver Public Library, ca. 1926; No. 22215.*)

5. Tacoma Pantages Theater (now Broadway Center for the Performing Arts), Tacoma, ca. 1916-18 (altered), B. Marcus Priteca. A significant presence in Tacoma's cultural life for almost eighty years, this building was restored in the early 1990s. (*Washington State Historical Society Library, Tacoma; April 2, 1925; Boland Collection, 12204.*)

6. Congregation Bikur Cholim Synagogue (now Langston Hughes Cultural Center), Seattle, 1912-15 (altered), B. Marcus Priteca. Emblematic of synagogue architecture at the time, this was heavily indebted to the Touro Synagogue, New Orleans, Louisiana (ca. 1909), that was illustrated in the *American Architect* in October 1909. *(Richard F. McCann Collection; ca. 1912-1915.)*

(1914-16; destroyed). He also designed the Longacres race track, Renton (1933-34; partly destroyed), warehouses, wartime public housing, government buildings, a number of retail shop exteriors and interiors, and several residences. Priteca also acted as consultant for the new Temple de Hirsch Sinai (1959-60) with Detlie & Peck, and for the Opera House (1959-62), with James J. Chiarelli, at Seattle Center.

Priteca made a major contribution to Seattle's urban fabric during the first third of the twentieth century. He is internationally known for his theaters, found throughout the United States and across Canada, which played a major role in the development of this building type in North America.

7. Jewish Settlement House Educational Center, Seattle 1914-16 (destroyed), B. Marcus Priteca. This nontheater building shows Priteca's predilection for the use of classical design elements. *(University of Washington Libraries, Manuscripts and University Archives Division, Jewish Archives.)*

In 1951, Priteca was elected a Fellow by the American Institute of Architects. At the time of his death on October 1, 1971, he was the only theater architect to have been so honored. Posthumously, the Theatre Historical Society referred to him as "the last of the giants" and bestowed upon him honorary membership.

8.   Orpheum Theatre, Seattle, 1927 (destroyed), Priteca & Peters. Priteca's continuing practice as a designer was well represented by this acoustically outstanding brick and terra-cotta theater, which was situated at the north end of downtown Seattle. *(Museum of History and Industry, Seattle; Seattle Historical Society Collection; ca. 1927; 11508.)*

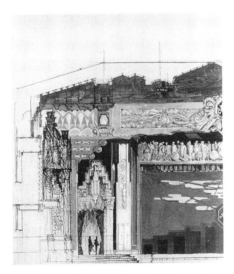

9.   Hollywood Pantages Theater, Hollywood, California, 1929-30, B. Marcus Priteca. This watercolor study of the proscenium arch, attributed to Priteca, depicts his development of Art Deco motifs for this theater interior. *(Richard F. McCann Collection; ca. 1929.)*

10.   Hollywood Pantages Theater, Hollywood, California, 1929-30, B. Marcus Priteca. This theater foyer shows the flamboyant version of the Art Deco style developed by Priteca; it is considered to be one of the first such interior in the history of motion picture theater architecture. *(Richard F. McCann Collection; ca. 1930.)*

Robert C. Reamer

DAVID L. LEAVENGOOD

Like many architects in early twentieth-century Seattle, Robert Chambers Reamer (1873-1938) adapted national design trends to suit the local architectural style of the emerging city. Reamer distinguished himself from others, however, in his unique ability to express both style and function in his designs, and in his mastery of a wide range of architectural idioms. While he is best known nationally for his Yellowstone National Park projects, his Seattle area buildings also exhibit his distinctive style and contribute significantly to the character of the city.

Born September 12, 1873, in Oberlin, Ohio, Reamer attended public school until the age of twelve, when, according to his

Robert Chambers Reamer, about 1926. *(Special Collections Division, University of Washington Libraries.)*

1. Old Faithful Inn, Yellowstone National Park, Wyoming, 1902-3, Robert C. Reamer. Old Faithful Inn was the first of Reamer's many Yellowstone structures. It was also the first in which he explored the use of natural, "rustic" materials as elements of an architectural language appropriate to a park setting. *(Montana Historical Society; ca. 1910; Haynes Foundation Collection.)*

2. Skinner Building/Fifth Avenue Theater, Seattle, 1925-26, Robert C. Reamer. A remarkably well-scaled facade developed using restrained Renaissance motifs makes this a particularly successful urban building. *(University of Washington Libraries, Special Collections Division; photo by Asahel Curtis, 50868.)*

3. Fifth Avenue Theater, Seattle, 1925-26, Robert C. Reamer (with the theater designer J. L. Skoog). Comparable to the finest "atmospheric" theater interiors of the period, the Fifth Avenue was inspired by the traditional Chinese decorated wood structures of the Forbidden City. *(University of Washington Libraries, Special Collections Division; UW14777.)*

7. Seattle Times Building, Seattle, 1930, Robert C. Reamer. This rendering of the simply detailed headquarters building for the *Seattle Times* demonstrates Reamer's mastery of the Art Deco mode. *(Private collection.)*

Bellingham Hotel (ca. 1930), the Lewis and Clark Hotel, Centralia (1926), and the Lake Quinault Lodge, Quinault (1926). Residential projects by Reamer include the French Normandy style Donald Graham house, Seattle (1931-32), and the Weyerhaeuser Experimental House, Seattle (1935). The latter residence, a prototype design sponsored by the Weyerhaeuser Company to showcase wood products, was innovative in its use of modular design and in its distinctly modern style. A similar design was exhibited at the 1937 Chicago World's Fair.

The last major building Reamer completed before his death was the Edmond Meany Hotel, Seattle (1930-32), near the University of Washington campus, now sadly altered. It was selected in 1938 to be included in the American Institute of Architects traveling exhibition of one hun-

8. Fox Theater (now Act Three Fox Tri-Cinema), Spokane (1931; altered), Robert C. Reamer. Reamer's reputation as a designer of theaters, achieved as a result of his Fifth Avenue Theater in Seattle, brought him this commission in Spokane. *(Private collection; Libby Photographers, Spokane; ca. 1945.)*

dred representative and distinguished buildings in America. Executed in the Art Deco
style, the hotel was the first continuously
poured slip-formed concrete structure in
the Northwest.

Robert C. Reamer worked in Seattle in a
period of rapid expansion. His special contribution was a sensitive and assured amal-
gam of style and function, often utilizing
playful, intricate detailing. Reamer's eclecticism grew out of his understanding, appreciation, and personal exploration of the
major design currents of the first three
decades of this century. His architectural
works were significant in their exceptional
refinement and in their contribution to
Seattle's image as a leading West Coast city.

9. Edmond Meany Hotel (now Meany Tower
Hotel), Seattle, 1930-32 (altered), Robert C.
Reamer. Reamer's design incorporated the
technological sophistication of a continuously
poured slip-formed concrete structure as an
influence on its extruded vertical form. *(Museum
of History and Industry, Seattle; PEMCO Webster
& Stephens Collection, 83.10.4302.4)*

10. Weyerhaeuser Experimental House, Seattle, 1935, Robert C. Reamer. This project was designed to
show the possible applications of a wide array of wood products. The simple rectangular forms
represent a move toward Modernism, while the decorative frieze band is clearly related to the Art
Deco. *(Photo by T. William Booth, 1993.)*

Henry W. Bittman

CATERINA PROVOST

Spanning nearly half the twentieth century, the prolific architectural and engineering practice of Henry W. Bittman (1882-1953) adorned the north end of Seattle's downtown with a string of terra-cotta jewels, and contributed over 250 new and remodeled buildings to business and civic districts throughout Washington and Alaska.

The oldest of four children, Henry W. Bittman was born July 15, 1882, and grew up in Greenpoint, New York, a suburb of New York City. His father, John Bittman, a prominent and prosperous interior designer, no doubt instilled both design and business sense in his son. Henry Bittman studied engineering at Cooper Union, then worked briefly in Chicago as a bridge engineer. In 1906 he came to Seattle, where he practiced for a year with architect William Kingsley. By 1908 he had his own structural engineering practice, specializing in the de-

Henry W. Bittman, date unknown. *(Courtesy of Martha Lamb. Photo by Ken Ellis, ca. 1950.)*

sign of structural steel skeletons for Seattle's new buildings. He also served from 1914 until 1919 as representative of Puget Sound and Alaska Powder Company, an explosives supplier.

1. Home of Henry and L. Jessie Bittman, Seattle, 1914-15, with additions in 1929 and 1949, Henry Bittman. This Tudor house was one of Bittman's few residential designs, and may have been his first foray into architecture. *(Washington State Archives. Puget Sound Branch, King County Assessor Real Property Record, Record Group KG317/1-4.)*

In 1923, Henry Bittman was licensed as an architect in Washington State, and shortly thereafter, marshaling a talented design team, he became a successful and respected commercial architect. Combining his engineering ability with business savvy and artistic sensibility, Bittman was able to attract and retain both a devoted clientele and a loyal and capable staff, notably architect Harold Adams, a talented designer. For forty-five years, until his death, Bittman continued in this Seattle practice, building a reputation for reliability, straightforwardness, integrity, and cost-consciousness.

In 1914-15, Bittman designed a permanent Seattle home for himself and his wife Jessie, an active, college-educated woman and an award-winning horticulturist. This home still stands, featuring an enormous living room with cathedral ceiling and murals of Lake Union. Here the couple, who never had children, entertained frequently and with flair. They crowned each year with an elaborate New Year's Eve party, where, at the stroke of midnight, a specially designed dining table would split open and a sculpture commemorating the year would arise and revolve.

Bittman was an urban architect, specializing in the commercial store and loft block, and also designing industrial buildings, apartment buildings, hotels, civic buildings, and theaters. Nearly all his work conformed rigidly to the rectangular urban block form, hugging the street front. Yet he approached each building type differently. From an artistic standpoint, Bittman's most successful buildings were those of several stories, where the strong vertical lines worked in harmony with the height of the building, anchored at the bottom by a strong, heavy base of storefront openings and crowned by a cornice neither too heavy nor too insubstantial. It seems likely that Bittman, who had worked in Chicago, was influenced by the modern idiom of the Chicago School. Bittman's loft buildings often incorporated Chicago-style windows—that is, a picture

2. Terminal Sales Building, Seattle, 1923, Henry Bittman. This building was modeled functionally on sales "terminals" in New York, Chicago, and San Francisco, and is very similar in form to several Bittman warehouses. (*Bittman Vammen Taylor, P.S., Collection; photo by Webster & Stevens, ca. 1923.*)

window flanked by two narrow operable windows.

Bittman's masterpieces were his two Seattle skyscrapers, the Terminal Sales Building (1923) and the United Shopping Tower (now Olympic Tower, 1928-31; altered), and his Eagles Temple (1924-25; altered). The Terminal Sales Building's dressed-up industrial style is a refreshing departure from the conventional office building with the detailing best described as Jacobethan. The United Shopping Tower, on the other hand, was clearly conceived in the New York Art Deco tradition, and embraces ideals of urban form which many architects today are striving to readdress. The Eagles Temple utilizes classical detail, but again successfully

3. Eagles Temple, Seattle, 1924-25 (altered), Henry Bittman. This sumptuous building, recalling the Italian palazzo in its form, was national headquarters of the Fraternal Order of Eagles, of which Bittman was a member. Traditional classical details in terra cotta ornament this ceremonial building. *(Bittman Vammen Taylor, P.S., Collection; photo by Webster & Stevens, ca. 1925.)*

4. Monte Cristo Hotel, Everett, 1924-25, Henry Bittman (A. H. Albertson, consulting architect). The cast stone ornament creates strong horizontal base and crown bands, while the cast stone quoins and finials emphasize stately vertical lines. *(Bittman Vammen Taylor, P.S., Collection; photo by Webster & Stevens, ca. 1925.)*

5. Seattle Recreation Building (Von Herberg Kelly Building), Seattle, 1928-30 (destroyed), Henry Bittman. This building type, the in-town store and loft building, was a typical 1920s commission, featuring Chicago-style windows, strong vertical lines, and Baroque terra-cotta ornament. *(Bittman Vammen Taylor, P.S., Collection; photo by Webster & Stevens, ca. 1930.)*

6. Music Box Theater, Seattle, 1928 (destroyed), Henry Bittman. Baroque motifs characterize this late 1920s theater. The interior featured a lavish and colorful marble-columned lobby and ornately decorated house. *(Bittman Vammen Taylor, P.S., Collection; photo by Webster & Stevens, ca. 1928.)*

7.   United Shopping Tower (Olympic Tower), Seattle, 1928-31 (altered), Henry Bittman. A refined Art Deco office tower set back from a base of street-front shops with Chicago-style windows and strong vertical lines. *(Bittman Vammen Taylor, P.S., Collection; photo by Webster & Stevens, ca. 1931.)*

resolves vertical and horizontal emphases. It also features a grand theater and ballroom, completely concealed from the outside. Other Bittman theaters in Seattle include the Music Box (1928; destroyed) and the Embassy Theater in his Mann Building (1926). A Tacoma Hamrick theater, featuring geometric Art Deco ornament, was commissioned in 1930 but apparently never built.

Bittman's prosperity during the 1920s allowed him to weather the Depression. He had invested in several buildings, which earned enough to help him pay the bills. About 1937, he designed a large mausoleum in Seattle, for the Clise family, a lifelong client, but it was never built. In the 1940s, work

picked up again, most of it for one- and two-story offices, and storefront remodels, where Bittman's structural knowledge and ability to communicate with builders was a great asset. During the late 1930s and early 1940s he followed the Streamlined Moderne style, and later moved into the International Style and shunned ornament altogether. One of his last major commissions was as associate architect and resident engineer for the new Seattle Post-Intelligencer Building (1947, now altered for use by Group Health), designed by Lockwood & Greene Engineers of New York City.

Bittman practiced until his death in Seattle on November 16, 1953.

8. King County Courthouse and City Hall, Seattle (first five stories, 1914-17, Augustus Warren Gould), remodel and addition of upper six stories, 1929-31, Henry Bittman, with J. L. McCauley. Bittman's addition is sympathetic with the original proposed scheme as rendered by Gould, which showed six very similar upper stories topped by a set-back tower. *(Bittman Vammen Taylor, P.S., Collection; photo by Webster & Stevens, ca. 1931.)*

9. William Volker Building, Seattle, 1928, Henry Bittman. This concrete post-and-slab structure allows enormous windows all around. Despite the warehouselike exterior, the lobby boasts marble walls, plaster friezes, and ornamental brass railings. *(Bittman Vammen Taylor, P.S., Collection; photo by Webster & Stevens, ca. 1928.)*

Floyd A. Naramore

DUANE A. DIETZ

Floyd A. Naramore (1879-1970), a native of Warren, Illinois, was born July 21, 1879. He began his career during his engineering studies at the University of Wisconsin, working as a bridge draftsman for the Chicago & Northwestern Railroad (1900-1903) and with architect George Fuller on construction of the Chicago & Northwestern Office Building, Chicago (1904-5). He studied at the Massachusetts Institute of Technology, receiving an architectural degree in 1907. Naramore then found draftsman's work with John McEwen & Co. in Chicago but soon moved to Portland, Oregon. His previous bridge experience led to a position with Northwest Bridgeworks, Portland (1909-12), where he became a skilled cost estimator. That skill benefited him in his appointment as Architect and Superintendent of Properties for the Portland school system, where he gained national attention for his design of Couch Elementary School (1914-15). Impressed by both his design work and

Floyd A. Naramore, date unknown. *(NBBJ Collection.)*

ability to control costs, the Seattle School Board hired Naramore to succeed Edgar Blair as architect for the Seattle School District in 1919. After World War I the state had passed a compulsory attendance law, and the district was faced with a need for many new school buildings to accommodate growing enrollment.

1. John Hay Elementary School, Seattle, 1920-21, Floyd Naramore. The use of architectural ornamentation (terra-cotta pilasters) on the corners of the buildings rarely appeared in Naramore's later work. The older John Hay School remains on the site as well. *(Seattle Public Schools Archives; ca. 1926; #234-4)*

2. Roosevelt High School, Seattle, 1921-22 (1928 addition by Naramore; altered), Floyd Naramore. This was the first high school designed by Naramore and the first of his buildings to use a monumentally scaled entry pavilion. *(Seattle Public Schools Archives; ca. 1925; #017-5)*

Naramore's first Seattle School District project was the design of Highland Park Elementary School (1919-21), followed quickly by a free-standing addition to John Hay Elementary School (1920-21; now an alternative school), Roosevelt High School (1921-22), Martha Washington Girls Parental School (1920-21; destroyed), and Bailey Gatzert Elementary School (1921-22; destroyed), all in the modernized Georgian mode preferred by Naramore. In contrast, his Columbia Elementary School (1922; now an alternative school) is the only Mission Revival school in the district and also the only school Naramore executed with exterior stucco. James Garfield High School (1922-23) was Naramore's single attempt at the Jacobean style.

Passage of successive bond issues in 1923, 1925, and 1927 allowed the school district to construct Montlake Elementary School (1923-24), Dunlap Elementary School (1923-24), E. C. Hughes Elementary School (1925-26, a twin of Dunlap), Bryant Elementary School (1926), Magnolia Elementary School (1926-27; now an alternative school), Alexander Hamilton Junior High School (1926-27), John Marshall Junior High School (1926-27), Grover

Cleveland High School (1926-27), and Laurelhurst Elementary School (1928-29)—all Georgian compositions by Naramore. His only experiment with Art Deco styling resulted in the whimsical cast stone ornamentation that graces Bagley Elementary School (1928-30). The second Whittier Elementary School (1927-28) and James Madison Junior High School (1928-29) were his only forays into the Collegiate Gothic style and were most likely influenced by the recent completion of Suzzallo Library on the University of Washington campus. In the early 1930s, Naramore returned to his preferred Georgian mode with the James Monroe Junior High School (1930-31; now Monroe Building, West Woodland Elementary School), and Loyal Heights Elementary School (1931).

Naramore favored siting a building to present an imposing facade, as can be seen at Cleveland High School and Roosevelt High School, and to a lesser extent at John Hay Elementary School. His use of terraces and entry stairs not only enhanced the orderly structure of the Georgian facades but also created a symbiotic connection between building and landscape well suited to the institutional mission of the school.

3. Garfield High School, Seattle, 1922-23 (1929 addition by Naramore; altered), Floyd Naramore. The entry is one of the best examples of Jacobean detailing within the school district. *(Seattle Public Schools Archives; ca. 1923; #014-7)*

Naramore formed a partnership with Alvin Menke from 1924 to 1929, designing schools in Ellensburg and Aberdeen and also acting as consulting architect to various school building projects in Longview and Bellingham. However, the Depression, and the attendant lack of public funds for school construction, soon led the two men to dissolve the partnership. The completion of Loyal Heights Elementary School in 1931 represented the end of construction within

the Seattle School District for some time, and Naramore resigned the following year. In the 1930s, his knowledge of institutional design and construction enabled him to continue to win projects, often in collaboration, as exemplified by Bagley Hall at the University of Washington (1935-36; altered) designed with Grainger & Thomas and Bebb & Gould.

Naramore was elected a Fellow of the AIA in 1935 and served as Washington State

4. Columbia Elementary School, Seattle, 1922 (altered), Floyd Naramore. The main entry arch, white stucco exterior walls, and small ornamental details above the windows are typical elements in recognizing the only Mission Style building in the district. *(Seattle Public Schools Archives; ca. 1925; #213-4.)*

5. Dunlap Elementary School, Seattle, 1923-24 (1925 addition by Naramore; altered), Floyd Naramore. Dunlap is one of the best examples of Naramore's work in the Georgian style. The peaked entry, cornice, and regimented windows are typical elements of the Modern Georgian mode. Hughes Elementary School is nearly identical in its detailing. *(Seattle Public Schools Archives; ca. 1924; #219-2.)*

AIA chapter president from 1939 to 1940. In 1939, he formed a partnership with Clifton Brady to design temporary defense housing and schools in the Seattle area. With his design for T. T. Minor Elementary School (1940-41), he abandoned the symmetrical organization and eclectic facades of his earlier work in favor of a looser articulation of the building's spaces, bringing modern architecture to Seattle's schools.

6. Alexander Hamilton Junior High School, Seattle, 1926-27 (altered), Floyd Naramore. Hamilton was the first intermediate school in the district. Its facade is more muted than that of Dunlap, but still Modern Georgian in character. *(Seattle Public Schools Archives; ca. 1928, neg. #105-3.)*

7. Grover Cleveland High School, Seattle, 1926-27 (altered), Floyd Naramore. Cleveland is an excellent adaptation of eighteenth-century building and landscape concepts. The use of terraces creates a dignified entry sequence and a magnificent view of Boeing Field. *(Seattle Public Schools Archives; ca. 1927; #012-5.)*

8. Loyal Heights Elementary School, Seattle, 1931 (altered), Floyd Naramore. This building is a two-story version of his first design, Highland Park Elementary School (1919-20). These two schools, along with Montlake Elementary, are unique among Naramore's school buildings for their nonhierarchical entrances. *(Seattle Public Schools Archives; ca. 1936; #246-12.)*

The amount and scale of the work commissioned by the federal government during the war forced Naramore and other architects to form joint ventures to carry out the major federal projects. In addition to the partnership of Naramore & Brady, Naramore became involved in other combined practices between 1940 to 1943, such as Naramore, Grainger & Thomas; Naramore, Grainger & Johanson; and Naramore, Bain, Brady & Johanson. These partnerships completed nearly six thousand units of housing, a number of schools, and other facilities, such as Eastpark Community Center, Bremerton (1941-42).

In 1943, the Naramore, Bain, Brady & Johanson partnership (since succeeded by NBBJ) was found to be the best fit among the combinations attempted. At sixty-four, Naramore was named senior partner, with broad responsibilities for firm management. He passed on his experience in school planning, supervising design work for McKinley Elementary School, Olympia (1948-49; destroyed), and various other projects until his death, October 29, 1970.

9. Bagley Hall, University of Washington, Seattle, 1935-36 (altered), Floyd A. Naramore, Grainger & Thomas, and Bebb & Gould. The University of Washington's chemistry building, with a utilitarian and modified Gothic design, fits compatibly into its campus setting. Naramore's participation in the professional collaboration that brought the design to fruition presaged his involvement with similar teams in the later 1930s and early 1940s. *(University of Washington Libraries, Special Collections Division; photo by White Martin, IMS Series I, 5097C.)*

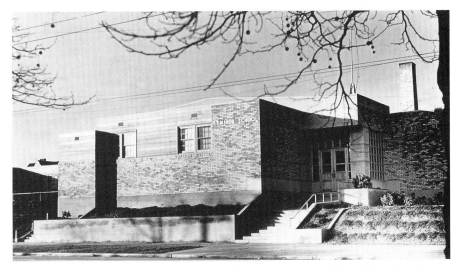

10. T. T. Minor Elementary, Seattle, 1940-41 (altered), Naramore & Brady. This building, Seattle's first school in the International Style, is characterized by the lack of ornamentation and the flat planes of the facades. *(Seattle Public Schools Archives; ca. 1942; #254-14.)*

J. Lister Holmes

DUANE A. DIETZ

J. Lister Holmes (1891-1986) was one of a handful of Northwest architects who successfully crossed from the Beaux-Arts design tradition to the International Style. Born in Seattle July 6, 1891, Holmes studied civil engineering at the University of Washington for two years and then transferred to the architecture program at the University of Pennsylvania, receiving a degree in 1913. The University of Pennsylvania's Beaux-Arts curriculum emphasized the use of applied ornamentation, generous scale, and the systematic adaptation of past architectural styles.

After a series of short-lived jobs in Philadelphia and Montana, Holmes returned to Seattle in 1920, where he worked briefly for Bebb & Gould, Schack, Young & Myers, and B. Marcus Priteca (see essays). A series of successful residential projects and the promise of future work encouraged Holmes to set

J. Lister Holmes. *(University of Washington Libraries, Special Collections Division; UW14553.)*

out on his own in 1922. His Beaux-Arts education enabled him to design in a variety of architectural idioms. He designed English Tudor homes for Harry Lawton in Seattle

1. Harry Lawton house, Seattle, 1926-27, J. Lister Holmes. An English Tudor revival style home. *(University of Washington Libraries, Special Collections Division; ca. 1931; UW14548.)*

2. O. W. Fisher, Jr., house, Seattle, 1926, J. Lister Holmes. A 1926 sketch emphasizing the Normandy Provincial style of the facade. This style defined the early period of Holmes's career. *(University of Washington Libraries, Special Collections Division; UW14552.)*

(1926-27), and Phil Polsky in Beaverton, Oregon (1932-33). A loose interpretation of the Spanish Colonial style for J. N. Donovan, Bellingham (1923-25), was replete with red tile roof and a whitewashed stucco exterior. Holmes's own home in Seattle (1928-30) was done in the Normandy Provincial mode while designs for the O. W. Fisher, Jr., house, in Broadmoor (1926), Collinswood (now the Bloedel Reserve), Bainbridge Island (1930-32), and the Phillip Baillargeon House in Seattle (1936-37) were executed in an eighteenth-century French idiom. His design of the Case Jones house, Seattle (1936), is in a more subdued American Colonial Revival mode.

As the Depression deepened in the 1930s, residential construction in Seattle slowed considerably. The International Style began to make serious inroads among local architects. Many were attracted to the simplicity derived from the lack of ornamentation, cubist effects achieved by windows mounted flush with wall surfaces, overhanging flat roofs, and white exterior walls. Holmes's first effort in this new design vein was the Weinir Dental Clinic, Seattle (1936; destroyed). His next design, the Arnold Dessau house, The Highlands (1937-39; altered), was quickly recognized for its blend of the International Style with distinctly regional vernacular elements. Holmes told an associate: "They [the clients] do not know it yet, but the theme for that house is to be a cross between Modern and Japanese, which has many of the elements of Modern in it." The Katherine Coulon house, Seattle (1939-40), shared many of the modern elements of the Dessau house, but was sited in a manner more sympathetic to the climate of the Northwest.

The local recognition garnered by the Dessau house led to Holmes's involvement in the design of the Washington State Pavilion (with Victor Jones and Carl F. Gould, 1938-39; demolished) for the 1939 New York World's Fair. He was then asked by the Seattle Housing Authority to serve as chief architect in the planning and design of Seattle's first large-scale slum-clearance housing project, Yesler Terrace (1940-43). Holmes also directed architects in other Seattle housing projects such as Gatewood Heights (1941-43) and Seward Park (1941-43). Another wartime commission was the Rainier Vista Elementary School (1942-43; now a Head Start facility), which he designed with William J. Bain, Sr.

3. Collinswood (Bloedel Reserve), Bainbridge Island, 1930-32 (with addition and alterations 1951-52), J. Lister Holmes. This 1951 drawing shows the original 1932 French Manor style house and Holmes's matching 1952 addition of garage, storage, and workshop spaces. *(The Bloedel Reserve Archives.)*

During World War II, Holmes's private practice was put on hold. This changed in 1945 with the design of the Industrial Branch of Seattle First National Bank (1945-47). He then executed designs for the Samuel Rubinstein house (1945-47), Harvard Square Medical and Dental Clinic (1946-47), Seattle Public Schools Adminis- tration Building (1946-48), the Ida Culver house (1948-49), and Catherine Blaine Junior High (now Elementary) School (1949-52). The Rubinstein house best represents Holmes's fusion of the Northwest vernacular with International Style elements, while Catherine Blaine Junior High was his purest Modern effort.

4. Weinir Dental Clinic, Seattle, 1936 (destroyed), J. Lister Holmes. This exterior elevation typifies the elements of the International Style: overhanging flat roofs and horizontal strip windows flush to white exterior walls. *(University of Washington Libraries, Special Collections Division; ca. 1937; Dearborn-Massar Collection, DM-1881.)*

5. Arnold Dessau house, The Highlands, 1937-39 (altered), J. Lister Holmes, architect; Butler S. Sturtevant, landscape architect. This Modern house featured severe rectilinear volumes and strong horizontal elements. The lanai feature was unique in the Northwest at the time. *(University of Washington Libraries, Manuscripts and University Archives Division; J. Lister Holmes Papers, Acc. 3789.)*

Holmes recognized the importance of city planning and served as a member of the Seattle Planning Commission (1947-55, chairman 1948-50), and on the national board of the American Society of Planning Officials (1948-51). His planning experience enabled him to execute his largest planning work, the Fort Lewis Peacetime Development Master Plan (1950-52). This project provided a framework for planning site circulation, troop housing, community buildings, commercial areas, and other facilities in the Fort Lewis area.

By the mid-1960s, Holmes had reduced the workload of his office, executing selected projects for favored clients. The United Parcel Service distribution buildings in Seattle (1950-51; destroyed), and in California in Pasadena (1951-52), San Diego (1951-52), Los Angeles (Headquarters, 1956), San Francisco (1962-63), and Los Angeles (1965), and a seven-acre complex in Seattle (1968-70) represent the last major works in his career. Holmes was elected a Fellow of the American Institute of Architects in 1955. He died in Seattle on July 18, 1986.

6. Yesler Terrace Defense Housing Project (Yesler Terrace), Seattle, 1940-43, J. Lister Holmes, chief architect; William Bain, William Aitken, George W. Stoddard, and John T. Jacobsen, associate architects; Butler S. Sturtevant and E. Clair Heilman, landscape architects. Yesler Terrace, with 878 units on a 43-acre site overlooking Puget Sound, proved that low-cost housing could be both energy efficient and aesthetically pleasing. *(University of Washington Libraries, Special Collections Division; photo by Ernst Kassowitz, ca. 1943; UW 8301.)*

7. Samuel Rubinstein house, Seattle, 1945-47, J. Lister Holmes & Associates. Holmes's refinement of Modernism includes the use of regional materials. A raised cubical space enhances the vertical movement of a stairway. *(University of Washington Libraries, Special Collections Division; ca. 1948; Dearborn-Massar Collection, DM-1825.)*

8. Seattle Public Schools Administration Building, Seattle, 1946-48, J. Lister Holmes & Associates. Holmes used a glazed volume to contain a stairway and added strong vertical elements in the glass facade similar to that of the Rubinstein house. *(University of Washington Libraries, Special Collections Division; ca. 1950; Dearborn-Massar Collection, DM-1850.)*

9. Catherine Blaine Junior High (now Elementary) School, Seattle, 1949-52, J. Lister Holmes & Associates; Robert H. Dietz & Charles Graham MacDonald, associate architects. This view, north to the library courtyard, shows the angular music wing on the left and the school administration and Seattle Parks Department offices on the right. *(University of Washington Libraries, Special Collections Division; ca. 1950; Dearborn-Massar Collection, DM-1801.)*

10. United Parcel Service Sorting Building, Seattle, 1950-51 (destroyed), J. Lister Holmes & Associates. The first of a series of large package-sorting buildings designed by Holmes that incorporated modular design. *(University of Washington Libraries, Special Collections Division; ca. 1952; Dearborn-Massar Collection, DM-1876)*

Elizabeth Ayer

S. SIAN ROBERTS &
MARY SHAUGHNESSY

Elizabeth Ayer (1897-1987) was born in Thurston County, Washington, October 13, 1897, to Cora Ellis and Charles Henry Ayer. Cora Ellis Ayer was an artist; Charles Henry was a successful lawyer and judge, and was elected mayor of Olympia in 1895. His forebears were Pacific Northwest pioneers who arrived in Washington Territory in 1852. In 1930, Elizabeth Ayer followed the pioneering tradition of her family by becoming the first woman to be registered as an architect in the state of Washington. During her long and prolific career, she helped to shape many of the residential neighborhoods of Seattle and the Puget Sound region.

Elizabeth Ayer, 1939. *(University of Washington Libraries, Manuscripts and University Archives Division.)*

1. Langdon C. Henry residence, The Highlands, 1927-28, Edwin Ivey, Architect. Described by Ayer as "French Colonial," this house was one of several of the firm's projects in The Highlands. Ayer, who prepared the majority of the drawings, later identified the Henry residence as one of her favorite projects. *(University of Washington Libraries, Special Collections Division; UW14713.)*

2. Seattle Children's Home, Seattle, 1930-31 (destroyed), Edwin Ivey, Architect. According to the firm's records, Ayer was heavily involved in this project, which was one of only a few institutional buildings undertaken by the firm. It was later described by Ayer as a career highlight. *(University of Washington Libraries, Manuscripts and University Archives Division; MSS&UA 533.)*

In 1916, Ayer enrolled at the University of Washington, and in 1921 became the fourth graduate, and the first woman graduate, of the recently established architecture program. She worked briefly for the Seattle architect Andrew Willatsen (see Willatsen essay), and then was hired by Ivey & Riley, Architects, as an "office girl." In the years that followed, Edwin J. Ivey (1883-1940) was

to become Ayer's mentor and her major architectural influence.

Due to financial difficulties, the Ivey & Riley partnership dissolved in 1921, but Ayer continued with the firm of Edwin Ivey, Architect. During the 1920s, when work was occasionally scarce, Ayer took two leaves of absence. In 1922, she moved to New York City. Provided with references by Ivey, who

3. Aubrey Naef residence, Seattle, 1935-36, Edwin Ivey, Architect. Described by Ayer as "Modern Colonial," this house exemplifies the design versatility of the firm. *(University of Washington Libraries, Special Collections Division; UW14715.)*

4.   Winston W. Chambers residence, Seattle, 1937, Edwin Ivey, Architect; Elizabeth Ayer, Associate.
This modest but imposing Colonial house in Laurelhurst is on a hill overlooking Lake Washington.
When this was published the captions credited both Ivey and Ayer. From *Architectural Record,* 87
(January 1940); photo by Roger Sturtevant. *(University of Washington Libraries, Special Collections
Division; UW14732.)*

5.   Albert Schafer Castle, Hood Canal, Washington, 1938-39, Edwin Ivey, Architect; Elizabeth Ayer,
Associate. This project was developed from an early sketch done by Ayer for this pioneering Washing-
ton timber family. The Norman details were designed by Ayer and produced by craftsmen in the
Schafer mills. *(Photo by Larry Steagall,* Bremerton Sun, *1990.)*

6. Lee Doud residence, Tacoma, 1948-51, Ayer & Lamping. This house illustrates the application of the modern free-plan concept. Although the exterior is characterized by residential forms and detailing typical of the time, the interior is noticeably more modern. *(University of Washington Libraries, Special Collections Division; ca. 1951; Dearborn-Massar Collection, DM-89.)*

7. Doud residence, Tacoma, 1948-51, Ayer & Lamping. This explicitly modern kitchen employs planar surfaces and minimalist detailing. *(University of Washington Libraries, Special Collections Division; ca. 1951; Dearborn-Massar Collection, DM-97.)*

had received his architecture degree from the University of Pennsylvania in 1910, she found work as a draftsperson with the firm of Cross & Cross, and with Grosvenor Atterbery. After a year in New York City, she returned to the Pacific Northwest, and to Ivey's firm. In 1927, Ayer traveled to Europe for a year, spending most of her time in Italy. During her travels she maintained an active correspondence with Ivey, in which she described her impressions of architectural sights that he had recommended from his own travels abroad.

In the period following Ayer's return from Europe, the firm of Edwin Ivey, Architect, designed several grand homes in exclusive neighborhoods such as Broadmoor and The Highlands, employing a number of different but traditional residential styles. The plans largely conformed to the schemes typical of the architectural style selected. It was not until the late 1930s and early 1940s that the expression of progressively freer plans began to transform the symmetrical, formal nature of their projects.

8. W. Hilding Lindberg residence, Tacoma, 1948-52, Ayer & Lamping. The traditional detailing of this large house illustrates Ivey's influence in Ayer & Lamping's work. (*University of Washington Libraries, Manuscripts and University Archives Division; MSS&UA 532.*)

9. William E. Forland residence, Seattle, 1961-63, Ayer & Lamping. This large house appeared very traditional from the front, but the back and interior were more freely composed, showing a mix of traditional and modern attitudes in design. (*Photo by S. Sian Roberts, 1993.*)

10. Robert F. Linden residence, Bainbridge Island, 1962, Ayer & Lamping. This one-story house was completed near the end of Ayer's career. A free plan, allowing the creation of an exterior courtyard, and the use of corner windows illustrate a level of modernism in Ayer's design approach. *(University of Washington Libraries, Special Collections Division; UW14717.)*

In 1940, Edwin Ivey was killed in an automobile accident. Ayer and another of Ivey's employees, Rolland Lamping (1907-?), continued the practice under Ivey's name. Like Ayer, Lamping had received his architectural degree from the University of Washington. After a short tenure with Smith, Carroll & Johanson in Seattle, he had joined Ivey's firm in 1936. Following World War II, during which both Ayer and Lamping served as architects for the U.S. Engineers Office, the partnership of Ayer & Lamping Architects was established. Although the two principals continued to focus on residential design, their projects included comparatively few of the large estates completed during their tenure with Ivey. Their practice consisted primarily of modest single-family homes, residential remodels, and small commercial projects.

Like many of their contemporaries, Ayer & Lamping began developing plans that emphasized functional rather than stylistic requirements. Functionally related spaces were often expressed individually on the exterior, creating an informally organized collection of volumes. Yet, while the plans of their houses became increasingly modern,

Ayer & Lamping resisted the modern imagery favored by many of their contemporaries. Between 1940 and 1970, Ayer & Lamping produced a remarkably consistent body of work which successfully adapted traditional models to modern functional needs. Throughout this period, they completed hundreds of projects in western Washington, most of which still stand, setting the tone for many typical Northwest neighborhoods.

After fifty years of practice, Ayer retired to Lacey, Washington, in 1970. In addition to her private practice, she served on Seattle's Board of Adjustments from 1960 to 1970, and remained active on the Lacey Planning Commission until 1980. Throughout her career, Ayer was known for her generosity, both personal and professional, and for her ability to understand and realize her clients' aspirations. By the time she retired, she had prepared designs for the grandchildren of some of her first clients. Ayer's successful and prolific career as the first woman registered architect in Washington paved the way for succeeding generations of Pacific Northwest women architects. She died August 4, 1987, in Lacey.

William J. Bain, Sr.

DUANE A. DIETZ

William James Bain, Sr. (1896-1985), a native of New Westminster, British Columbia, was one of Seattle's more prolific designers. Born March 27, 1896, he began his architectural education in 1915, apprenticing for W. R. B. Willcox, Arthur L. Loveless, and other Seattle architects (see Willcox and Loveless essays). After serving in France during World War I, Bain enrolled at the University of Pennsylvania, graduating with an architecture degree in 1921. The university's Beaux-Arts curriculum, directed by Paul Cret, reinforced design concepts familiar to Bain through his earlier apprenticeships.

William J. Bain, Sr. *(NBBJ Collection.)*

Upon his return to Seattle, Bain again worked briefly for Willcox, from 1921 to 1922, and for Loveless, from 1922 to 1923, and then in the Los Angeles office of Johnson, Kaufman & Coate, from 1923 to 1924, before opening his own office in Seattle in 1924. With his Beaux-Arts background and his engaging manner, Bain quickly developed a reputation for quality

1. Shoremont Apartments (now north half of Lake Court Apartments), Seattle, 1926-28, William J. Bain, Sr. Bain won a Washington State Chapter AIA Honor Award for his design of this apartment complex. Bain & Pries enlarged the complex with a compatible addition in 1930-31. *(Photo by Jeffrey Karl Ochsner, 1993.)*

2. Bel Roy Apartments, Seattle, 1930-31, Bain & Pries. This Moderne apartment building used enlarged bay windows on a zigzag floor plan to enable all units to view Lake Union and downtown Seattle. *(Photo by T. William Booth, 1993.)*

eighteenth-century French and English elements were blended in the Clarence Shaw house (1929), while the French Provincial mode is represented at the Shoremont Apartments (1926-28), Carman house (1928), Samuel J. Calderhead house (1936-38), and Herbert Schoenfeld house (1938-40), all in Seattle. The Georgian Revival was applied in the Viceroy Apartments (1930-31), the George Vance house (1938-39), and the James G. Pursley house (1939-40).

A tumultuous partnership with Lionel Pries from 1928 to 1932 (see Pries essay) was responsible for a number of sororities and apartment buildings around Seattle. Georgian details accent the Consulate Apartments (1929-30) and Envoy Apartments (1930). At the Moderne style Bel Roy Apartments (1930-31), the zigzag floor plan was designed to maximize views from all units. Two sororities north of the University of Washington campus, Gamma Phi Beta (1932-35) and Pi Beta Phi (1932-35), are textbook examples of the Georgian Revival.

residential architecture. His homes and apartment buildings in Seattle ran the gamut of architectural idioms popular in the twenties and thirties. A combination of

3. Pi Beta Phi Sorority House, Seattle, 1932-35, Bain & Pries, William J. Bain. The straightforward interpretation of Georgian detailing reflects the tendencies toward classicizing design among Beaux-Arts trained architects in the late 1920s. An early rendering of this building was drawn by Pries, but when the firm split, Bain retained the commission. *(Photo by Duane A. Dietz, 1992.)*

4. Herbert Schoenfeld house, Seattle, 1938-40, Wiliam J. Bain, Sr. The garden front of this house derives its form and simple detailing from French Provincial precedents. From *Architect and Engineer*, August 1941.

Residential work in the Seattle area diminished as the Depression progressed. Many of Bain's works during this period were small homes that could be built for between $6,000 and $10,000, far smaller than the large homes he had designed previously. However, by the late 1930s he was receiving a variety of commissions. His Albert Brygger house, Port Madison (1937-38), shows increasing horizontality and a more informal

5. Royal Crowne Cola Beverage Company building, Seattle, 1940-41 (destroyed), William J. Bain, Sr. Bain's solution for this emerging building type drew on the Streamline Moderne style generally favored by soft drink companies at the time. From *Architect and Engineer,* August 1941.

6. Louis T. Dulien house, Seattle, 1939, William J. Bain, Sr. The use of low overhanging eaves and a trilevel floor plan characterized Bain's homes during the early 1940s. (*University of Washington Libraries, Special Collections Division; ca. 1944; Dearborn-Massar Collection, DM-320.*)

approach to planning, and the Royal Crowne Cola Company building (1940-41; destroyed), showed Bain experimenting with streamlined forms. After 1940, the war effort started to improve architectural fortunes in Seattle. Bain served as Washington State AIA chapter president from 1941 to 1943 and became involved with J. Lister Holmes (see Holmes essay) and others on Yesler Terrace (1940-43), and with J. Lister Holmes on Rainier Vista Elementary School (1942-43; now a Head Start facility).

In 1942, Bain was named camouflage director for the state of Washington. One of his better known projects was the camouflaging of the Boeing assembly plant in Seattle. By covering the roof with false buildings, fences, and other realistic features, Bain was able to make the assembly plant look like a residential neighborhood from the air.

Several large projects commissioned by the federal government during the war forced Bain and other architects to work together in joint ventures. In 1943, Floyd Naramore, William Bain, Clifton Brady, and Perry Johanson found that their personali-

ties were compatible and thus formed a lasting partnership, known informally as "The Combine" (currently known as NBBJ). Bain's work there included design and staff supervision of such projects as the Boeing Pre-Flight Facilities in Renton and Moses Lake (1956-58), and Seattle's Scottish Rite Temple (1958-62) and First Presbyterian Church (1965-70).

Bain was elected a Fellow of the AIA in 1947. That same year he formed a partnership with Harrison Overturf which, until 1970, enabled Bain to maintain a residential practice separate from the Naramore, Bain, Brady & Johanson partnership. Homes such as the John L. Scott house (1948-49, Bain & Overturf) and his own home (1950-51, Bain & Overturf), both in Seattle, successfully combined the forms of the Colonial Revival and New England Cottage with the new Modern approach to residential design in vogue on the West Coast.

By 1975, Bain was semi-retired but continued to work at the NBBJ offices, developing a prefabricated utility core for low-income housing, until his death January 22, 1985.

7. Camouflaged Boeing assembly plant, Seattle, 1942-43, William J. Bain, Sr., camouflage director. Unlike the practice in California, where ersatz neighborhoods were simply painted on building roofs, Bain designed false houses and working victory gardens to enhance the realism of Washington camouflage projects. (*The Boeing Company Archives; ca. 1944; # X1228.*)

8. John L. Scott house, Seattle, 1948-49, Bain & Overturf. An intriguing Modern residence, this is characterized by a white exterior, angular overhangs, and rectangular volumes. (*University of Washington Libraries, Special Collections Division, ca. 1951; Dearborn-Massar Collection DM-360.*)

9. Scottish Rite of Freemasonry Temple, Seattle, 1958-62, Naramore, Bain, Brady & Johanson; William J. Bain, Sr., partner-in-charge. This structure shows the simple forms and clear linear detailing that characterized Bain's approach within the NBBJ firm. *(Photo by Duane A. Dietz, 1993.)*

10. First Presbyterian Church, Seattle, 1965-70, Naramore, Bain, Brady & Johanson; William J. Bain, Sr., partner-in-charge. This structure displays a traditional gabled form but is executed in unfinished concrete with restrained detailing reflecting Bain's design approach. *(Photo by T. William Booth, 1993.)*

Frederick William Anhalt

DAVID A. RASH

& THOMAS ESTEP

While coming to architecture from the building trades was a frequent path for designers in the nineteenth century, it has become much less common in the twentieth. However, the career of Frederick William Anhalt (b. 1896), who is best known for his design of high quality residential apartments in Seattle, followed this unusual trajectory.

Born on a farm near Canby, Minnesota, March 6, 1896, Anhalt moved with his family to North Dakota when he was eleven. At the age of fourteen he left home to work in the butcher business and seek his fortune. After several stops in the Midwest, where he worked in a number of trades related to the grocery and butcher businesses, he settled in Seattle, perhaps as early as 1924.

Frederick William Anhalt, ca. 1929. (*Fred Anhalt Collection*).

By 1925, Anhalt was working as a salesman in Seattle and surrounding areas for the Hurley Store Fixtures Company. After some initial success in selling store fixtures to mer-

1. Cora M. Graham Store Building, Seattle, 1926, William H. Whiteley, architect, Victor F. Sandberg, contractor; Western Building & Leasing Company, developer. Like many commercial buildings developed by Western Building & Leasing Company, this has residential units along the rear. The simple one-story mass is embellished with Classical Revival motifs. (*Photo by David A. Rash, 1993.*)

2. Western Building & Leasing Company bungalow apartments, Seattle, 1926-27, Victor F. Sandberg, designer-builder. This two-building complex was the first strictly residential development by Western Building & Leasing Company and was the first of several of the company's apartment buildings in which Anhalt chose to reside. *(Photo by David A. Rash, 1993.)*

chants, Anhalt saw an opportunity to sell fixtures by leasing empty commercial buildings in the outlying districts of Seattle as markets and butcher shops. In this development scheme, he was joined by a fellow former butcher, Jerome B. Hardcastle, Jr., whose father happened to be a carpenter. Anhalt and Hardcastle established their development organization as the Western Building & Leasing Company. By mid-1926,

they were constructing new buildings rather than leasing existing ones. Initially, Western Building & Leasing utilized architects and contractors to design and construct their buildings, but Anhalt increasingly made both design and construction an in-house function of the company. During 1928, to centralize control further, Anhalt arranged to buy out his partner's interest in the company.

3. Western Building & Leasing Company apartment building, Seattle, 1927, William H. Whiteley, architect; Western Building & Leasing, contractor. This Mediterranean Revival style courtyard apartment building was apparently the only apartment building that Whiteley designed for Anhalt; however, Whiteley did design some half-dozen apartment buildings for Anhalt's partner, Jerome B. Hardcastle, Jr. From "Apartments by Anhalt," 1930. *(University of Washington Libraries, Special Collections Division; UW14780.)*

4. Western Building & Leasing Company apartment building, Seattle, 1927, Western Building & Leasing Company, designer-builder. The Medieval English style of this apartment building established the exterior appearance of virtually all of Anhalt's subsequent apartment buildings. From "Apartments by Anhalt," 1930. *(Collection of Frederick A. Graham.)*

During this time, Western Building & Leasing had no particular focus to its work. The company built bungalow apartments, courtyard apartments, commercial buildings, and houses in Seattle neighborhoods, including Ballard, Queen Anne, Capitol Hill, Beacon Hill, and West Seattle. Stylistically, the commercial buildings were typically Classical Revival in derivation, the bungalow apartments English Tudor, and the courtyard apartments Mediterranean Revival.

In late 1928, Mark B. Borchert of Portland, Oregon (perhaps a relative of Cresence Borchert Anhalt, Frederick's wife), established the Borchert Company with the intention of building luxury apartments in Seattle using money provided by Portland investors. The Borchert Company realized three Seattle apartment buildings between December 1928 and mid-1929, at 1201 East John Street (1928-29), 417 Harvard Avenue East (1928-29), and 1516 East Republican Street (1929; now the Twin Gables). Western

5. The Borchert Company apartment building (now Twin Gables), Seattle, 1928-29, Western Building & Leasing Company, designer-builder. The drawings for this, the last of the three Borchert apartment buildings (and 417 Harvard Avenue East, as well), bear Edwin E. Dofson's initials. Dofson, a designer in Anhalt's employ, was involved in transforming Anhalt's design ideas into graphic form on a number of his projects. From "Apartments by Anhalt," 1930. *(Collection of Frederick A. Graham.)*

6. The Anhalt Company apartment building (now Belmont Court), Seattle, 1929-30, the Anhalt Company, designer-builder. This was typical of the scale of Anhalt's later apartment buildings. Some six months elapsed between the completion of the plans and the issuance of the building permit, with another five months required for construction. *(Collection of Paul Dorpat; photo ca. 1930.)*

7. The Anhalt Company apartment building, Seattle, 1929-30, the Anhalt Company, designer-builder. This was the largest and most elaborate of Anhalt's apartment buildings. With its companion across East Roy Street, this was the first to incorporate cast-stone ornament into its brick veneer exterior. From "Apartments by Anhalt," 1930. *(University of Washington Libraries, Special Collections Division; UW14779.)*

Building & Leasing constructed all three buildings and designed at least the latter two.

Within two weeks of the issuance of the building permit for the last of the Borchert apartment buildings, Anhalt announced plans for construction of a new apartment building at 730 Belmont Avenue East (1929; now Oak Manor). Curiously, Western Building & Leasing was now transformed into the Anhalt Company, which soon was

building five additional luxury apartment buildings, one house, and a commercial alteration, before the Depression brought a virtual halt to construction in late 1930 and early 1931. By 1930, the Anhalt Company had also acquired the apartment buildings previously owned by the Borchert Company.

With the focus on the luxury apartment segment of the rental market, Anhalt's later work was located in the Capitol Hill neigh-

8. The Anhalt Company apartment building (now The Belmont), Seattle, 1929-30, the Anhalt Company, designer-builder. The long, narrow site with frontage on both Belmont Place and Boylston Avenue resulted in a more conventional design with double-loaded corridors for this apartment building, while retaining Anhalt's trademark Medieval English style. From "Apartments by Anhalt," 1930. (*University of Washington Libraries, Special Collections Division; UW14778.*)

9. Edwin C. Kellogg house, Seattle, 1935, Galen W. Bentley, architect; Anhalt, Inc., contractor. As early as 1929, Anhalt began incorporating "early American" elements into some of the interiors of his apartment buildings. During the 1930s, this appreciation extended into Colonial Revival style houses. (*Photo by David A. Rash, 1993.*)

borhood of Seattle. The buildings were larger in scale and stylistically derived from Medieval English and Norman prototypes. These later apartment buildings usually retained the individualized entrances of the earlier bungalow apartments, allowing the apartments to have a "home-like" quality that Anhalt preferred and stressed in his promotional literature. He also stressed the high level of maintenance that his company provided, plus amenities like wood-burning fireplaces and "electric dish-washing machines."

Although Anhalt was able to construct his four largest apartment buildings after the stock market crash of October 24, 1929, the unavailability of new capital doomed his most ambitious project and eventually forced the Anhalt Company into bankruptcy. Until he abandoned the construction trades in 1942 for his increasingly thriving nursery business, Anhalt's building activity was limited primarily to speculative and custom homes. He later retired and in 1994 was living in California.

Throughout his years as a developer-builder-designer, Anhalt worked to achieve quality in everything he undertook. Sixty years later his apartments are still sought after, and his name has become synonymous with a standard few achieve in apartment building today. While he never became an architect, Frederick Anhalt was made an honorary member of AIA-Seattle in 1993—a fitting tribute to his contribution to Seattle's urban environment.

10. Saint Stephen Episcopal Church, Seattle, 1940-42 (altered), Thomas, Grainger & Thomas (architect), W. C. Brown (contractor, 1941), Frederick Anhalt (contractor, 1941-42). Among the very last of Anhalt's constructed works was his only church, where he served on the building committee and eventually assumed the role of contractor after difficulties with the initial contractor. *(Photo by David A. Rash, 1993.)*

Lionel H. Pries

DREW ROCKER

Lionel H. "Spike" Pries (1897-1968) profoundly influenced architecture students at the University of Washington for over thirty years. For many young, provincial Washingtonians, he provided an introduction to a larger world, which encompassed foreign travel, classical music, art history, crafts, and fine arts as well as architecture. For many students from the 1930s to the 1950s (including Victor Steinbrueck, Minoru Yamasaki, Roland Terry, Paul Kirk, Fred Bassetti, Keith Kolb, Wendell Lovett, Astra Zarina, and others), Pries was the center of the school.

Lionel H. Pries was born in San Francisco on June 1, 1897, to a cultured and international family. He attended the Uni-

Lionel H. Pries, ca. 1930. From *Washington Alumnus*, December 1931. *(University of Washington Libraries, Special Collections Division; UW14755.)*

1. Bothin Building, Santa Barbara, California (1925), Lionel H. Pries, architect for reconstruction (W. H. Aiken and J. V. Elliott for original building, 1902). Initially a three-story structure in brick, this was heavily damaged in the 1925 earthquake. Reconstructed as a two-story structure, and conforming to city's ordinance in regard to style, Pries's Bothin Building has been characterized as "one of the really distinguished examples of the Spanish Colonial Revival in Santa Barbara." *(Photo by Deborah Walker, 1993.)*

2.   Residential project, location unidentified, ca. 1928-29, Bain & Pries. This rendering is representative of many of the Bain & Pries projects based on sophisticated interpretations of English precedents, probably reflecting their knowledge of contemporary Philadelphia architects. *(University of Washington Libraries, Special Collections Division; UW14404.)*

3.   Convalescent Home for Crippled Children, Seattle, 1928-30 (altered), Bain & Pries. This building provided living quarters for forty children as well as nurses' quarters and space for supervised play. The three-dimensional composition style gives a residential character to this institutional structure. Pries was no doubt also responsible for the playful figures of children that were integrated into the design. From *Architect and Engineer*, August 1941.

versity of California at Berkeley, studying under John Galen Howard, and receiving his B.Arch. in 1920. He went on to the University of Pennsylvania, earning his M.Arch. in 1921, while also serving as assistant critic to the legendary Paul Cret. That year he tied for first place in the American Academy in Rome Competition, and from 1921 to 1923 he studied in Europe as winner of the LeBrun Travelling Scholarship.

In 1924, Pries returned to the West Coast, entering private practice in San Francisco. After the 1925 earthquake, he received multiple commissions in Santa Barbara and was responsible for designing the reconstruction of several downtown buildings in the Spanish Colonial Revival style (as required by ordinance) including the Bothin Building (1925), McKay Building (1925-26), and Auto Show Rooms and Seaside Oil

BROADMOOR RESIDENCE FOR DR. GLENN BORGENDALE

4. Dr. Glenn Borgendale house project, Seattle, 1935 (unbuilt), Lionel H. Pries. Although Pries opposed modern teaching methodologies, he was interested in adopting Modern approaches within the Beaux-Arts tradition. This watercolor reflects his skills as a delineator. *(University of Washington Libraries, Special Collections Division; UW14403.)*

Company Building (1926). Other projects included the Mission Style Abracadabra Club, Berkeley (1927-28; destroyed), and residences in a variety of Bay Area communities. Pries was also published as a delineator.

In 1928, Pries relocated to Seattle and entered the partnership Bain & Pries with his former Pennsylvania classmate William J. Bain, Sr. (see Bain essay). Projects of the partnership reflected a sophisticated approach to eclectic design, with buildings in Seattle including the George Youell house (1929), the Karl A. Krueger house (1928-29), the Convalescent Home for Crippled Children (1928-30; altered), and the Bel Roy Apartments (1930-31).

Pries also began as a part-time instructor in architecture at the University of Washington in 1928, and from 1930 to 1932 he was director of the Seattle Art Institute. When the partnership with Bain dissolved in 1932, Pries became an assistant professor, beginning the full-time teaching career for which he is most remembered. He was promoted to associate professor in 1938 and to professor in 1948.

5. Colonel Julian P. Willcox house, Holly (near Bremerton), Washington, 1937 (altered); Lionel H. Pries. Combining modernity and tradition, new materials (hexagonal shingles) and traditional crafts (Native totem poles), this extraordinary house may reflect Pries's personal reinterpretation of the new architecture he had seen in Mexico. Unfortunately, the totem poles were removed by a later owner. *(University of Washington Libraries, Special Collections Division; ca. 1938; Dearborn-Masser Collection, DM-3821.)*

Pries accepted occasional commissions, continuing to explore ideas in design. He was increasingly interested in the possibility of combining modern and traditional techniques. His Colonel Julian P. Willcox house, Holly, Washington (1937; altered), presented a mix of materials and textures, including log construction, applied within a framework free of direct historical reference. The incorporation of Native American totem poles reflects Pries's understanding of the work of leading contemporary Mexican architects, whose architecture combined modernity and traditional arts and crafts (work that Pries knew from his travels). Pries's own house in Seattle (1948-50; altered), similarly explored the relationships between architecture and the visual arts and between machine-made materials and hand-crafted elements.

Although Pries was an inventive designer and artist, he was most influential as an educator, described by some as a "magician" in that role. Idiosyncratic and demanding, he had set the highest standards for himself in

6. Colonel Willcox house, gatehouse, Holly (near Bremerton), Washington, 1937, Lionel H. Pries. In 1989, this house was restored and altered as necessary for its current use as a bed and breakfast inn. (*University of Washington Libraries, Special Collections Division; Dearborn-Massar Collection, DM-3823.*)

7. Richard Lea house, Lopez Island, 1946-47 (altered), Lionel H. Pries. With its long ground-paralleling eaves and sod roof, this house nestles into the landscape of the shoreline at Lopez Island. (*Private collection; photo ca. 1950.*)

8. Lionel H. Pries house, Seattle, 1948-50 (altered), Lionel H. Pries. This watercolor rendering shows the house as Pries envisioned it in 1948. Two unsympathetic remodelings have obscured the original design. The watercolor remains with the house. *(Private collection.)*

his own education, and he expected no less of his students. Regarded as a strict teacher, he was most comfortable with the brightest and best students, measuring their potential by their design aptitudes. He developed a reputation for erasing or sponging out work he did not find acceptable. At the same time, he was known to be devoted to his students, and could be found in studio offering critiques late into the evening. He also invited them to his home to see his collections of Northwest Native American art, Piranesi etchings, Latin American and European textiles, and architectural books.

After World War II, the architecture program at the University of Washington grew rapidly and was influenced by the postwar emphasis on operational efficiency, expediency, and strict "functionality." Pries was generally considered outdated by his new colleagues in the post-war era. Yet Pries's breadth continued to make him influential with students.

In the period after World War II, American architecture schools turned away from traditional methods, but not until Pries's forced departure did the Beaux-Arts era end completely at the University of Washington. In an atmosphere increasingly incompatible

9. Lionel H. Pries house, Seattle, 1948-50 (altered), Lionel H. Pries. The front door and frame were fabricated from a Burmese bedstead collected by Pries. The contrast of the fine detailing of these elements and the concrete block wall of the house are indicative of Pries's interest in mixing machine-made materials and finely crafted objects. *(Private collection; ca. 1950.)*

with the approaches he had so successfully expounded, and in the moral climate of the time, Pries's homosexuality became the basis for his dismissal from the University in 1958. Without significant income or other resources to draw upon, Pries became associated with several Seattle offices. In 1959 and 1960, he worked at Durham, Anderson & Freed, adding a sparkle to their work, as exemplified by the crucifix he designed and made for Faith Lutheran Church, Bellingham (1960). From 1961 to 1963 he worked for John Graham & Company. His last projects were the Max A. Gurvich house, Seattle (1964-65), and the Robert W. Winskill house, Mill Valley, California (1968-70). He died in Seattle on April 7, 1968.

Pries left the University at a time of changing values and goals that cast a shadow over what had been a brilliant teaching record. Yet, in any survey of architecture alumni of his decades, "Spike" Pries is cited again and again for the central place he occupied in their lives and continues to occupy in their memories.

10. Richard Lea house remodeling, Seattle, 1956, Lionel H. Pries. The remodeling of the Lea house involved substantial reconstruction. The resulting design provided modern spaces which served as settings for the display of a variety of art objects. *(Photo by Art Hupy, 1956.)*

Butler Sturtevant

DUANE A. DIETZ

The career of Butler Stevens Sturtevant (1899-1970) spanned the years from the waning days of the Beaux-Arts period to the heyday of Modern design. He is considered a prototypical landscape architect given the broad range of his practice, which included the design of private estates, college campuses, planned communities, and airports.

Sturtevant was born September 1, 1899, in Delevan, Wisconsin. He received an undergraduate degree in horticulture at the University of California, Southern Branch (now UCLA), in 1921. He then studied at Harvard University in the landscape architecture graduate program from 1922 to 1924, where he completed all work but his thesis. His classmates included Thomas Church and Charles Eliot II. Sturtevant worked through a series of offices (Cook, Hall & Cornell, Los Angeles, 1924-25; Stiles

Butler Stevens Sturtevant. From *Architect and Engineer,* March 1936.

& Van Kleek, Boston, 1925-26; Fletcher Steele, Boston, 1926-27; and Gardner, Gardner & Fischer, Los Angeles, 1927-28) before opening an office in Seattle in 1928 to

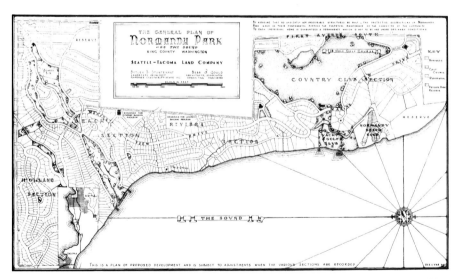

1. General Plan of Normandy Park, Seattle, 1928-29, Butler S. Sturtevant, landscape architect; Bebb & Gould, architects. This plan by Sturtevant reflects the experience gained through his subdivision work with Stiles & Van Kleek and at the office of Cook, Hall & Cornell. *(University of Washington Libraries, Special Collections Division; ca. 1929; UW13573.)*

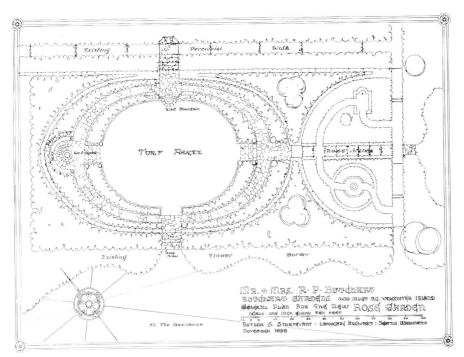

2. New Rose Garden Plan for Mr. and Mrs. R. P. Butchart, Victoria, British Columbia, 1928-29, Butler S. Sturtevant. This plan for the Rose Garden represented the first outside involvement in the development of what eventually became Butchart Gardens. (*University of Washington Libraries, Special Collections Division; ca. 1928; UW13574.*)

participate with Bebb & Gould in the design of the Normandy Park Subdivision Master Plan (1928-29).

A recommendation from Carl Gould led to Sturtevant's design for the New Rose Garden at Butchart Gardens, Victoria, British Columbia (1928-33), and a courtyard garden at Children's Orthopedic Hospital, Seattle (1930-31; destroyed). Gould also recommended Sturtevant for the landscape architect's staff position at the University of Washington, a position he held from 1931 to 1939. He directed nearly nine hundred Works Progress Administration laborers in the planting of Anderson Hall (1930-32), construction of a new 2 1/2 acre Medicinal Herb Garden (1934-36), reconstruction of Rainier Vista (1935-37), renovation of Drumheller Fountain (1935-36), and the planting of cedar trees on Stevens Way (1938).

Sturtevant's design work surrounding Anderson Hall led to his involvement in the design of the campus plan for Principia College, a small Christian Science school in Elsah, Illinois (1931-38). His relationship with the architect, Bernard Maybeck, was tumultuous, and the client had to beg Maybeck to continue working with Sturtevant, acknowledging that Sturtevant was "tactless and impulsive and has not always remembered that we began with the definite understanding that the architect was to have general supervision of the landscape plans," but noting that Sturtevant was enthusiatic and "unquestionably in love with his work here." Maybeck completed his portion of the commission, leaving Sturtevant to work on various campus projects until 1969.

Sturtevant's work at the Frederick Remington Green Garden in The Highlands (1931-33) and the William O. McKay Roof

3.   Grounds and Chapel, Principia College, Elsah, Illinois, 1933, Butler Sturtevant, landscape architect, Bernard Maybeck; architect. This former cornfield was chosen by Sturtevant and Maybeck to be the religious center of the campus. Its panoramic view over the Mississippi is unrivaled in the Midwest. *(Photo by Duane A. Dietz, 1991.)*

4.   Boys' Dormitory, Principia College, Elsah, Illinois, 1933-35, Bernard Maybeck, architect; Butler Sturtevant, landscape architect. Sturtevant's design of the landscaped setting provides an effective complement to Maybeck's building and focuses attention on the entry. *(Photo by Duane A. Dietz, 1991.)*

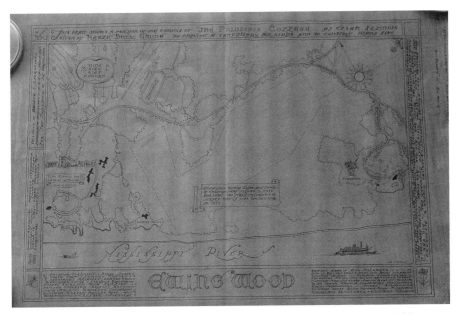

5. Principia College Plan—Ewingwood Addition, Elsah, Illinois, 1934, Butler Sturtevant. This addition of 1,200 acres doubled the area of the campus. Sturtevant set aside the entire parcel as a nature preserve, an unheard of action in the 1930s. *(Principia College Archives.)*

6. Medicinal Herb Garden, University of Washington, Seattle, 1934-36 (partly destroyed), Butler S. Sturtevant. This aerial view highlights Sturtevant's work on the Medicinal Herb Garden, the planting of cedar trees along Stevens Way, and the reconstruction of Drumheller Fountain. *(University of Washington Libraries, Special Collections Division; ca. 1939; UW6061.)*

7. Ambrose Patterson Garden, Seattle, 1936-37, Butler S. Sturtevant. Ambrose and Viola Patterson, professors of art at the University of Washington and members of the Northwest Group of Seven, wanted a new Modern garden to match their new Modern house by architect John Sproule. *(Photo by Duane A. Dietz, 1993.)*

Garden in Seattle (1931-32) established his reputation as a residential landscape designer. His design for the Ambrose Patterson Garden in Seattle (1936-37) was shown at the San Francisco Museum of Art's exhibition entitled "Contemporary Landscape Architecture and Its Sources" as Seattle's first modern garden. He collaborated with J. Lister Holmes (see essay) on the Arnold Dessau house in The Highlands (1937-39), to "bring the outdoors inside." Across the road, another project, the Paul Piggott residence (1943-45; formerly Norcliffe), includes a cliffside pool; this feature is unique in the Northwest, and may have influenced Sturtevant's friend, landscape architect Thomas Church, in his design of

8. Arnold Dessau house, The Highlands, Washington, 1937-39 (altered), J. Lister Holmes, architect; Butler S. Sturtevant, landscape architect. The lanai feature is an innovation used by Sturtevant to "bring the landscape indoors." *(University of Washington Libraries, Manuscripts and University Archives Division; J. Lister Holmes Papers, Acc. 3789.)*

the Dewey Donnell Garden in Sonoma, California.

When Sturtevant joined the Army Air Corps in 1941, he formed a partnership with Edwin Grohs to maintain his practice. This partnership allowed Sturtevant to work on housing projects such as Yesler Terrace (1940-43) and Holly Park (1942-43) in Seattle, and on Westpark (1940-42), Eastpark (1942-44), and Bremerton Gardens (1943-44) in Bremerton while he was also involved in laying out airfields throughout the southern United States.

At the end of the war, Sturtevant opened a San Francisco office specializing in airport design (Western Engineers, 1945-46; Sturtevant & French, 1946-47), but only one of these commissions has been identified: the

Portland Airport in Portland, Oregon (1945-48). He also began to do larger land planning work, executing master plans for the Pope Estate in Burlingame, California (1946-47), and the Village of Hana, Island of Maui, Hawaii (1947-49).

Thereafter, Sturtevant moved back to his native Midwest, settling in St. Louis to work on the design of the Principia School campus (1948-69) for grades K-12. He also executed the American University Campus Master Plan, Beirut, Lebanon (1961-62), and work for John Brown University, Siloam Springs, Arkansas (1962-63), and the Mason Woods Development, St. Louis, Missouri (1966-69). His untimely death in St. Louis in February 1970 brought an abrupt end to a varied and wide-ranging career.

9. Piggott pool and garden terrace, The Highlands, 1943-45, Butler S. Sturtevant. Sturtevant used flat terraces and a borrowed landscape—Puget Sound—to create a space that is both intimate and expansive. This commission was a major extension of the existing landscape, which had been designed by the Olmsted Brothers. *(Photo by David Streatfield, 1978.)*

Kichio Allen Arai

DAVID A. RASH

Architecture has often been claimed to be an "old man's" profession, since it often takes years for an architect to establish a practice and to derive a comfortable income from it. While architecture may not always be amenable to young practitioners, in this country it has been even less amenable to ethnic minorities. Some of the best early African American designers, for example, found success only by designing churches for black congregations or by working for established practitioners. Members of other ethnic minorities have often fared little better. Locally, the first Asian American to graduate from the architecture program at the University

Kichio Allen ("A. K.") Arai; date unknown.
(Gerald Y. Arai Collection.)

1. Nichiren Buddhist Church, Seattle, 1928-29, A. K. Arai. The central sanctuary of this modest first work was designed prior to Arai's departure to pursue graduate work at Harvard University. The east addition (1933-35) was also by Arai, while the west addition (1956-57) was by T. Gregory Saito. *(Photo by David A. Rash, 1993.)*

Kichio Allen Arai (1901-66), the first native Asian American in Seattle to design buildings under his own name, is not surprisingly almost unknown locally.

Arai was born at Port Blakely, Washington, August 30, 1901, to first-generation Japanese American parents. By 1909, the Arai family had moved to Seattle. After graduation from Broadway High School, Arai entered the University of Washington in the fall of 1919. During this time, the teaching of the architecture faculty was modeled on the methods of the École des Beaux-Arts, which included numerous student design competitions during the academic year. Although he never won any of the major prizes, Arai often received favorable mentions locally and nationally under the auspices of the Beaux-Arts Society of Architects of New York City. He began signing his drawings "K. Allen Arai" as a sophomore, switching to "A. K. Arai" in his junior year and for the remainder of his professional career.

After graduation in 1925 with a B.A. degree in architecture, Arai obtained a position with Schack, Young & Myers, one of Seattle's leading architectural firms during

2. Nichiren Buddhist Church garage, Seattle, 1933, A. K. Arai. At a mere $50 building permit valuation, this simple garage building was undoubtedly Arai's least expensive built structure; however, during the Depression, any tangible work was good news. *(Photo by David A. Rash, 1993.)*

of Washington, Wing Sam Chinn, initially worked for Andrew Willatsen (1922-26) and later for Thomas, Grainger & Thomas (1928-34), where Donald P. Thomas, a near classmate of Chinn's and a son of Harlan Thomas, had become a principal of the firm.

3. Yakima Buddhist Bussei Kaikan, Wapato, 1936-41, 1950-65, A. K. Arai. Construction of this Art Moderne style gymnasium was accomplished by the congregation over a number of years during the fall and winter, beginning in 1939. Although the building was usable by 1941, final completion was interrupted by the internment of member Japanese Americans during World War II. *(Yakima Buddhist Church, 1974.)*

4. Seattle Buddhist Church, Seattle, 1940-41, Pierce A. Horrocks, architect; A. K. Arai, associate. Arai's lack of an architectural license necessitated the involvement of Horrocks as "architect of record" in the design of this striking church complex which combines traditional Japanese architecture with contemporary American construction techniques. *(University of Washington Libraries, Special Collections Division; photo by C. F. Todd, ca. 1941; 24988.)*

the 1920s (see essay). David J. Myers had been associated with the University's architecture program from 1917 to 1920, and his firm had designed the Japanese Baptist Church (1922-23), two factors which may have favored Arai's employment there. When Arai left Seattle to pursue graduate studies at Harvard University, he was better known for his abilities as the left-handed center-fielder "Anki" for the Nippon Athletic Club than for his design ability. Nonetheless, he did design his first independent building, the Nichiren Buddhist Church, Seattle (1928-29), prior to departing.

5. Idaho-Oregon Buddhist Temple, Ontario, Oregon, 1955-58, A. K. Arai. Although the groundbreaking ceremony occurred on January 13, 1952, Arai was not retained as architect until 1955. Construction proceeded as with the Yakima Buddhist Bussei Kaikan, beginning in 1955 and finishing in February 1958. *(Photo by David A. Rash, 1993.)*

6. White River Buddhist Temple, Auburn, 1963-64, Richard O. Parker, architect; A. K. Arai, associate. The penchant of practitioners of Modern architecture for rationalized, expressed structure is well exemplified in the wall construction of this building, while the structure of the roof over the sanctuary maintains the flavor of traditional Japanese architecture. *(Photo by David A. Rash, 1993.)*

Unfortunately, his return to Seattle with his M.Arch. degree coincided with the onset of the Depression. During the 1930s, Arai worked as a draftsman whenever such work was available and, until the age of thirty-one, continued to play semiprofessional baseball. Independently, he designed the Yakima Buddhist Bussei Kaikan (1936-41) at Wapato as well as some lesser buildings and renovations.

In 1940, the property of the first Seattle Buddhist Church (see Saunders essay) was condemned as part of the site for the Yesler Terrace housing project. Arai received the commission to design the replacement building, and construction began in late 1940 with the building being sufficiently complete for dedication on October 5, 1941. Barely two months after the dedication, Japan attacked Pearl Harbor. The hysteria that followed this attack resulted in the forced relocation of Japanese Americans from the West Coast. The local Japanese American community never fully recovered from this devastating relocation, nor did Arai's architectural career.

After World War II, the Arai family returned to Seattle, arriving in February 1947.

Arai found work with local firms, notably Naramore, Bain, Brady & Johanson and Durham, Anderson & Freed. His departure from the latter firm apparently coincided with his last two architectural commissions, which were designed under the firm name of Richard O. Parker and A. K. Arai Associate. This was not an attempt to establish his own practice, as Arai also worked full-time for the Olympian Stone Company and finally for Fentron Industries until his death October 13, 1966.

With only a handful of executed buildings spread out over some thirty-five years, Arai's independent career cannot be easily assessed. It is ironic that despite Arai's obscurity, a selected portion of his work has been more widely disseminated than that of possibly any other Seattle architect. In the late 1980s, a number of Arai's student drawings were reproduced as art prints by a friend of Arai's son, Gerald Y. Arai, a Seattle architect. Some 20,000 were printed and sold. These drawings as well as his several Buddhist structures well illustrate a talent that was underutilized and largely unrecognized.

7. Shinran Shonin 700th Anniversary Memorial Hall addition to the Seattle Buddhist Church, Seattle, 1963-64, Richard O. Parker, architect; A. K. Arai, associate. Nine years after the elevation of the Seattle Buddhist Church to the status of "Betsuin," the church complex was enlarged by a wing containing classrooms, chapel, and nokotsudo (columbarium). *(Photo by David A. Rash, 1993.)*

8. Shinran Shonin 700th Anniversary Memorial Hall addition to the Seattle Buddhist Church, Seattle, 1963-64, Richard O. Parker, architect; A. K. Arai, associate. Fittingly, this updated reinterpretation of his adjacent masterpiece church was Arai's final executed work. *(Photo by David A. Rash, 1993.)*

9. "A Romanesque Cloister" (student project), December 8, 1928, A. K. Arai. Arai rendered this exquisite solution of an *analytique* problem while a graduate student at Harvard University. It was one of a group of his student drawings reproduced in the 1980s as art prints. *(Private collection.)*

Paul Thiry

MEREDITH L. CLAUSEN

Paul Albert Thiry (1904-93) is known locally for introducing the architecture of the European Modernists to the Pacific Northwest in the mid-1930s, for his work on the Seattle Planning Commission in the late 1950s, and for his role as principal architect of the Seattle World's Fair in 1962. His international reputation, however, rests mainly on his modern houses and churches, designed in a regional variant of Modernism, and on his contribution to the planning and preservation of the United States Capitol, as a member of the National Capital Planning Commission and the President's Council on Pennsylvania Avenue from 1963 to 1975.

Paul Thiry. *(Paul Thiry Collection.)*

1. Lakecrest Apartment Court (now south half of Lake Court Apartments), Seattle, 1928-29, Taylor & Thiry. During at least part of the time while this project was in design and construction, James M. Taylor, Jr., was working as a draftsman for John Graham and Thiry was employed as a draftsman with Butler Sturtevant. This design, which presents a picturesque composition with motifs and details from French provincial sources, exemplifies Thiry's use of historical references in his early work. *(Photo by T. William Booth, 1993.)*

2. Paul Thiry house, Seattle, 1935-36, Paul Thiry. This project, Thiry's initial design in Seattle reflecting the influence of the Modern Movement, was considered extraordinarily radical when it was completed in 1936. *(Paul Thiry Collection; photo by Larry Novack, ca. 1940.)*

Thiry was born September 11, 1904, in Nome, Alaska, of French parents, and was educated at Saint Martin's, a Benedictine school near Olympia, Washington. After an abortive beginning in pre-med, he switched to architecture, receiving his degree from the University of Washington in 1928, at a time when the school was still fully immersed in the Beaux-Arts tradition. As part of his training, he spent a year abroad at the American School in Fontainebleau. After working briefly with Butler Sturtevant (see essay), he opened his own office in 1929, always working alone or, at most, with one or two people.

Thiry's early work consisted of apartment buildings and small private residences, mostly using conventional Norman or Colonial forms. In 1934, as work slackened during the Depression, Thiry again went abroad, taking a year-long trip around the world visiting Japan, China, India, Egypt, Europe, and Central America. While abroad, he met both Antonin Raymond, in Tokyo, and Le Corbusier, in Paris, encounters which greatly broadened his horizons. Upon his return to Seattle in 1935, he designed his own house in the then still radi-

cally new style of the European Modernists. However, his clients, were, for the most part, unprepared for his rigorously stark, cubical, white stuccoed forms and flush unornamented surfaces, and in much of his subsequent domestic work, done in partnership with Alban Shay under the name of Thiry & Shay (1935-39), he yielded to the demand for a softer, more regional variant, with gently sloped roofs and natural wood siding and trim.

During World War II, Thiry, in partnership with others (Jones, Thiry & Ahlson, in 1942; Jones, Bouillon, Thiry & Sylliaasen, from 1943 to 1944), was involved in several large-scale housing and military projects, including 6,000 dwellings and community facilities in Port Orchard (1940-44) and a Naval Advance Base Depot in Tacoma (1943-44). After the war, his practice flourished, with work ranging broadly from churches and houses to educational facilities, museums, libraries, and commercial buildings. He became active in city and regional planning as a member of the Seattle Planning Commission from 1952 until 1961, when he resigned in protest over plans for a new freeway. He was a member of the

3. Our Lady of the Lake Church, Seattle, 1940-41 (destroyed), Paul Thiry. While the gable roof forms and brick materials were traditional, the asymmetrical composition of simple volumes with almost no decorative detail represented Thiry's balancing of tradition and modernity in this religious structure. *(Paul Thiry Collection.)*

executive committee of the Puget Sound Regional Planning Council between 1954 and 1957, and an advisory member of the Washington State Joint Committee on urban area government.

Thiry began publishing articles on architecture in the 1950s. He also wrote *Churches and Temples* with R. Bennett and H. Kamphoefner (New York: Reinhold, 1953), a major work on modern religious architecture.

In 1957, Thiry was appointed principal architect of Century 21 (the Seattle World's Fair), a task that included site planning and the coordination of the work of the participating architects, as well as the design of the Coliseum (1958-62), a number of international exhibition buildings, and several temporary structures. During this time he also designed the U.S. Embassy residence in Santiago, Chile (1958-61).

4. Museum of History and Industry, Seattle, 1948-50 (altered), Paul Thiry. This museum brought Thiry's approach to Modernism to an institutional program. Unfortunately, the construction of State Highway 520 forced a radical reconfiguration that severely compromised Thiry's initial design. The building has also been enlarged several times. *(Paul Thiry Collection.)*

5. Washington State Library, Olympia, 1954-59, Paul Thiry. This building draws upon the classical precedent of the Capitol Group in its colonnaded form, but remains fully Modern in detail. *(Paul Thiry Collection.)*

As chair of the AIA Committee on the National Capitol Building in Washington, D.C., in 1963, Thiry was appointed to serve on the National Capital Planning Commission, an advisory committee set up to prepare and implement comprehensive plans for the nation's capital. It was in this capacity that Thiry, known for his strong opinions, became embroiled in the controversy over whether to extend or preserve the West Front of the Capitol Building, opposing the national AIA, which favored restoration.

Thiry is also known for his participation as architectural consultant for the Army Corps of Engineers' Libby Dam project in northwestern Montana. His work there be-

6. "Week-end Shelter," Kittitas Valley, Washington, 1956, Paul Thiry. Two gable roof forms above two simple platforms are the basic elements of Thiry's central Washington vacation cabin. Although this project was published, its exact location was never revealed. *(Photo by Art Hupy, 1956)*

7.   Seattle Center Coliseum, Seattle, 1958-62 (to be altered), Paul Thiry. This arena shows Thiry's continuing interest in dramatic concrete structures. The roof is suspended from the framework of concrete beams. The Coliseum has served as one of Seattle's primary indoor sports facilities since 1962, but was targeted for interior expansion (by lowering the floor) in the early 1990s. (*University of Washington Libraries, Special Collections Division; ca. 1962; UW14828.*)

8.   Mercer Island Presbyterian Church, Mercer Island, 1960-61, Paul Thiry. Thiry's experimentation with concrete structural technology is reflected in the extraordinary folded plate roof which seems to float above the sanctuary space of this church. (*Paul Thiry Collection; photo by Hugh Stratford.*)

9. Saint Demetrios Greek Orthodox Church, Seattle, 1964-68, Paul Thiry. Thiry's design mixes traditional and modern approaches in this unusual application of concrete vaulting techniques. *(Paul Thiry Collection.)*

gan in 1962, when he was commissioned to create a master plan as well as guidelines for the design of the dam, powerhouse, visitors' center, and associated structures. He saw the challenge as twofold: to accommodate visitors in an appealing yet safe and comfortable way, and to reconcile the conflicting demands of a large-scale engineered structure with the fragile beauty of the natural terrain.

Thiry remained interested in the development of building technology throughout his career, and he experimented with prefabrication, the use of plywood paneling, and precast and prestressed concrete, especially in the early years of his practice. As an architect, he advocated strong individual initiative and opposed the team approach, believing it too often resulted in "nobody pulling a full load." He pushed for quality, and regretted the tendency to measure the success of architects on the basis of their volume of business or size of operation.

Recipient of numerous awards, Thiry became an AIA Fellow in 1951, Chancellor of the College of Fellows for 1962-64, and in 1965 was granted a national AIA citation for his work in community design. Thiry remained active until the late 1980s, when failing health curtailed his ability to practice. He died of congestive heart failure at his home in Seattle on June 27, 1993.

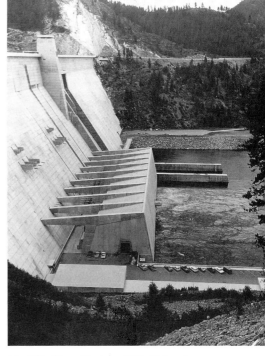

10. Libby Dam, Montana, 1962-84 (continung involvement), Paul Thiry, consultant to the Army Corps of Engineers. Thiry was responsible for the master plan of the complex and he established design guidelines for the powerhouse, visitors' center, and other associated facilities. The massive concrete forms and abstract composition are in the tradition established by American dams built in the 1930s. *(Paul Thiry Collection.)*

Paul Hayden Kirk

DAVID A. RASH

One legacy of the nineteenth century has been the perception that the Pacific Northwest is physically and culturally isolated from the rest of the country. This view has often been used to rationalize the relative dearth of nationally published work by local practitioners compared with other regions. While there may be some truth to this argument, the work of at least one local practitioner has been an exception. With his inclusion in some sixty articles in national architectural journals between 1945 and 1970, Paul Hayden Kirk (b. 1914) is possibly the most widely published of Seattle's architects.

Kirk was born in Salt Lake City, Utah, on November 18, 1914, and came with his family to Seattle in 1922. His architectural education was obtained at the University of Washington, where he received his degree in architecture in 1937. Prior to starting his own practice in 1939, he worked for Floyd A. Naramore, A. M. Young, and B. Dudley Stuart as a draftsman and for Henry Bittman as a designer (see essays on Naramore; Bittman; and Schack, Young & Myers).

Paul Hayden Kirk. *(University of Washington Libraries, Special Collections Division; 1962; Dearborn-Massar Collection, DM-2695.)*

Initially, Kirk's practice was essentially residential in scope and was characterized by a competent command of historicist forms and details. However, the seeds for the

1. Columbia Ridge tract house, Seattle, 1941-42, Paul Hayden Kirk. This was one of some two hundred houses designed for four independent construction firms working at this private development on Beacon Hill. *(Photo by David A. Rash, 1993.)*

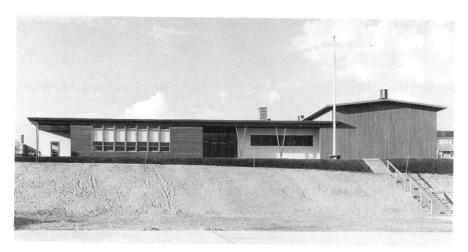

2. High Point School, Seattle, 1943 (destroyed), Stuart, Kirk & Durham, Associated Architects. This was Kirk's earliest institutional project and was the first of many to appear in the national architectural press. (*University of Washington Libraries, Special Collections Division; photo by P. A. Dearborn, 1943; Dearborn-Massar Collection, DM-2300.*)

elimination of historicism from his work can be found in the speculatively built Columbia Ridge housing development (1941-42), where economics dictated a simplification of form and detailing. His professed admiration of Pietro Belluschi, who designed the Harry W. Myers residence (1940-41) locally under the firm name A. E. Doyle & Associates of Portland, Oregon, may have further encouraged Kirk to turn toward a more Modern approach.

During World War II, Kirk practiced as part of Stuart, Kirk & Durham, Associated Architects, and for five years afterward as a principal in Chiarelli & Kirk. Notable projects from the partnership with James J. Chiarelli included the Crown Hill Medical-Dental Clinic (now 1422 Clinic) (1946-47), the William W. Corley residence (1947-48; destroyed?), and the Lakewood Community Church (1949).

From 1950 to 1957, Kirk was a sole practitioner. Although he would later dismiss the International Style as "an architecture which has been imposed on the land by Man," many of his best buildings from the early 1950s appear to have relied heavily on the tenets and forms developed by Ludwig Mies

van der Rohe. This is particularly evident with the Blair Kirk house (1951; altered) and the Lake City Clinic (1951-52; now Wu Building); however, where Mies preferred brick, steel, and glass for his structures, Kirk tended toward rough-cut stone, wood, and glass—materials allowing for a "Northwest" derivative of Mies's work.

In the ensuing years, the formal vocabulary of the International Style was increasingly abandoned, although Kirk continued to adhere to Mies's dictum that "God is in the details." As Kirk's work began to include religious and public buildings, intricate detailing, often in wood, became the hallmark of his most notable commissions, including the University Unitarian Church (1955-59), the Frank Gilbert residence at The Highlands (1956-57), and the McNair-Price Clinic in Medford, Oregon (1957-58; with Jack A. Edson of Medford superintending). Also, the influence of traditional Japanese architecture was discernible in his early use of shoji screens as interior partitions as well as in more overt formal responses on the exterior, as at the Japanese Presbyterian Church (1962-63) or the Blair Kirk residence on Mercer Island (1968-69).

3. C & K (now Lakeview Boulevard) Apartments, Seattle, 1949, Chiarelli & Kirk. This apartment building was developed by the architects and was one of their larger projects. *(University of Washington Libraries, Special Collections Division; 1952; Dearborn-Massar Collection, DM-1016.)*

4. Blair Kirk house, Seattle, 1951 (altered), Paul Hayden Kirk. This precisely detailed house translates the International Style into a Pacific Northwest wood idiom. It was built on a speculative basis by Paul Kirk's older brother. *(University of Washington Libraries, Special Collections Division; 1951; Dearborn-Massar Collection; DM-2363.)*

5. University Unitarian Church, Seattle, 1955-59, Paul Hayden Kirk. The intricately detailed glass screen and the exposed wood structure supporting it enliven the austere exterior in conjunction with the landscaping designed by William G. Teufel. (*University of Washington Libraries, Special Collections Division; 1960; Dearborn-Massar Collection, DM-2599.*)

6. Group Health Cooperative Northgate Clinic, Seattle, 1957-58 (destroyed), Paul Hayden Kirk & Associates. Ironically, this now demolished building was used to illustrate Kirk's work in the *Journal of the AIA* when he was elected a Fellow of the AIA in 1959. Landscaping was designed by William G. Teufel. (*University of Washington Libraries, Special Collections Division; 1958; Dearborn-Massar Collection, DM-2330.*)

As the scope of some of Kirk's work became more complex, the structure of his firm also changed. By 1957, the firm was known as Paul Hayden Kirk & Associates. By 1960, it became Kirk, Wallace, McKinley & Associates with the elevation of Donald S. Wallace and David A. McKinley, Jr., to full partnership. Projects like the Exhibition Hall, the Resident Theater (now Intiman Theater), and the parking garage at today's Seattle Center (all 1959-62), Jefferson Terrace (1963-67), the French Administration Building (1965-67) at Washington State University, and the Physio-Control headquarters (1973-74) in Redmond became more typical, although houses never disappeared completely from the firm's work prior to Kirk's official retirement in 1979.

7. Japanese Presbyterian Church, Seattle, 1962-63, Kirk, Wallace, McKinley & Associates. When this building was given a national AIA Merit Award in 1965, the jury commented, in part: "The church has a modest, serene quality." *(Photo by David A. Rash, 1993.)*

8. Magnolia Branch Library, Seattle, 1962-64, Kirk, Wallace, McKinley & Associates. This well-detailed post-and-beam structure is perhaps the quintessential "Kirk" building and is well complemented by the landscaping designed by Richard Haag & Associates. *(Seattle Public Libraries, 1968.)*

9. C. Clement French Administration Building, Washington State University, Pullman, 1965-67, Kirk, Wallace, McKinley & Associates. Although often referred to as "Fort French" by the students, the brick and precast-concrete exterior is perhaps the most intricately detailed of the firm's masonry-clad buildings. *(Photo by David A. Rash, 1992.)*

Ideally, at least fifty years should elapse before one attempts to assess objectively an architectural career. While it has been only some fifteen years since Kirk officially retired from active practice, and although some of his buildings still need to pass the test of time, many, such as the Blair Kirk house, the University Unitarian Church, and the Japanese Presbyterian Church, are as much admired today as when they were initially completed and they clearly indicate why Kirk was elected a Fellow of the American Institute of Architects in 1959. They also confirm *Architectural Forum*'s characterization of his work in August 1962: "clarity, suitability, and restraint."

10. Edmond S. Meany Hall for the Performing Arts, University of Washington, Seattle, 1966-74 (altered), Kirk, Wallace, McKinley & Associates. At a cost of $7.1 million, Meany Hall was the most expensive and complex building designed by Kirk's firm to that time. The adjacent undergraduate library and parking garage (1966-71) are also by Kirk's firm. *(University of Washington Libraries, Special Collections Division; ca. 1975; UW4846.)*

John Graham, Jr.

MEREDITH L. CLAUSEN

John Graham, Jr. (1908-91), son of architect John Graham, Sr. (see essay), and a Seattle native, gained an international reputation in the early 1950s as a pioneer in the design of the large-scale regional shopping center. Since then, his firm has gone on to design scores of similar large-scale suburban shopping centers, medical facilities, high-rise office buildings, hotels, schools, and churches, throughout the United States including Hawaii and Alaska, as well as Canada, England, Southeast Asia, and Australia.

Born in Seattle May 8, 1908, Graham attended the Moran School and then Queen Anne High School, graduating in 1925. He began his architectural training at the University of Washington in 1926, but transferred to Yale and finished in 1931 with a degree in fine arts. Facing a depressed economy, Graham eschewed architecture for a job in retailing, and worked as a trainee in statistical merchandising. This experience

John Graham, Jr. *(John Graham Associates Collection.)*

established his direction as an architect, more that of a businessman than artist.

In 1937, as the economy improved, Graham returned to Seattle, joined his father's architectural firm, and then shortly thereafter opened a branch office in New York City in partnership with the engineer William

1. Edgewater Apartments, Seattle, 1939-40, John Graham, Jr. These two-story apartment buildings of traditional character front on the adjacent streets and enclose a series of courtyards. The courtyards nearest Lake Washington open to the water. *(John Graham Associates Collection; photo ca. 1950.)*

2. Northgate Shopping Center, Seattle, 1946-50 (later enclosed), John Graham & Company. This cluster of stores, surrounded by ample parking and accessible from nearby highways, proved a paradigm for the development of the regional shopping center in post–World War II America. It also established John Graham & Company as national leaders in shopping center design. *(John Graham Associates Collection; ca. 1950.)*

3. Ala Moana Center, Honolulu, Hawaii, opened 1960 (altered), John Graham & Company. The firm's success in adapting Graham's concepts for shopping center design to multiple locations is well represented by this example from Hawaii. This building has since been expanded. *(John Graham Associates Collection; ca. 1960.)*

Painter, with quarters in the newly opened Rockefeller Center. From there, he oversaw the firm's work chiefly in department store design. With the outbreak of World War II, the New York office was closed and Graham turned to the design of war housing on his own, developing several large, FHA-financed housing projects on the East Coast. Among these was the Suburban Heights development in Washington, D.C.

In 1946, upon his father's retirement, Graham returned to Seattle, took over the Graham firm, John Graham & Company, and began the design of the Northgate Shopping Center (1946-50). The timing was perfect. As the postwar economy boomed and suburbanization of the Seattle area accelerated, Graham, with his background in retailing and experience in large-scale planning and private development, sensed an opportunity. He met with Rex Allison, president of the Bon Marché department store, and together they developed the Northgate concept. The shopping center opened in

4. Space Needle, Seattle, 1960-62, John Graham & Company with Victor Steinbrueck. The idea of the revolving restaurant had previously been proposed by Graham and was most likely his idea. Steinbrueck and others contributed to the resolution of the structural design and formal characteristics of this icon for the Seattle World's Fair. *(John Graham Associates Collection; ca. 1962.)*

1950, the first of its kind in the country.

An immediate, overwhelming financial success, the Northgate Shopping Center established Graham as a leader in the field. His firm went on to design over seventy large-scale, multimillion dollar regional shopping centers throughout the country and Canada. Among them are Gulfgate, Houston (opened 1962); Capitol Court, Milwaukee (opened 1957); NorthShore, Peabody, Massachusetts (opened 1958); Ala Moana, Honolulu (opened 1960); Lloyd Center, Portland (opened l960); Wellington Square, London, Ontario (opened 1960); Montgomery Mall, Bethesda, Maryland (opened 1968); and Clackamas Town Center, Portland (opened 1981). Graham's firm often maintained a continuing involvement in these centers, designing modifications for many of them in the years after they opened.

Known as an architect with an unflinching eye on the "bottom line," Graham was favored by developers and corporate and institutional clients. Among his buildings are the Edgewater Apartments (1939-40), Seattle Mason Clinic (1954), the Headquarters of Washington Natural Gas (1962-64), the Olympic Hotel parking garage (1963-65), and the 42-story Bank of California Building (1971-74), all in Seattle, as well as the Veterans Administration Hospital, Spokane (1946-1948), and the 44-story Wells Fargo Building, San Francisco (1960-66; now the 44 Montgomery Building).

One of the firm's most celebrated works is the 600-foot Space Needle for the Seattle World's Fair (1960-62), design of which has been claimed by both Victor Steinbrueck (see essay) and Graham. It appears likely that Graham, in whose office the work was done and who had previously designed a high-rise office building with a revolving restaurant in Honolulu (evidently a new concept for which Graham held U.S. patent, #3125189, granted March 17, 1964), came up with the basic concept, which was then developed formally by Steinbrueck and others on the design team.

5. Wells Fargo Building (now 44 Montgomery Street Building), San Francisco, California, 1960-66, John Graham & Company. Graham's move into high-rise office building design is exemplified by this early office structure in San Francisco. (*John Graham Associates Collection; ca. 1966.*)

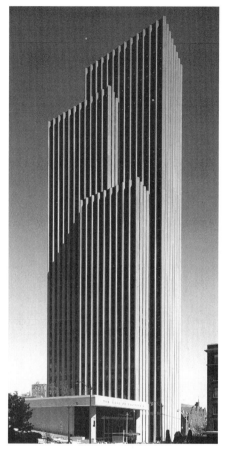

6. Bank of California Building, Seattle, 1971-74, John Graham & Company. Graham's design for this office building draws on the formal precedent set by Eero Saarinen's CBS Building in New York City. (*John Graham Associates Collection; ca. 1975.*)

In 1974, Graham entered into partnership with Roderick Kirkwood. Sometimes functioning as developer as well as architect, Graham built up a large, diverse, but tightly organized staff of architects, planners, engineers, and technical consultants. The firm specialized in large-scale, fast-track jobs known in general for their practicality rather than architectural distinction. Among their over 1,000 projects are the 1600 Bell Plaza (1976; now U.S. West), the Westin Hotel and Towers (1979-82), and the Sheraton Hotel and Towers (1978-82), all in Seattle; and the Alaska State Office Building,

Juneau, Alaska (1972-75; joint venture with Linn Forrest); the Naval Regional Medical Center, Bremerton (1978-81; joint venture with Sherlock, Smith & Adams); and the Madigan Army Medical Center, Tacoma (1984-86).

One of Graham's last projects before he retired in 1986 was the Stimson Center, a proposed $150 million, 45-story multi-use retail and office building, of which Graham and the Stimson family were to have been co-owners and developers, on the block bounded by Fifth and Sixth avenues and Pike and Pine streets in downtown Seattle. It remained unrealized. Graham died in Seattle on January 29, 1991.

Over the course of his career, Graham's practice grew to encompass a wide variety of large-scale building types, but he remains most recognized for his design solution for the regional shopping center. It was his Northgate Shopping Center in Seattle that became the model for many similar regional centers.

7. Alaska State Office Building, Juneau, Alaska, 1972-75, John Graham & Company with Linn Forrest. The irregular form of this building results from the stacking of concrete trays formally integrating the parking floors below with the office floors above. *(John Graham Associates Collection; 1977.)*

8. Bellevue Athletic Club, Bellevue, completed 1979, John Graham & Company. This complex building houses a variety of athletic facilities. The form is composed of an irregular series of interconnecting white stucco boxes. *(John Graham Associates Collection; 1980.)*

9. Naval Regional Medical Center, Bremerton, 1978-81, John Graham & Company. The breadth of the John Graham firm's practice by the late 1970s is represented by this medical facility in Bremerton. *(John Graham Associates Collection.)*

10. Sheraton Hotel and Towers, Seattle, 1978-82, John Graham & Company. The form of this building results from the juxtaposition of the triangular residential tower rising from a horizontal base including lobby, restaurants, meeting rooms, and ancillary facilities. *(John Graham Associates Collection; 1982.)*

Benjamin F. McAdoo, Jr.

ESTHER HALL MUMFORD

Benjamin F. McAdoo, Jr., 1981. (*Thelma McAdoo Collection.*)

Benjamin Franklin McAdoo, Jr. (1920-81), was the first African American architect to operate a long-term practice in the state of Washington. During his career he was responsible for over four hundred designs encompassing a range of building types from single and multifamily residential projects to larger commercial and institutional structures.

McAdoo was born October 29, 1920, in Pasadena, California, to Benjamin F. McAdoo, Sr., and Alfaretta DeRoussel McAdoo. After a two-year course at Pasadena City College, he spent one year at the University of Southern California. He transferred to the University of Washington in 1944. Throughout his studies McAdoo worked nights and attended daytime classes, graduating with a B.Arch. from the University of Washington in 1946.

His career falls neatly into two parts. In the period before 1962 his work was primarily renovations, residences, and small churches. In the later 1960s and 1970s, after an absence from the city, he received many larger commissions from public and commercial institutions.

1. Herbert Rivkin residence, Mercer Island, Washington, 1954-55, Benjamin F. McAdoo, Jr. The simple forms, shallow sloping roof, exposed wood frame structure, and large expanses of glass in this house show McAdoo's adaptation of elements of the developing Northwest regional approach to Modern architecture. (*Photo by Art Hupy, 1955.*)

2. Donald Hochberg residence, Mercer Island, 1953-54, Benjamin F. McAdoo, Jr. McAdoo's continuing development of regional themes, including strong horizontal lines, natural materials, and large expanses of glass, marked his first Home of the Month award-winning design. *(Thelma McAdoo Collection; photo by Elizabeth Green, 1954.)*

3. George H. Hage residence, Seattle, 1955-56, Benjamin F. McAdoo, Jr. Sited at the brow of a hill, this home turns a relatively opaque face to the street, but opens through a glass wall to the views beyond. This house, selected as the best *Seattle Times*/AIA Home of the Month for 1956, brought McAdoo wide recognition. *(Photo by Art Hupy, 1956.)*

4. Benjamin F. McAdoo, Jr., residence, Bothell, 1957-58, Benjamin F. McAdoo, Jr. This house for his own family is probably the best expression of McAdoo's personal interpretation of Modernism in the setting of the Northwest. *(Thelma McAdoo Collection; photo by Vern and Elizabeth Green, 1961.)*

5. Concrete modular house, Jamaica, 1961-1962, Benjamin F. McAdoo, Jr., AID, Jamaica. Unlike an earlier AID prototype concrete block house, this design by McAdoo, adopted by the Jamaican government, could be assembled by unskilled workers. Here McAdoo stands in the middle of a partly erected house. (*Thelma McAdoo Collection.*)

McAdoo began his private practice in 1947 at a time when Modern architecture was emerging and building materials released from wartime industry were feeding a house-building boom in Seattle. That year he received his first commission for a complete house design, the John P. Browning residence (1947).

In the 1950s, McAdoo became known for his innovative Modern residential designs. His projects, with their horizontal lines, revealed structure, large areas of glass, site integration, and use of wood, reflected his personal combination of Modernist and regionalist sensibilities. With the publication of the William Moorhouse residence (1948-49) in the *Seattle Times* in July 1949, his residential work began to receive attention in the press and by the mid-1950s his commissions were being regularly published and frequently were receiving recognition through the *Seattle Times*/AIA Home of the Month program beginning with the Donald Hochberg residence, Mercer Island (1953-54), the first year the awards were given.

This was followed by the Kenneth Ota residence (1955-56) and the George H. Hage residence (1955-56). Perhaps the best example of McAdoo's approach was his own house, located between Kenmore and Bothell (1957-58), which was extensively covered by the *Seattle Times*.

McAdoo participated in several community activities. He broadcast a weekly radio commentary on social issues in the mid-1960s and served for four years as president of the local chapter of the National Association for the Advancement of Colored People (NAACP). His activity in the state Democratic Party, including an unsuccessful run for the legislature, led to his appointment as administrator of a housing program in Jamaica for the U.S. Agency for International Development (AID) in 1961. While in Jamaica, he administered construction of a concrete block house prototype used by the agency, and he also designed a concrete block modular house which untrained workers could assemble. The success of McAdoo's version led to its adoption by the Jamaican government, which established plants to manufacture the modular units on the island.

McAdoo returned to the United States in 1963 and worked in Washington, D.C., where he helped to set up the Latin American Division of the AID before transferring to the General Services Administration's Public Building Service. While at the latter agency he was a coordinating architect, with Edward Stone, for the John F. Kennedy Center for the Performing Arts, and for the National Fisheries Center and Aquarium.

Opportunities for African Americans, lacking prior to 1961, were expanding when McAdoo returned to the Seattle area in 1964. He worked in the Auburn office of the Public Building Service, where his responsibilities included supervision of the design and construction of federal buildings in the Northwest. At the same time, he maintained an office in Seattle, eventually resuming full time private practice in the late 1960s.

6. King County Central Blood Bank, Southcenter Branch, Tukwila, 1967-70, Benjamin McAdoo & Company. This building is based on a system of pre-cast concrete exterior wall panels that provide sun control and allow flexibility in the interior. *(Thelma McAdoo Collection; photo by Photographic Illustrators, 1155, ca. 1972.)*

7. Fire Station No. 29 (West Seattle), Seattle, 1969-72, Benjamin McAdoo & Company. The strong horizontal lines of the roofs unify this composition of rectangular volumes clad in brick. *(Thelma McAdoo Collection; photo by Photographic Illustrators, 1257, ca. 1972.)*

8. Ethnic Cultural Center, University of Washington, Seattle, 1970-72, Benjamin McAdoo & Company. This building features asymmetrical wood-clad forms with clerestories that bring light into the interior. (*Thelma McAdoo Collection; photo by Photographic Illustrators, 1304, ca. 1972.*)

While McAdoo received few high-profile commissions, his reputation for sound work brought him a number of larger projects such as the King County Central Blood Bank, Southcenter Branch (1967-70). During the last ten years of his life, his firm engaged primarily in institutional work as exemplified by the renovation of several buildings at the University of Washington (such as Smith Hall, 1974-78), design of the UW Ethnic Cultural Center (1970-72), and Forward Thrust projects such as Fire Station No. 29 (West Seattle, 1969-72) and the Queen Anne Pool (1974-78).

After 1951, McAdoo's office was located in a remodeled house at Olive Way and Boylston Street on Capitol Hill. Over the years, he altered and enlarged this building, creating a mixed-use complex with retail and residential spaces as well as his office. Early in 1981 he completed an upper floor addition, which was to be a residence for his wife and himself; however, he was able to enjoy living there only a short time for he died June 18, 1981.

During his career McAdoo employed a number of young architects; two of them, Garold Malcolm (b. 1940) and Richard Youel (b. 1943), continued the business after McAdoo's death as McAdoo, Malcolm & Youel, retaining McAdoo's name in honor of the founder.

9.   Seattle First National Branch Bank, Wedgwood, Seattle, 1970, Benjamin McAdoo & Company. This small branch bank was the first of a group of three commissioned by the bank that were built from a single prototype design. The others are the branches at Rainier Beach, Seattle (1972), and at Lake Hills, Bellevue (1971). *(Photo by T. William Booth, 1993.)*

10.   Queen Anne Forward Thrust Swimming Pool, Seattle, 1974-78, Benjamin McAdoo & Company. One of the last projects funded from the Forward Thrust bond issue, this community pool building is a simple composition of brick-clad volumes housing the pool, locker rooms, ancillary facilities, and support spaces. *(Thelma McAdoo Collection; photo by Gregg Krogstad, 1982.)*

Roland Terry

THOMAS VEITH

Roland Terry (b. 1917), who generally practiced in a wood-based idiom often associated with the work of Northwest Modernists in the 1950s, earned a reputation for attention to detail and the intergration of architecture with interior and landscape design.

Terry was born in Seattle on June 2, 1917. He graduated from Lincoln High School and entered the architecture program at the

Roland Terry. *(Roland Terry Collection.)*

1. Florence B. Terry residence, Seattle, 1937-38 (altered), Roland Terry. Terry consulted his teacher, Lionel Pries, in the course of designing this house for his mother. Terry came to share Pries's penchant for integrating architecture, landscape design, and interior design, and for incorporating the work of local artists. *(University of Washington Libraries, Special Collections Division; Dearborn-Massar Collection, DM-4378.)*

University of Washington in 1935, taking summer employment with William J. Bain, Sr. (see essay), in 1935 and 1936, and with J. Lister Holmes (see essay) from 1937 to 1940. In his sophomore year, Terry designed a house for his mother, Florence Beach Terry (1937-38; altered). After receiving a bachelor of architecture degree in December 1940, Terry again took employment with Holmes but left for San Francisco in October 1941 to embark on a tour of South America made possible by an AIA Langley Scholarship; he returned in May 1942.

Following military service from 1942 to 1946, Terry and former schoolmates Bert A. Tucker (1910-83) and Robert M. Shields (b. 1917) formed the partnership of Tucker, Shields & Terry. The principals built their own office (1946-47; destroyed), then designed a number of custom houses as well as Canlis' Charcoal Broiler in Seattle (1949-51; with Wimberly & Cook, Architects of Honolulu; altered). In 1949, Terry traveled to Spain and Italy and then, in the winter of 1949-50, studied painting at the Académie Julian in Paris. Terry left the partnership (which continued as Tucker & Shields) in 1951.

Late in 1952, Terry became associated with Philip A. Moore (1903-72) in the partnership of Terry & Moore. The firm com-

2. Canlis' Charcoal Broiler, Seattle, 1949-51, Wimberly & Cook, Architects, Honolulu, with Tucker, Shields & Terry, Architects and Interior Designers, Seattle (altered, 1951-52, by Tucker & Shields; 1957-58, by Terry & Moore). This building, shown here shortly after the renovation by Terry & Moore, helped establish Terry's reputation for interior design in commercial work and led to a large number of restaurant commissions. (*University of Washington Libraries, Special Collections Division; Dearborn-Massar Collection, DM-4505.*)

pleted a large number of residences, including houses for John H. Hauberg, Jr. (1953-54; altered), and William K. Blethen (1955-57). Terry was not only responsible for the architectural design of these two structures, but planned their gardens as well. He collaborated with Warren Hill, who designed most of the furniture at the Hauberg residence, in the development of that project's interior layout, and in a similar manner, worked with Allen Vance Salsbury at the Blethen residence. Antiques and art objects collected by these clients were accommodated in the two projects, as were the commissioned works of local artists.

Terry & Moore's subsequent works included a country house for Hauberg on Bainbridge Island (1955-57; altered) and the Lawrence B. Culter residence in Vancouver, British Columbia (1957-58). Post-and-beam construction, consisting of peeled log columns and rough-sawn beams, sliding screens used as room dividers, and glass panels that can be removed to open living spaces completely to the outdoors are elements introduced in these two houses which often appeared in Terry's later residential work.

Prominent restaurateur Walter Clark hired Terry & Moore to design several restaurants, beginning with Clark's New Crabapple, Bellevue (ca. 1954; destroyed), and including Clark's Red Carpet (1956; destroyed), the Lakewood Terrace Dining Room (now the Terrace Restaurant), Tacoma (1957; altered), and the Dublin House (1960; destroyed). These projects solidified the firm's reputation for the design of nonresidential interiors.

Terry's international collecting expeditions on behalf of Clark and other clients, his habit of secluding himself while developing schemes for new projects, and his willingness to reconsider and rework major elements of his designs late in their development sometimes complicated his design process. Yet it was this constant refinement of detail and the integration of the other visual arts that gave Terry's work its unique character. His approach to design may reflect the influence of Lionel Pries (see essay) and of Hope Foote, two of his teachers at the University of Washington.

Independent practice as Roland Terry & Associates began in 1960. The firm's designs included houses, such as the Paul Roland Smith (1961-62) and Philip A. Stewart (1961-63) residences; the Washington Park Towers (1964-69), a high-rise condo-

3. John Hauberg, Jr., residence, Seattle, 1953-54 (altered), Terry & Moore, Architects. The elegant, wood-clad volumes that make up this house were organized to open onto landscaped gardens. The mosaic paving around the pool at the left was designed by Guy Anderson; Everett DuPen did the sculpture. *(University of Washington Libraries, Special Collections Division; Dearborn-Massar Collection, DM-6294.)*

4. William K. Blethen residence, Seattle, 1955-57, Terry & Moore, Architects. Despite the floor-to-ceiling windows, flat roof, and tall slender columns (all typical of Modern design in the 1950s), this could be considered an eclectic structure. It borrows from Pompeiian villa architecture and from Asian residential interiors. *(University of Washington Libraries, Special Collections Division; Dearborn-Massar Collection, DM-4470.)*

5. Lawrence B. Culter residence, Vancouver, British Columbia, 1957-58, Terry & Moore, Architects. Peeled logs, built-in furniture, and removable glass wall panels all became typical in Terry's later houses. Terry often collaborated with Irene McGowan, who designed the lighting fixtures. (*University of Washington Libraries, Special Collections Division; Dearborn-Massar Collection, DM-4594.*)

Killingsworth & Associates of Long Beach, California, and interior designer David T. Williams of New York), became Terry's partner in 1974. Terry & Egan's designs included the interiors at Halekulani Hotel, Honolulu (1978-83; also with Killingsworth & Associates). This partnership was dissolved in 1987.

Terry was elected a Fellow of the AIA in 1980 and received the Seattle Chapter Medal in 1991, the year he completed his retreat on Lopez Island, begun in 1965 and considered by Terry to be his best work. Terry, now semi-retired, resides in Mount Vernon, Washington.

6. Washington Park Towers, Seattle, 1964-69, Roland Terry & Associates. The design for this condominium tower was controversial because of its height, although Terry argued that the design preserved views to the lake by limiting the building's footprint to only twelve percent of the landscaped site. (*Photo by Thomas Veith, 1993.*)

minium development on the shore of Lake Washington; the Episcopal Church of the Redeemer, Kenmore (1964); and a number of joint ventures in which Terry's office was generally responsible for the interiors. Additional work for Peter Canlis included restaurants in Honolulu (1960-61), at the Hilton Hotel in Portland (1962-63; now Alexander's), and at the Fairmont Hotel in San Francisco (ca. 1968; destroyed).

Robert H. Egan (b. 1922), a long-time associate, who was deeply involved in the design of the Double Tree Inn, Tukwila (1967-69), and the interiors at the Kahala Hilton Hotel, Honolulu (1967-69; with

7. Nordstrom Department Store, Seattle, 1971-74, Roland Terry & Associates, Seattle, and Skidmore, Owings & Merrill, Architects, San Francisco. This structure's marquee steps down at each entrance to follow the grade of the adjacent streets. The travertine facing integrates several buildings and lends this well-known Seattle retailing establishment what Terry has called an "informal and friendly elegance." *(Photo by Thomas Veith, 1993.)*

8. Bank of California Main Banking Hall, Bank of California Building, Seattle, 1971-74 (altered), Roland Terry & Associates. Although John Graham & Company designed the building itself, the interiors of the bank's corporate offices (which occupy the first ten floors) and of the bank's public rooms were designed by Terry's firm. *(From Terry & Egan promotional brochure.)*

9. Roland Terry residence ("Baycourt"), Lopez Island, Washington, 1965-91, Roland Terry. The sod-roofed buildings and the surrounding gardens were developed over a period of many years. Terry has described the main house as a Palladian structure executed in the "Northwest Modern" idiom and considers it to be his best design. *(Roland Terry Collection.)*

10. Wilson Bradley, Jr., residence, Carpinteria Valley, California, 1982-84, Terry & Egan AIA & Associates, architects; Jean Jongeward ASID, interior designer. Although this house shares many elements with Terry's earlier residential designs, the choice of materials, formal expression, and garden scheme place this project squarely in the tradition of the Italian villa. *(Roland Terry Collection.)*

Victor Steinbrueck

THOMAS VEITH

Victor Eugene Steinbrueck (1911-85) was born December 15, 1911, in Mandan, North Dakota, and moved with his family to Seattle in 1913. He grew up in Seattle and graduated from Franklin High School. In 1928, he entered the University of Washington School of Fisheries, but shifted to architecture in 1930. After graduating in 1935, in the midst of the Depression, he worked with the Civilian Conservation Corps and traveled with the sculptor James FitzGerald (a schoolmate), continuously sketching and painting, as would become his lifelong habit. He completed his architectural training in the offices of several local architects, including William J. Bain, Sr., in 1935 (see essay), J. Gordon Kaufmann in 1936, James Taylor in 1936, and Bjarne Moe in 1937-38. He entered private practice in 1938 and later became involved with the Yesler Ter-

Victor Steinbrueck sketching in downtown Seattle. *(Photo by Mary Randlett.)*

race Housing Project (1940-43) by architects Aitken, Bain, Jacobsen, Holmes and Stoddard.

After military service from 1942 to 1946, Steinbrueck joined the faculty of the University of Washington as acting instructor in

1. Alden Mason residence, Seattle, 1949, Victor Steinbrueck. Steinbrueck's residential work included several houses that were modest in size and budget, and that were characterized by a minimalist approach to structure and an economical use of space. *(University of Washington Libraries, Special Collections Division; Dearborn-Massar Collection, DM-4201.)*

2. Steinbrueck residence, Seattle, 1949-53, Victor Steinbrueck. The plywood-clad north and east elevations of this house, seen here from across the street, contrast markedly with the garden side of the structure, which is mostly glass. (*University of Washington Libraries, Special Collections Division; Dearborn-Massar Collection, DM-4234.*)

architecture. An idealistic advocate of an architecture of social responsibility, he sought to integrate technology with the changing needs of modern society and focused on the contribution of Modern architecture to the development of a new regionalism. He served as acting chairman of the newly organized Department of Architecture from 1962 to 1964 and retired as professor emeritus in 1976.

Steinbrueck's contribution to Seattle architecture and urban design was extensive and varied. The designs for his own house (1949-53) and the Alden Mason house, Richmond Beach (1951; destroyed), both received Seattle AIA Honor Awards and exemplify the simplicity and understated approach of his early residential work. Other small commissions were completed, including an earlier house for Alden Mason in Seattle (1949), and residences for William T. Stellwagen (1951-55) and Earl L. Barrett (1954-56). In 1957, Steinbrueck relocated briefly to Michigan to work with classmate Minoru Yamasaki, but soon returned to Seattle, where he completed several additional houses, including the Frederick Anderson (1958) and T. H. Terao (1959-61; altered)

residences. Steinbrueck also participated with Paul Hayden Kirk & Associates in the design of the University of Washington Faculty Center Building (1958-60; also called the Faculty Club), which received a Seattle AIA Honor Award in 1960.

3. William T. Stellwagen residence, Seattle, 1951-55, Victor Steinbrueck. This house was designed to be constructed by the clients. It continues the pattern of closing off views from the street and opening the interior of the house to the garden beyond. (*University of Washington Libraries, Special Collections Division; Dearborn-Massar Collection, DM-4266.*)

4. Faculty Center Building (Faculty Club), University of Washington, Seattle, 1958-60, Paul Hayden Kirk & Associates and Victor Steinbrueck, Associated Architects. This regional interpretation of the principles of Modern architecture and the work of Mies van der Rohe replaced Ellsworth Storey's Hoo-Hoo House. *(University of Washington Libraries, Special Collections Division; Dearborn-Massar Collection, DM-2665)*

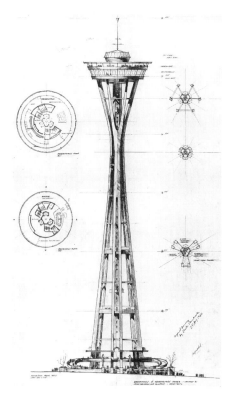

Perhaps more important than his design work was Steinbrueck's ability to engage the interest of the average citizen in the city's architectural heritage, beginning with the publication of his *Guide to Seattle Architecture, 1850-1953,* sponsored by the AIA in 1953. He was able to communicate the quality of the city through the publication of his sketches in *Seattle Cityscape* (1962), *Market Sketchbook* (1968), and *Seattle Cityscape #2* (1973). His architectural critiques took a variety of forms, beginning as columns and sketches in *Argus,* a local periodical, and later ranging from letters to the editor to direct political action.

5. Space Needle, Seattle, 1960-62, John Graham & Company with Victor Steinbrueck. The notation "original drawing by Victor Steinbrueck, 24 August 1960" occurs on this drawing from Graham's office. Although Steinbrueck is often credited with responsibility for the architectural form of this Seattle landmark, its authorship is still a matter of question because Graham had previously patented a scheme for a revolving restaurant. *(University of Washington Libraries, Special Collections Division; UW14798.)*

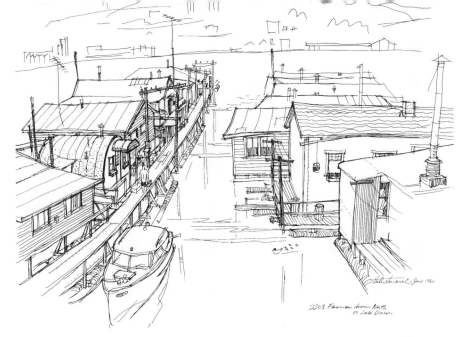

6.   Steinbrueck's three sketchbooks were intended to document the city's life as represented by its architecture. Through his drawings, he attempted to communicate the full range of Seattle's built environment, including its vernacular fabric as exemplified by these houseboats, from *Seattle Cityscape*. (*University of Washington Libraries, Special Collections Division.*)

7.   In this sketch panorama, from *Seattle Cityscape #2*, Steinbrueck attempted to elucidate the important relationship between Seattle and the surrounding region, subtly warning that the city's connection to its beautiful physical setting was in danger of being lost. (*University of Washington Libraries, Special Collection Division.*)

8. Capitol Hill Viewpoint Park (now called Louisa Boren Park), Seattle, 1975, Victor Steinbrueck, with landscape consultant Richard Haag. Steinbrueck was concerned that publicly owned "leftovers" be used to best advantage—in this case, to further the appreciation by Seattle citizens of their physical suroundings. The cor-ten steel sculpture is by Lee Kelly. *(Photo by Thomas Veith, 1993.)*

In the 1960s, he began to emphasize the importance of buildings to people as an embodiment of local culture. As a spokesman for the preservation of Pioneer Square, he noted the interrelated nature of buildings and public spaces. In his advocacy for the preservation of the Pike Place Market, he used his considerable artistry in words and sketches to bring the lessons of Lewis Mumford and Jane Jacobs to the public. He founded the Friends of the Market, which successfully resisted the City of Seattle's urban renewal plans and helped pass an initiative to preserve the Market in 1971. The resulting ordinance was unique in seeking, through the intergration of low-income housing and attention to social concerns, to preserve the character of the Market, and to support the diversity of life within the heart of the city.

Steinbrueck's battles with government bureaucracies were symptomatic of an un-tiring commitment to developing Seattle's sense of itself. He contributed to the design of a number of projects that promote civic awareness, such as the Space Needle (1960-62), completed with John Graham & Company, and several parks—including Capitol Hill Viewpoint Park (1975; now called Louisa Boren Park) and Betty Bowen Viewpoint/Marshall Park (1977), both planned with Richard Haag as landscape consultant, and Market Park (1981-82; now called Victor Steinbrueck Park), designed in association with Haag.

A protracted battle over publicly accessible open space at Westlake Park was perhaps the most demanding of Steinbrueck's involvements with city politics and alienated both Steinbrueck and fellow combatant Folke Nyberg from much of Seattle's "establishment." The debate called attention to the significance of the Westlake diagonal and led to renewed calls for more open space in

9. Residence for Steinbrueck, Inc., Seattle, 1979-80, Victor Steinbrueck. This speculative house is situated in the midst of several cottages designed by Ellsworth Storey near Colman Park and is intended to complement them. The new structure was built by Steinbrueck's son, Peter, the elder man's partner and design associate for this project. It was Victor Steinbrueck's last architectural commission. (*Photo by Thomas Veith, 1980.*)

downtown Seattle. In addition, the enclosure of public space within a private building using the city's power of eminent domain raised a number of legal issues concerning the definition of public space. In the end, Steinbrueck and Nyberg were successful in ensuring access to the park for all citizens and making it difficult for the private developer to prevent civic activities such as political demonstrations from occurring there.

Steinbrueck died in Seattle on February 14, 1985, leaving, as a legacy, his conviction that "realistic hope for the future depends upon public and private awareness, concern, and civic involvement, with a real commitment to human values above material considerations. It is to this commitment, and the vital part it must play in building a good and livable city, that we must dedicate ourselves."

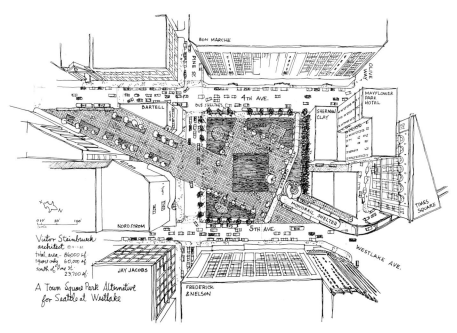

10. Alternate Scheme for Westlake Park, Seattle, 1981, Victor Steinbrueck. The Westlake controversy brought Steinbrueck into direct confrontation with some of Seattle's most influential business interests as well as many patrons of the arts. Folke Nyberg and Victor Steinbrueck both prepared a number of alternate schemes for the project. (*University of Washington Libraries, Special Collections Division.*)

Vernacular and Popular Architecture in Seattle

GAIL DUBROW &

ALEXA BERLOW

The study of vernacular and popular architecture is the study of ordinary buildings. It embraces elements of the built environment that are at once common and familiar, aspects of the urban fabric that often play a greater role in most residents' daily lives than their high-style counterparts. Vernacular and popular architecture can be seen as embodying social process; the built form reflects the influences of various social groups and societal forces. An understanding of it requires that information be drawn from a wide range of sources and multiple disciplines in conjunction with in-depth field work.

The term "vernacular" was initially applied to the architecture of folk cultures or preindustrial societies. However, the two categories, vernacular (or folk) and elite (or high-style, usually architect-designed), have not been able to account adequately for the broad range of buildings constructed during the last two centuries. These relatively recent products of industrial culture have been characterized as "popular," yielding a tripartite model—"vernacular," "popular," "high-style"—for defining all of the built environment.

While cultural resource surveys of Seattle's built environment have been conducted, an overall analytical framework for local urban vernacular and popular architecture has yet to be developed. The published survey of Seattle neighborhoods by Nyberg and Steinbrueck between 1975 and 1977 and subsequent city inventory work have identified neighborhood resources; however, no synthesis of existing surveys has

1. Railroad Avenue (Alaskan Way), Elliott Bay waterfront, 1890. From the founding of Seattle, the waterfront has been the site of utilitarian structures serving the needs of industrial users. Early wharves, piers, warehouses, and similar structures were all dependent on connections to rail and water. (*Museum of History and Industry, Seattle; Seattle Historical Society Collection, 13,292.*)

2. Gee How Oak Tin Benevolent Society, Seattle, 1908-9 (altered), Charles Haynes. This single-room-occupancy (SRO) hotel opened in 1909 as the Hotel Hudson, but was later acquired by a Chinese family association. The recessed balcony, metal railing, and tile roof are the result of alterations in 1936 designed by Bockerman & Chinn, based on traditional Chinese architecture. *(Photo by Alexa Berlow, 1993.)*

proach to building, at least for a short time. Oral accounts suggest that Scandinavian immigrants were well represented among workers in the Seattle building trades and were responsible for the construction of many late nineteenth- and early twentieth-century structures. Clearly, Asian and Pacific immigrants have left their impact on major portions of the urban fabric, as is evident in Seattle's International District. For the most part, Chinese and Japanese immigrants occupied and modified standard American building types, although significant alterations could be made for culturally distinct uses such as association halls, language schools, bathhouses, and similar buildings. The decorative details associated with Chinatowns have been studied more thoroughly than the architectural influence of other Asian and Pacific groups.

yet been undertaken. As a result, many basic questions regarding Seattle's built environment remain unanswered and this essay can only suggest possible directions for future study.

Because the Euro-American settlement of Seattle dates only to the early 1850s, early building appears to have been heavily influenced by established types and forms drawn from elsewhere in the United States. Early Seattle builders responded within the context of local conditions to the pervasive influence of American industrial production and mass culture. Seattle's rapid growth after 1880 was fueled primarily by immigration, but the influence of immigrants' building traditions on Seattle's architecture remains largely unstudied. Builders appear to have followed common models, published in pattern books, builders' guides, and periodicals (see Pattern Books, Plan Books, Periodicals essay), but some ethnic influence may be present as well. Recent research has revealed that Scandinavians, particularly in Washington's rural areas, managed to retain their traditional ap-

3. Finnish Temperance Society (now Lafurno's Italian Restaurant), Seattle, 1902 (altered; to be demolished). Built to provide an alcohol-free environment for members of the Interbay Finnish community, this soon became an important local gathering place. The narrow, one-room width and single prominent elevation are similar to features of buildings found in rural towns in Finland, although the facade derives primarily from American precedents. *(Photo by Alexa Berlow, 1993.)*

4. Novelty Mill, Seattle, 1905 (destroyed). This lumber mill, located not far from Duwamish Head, consisted of a collection of simple rectilinear forms. One of the earliest lumber mills in West Seattle, it provided employment for many residents of the area until the 1930s. *(Museum of History and Industry, Seattle; PEMCO Webster & Stevens Collection, 83.10.7379.)*

Vernacular and popular architecture can also be considered in terms of its location in the urban fabric. Since the late 1880s, the architectural profession has assumed primary responsibility for major commercial and institutional structures. Nevertheless, most residential and commercial buildings, as well as many utilitarian and industrial structures, were not products of architectural custom design. Thus, Seattle's vernacular-popular architecture is found primarily in areas such as railroad corridors, industrial zones, commercial strips, and residential neighborhoods.

Seattle's industrial buildings have been located along the city's waterways and rail routes since the period of initial settlement. Early wharves and piers were simple shed structures which drew on the abundant supply of native softwoods as a construction material. Such sheds proved to be a flexible building type for the city's working waterfront, accommodating various enterprises including fish processing plants, warehouses, ice plants, and creameries. Similarly, lumber, shingle, brick, and steel mills were located in areas easily accessible by rail and water. Their simple forms, like those of the wharves and piers, accommodated a variety of industrial processes. Many appear to have been erected according to established construction practices or standard repetitive designs, although some may have been designed by professional architects. These utilitarian buildings often responded primarily to the demands of the processes which they housed, and their designs were seldom generated by abstract intellectual concepts, although some details may occasionally reflect aesthetic rather than utilitarian intent.

5. Western Mill, Seattle, 1909 (destroyed). This mill recalls the time when Lake Union's waterfront primarily served industrial and commercial uses. Located at the south end of the lake, the mill employed many residents of the Cascade neighborhood. *(Museum of History and Industry, Seattle; ca. 1909; Seattle Historical Society Collection, 9881.)*

Seattle's residential neighborhoods include a variety of vernacular and popular buildings. The character of the residences themselves was clearly influenced by regional and national models as published in pattern books and popular periodicals (see essay), but these neighborhoods also include other ordinary building types. For example, small corner grocery stores followed the pattern of streetcar stops. These two-story structures accommodated ground-level businesses and second-floor residences, al-

6. Corner of East Pike and Broadway Avenue, Seattle, ca. 1915 (destroyed). This cluster of one- and two-story buildings was in one of Seattle's neighborhood commercial centers. Such areas of commercial and social life usually developed near the city's streetcar lines. Many of these neighborhood centers remain today, recalling the pattern of streetcar lines that were abandoned in 1939. *(Museum of History and Industry, Seattle; PEMCO Webster & Stevens Collection, 83.10.1926.)*

7. The Durn [Good] Grocery Store (now Roadrunner Coffeehouse), Seattle, ca. 1920. This building in Wallingford looks today much as it did more than sixty years ago. Originally named Durn Grocery after an early owner, the "Good" was added by a later proprietor. This structure is now a coffee and comic book store, but the Durn Good Grocery also survives, on a corner three blocks west in a former butcher shop. *(Photo by Alexa Berlow, 1993.)*

lowing the owners to both run a business and raise a family on a limited budget. Some look and function much as they did more than sixty years ago, showing remarkable resilience as a type. Others have been adapted to new uses, such as the Wallingford Building now known as the Daylight Glass Studio (ca. 1912; remodeled 1955, 1973). Still others were replaced by supermarkets and parking lots as former streetcar suburbs adapted to the age of automobiles and centralized services.

Vernacular and popular building also can be considered in relation to the influence of particular social groups. Only a few of these building types have been studied to date. One example is the single-room-occupancy (SRO) hotel, a building type that reflects the contributions of single working men to the economic development of the city. These three- to six-story mixed-use buildings generally included small retail and wholesale establishments on the ground

8. Youngstown Improvement Club (now Disabled American Veterans, Chapter 23), Seattle, 1924. Located in the Delridge neighborhood of West Seattle, this meeting hall was built by the club members to boost the image of the small steel mill neighborhood. The club functioned as a community center until World War II, when the Youngstown area became a site for military activity. Although the building has changed hands, the community hall facilities continue to function much as they did in the 1920s and 1930s. *(Photo by Alexa Berlow, 1993.)*

9. Twin Teepees, Restaurant, Seattle, 1936 (altered), Dell W. Harris, Architect. The impact of the automobile is reflected in the architecture of Seattle's commercial strips. Twin Teepees, on Aurora Avenue across from Green Lake, demonstrates the tendency of early automobile-oriented buildings to call attention to themselves with unique forms. *(Photo by Alexa Berlow, 1993.)*

floor and single-room residences on the upper levels, and were found in close proximity to the working waterfront and in Pioneer Square and the International District. Surviving buildings of this type continue to provide a significant stock of low-income housing in the downtown neighborhoods.

Social club buildings are another example where the influence of particular groups has been significant. Club buildings were built by groups with ethnic, religious, or work-related affiliations. First appearing in Seattle in the late nineteenth century, these structures offered individuals with common interests or backgrounds comfortable gathering places, as well as quarters for mutual benefit associations, and other political or social organizations. Club buildings also provided members of various ethnic groups, from Finnish to Filipino, with a center for the continuation of their cultural heritage. Social, commercial, and residential functions have often been combined in Chinese association halls, which have been gathering places for family, district, and business organizations. These typically contain ground floor retail stores and single rooms upstairs that serve as residences for working men. The presence of the association hall can be identified from the street by a recessed or projecting balcony with metal railings, usually overhung by a tiled roof with flared edges.

While some organizations, such as the Fraternal Order of Eagles or the Independent Order of Odd Fellows, built large architect-designed structures (see essays for Bittman and for Breitung & Buchinger), many built on a much more modest scale. Members of a Youngstown business association, in West Seattle, for example, built the Youngstown Improvement Club (1924), a gable-roofed structure similar to adjacent residences.

10. Residential neighborhood southeast of Rainier Avenue and South Charles Street, between the Central District and Beacon Hill, 1959. The residential fabric of this Seattle neighorhood reflects a variety of influences, national and local, and the interpretations of individual builders. This area was slated for demolition to allow new construction associated with urban renewal. *(Museum of History and Industry, Seattle; Seattle Historical Society Collection, 3685.)*

The middle and late twentieth century have generated popular structures that reflect contemporary social patterns. Just as streetcars fueled the first wave of suburban growth in the early twentieth century, the automobile has since shaped the pattern of urban development. Small-scale roadside commercial/retail establishments have sprung up along urban arterials to serve middle class motorists and suburbanites. "Novelty buildings," such as the Twin Teepees Restaurant (1936) near Green Lake, have taken on the function of billboards, using architectural form to advertise retail services. Dick's Drive-In, in Wallingford (1954), is an example of later roadside structures, which have tended to be simpler in form, surrounded by oversized parking lots, and more dependent on signage for identity. Such buildings have been criticized for eroding the traditional relationship of building to place and undermining the pedestrian environment by creating auto-oriented strips on the urban periphery.

The vernacular and popular elements of Seattle's built environment provide enduring reminders of each successive stage in the city's development. Research in Seattle has just begun to address the full range of vernacular and popular building types. Nonetheless, such common and ordinary elements of the architectural landscape play a critical role in providing a sense of continuity between the past and the present, and are critical to an understanding of the city's form and character.

APPENDIXES

tecturally (Seattle, 1902). Some of their drawings can be found at the Special Collections Division of the University of Washington Libraries.

Useful summaries relative to Bebb's life and career are in *Pacific Builder and Engineer,* November 26, 1910, and January 17, 1914, as well as *A Volume of Memoirs and Genealogy of Representative Citizens of the City of Seattle and County of King, Washington* (New York and Chicago, 1903), and Clarence Bagley, *History of Seattle* (Chicago, 1916). Jeffrey Karl Ochsner and Dennis Alan Andersen deal with Bebb's introduction to Seattle in "Adler and Sullivan's Seattle Opera House Project," *Journal of the Society of Architectural Historians* 48 (September 1989): 223-31. Bebb's obituaries are found in the *Seattle Post-Intelligencer* and *Seattle Times* for June 23, 1942.

For Mendel, similar biographical information is available in *Spike's Illustrated Description of the City of Tacoma* (Tacoma, 1891), *Pacific Builder and Engineer,* June 25, 1910, and March 21, 1914. Mendel's obituaries are found in the *Seattle Post-Intelligencer* and *Seattle Times,* June 11, 1940.

In addition, Bebb was the author of a number of published articles including: "Fire Losses in Fire-Proof Buildings," *The Engineering Magazine,* February 1893; "Modernity in Architecture," *Pacific Builder and Engineer,* May 28, 1910; and "The Art of Designing Commercial Buildings," *Pacific Builder and Engineer,* April 13, 1912. Mendel also published several lead articles in early issues of *Washington State Architect.*

Beezer Brothers

There is no convenient reference source of information regarding the Beezer Brothers. Documentation for individual buildings can be gleaned from building permits, *The American Architect and Building News, Pacific Builder and Engineer,* and the *Seattle Daily Journal of Commerce,* as well as a vari-

ety of other periodicals. Information for the brothers themselves is even more scarce, with the best sources being their respective death certificates, the obituary for Louis Beezer in *Architect and Engineer,* January 1929, and the obituary for Michael J. Beezer in the *Seattle Daily Journal of Commerce,* September 16, 1933. An article by M. J. Beezer, "Domestic Architecture," *Pacific Builder and Engineer,* September 14, 1907, provides some insight concerning the firm's design philosophy.

Henry W. Bittman

The primary source for information about Henry Bittman is the company records of Bittman Vammen Taylor, P.S., Seattle. The company records include an extensive listing of projects dating back to 1914, with plans for most of them, photographs of some, and a few cost estimates. Some additional plans and an advertising pamphlet for the Terminal Sales Building are held in the University of Washington Libraries Special Collections Division. Information about Bittman and his office is also available from a variety of individuals, including Herbert Bittman (principal at Bittman Vammen Taylor and nephew of Henry Bittman), Martha Lamb (niece of Henry Bittman), Ernest "Bud" Anderson (whose aluminum window business, Durelle Products, supplied many of Bittman's projects between 1947 and 1953), and Paul Hayden Kirk (who worked briefly in Bittman's office). Seattle Landmarks Preservation Board files on the Mann Building, the Decatur Building, the Terminal Sales Building, the Olympic Tower, the Music Box Theater, and the Eagles Temple are helpful, although the landmark nomination form erroneously attributes the Mann Theater to Sherwood Ford, a claim disputed at the Landmarks Board hearing. This error was carried into Karin Link's generally good essay, "Architect and Engineer: Henry Bittman," in the book *Impressions of Imagi-*

nation: Terra-Cotta Seattle (Seattle: Allied Arts of Seattle, 1986), which also contains some mislabeled photographs, fails to attribute the Securities Building addition to Bittman, and contains a few factual errors about Bittman's education and early employment. *King County Courthouse Restoration Study,* by Cardwell/Thomas & Associates, Architects (Seattle, 1991), available at the King County Department of Cultural Resources, provides some historical information. Additional information may be culled from Seattle Building Permit Records, *Polk's Seattle Directory,* obituaries in the *Seattle Post-Intelligencer* and *Seattle Times,* and articles in *Pacific Building and Engineering Record* on December 22, 1906, and March 16, 1907.

William E. Boone

The chief sources of information on the life and career of William E. Boone are the many Seattle newspaper reports of the period in which he was designing. The work of Boone & Willcox was featured in *Northwest Magazine* in February 1891. Brief biographies of Boone appeared in Julian Hawthorne, *History of Washington, the Evergreen State* (New York, 1893), pp. 396-97, and in *A Volume of Memoirs and Genealogy of Representative Citizens of the City of Seattle and County of King, Washington* (New York and Chicago, 1903), pp. 230-32, but both are relatively inexact. Boone's obituary apeared in the *Seattle Post-Intelligencer* on October 31, 1921, but this, too, provides limited information.

Breitung & Buchinger

Information regarding the firm Breitung & Buchinger and its two principals is surprisingly scarce. Brief biographical accounts of Carl Alfred Breitung can be found in early articles in *The Commonwealth* (a Seattle weekly journal), in scattered articles and notices in *Pacific Record* and *Pacific Builder*

and Engineer, and in *Seattle Daily Bulletin.* A portrait with accompanying notes is found in *Men of the Pacific Coast* (San Francisco, 1902). The early career of Theobald Buchinger is outlined in *Seattle of To-Day* (Seattle, 1907), and in the Tacoma German-language newspaper, *Wacht am Sunde,* June 7, 1917. Photographs of projects can be found in the Special Collections Division of the University of Washington Libraries, the Museum of History and Industry in Seattle, and in the archives of some of the institutions that inhabit buildings designed by the partners. Buchinger's obituary is found in the *Seattle Times,* December 26, 1940. Information about Breitung's life and career after his departure from Seattle has not been discovered. (Although records in Seattle indicate that he intended to relocate to San Antonio, Texas, no evidence of his presence in San Antonio or Texas has yet been found.)

Édouard Frère Champney

Brief biographical accounts of Champney's life up to 1914 can be found in Snowden's *History of Washington State* (Seattle, 1915) and Bagley's *History of Seattle* (Chicago, 1916). Both contain information previously published in articles in *Pacific Builder and Engineer* and *Pacific Coast Architect.* Photographs of Champney's major projects, including those of Gould & Champney, as well as construction photographs of Saint Mark's Cathedral, can be found in the Special Collections Division of the University of Washington Libraries, the photography collections of the Museum of History and Industry in Seattle, and the Seattle Public Library. Brief menton of individual projects or construction notices may be found in *Pacific Builder and Engineer, Northwest Architect, Pacific Coast Architect,* and *Western Architect.* (A number of volumes from Champney's personal library, including folios illustrating the buildings and grounds of the 1900 Paris International

though the banking floor was not; the estimated date of completion is given in this publication as August 15, 1924. Grant Hildebrand's essay in Lydia S. Aldredge, ed., *Impressions of Imagination: Terra-Cotta Seattle* (Seattle: Allied Arts of Seattle, 1986), discusses major buildings by Graham that employ terra-cotta facing and includes many structures by Graham not included herein because of limitations of length and demands of breadth. Many of Graham's buildings are cited in Sally B. Woodbridge and Roger Montgomery, *A Guide to Architecture in Washington State* (Seattle: University of Washington Press, 1980), although dating of the Bank of California Building is incorrect. (The date herein is from *Seattle Daily Journal of Commerce,* which lists the date of permit as May 1923, opening as August 1924.) Woodbridge and Montgomery also wrongly suggest that the Doric columns of the Dexter Horton "express the original height of the lobby."

Olof Hanson

The major source of information for Olof Hanson is the Gallaudet University Archives in Washington, D.C. Collections there include many of Hanson's drawings, a selection of his papers, and photographs of many of his buildings. A complete index of these materials, which runs to nearly 100 pages, can be interloaned from the Gallaudet University Library. Some material on Hanson's Minnesota career is available in Faribault, Minnesota, from the Rice County Historical Society. A copy of a prospectus for Thayer & Hanson (evidently prepared in 1901), including a list of Olof Hanson's buildings prior to that date, is held by the Northwest Architectural Archives of the University of Minnesota. The most complete published source on Hanson is his "An Autobiography," published by Gallaudet College in *The Companion* 16 (May 5, 1932). An insightful article on Hanson's life and work, by Judy

Mannes, is found in John V. Van Cleve, ed., *Gallaudet Encyclopedia of Deaf People and Deafness,* vol. 2 (New York, ca. 1987). Hanson himself published an articulate description of Seattle shortly after his arrival, "The Architectural Beauties and Possibilities of This Enterprising City," in *Seattle Daily Bulletin* 12 (January 1903; New Year's Edition): 18. Of the newspaper obituaries, that of the *University Herald* 12 (September 1933) offers the most complete information about Hanson and his family.

J. Lister Holmes

The University of Washington Libraries are an excellent source of information regarding J. Lister Holmes's career. His firm biography, office records, and correspondence are located in the Manuscripts and University Archives Division (Accession No. 3789), while the Special Collections Division has a substantial collection of his drawings and project photographs. Published information is available regarding the Dessau house in *Architectural Forum* 75 (July 1941): 54-55; the Yesler Terrace Defense Housing Project in *Pencil Points* 22 (November 1941): 684-89; the Rubinstein house in *Architectural Record* 110 (August 1951): 114-19; the Catherine Blaine Junior High School in *Architectural Record* 116 (July 1954): 123-127, and in *Vitrum,* no. 56 (an Italian architectural magazine); and the Seattle School District Headquarters in *Progressive Architecture* 32 (March 1951): 57-64. (The O. W. Fisher house was also published, but was erroneously attributed to A. L. Loveless.) Also, Lawrence Kreisman, *The Bloedel Reserve: Gardens in the Forest* (Seattle: Arbor Fund/Bloedel Reserve, 1988), provides an interesting, client-based biographical look at Holmes's involvement in the design and construction of Collinswood. Holmes's obituary appeared in the *Seattle Times,* July 19, 1986.

Edwin W. Houghton

The chief sources of information on the life and career of Edwin W. Houghton are the many Seattle newspaper reports of the period noting his buildings. Projects are also noted in contemporary professional publications including *Northwestern Architect, Pacific Builder and Engineer,* and in *Seattle Daily Journal of Commerce.* Early work by Edwin Houghton is presented in the booklet *Illustrated and Descriptive Book of Buildings by E. W. Houghton, Architect* (Seattle, 1902). In addition, very brief and inadequate summaries of Houghton's career appeared in his obituaries in the *Seattle Times* and *Post-Intelligencer* May 17, 1927. John Cort and the commissions for the Grand Opera House and Moore Theater in Seattle are discussed in Richard Engeman, "The 'Seattle Spirit' Meets *The Alaskan:* A Story of Business, Boosterism and the Arts," *Pacific Northwest Quarterly* 81 (April 1990): 54-66. Published renderings from the Saunders & Houghton office can be found in Jeffrey Karl Ochsner, "A. B. Chamberlin: The Illustration of Seattle Architecture, 1890-1896," *Pacific Northwest Quarterly* 81 (October 1990): 130-44. The involvement of Saunders & Houghton with the Seattle Schools is discussed in Jeffrey Karl Ochsner and Dennis Alan Andersen, "Architecture for Seattle Schools, 1880-1900," *Pacific Northwest Quarterly* 83 (October 1992): 128-43. In addition, some records of Houghton's life and practice are held by his grandson, John Houghton, who now lives in Oakland, California.

Daniel R. Huntington

Some biographical information on Daniel R. Huntington is available in two articles: "Daniel R. Huntington," *Pacific Builder and Engineer,* October 1916, p. 12; and "Ace Men of the Pacific Northwest," *Pacific Builder and Engineer,* October 6, 1928, p. 44. The opening of his first Seattle office is noted in *Pacific Record,* May 20, 1905, p. 4. Less reliable biographical information is provided by lecture notes recorded in the biographical index at Seattle Public Library. The Burwell house, by Huntington, and a few projects by Schack & Huntington are illustrated in Frank Calvert, ed., *Homes and Gardens of the Pacific Coast, Volume 1: Seattle* (Beaux Arts Village, Lake Washington: Beaux Arts Society Publishers, 1913). Despite the fact that Huntington served as city architect for a number of years, the City of Seattle has no record of his service. Susan Boyle's landmark nomination document for the Lake Union Steam Plant is available through the City of Seattle Department of Neighborhoods, and the Steam Plant is also discussed and illustrated in a student research paper by James T. Blomquist, "The Optimism of the Machine: The Lake Union Generating Plants, Eastlake Avenue East and Nelson Place," in the College of Architecture and Urban Planning Library at the University of Washington. Information on the Seventh Street Theater (which is listed in the National Register of Historic Places) and Hoquiam City Hall is available through the Washington State Office of Archaeology and Historic Preservation. Unfortunately, most of Huntington's records and drawings, except for some nonarchitectural watercolors and oil paintings in the possession of his grandson, Daniel R. Huntington III, have been destroyed. Construction drawings for a few of Huntington's buildings are available at the Special Collections Division, University of Washington Libraries. Additional information about his work may be culled from the *Seattle Daily Bulletin,* the *Seattle Daily Journal of Commerce,* and the *Seattle Post-Intelligencer,* although the information contained there is not always reliable and must be confirmed using Seattle Department of Construction and Land Use records, which are, unfortunately, incomplete.

Paul Hayden Kirk

Despite the frequent publication of individual buildings in the architectural press, which can be located via the various periodical indexes, the only available survey of Kirk's career is a student paper in the Architect's Reference Files at the Special Collections Division of the University of Washington Libraries by Evelyn Rubenstein titled "Paul Hayden Kirk: A Northwest Architect" (1976); this paper does contain some errors in dating and occasional lapses in critical inquiry and only discusses work prior to 1960. Special Collections also has a large collection of drawings from Kirk's office for the period from the late 1940s to the early 1960s. The Dearborn-Massar photograph collection at Special Collections contains excellent images of many of Kirk's published projects. Both Victor Steinbrueck, *A Guide to Seattle Architecture* (New York: Van Nostrand Reinhold, 1953), and Sally B. Woodbridge and Roger Montgomery, *A Guide to Architecture in Washington State* (Seattle: University of Washington Press, 1980), provide useful commentary on the many buildings they cite that were designed by Kirk's firms; however, both are sometimes unreliable in regard to dates and attributions. Insight into Kirk's design practice and philosophy can be obtained from his book, Paul Hayden Kirk and Eugene D. Sternberg, *Doctors' Offices and Clinics* (New York, 1955), and from the article "Fields of Practice: Clinics," *Progressive Architecture* 41 (February 1960): 143-59.

Arthur L. Loveless

At this time, the best source of information on Loveless is Thomas Veith, "An Analysis of the Work of Arthur L. Loveless with an Emphasis on Human Aesthetic Responses" (M. Arch. thesis, University of Washington, 1991). Earlier work by students at the University of Washington may also be of interest, particularly Lois Wardell, "Arthur Lamont Loveless" (typescript research paper, University of Washington, Department of Architecture, 1969). Several houses designed by the partnership of Wilson & Loveless are illustrated in Frank Calvert, ed., *Homes and Gardens of the Pacific Coast: Volume 1: Seattle* (Beaux Arts Village, Lake Washington: Beaux Arts Society Publishers, 1913) as well as in various issues of *Pacific Coast Architect*. Articles on a number of Loveless's buildings occur in the architectural press. Of interest are Arthur L. Loveless, "Honor Awards Washington State Chapter A.I.A.," *Architect and Engineer* 19 (December 1927): 35-37, 48, 52-53, 73, 77; "Seattle Honor Awards, Washington State Chapter, A.I.A.," *American Architect* 133 (February 5, 1928): 185-90; and "Studio Building, Seattle, Washington," *American Architect* 143 (November 1933): 49-54. Loveless's own residence was published in "Hollyhock House: Submitted in Our Small-House Competition by the Owner and Architect Arthur L. Loveless," *House Beautiful* 64 (October 1928): 380-81. A very brief essay by Loveless occurs in "A Northwest Architecture — A Symposium by 5 Seattle Architects," *Town Crier* 28 (December 16, 1933): 12-14. Loveless's buildings were (and still are) occasionally discussed in the popular press, particularly in the *Seattle Times* and the *Seattle Post-Intelligencer,* though the historical data recorded there are not always reliable. Drawings and photographs of several structures designed by Loveless may be found in the Special Collections Division at the University of Washington.

Donald MacKay

There is no convenient source of information regarding Donald MacKay. Documentation for individual buildings has been gleaned primarily from the *Seattle Post-Intelligencer* and the *Tacoma Daily Ledger.* Relevant biographical information readily available in the Seattle area is limited to

MacKay's obituary in *The Oregonian* (Portland), April 25, 1926. Some of MacKay's political involvements are mentioned in E. Kimbark MacColl's *Merchants, Money, and Power* (Portland, Oregon: Georgian Press, 1988).

Benjamin F. McAdoo, Jr.

The best source of information regarding Benjamin McAdoo's career is the collection of records and drawings at the successor firm, McAdoo, Malcolm & Youel, Architects, in Seattle. (A list of projects completed by McAdoo from 1947 to 1981 is also available.) Drawings and photographs of some of the houses and other buildings designed by McAdoo are found in the *Seattle Times* after 1949, especially his AIA "Home of the Month" projects. For example, the Hage house was covered extensively in the *Seattle Times,* February 24, 1957; McAdoo's own house was covered extensively in the *Seattle Times,* February 18, 1962, and Februrary 25, 1962. A lengthy article on McAdoo at the time of his move from Bothell to Capitol Hill appeared in the *Seattle Post-Intelligencer,* May 17, 1981. (These articles and many others may be found in the verical file and in the architect scrapbooks in the Art Department of the Seattle Public Library.) McAdoo's obituaries are found in the *Seattle Post-Intelligencer,* June 19, 1981; *Seattle Times,* June 20, 1981, and *Seattle Daily Journal of Commerce,* June 22, 1981. Information about McAdoo is also available from his partners in the second half of his career, Garold Malcolm and Richard Youel, and from his widow, Thelma McAdoo (who continues to reside in Seattle).

Mother Joseph of the Sacred Heart (Esther Pariseau)

Unpublished sources regarding Mother Joseph can be found in the Mother Joseph Collection at the Sisters of Providence Archives (4800 37th Avenue S.W., Seattle, Washington 98126), which documents her work in the Pacific Northwest between 1856 and 1902. The records include original correspondence; a diary of her 1856 voyage to Fort Vancouver, Washington Territory; legal documents; biographical information; West Coast Lumbermen's Association and American Institute of Architects awards; and records of the Statuary Hall nomination, selection, and dedication, 1969-80. Information on Mother Joseph's architectural work can be found in this collection as well as in the archival collections for the individual schools and hospitals she designed. There are several general published sources regarding Mother Joseph. The most recent biography is Mary Gleason, S.P., *He Has Given Me a Flame* (Montreal, 1992). An earlier biography is Sister Mary of the Blessed Sacrament McCrosson, S.P., *The Bell and the River* (Palo Alto, 1956). Rita Bergamini, S.P., and Loretta Zwolak Greene, *Mother Joseph Of the Sacred Heart: A Bibliography* (Seattle, 1986), lists books, periodicals, and newspaper articles about Mother Joseph and the nomination and dedication of the Mother Joseph statue in Statuary Hall, Washington, D.C., 1980. Another publication from the Statuary Hall dedication is 96th Congress, 2nd Session, Senate Document No. 96-70, *Acceptance of the Statue of Mother Joseph (Esther Pariseau) Presented by the State of Washington: Proceedings in the Rotunda of the United States Capitol, Washington, D.C., May 1, 1980* (Washington, D.C., 1980). (In addition, a 17-minute documentary video entitled *Mother Joseph, a Sister of Providence, 1823-1902* [Seattle, 1979] is available for loan from the Sisters of Providence, 520 Pike Street, C-11038, Seattle, Washington 98111, Attn: Public Relations Department. The video is based on manuscripts, photographs, and artifacts in the Archives.)

Information regarding the Providence Hospital commission in Seattle (indicating MacKay's role) can be gleaned from newspaper reports of the time, especially the *Seattle Post-Intelligencer,* April 19, April 26, April 29, and October 29, 1882.

Floyd A. Naramore

Sources of information regarding Naramore's career are somewhat scattered. The only national recognition occurs in a brief article in the *American Architect,* September 15, 1915, which contains photographs and plans of Couch Elementary School in Portland, Oregon. Local sources cover much of Naramore's Seattle School District Work. Patricia C. Erigero's *Seattle Public Schools: Historic Building Survey* (Seattle: Historic Seattle Preservation and Development Authority, 1989) summarizes and describes most surviving school buildings by Naramore for possible Historic Register designation. A master's thesis by William Gregory Robinson, "A History of Public School Architecture" (University of Washington, 1989), discusses the history of Seattle School District architecture. The Seattle School District Archives have many of Naramore's drawings, specifications, and notes. Personal information regarding Naramore can be found in AIA membership files at the University of Washington Manuscripts and Archives Division, which has Naramore's AIA membership application briefly describing his pre-Seattle work. Obituaries in the *Seattle Post-Intelligencer,* October 31, 1970, and the *Seattle Times,* October 30, 1970, provide valuable background information. The archives at NBBJ may have additional information regarding Naramore's school work in the partnership, but due to the length of time that has passed, correct attribution of specific projects has proved difficult to ascertain.

Native American Architecture on Puget Sound

For a general view of the Native people and sources, see "Central Coast Salish" and "Southern Coast Salish," in *Handbook of North American Indians,* vol. 7, *Northwest Coast* (Washington, D.C.: Smithsonian Institution, 1990). Still useful is T. T. Waterman and R. Greiner, "Indian Houses of Puget Sound," *Indian Notes and Monographs,* misc. ser. 9 (New York: Museum of the American Indian, 1921). J. E. Mauger, "Shed Roof Houses at the Ozette Archaeological Site: A Protohistoric Architectural System" (Ph.D. dissertation, Washington State University, 1978), deals with this type from an archaeological perspective, while W. Suttles, "The Shed-Roof House," in R. K. Wright, ed., *A Time of Gathering: Native Heritage in Washington State* (Seattle: Burke Museum and University of Washington Press, 1991), pp. 212-22, offers an ethnographic perspective. For Old Man House, see George Gibbs, "Tribes of Western Washington and Northwestern Oregon," in *Contributions to North American Ethnology* (Washington, D.C., 1877), and for Chowitsoot's house, see Edmond S. Meany in the *Seattle Post-Intelligencer,* October 1, 1905. Gable-roof houses are described in W. W. Elmendorf, *The Structure of Twana Culture* (Pullman: Washington State University Press, 1960/1992), and M. W. Smith, *The Puyallup-Nisqually* (New York: Columbia University Press, 1940). Hilary Stewart, *Cedar: Tree of Life to the Northwest Coast Indians* (Seattle: University of Washington Press, 1984), illustrates woodworking tools, methods, and products. P. Nabokov and R. Easton, *Native American Architecture* (New York: Oxford University Press, 1989), has excellent illustrations, but the section on this region is unfortunately marred by errors of historical and ethnographic fact and inaccurate identification of photographs. Paul Kane's early sketches of Coast Salish dwellings are reproduced in J. R. Harper,

Paul Kane's Frontier (Austin: University of Texas Press, 1971).

John Parkinson

The chief source of information on John Parkinson's life is his autobiography, *Incidents by the Way* (Los Angeles, 1935). Robert Howard Tracy, "John Parkinson and the Beaux-Arts City Beautiful Movement in Downtown Los Angeles, 1894-1935" (Ph.D. dissertation, University of California-Los Angeles, 1982), summarizes Parkinson's Seattle career, but is primarily dependent on *Incidents by the Way* as a source of information. The chief sources of information on Parkinson's Seattle career are newspaper reports between 1888 and 1894 describing his buildings. A brief, illustrated discussion of Parkinson's Seattle work is Dennis Andersen, "A John Parkinson Album," *Pacific Northwest Quarterly* 69 (April 1978): 71-74. Most of the published renderings from Parkinson's Seattle office can be found in Jeffrey Karl Ochsner, "A. B. Chamberlin: The Illustration of Seattle Architecture, 1890-1896," *Pacific Northwest Quarterly* 81 (October 1990): 130-44. Parkinson's involvement with the Seattle schools is discussed in Jeffrey Karl Ochsner and Dennis Alan Andersen, "Architecture for Seattle Schools, 1880-1900," *Pacific Northwest Quarterly* 83 (October 1992): 128-43.

Pattern Books, Plan Books, Periodicals

A brief general introduction to the subject of pattern books in a national context is David Gebhard, "Pattern Books," in Diane Maddex, ed., *Master Builders: A Guide to Famous American Architects* (Washington, D.C.: Preservation Press, 1985), pp. 68-73.

To date there has been no detailed study of plan books and periodicals for the pre-1900 period in Washington Territory and State. A discussion of Stevens's purchases for the Territorial Library may be found in

Hazel E. Mills, "Governor Isaac I. Stevens and the Washington Territorial Library," *Pacific Northwest Quarterly* 53 (January 1962). Architect W. E. Goodrich published plans for a double house in the *Seattle Post-Intelligencer,* October 1, 1882, perhaps the earliest such publication. The published *Catalogue of the Public Library of the City of Seattle* (Seattle, 1893) contains the list of architectural monographs, plan books, and periodicals held by the library at that time. In addition to newspapers which featured plans and advertisements for plans and pattern books, early building is discussed in the regional publications of the period, including *The Coast, The West Shore, Northwest Magazine,* and *Washington Magazine.* Copies of many plan books, periodicals, and ephemeral items can be found in the collections of the Seattle Public Library, the Special Collections Division and the Architecture and Urban Planning Library of the University of Washington Libraries, the Museum of History and Industry, Seattle, and the Washington State Historical Society, Tacoma.

For the post-1900 period, periodicals, plan and pattern books, and a variety of local publications may be found in these collections. Illustrated architectural brochures appeared after the turn of the century including *Seattle Architecturally* (Seattle, 1902) and *Seattle of To-Day Architecturally* (Seattle, n.d.), as well as individual publications by practitioners such as Edwin Houghton and Bebb & Mendel. Publications by the Craftsman Bungalow Company, including *Bungalow Magazine,* are available at the Special Collections Division, University of Washington Libraries, and the Seattle Public Library. The Seattle Public Library collection currently includes over 250 plan books for historic and contemporary domestic architecture, including the locally issued E. Ellsworth Green, *Practical Plan Book* (Seattle, 1912), and Victor W. Voorhees, *Western Home Builder* (Seattle, 1911). A relatively authoritative analysis of Seattle bungalows was prepared by Rob Anglin, "Report on Bungalows in Seattle" (typescript, 1979), and submitted to the city's Office of Urban Conservation. Copies of this study and "Bungalow: Landmark Nominations, City of Seattle Office of Urban Conservation" (typescript, 1982) are available at the Architecture and Urban Planning Library, University of Washington. "Criteria for Evaluating Classic Boxes" (typescript, 1979), a report prepared by Shirley M. Courtois for the Office of Urban Conservation, provides an analysis of the Classic Box house type and is available at the Special Collections Division, University of Washington Libraries. John Owen, "The Evolution of Popular Houses in Seattle" (M.Arch. thesis, University of Washington, 1975), discusses the influence of pattern and plan books on the design of residential architecture in Seattle.

Lionel H. Pries

Unfortunately, materials on Pries have remained scattered, and the full history of his life and work have not yet been the subject of extensive research. A selection of his original drawings can be found at the Special Collections Division, University of Washington Libraries. His collection of Northwest Native art is on loan from his heir to the State Capital Museum in Olympia. His collection of Piranesi etchings was given to the University of Washington for a token fee during his lifetime. Pries's books, papers, and other materials remain in the possession of his heir, Robert Winskill.

Pries's early life is summarized in the announcement of his winning the LeBrun Travelling Scholarship in *Pencil Points* 3 (May 1922): 35; his winning project was published in *American Architect* 121 (May 10, 1922): 389-90. The best overview of Pries's teaching career is probably Drew Rocker, "Lionel H. Pries: Educator of Architects," *ARCADE* 4 (April-May 1984). A student paper, "Lionel Pries," by Julia

Calloway, which can be found in the College of Architecture and Urban Planning Library at the University of Washington, lists many of Pries's projects in Seattle, but there are projects which are omitted (and, unfortunately, some projects which the paper attributes to Pries, such as the Medico-Dental Building, San Francisco, were by other architects). Several of Pries's Santa Barbara projects are identified in Rebecca Conrad and Christopher H. Nelson, *Santa Barbara: A Guide to El Pueblo Viejo* (Santa Barbara: Capra Press, 1986), pp. 73, 78, 81.

During Pries's California years his drawings and sketches were frequently published; *Pacific Coast Architect* 31 (February 1927) devoted eleven pages and the cover to his sketches. Pries sketches also appeared in the January 1927 issue and graced six of the twelve covers in 1928. A watercolor by Pries was published in *Pencil Points* in September 1931. Some work by Bain & Pries was published in *Architect and Engineer,* August 1941; and the Richard Lea house, on Lopez Island, appeared in *Architectural Record* 111 (April 1952). Pries's obituary appeared in the *Seattle Times,* April 10, 1968, and in the *Seattle Post-Intelligencer,* April 11, 1968. Finally, the recollections of many of Pries's former students and colleagues are an important source for knowledge of his life, work, and personality.

B. Marcus Priteca

The most substantive sources on Priteca are the Jewish Archives in the Manuscripts and University Archives Division, University of Washington Libraries; Richard McCann, successor to the Priteca practice and heir to a sizable collection of correspondence, drawings, and photographs; and the Theatre Historical Society publications at the University of Washington Drama Library, which include the quarterly journal *Marquee,* with reprints from older sources, and the same society's *Annuals* (the Hollywood

Pantages appears in the 1973 edition). Terry Helgesen, a contributor to many publications, has vast knowledge and an extensive collection of photographs and drawings on theater architecture, but at this writing (1994) is in failing health. The Huntington Museum in Los Angeles is establishing a room dedicated to the movie theater, which will include materials from McCann and Helgesen. The publication *Impressions of Imagination* (Seattle: Allied Arts of Seattle, 1986) includes an essay by Richard F. McCann; and Priteca's involvement with the Stimson family is discussed in Lawrence Kreisman, *The Stimson Legacy: Architecture in the Urban West* (Seattle: Willows Press/University of Washington Press, 1992).

From time to time articles about Priteca have appeared in the *Seattle Times* and *Seattle Post-Intelligencer*. Of particular note is Victor Steinbrueck's article, "An Oscar for an Architect," *Seattle Post-Intelligencer,* April 17, 1966. Priteca's obituaries appeared in the *Seattle Times,* October 3, l971, and in the *Seattle Post-Intelligencer,* October 3 and 5, l971. The Architects' Reference File at the University of Washington Libraries Special Collections Division contains a 1988 student paper by Mark McIntire with an extensive bibliography. The Washington State Office of Archaeology and Historic Preservation, a repository for National Register nominations, includes material specific to the Tacoma Pantages Theater.

Canadian sources include the Fine Arts Reference Library at the University of British Columbia, Vancouver, and the Vancouver Public Library. Doug McCallum published an article on Vancouver's Orpheum for the City of Vancouver in 1984.

Priteca's first name appears as Benjamin on his high school diploma and as Bernard on the death certificate. Sources also differ on Priteca's birth date; the mausoleum marker and the death certificate both read 1889.

Robert C. Reamer

There are multiple sources of information for the life and career of Robert C. Reamer. Drawings of his work for the Metropolitan Building Company, Seattle, are held in the Laird Norton Collection, Archives of the Metropolitan Building Company. A very small number of drawings are held by the Special Collections Division, University of Washington Libraries. Drawings of many of Reamer's Yellowstone projects are held in the Haynes Foundation Collection at the Montana Historical Society. Reamer's work was occasionally published during his life; see, for example, "Seattle Honor Awards, Washington State Chapter A.I.A.," *American Architect* 133 (February 5, 1928): 185-90; and "Hotel Edmond Meany, Seattle, Washington, *Architectural Record* 71 (March 1932): 179. Recent writing on Reamer's early career includes David L. Leavengood, "A Sense of Shelter: Robert C. Reamer in Yellowstone National Park," *Pacific Historical Review* 54 (November 1985): 495-513; David L. Leavengood, "The Mountain Architecture of R. C. Reamer," *Mountain Gazette,* 47:6; Richard A. Bartlett, "Old Faithful Inn," *American West* 16 (July-August 1979); and David L. Leavengood, "The Green Meadow Ranch," *Perspecta: The Yale Architectural Journal* 17 (1980): 56-65. Some of Reamer's Seattle work has been discussed in Lawrence Kreisman, *The Stimson Legacy: Architecture in the Urban West* (Seattle: Willows Press/University of Washington Press, 1992), and Lawrence Kreisman, "Weaver of Dreams," *Seattle Times Magazine,* January 8, 1989, p. 16. In addition, a very brief summary of Reamer's career appeared in his obituary in the *Seattle Times,* January 7, 1938.

Willis A. Ritchie

The chief sources of information on Willis A. Ritchie's life and career are several descriptive summaries that appeared between

1890 and 1915. These include the brief biographies in *Pacific Magazine* 3 (December 1890): 300-301; *A General Historical and Descriptive Review of the City of Seattle, Washington* (San Francisco, 1890), p. 27; Harvey K. Hines, *An Illustrated History of the State of Washington* (Chicago, 1893), pp. 362-64; and Nelson W. Durham, *Spokane and the Inland Empire* (Spokane, 1912), 3: 122-23. Also, the Seattle-based periodical, *Northwestern Real Estate and Business Review,* May 1891, includes an article that focuses on the first two years of Ritchie's practice in Washington. However, all of these sources must be used with caution since they include some inaccuracies and exaggerations.

Charles W. Saunders

The chief sources of information on the life and career of Charles W. Saunders are the many Seattle newspaper reports of the period noting his buildings. The work of Saunders & Lawton was prominently featured in the book *Seattle Architecturally 1902* (Seattle, 1902), which the firm co-published with Bebb & Mendel and deNeuf & Heide. In addition, brief summaries of Saunders's architectural career appeared in his obituaries in the *Seattle Times,* March 14, 1935, and *Architect and Engineer,* May 1935. Material regarding Saunders's legislative career may be found in the State Archives. Published renderings from the Saunders & Houghton office can be found in Jeffrey Karl Ochsner, "A. B. Chamberlin: The Illustration of Seattle Architecture, 1890-1896," *Pacific Northwest Quarterly* 81 (October 1990): 130-44. The involvement of the Saunders & Houghton office with the Seattle Schools is discussed in Jeffrey Karl Ochsner and Dennis Alan Andersen, "Architecture for Seattle Schools, 1880-1900," *Pacific Northwest Quarterly* 83 (October 1992): 128-43.

Schack, Young & Myers

Biographical material for the three principals of Schack, Young & Myers is relatively meager. For James H. Schack, *Men of the Pacific Coast* (San Francisco, 1903) provides a portrait and information regarding his birth and arrival in Seattle, while the obituary by A. M. Young in the *Monthly Bulletin* of the AIA Washington State Chapter March 1933 provides some useful biographical information but misstates Schack's age; curiously, Schack's death certificate lists his birth date as November 29, 1871. For A. M. Young, a short biographical sketch in *Pacific Builder and Engineer,* January 18, 1913, and his obituary in the *Seattle Times,* June 28, 1954, are useful. For David J. Myers, a biographical sketch in *Pacific Builder and Engineer,* November 26, 1910, and his obituary in the *Seattle Times,* May 10, 1936, are useful. A short summary of each principal's career was published in the *Seattle Daily Journal of Commerce,* August 17, 1920, announcing the formation of the firm. The successor firm, TRA, does maintain a history of the firm that goes back, in a general fashion, to Schack's arrival in Seattle in 1901; however, this document is most reliable for the period after World War II. TRA has donated most of the firm's architectural drawings from the 1900s to the 1940s to the Special Collections Division of the University of Washington Libraries. Only Myers published readily available articles that provide insight into his design practice and philosophy; these include: "The 'City Beautiful' Takes Firm Hold in Seattle," *Northwest Architect,* March 1910; "The Modest Home for the Northwest," *Northwest Architect,* April 1910; "Architecture Defined—American Library, Station and Bank Buildings—'Principles,'" *Pacific Builder and Engineer,* December 14, 1912; "A Good Plan and the Correct Proportions," *Pacific Builder and Engineer,* April 19, 1913; and "Coast Exhibits and How to Manage Them," *Pacific Builder and*

Engineer, June 21, 1913.

Edward Otto Schwagerl

As with most late nineteenth- and early twentieth-century designers in the Pacific Northwest, documentation of individual projects by Schwagerl is derived mainly from local newspapers: *Morning Oregonian* (Portland), *Tacoma Daily Ledger, Seattle Post-Intelligencer,* and *Seattle Times.* The most comprehensive biographical sketch available on Schwagerl occurs in *A Volume of Memoirs and Genealogy of Representative Citizens of the City of Seattle and the County of King, Washington* (New York and Chicago, 1903), pp. 353-57; however, many of the specific facts and dates provided in this sketch remain to be verified. Information on his work for the Tacoma Board of Park Commissioners can be found in chapter 50 of Herbert Hunt, *Tacoma: Its History and Its Builders* (Chicago, 1916). Information on his tenure as Superintendent of Public Parks in Seattle can be found in chapter 25 of Clarence B. Bagley, *History of Seattle* (Chicago, 1916). The influence of his parks and boulevards plans for Seattle is discussed in William H. Wilson, *The City Beautiful Movement* (Baltimore: Johns Hopkins University Press, 1989), which unfortunately gives Schwagerl's first name incorrectly as "Eugene," and has other minor biographical errors. His death notice appeared in the *Seattle Post-Intelligencer,* January 29, 1910, while obituaries appeared in the *Seattle Times* of January 28, 1910, and the March 1910 issue of *The Northwest Architect.*

Somervell & Coté

The most readily available source of information regarding W. Marbury Somervell and Joseph S. Coté is Clarence B. Bagley's *History of Seattle* (1916), pp. 832-33 (for Somervell) and p. 965 (for Coté). Also informative are three articles in *Pacific Builder and Engineer,* July 4, 1906 (Somervell & Coté), July 21, 1913 (Somervell & Putnam), and November 28, 1914 (Somervell & Putnam). Somervell's obituary was published in *Architect and Engineer,* July 1939. An article by Sean Rossiter, entitled "Seattle's Forgotten Architect," in the August 26, 1987, issue of *Seattle Weekly,* is less useful, as it contains multiple errors and exaggerations.

Victor Steinbrueck

Some biographical material on Victor Steinbrueck is available in the *Seattle Daily Journal of Commerce,* May 20, 1963. The significance of Steinbrueck's work is suggested by the front page news articles and prominent obituaries published the day after his death: Lansing Jones and Charles E. Brown, "Death Ends Steinbrueck's Long Love Affair with Seattle," *Seattle Times,* February 15, 1985; Charles E. Brown, "City Loses a Friend in Death of Architect Victor Steinbrueck," *Seattle Times,* February 15, 1985; "Pike Market's 'Father' Victor Steinbrueck Dies," *Seattle Post-Intelligencer,* February 15, 1985; Mary Rothschild and John Harris, "Friends Mourn the Loss of an Urban Hero," *Seattle Post-Intelligencer,* February 15, 1985. An obituary also was published in the architectural press: "Victor Steinbrueck, FAIA, Urban Activist in Seattle," *Architecture* 74 (April 1985): 29, 34.

Steinbrueck's house was published in "Northwest: Current Work," *Progressive Architecture* 34 (June 1953): 75; the Mason house in Richmond Beach is mentioned in *Architectural Record* 114 (September 1953): 48-2 to 48-3; and the Mason residence in Seattle (a different building) appeared in *Architectural Record* 113 (April 1953): 159-63. The Pioneer Square competition, in which Steinbrueck won the first prize ($300), is discussed in "Seattle's Pioneer Square to Be Remodeled: City Plans Renovation of Other Landmarks," *Architectural Record* 116 (October 1954): 48-6, and

"Landmarks Preserved in Remodeled Square," *Architectural Record* 117 (March 1955): 322. The design for the University of Washington Faculty Center Building was published in "Faculty Club," *Progressive Architecture* 42 (February 1961): 115-21. Several of Steinbrueck's houses were also published in the *Seattle Times.* Photographs of six of his houses may be found in the Dearborn-Massar Collection, Special Collections Division, University of Washington Libraries. Drawings of several projects are also available at the Special Collections Division, including measured drawings of several buildings in the Pioneer Square Historic District.

In his four books, Steinbrueck attempted to document the life and shape of the city, two characteristics which he viewed as intimately connected; see Victor Steinbrueck, *A Guide to Seattle Architecture, 1850-1953* (New York: Reinhold Publishing Corporation, 1953); *Seattle Cityscape* (Seattle: University of Washington Press, 1962); *Market Sketchbook* (Seattle: University of Washington Press, 1968); and *Seattle Cityscape #2* (Seattle: University of Washington Press, 1973). With Folke Nyberg he published *A Visual Inventory of Buildings and Urban Design Resources for Seattle, Washington* (Seattle: Historic Seattle Preservation and Development Authority, 1975-77). Steinbrueck was also published quite often in Seattle's popular press.

An extensive, although still incomplete, bibliography is included in Lisa J. Chin, "Victor Steinbrueck: The City Is People" (M.Arch. thesis, University of Washington, 1991). Chin's thesis is very brief in its presentation of biographical information on Steinbrueck, but suggests the significance of his involvement with a number of major civic projects and private developments and outlines some of his arguments for an architecture guided by social and community needs rather than economic and political expedience.

James Stephen

Washington State University, Manuscripts, Archives and Special Collections, is the repository for several volumes of business records and ledgers associated with Stephen & Josenhans, James Stephen, and Stephen & Stephen, and for architectural photographs taken by James Stephen in Alaska (ca. 1887) and Mexico (1908). The Seattle Public Schools Facilities Department retains important primary source materials, including the original specifications, plans, and drawings for all extant and some demolished schools designed by Stephen. The Seattle School District Archives include an extensive collection of historic photographs, district records, and architectural plans of demolished and surplused or sold schools designed by Stephen (as well as a lengthy chronology of model plan schools developed by Peter Staten in conjunction with his research for "Neighborly Schools," *Seattle Weekly,* April 6, 1988). *Seattle Public Schools—Historic Building Survey* (Seattle, 1990), prepared by Patricia C. Erigero for Historic Seattle Preservation and Development Authority, provides a thorough description of Seattle school building history and architecture as well as the role of James Stephen. The work of Stephen & Josenhans at Washington State University is presented in J. M. Neil, "Administrators, Architects and Campus Development: Washington State University, 1890-1905," *Journal of the Society of Architectural Historians* 29 (May 1970): 144-55. Works by Stephen, including buildings other than schools, can be identified from contemporary reports in *Pacific Builder and Engineer* and *Seattle Daily Journal of Commerce.* A particularly detailed description of Stephen's Queen Anne High School is found in *Pacific Builder and Engineer,* November 13, 1909, pp. 444-50. Stephen's obituary appeared in the *Seattle Times,* September 28, 1938. Descendants of James Stephen who remain in the region may also be a source of information.

Biographical information was obtained from personal communications and interviews with the late James Howard Stephen and other Stephen family members.

Ellsworth Storey

A biographical essay by Storey's daughter Eunice, a key document for personal data, may be found at the Architecture and Urban Planning Library at the University of Washington. The Special Collections Division, University of Washington Libraries, holds surviving drawings from Storey's office and a selection of photographs of his projects. The Architects Reference File at Special Collections also includes several incomplete lists of Storey's buildings. Some of Storey's work was published in his lifetime: for the Hoo-Hoo House, see *Pacific Builder and Engineer,* June 12, 1909; for several residential projects see *Chapters on Architecture,* June 1911; *Bungalow Magazine,* October 1914 and June 1916; and *Washington State Architect,* November 1927. Many of Storey's buildings are cited in Sally B. Woodbridge and Roger Montgomery, *A Guide to Architecture in Washington State* (Seattle: University of Washington Press, 1980). Victor Steinbrueck, *Seattle Cityscape* (Seattle: University of Washington Press, 1962), illustrates and discusses the Henry C. Storey and Ellsworth Storey houses and the cottages (Steinbrueck lived in the Henry C. Storey house for several years). Steinbrueck also discusses the Storey cottages in *Pacific Architect and Builder* 66 (June 1960): 21-24. For a brief discussion of the Hoo-Hoo House, see James F. O'Gorman, "The Hoo-Hoo House, Alaska-Yukon-Pacific Exposition, Seattle, 1909," *Journal of the Society of Architectural Historians* 48 (October 1960): 123-25. An abstract of Grant Hildebrand's presentation on Storey to the Society of Architectural Historians appears in *Journal of the Society of Architectural Historians* 31 (October 1972): 223 (although Hildebrand notes that

dates given therein for the cottages are wrong, as is the attribution to Storey of the Denny Blaine bus shelter). (In addition, it should be noted that the H. C. Storey house has sometimes been misidentified as the Mulliken house in some of the literature on Storey.)

In 1993, Christine Carr, a graduate student in the Department of Architecture at the University of Washington, initiated a detailed research project on Storey. Her M.Arch. thesis, "The Houses of Ellsworth Storey: Frames and Patterns," was completed in June 1994.

Butler Sturtevant

There are very few sources of reliable information concerning Sturtevant's career. There are several drawings in the Special Collections Division, University of Washington Libraries, and some correspondence in the Ambrose Patterson Manuscripts Collection and in the J. Lister Holmes Collection in the Manuscripts and University Archives Division, University of Washington Libraries, where Sturtevant's work on the University campus can also be found in the collection of University Records. Only one out-of-state source has been located, that being Principia College in Elsah, Illinois. That school's collection contains client correspondence, as well as some drawings and photographs of Sturtevant's work on the Principia campus. A large collection of his drawings for the St. Louis campus, dating from the late 1950s to 1969, are kept in the Principia School offices. Published works include the "Frederick Remington Green Garden," *Country Life,* January 1936, pp. 31-33; "Houses for Defense: Westpark, Bremerton," *Architectural Forum,* December 1941, pp. 410-16; and "Holly Park Housing Project," *Architectural Forum,* July 1945, pp. 101-3.

Sturtevant's death in a St. Louis suburb in February 1970 remains something of a mystery. A death certificate could not be located and no obituary or death notice has been found in the St. Louis newspapers.

Roland Terry

Roland Terry, who currently lives in Mount Vernon, Washington, is an obvious source of information concerning his own life and career. Other sources include records of the AIA (Seattle Chapter) at the Manuscripts and Archives Division of the University of Washington Libraries, numerous articles in the *Seattle Times* and *Seattle Post-Intelligencer,* and an interesting portrait of Terry written by Barry Head entitled "Master of Costly Design" in *Seattle Magazine* 4 (June 1967): 37-41. Terry's work was widely published in the 1950s and early 1960s. The Florence B. Terry house and four buildings by Tucker, Shields & Terry are included in Victor Steinbrueck's book, *Guide to Seattle Architecture, 1850-1953* (New York: Reinhold, 1953). The Hauberg country house on Bainbridge Island and Terry's retreat on Lopez Island ("Baycourt") are illustrated in *Contemporary Homes of the Pacific Northwest* (Seattle: Madrona Press, 1980). "Baycourt" is also discussed in Jon Krakauer's article, "In the San Juan Islands: Driftwood and Sod Shape a Seattle Architect's Residence," *Architectural Digest* 46 (June 1989): 188-93. Other useful magazine articles include "Hillside Restaurant Gives Seattle Diners a View of Their City from a Building That Mixes Northwest Rusticity with Lush Hawaiian Decor," *Architectural Forum* 98 (May 1953): 148-49; and "Three Restaurants by Terry & Moore," *Pacific Architect and Builder* 64 (November 1958): 11-17. The Blethen and Hauberg residences in Seattle are extensively illustrated in "How People Are Achieving a New Elegance," *House Beautiful* 102 (November 1960): 197-202, 204-13; Curtis Besinger discusses the Paul Roland Smith residence in "An Atrium for All the Seaons," *House Beautiful* 105 (August 1963): 58-67; and the Culter residence is described in "How to

Have a View Wherever You Look," *House and Garden* 120 (October 1961): 161-73. The extent of Terry's reputation as a fine interior designer is suggested by articles such as "A Self-effacing Scheme for a Creative Florist in Seattle," *Interiors* 115 (July 1956): 52; "Japan Air Lines: Oriental Serenity in Seattle," *Interiors* 120 (September 1960): 152; and "Bavarian Decor and American Cuisine in an A-frame by Architects Terry and Moore of Seattle, " *Interiors* 122 (February 1963): 65-67.

Paul Thiry

Sources for information on Thiry and his work are extensive. Among the more important are Robert E. Koehler, "Profile III: Paul Thiry," *Pacific Architect and Builder,* February 1961; Nelson and Wright, *Tomorrow's House* (New York, 1945; on his houses); Albert Christ-Janer and Mary Mix Foley, *Modern Church Architecture* (New York: McGraw-Hill, 1962; on his churches); Esther McCoy, "West Coast Architects IV/ Paul Thiry," *Arts + Architecture,* February 1965; "Seattle Center Coliseum," *Vitrum* (Milan), October 1967; Andrea O. Dean, "A Dam Designed as a Powerful, Respectful Work of Architecture," *AIA Journal,* April 1977, pp. 36-40; "Paul Thiry," in *Contemporary Architects* (New York: St. Martin's Press, 1980), pp. 810-12; and Meredith L. Clausen, "Paul Thiry: The Emergence of Modernism in Northwest Architecture," *Pacific Northwest Quarterly* 75 (July 1984): 128-39. See also the architect scrapbooks and the vertical file at the Art Department of Seattle Public Library; the taped and transcribed interview published by the Smithsonian Institution as part of the Archives of American Art, Meredith L. Clausen, interviewer, September 1983; and the Oral History interview, Seattle Center Foundation, Lorraine McConaghy, interviewer, November 1991. Thiry's obituary appeared in the *Seattle Times,* July 3, 1993.

Harlan Thomas

Although Harlan Thomas played a significant professional role as both practitioner and educator, there is relatively little material available on his career. The key reference is a manuscript, "A Chronicle of Harlan Thomas—Designing Architect," prepared by the Department of Community Development, City of Seattle, October 1975, a copy of which is in the Special Collections Division, University of Washington Libraries. Unfortunately, the photographs originally a part of the manuscript have disappeared except for their rather unsatisfactory copy machine reproductions. Recently, however, the Special Collections Division, University of Washington Libraries, received a portfolio of photographs of many Thomas projects. Thomas is mentioned early in his career in Clarence B. Bagley, *History of Seattle* (Chicago, 1916), 3: 13-14, and in the *Seattle Times,* August 2, 1951, which noted an exhibit of his paintings. Some of Thomas's buildings appeared in contemporary publications; for example, for Thomas's high schools, see *Pacific Builder and Engineer* 12 (November 11, 1911): 312-15. His obituary appeared in the *Seattle Post-Intelligencer,* September 8, 1953. Information is also available from Thomas's former students (such as Professor Emeritus and Mrs. John Rohrer, who provided information for this essay).

Vernacular and Popular Architecture in Seattle

For a general introduction to the current state of research on vernacular and popular architecture, see Dell Upton and John Michael Vlach, eds., *Common Places: Readings in American Vernacular Architecture* (Athens: University of Georgia Press, 1986). Two articles that present an overview of the field from somewhat different viewpoints are Dell Upton, "The Power of Things: Recent Studies in American Vernacular Architecture," *American Quarterly* 35 (1983): 262-79; and Thomas C. Hubka, "American Vernacular Architecture," in Ervin H. Zube and Gary T. Moore, *Advances in Environment, Behavior and Design,* (New York and London: Plenum Press, 1991), 3: 153-84. Dell Upton, ed., *America's Architectural Roots: Ethnic Groups that Built America* (Washington, D.C.: Preservation Press, 1986), is a brief introduction to the contributions of various ethnic groups to the built environment of the United States.

The Vernacular Architecture Forum (VAF) fosters communication among scholars working in this field. Selected papers from VAF meetings are published in *Perspectives in Vernacular Architecture,* 4 vols. (Columbia: University of Missouri Press, 1986-92). (Unfortunately, the paper, "Patterns of Acculturation and Social Differentiation in Ethnic Vernacular Architecture of Washington State," which addressed the Scandinavian contribution to the architecture of Washington State, presented by Robert E. Walls at the VAF meeting in Lexington, Kentucky, May 12, 1990, is not included in these volumes.)

While a large number of cultural resource surveys have been undertaken in Washington State at the city, county, and state level, no general framework has been developed nor are these surveys always comparable in terms of form, methodology, level of detail, and the like.

In recent years, the Washington State Office of Archaeology and Historic Preservation has commissioned studies ("context documents") that provide a historic context for properties associated with the state's African American heritage and with the state's Asian and Pacific American heritage; see, for example, Gail Dubrow, Gail Nomura, et al., The *Historic Context for the Protection of Asian/Pacific American Resources in Washington State* (Olympia: Office of Archaeology and Historic Preservation, 1993). A broad context document addressing residential vernacular architecture may also be developed. In 1986, Leonard Garfield and Greg Griffith, in the Office of Archaeology and Historic Preservation, did prepare a Multiple Property Documentation form on rural schools in Washington, which provides a context for that building type. The King County Landmark and Heritage Commission primarily focuses on unincorporated areas of King County. One recent effort is directed toward a "multiple property designation" which may allow recognition of many types of vernacular buildings (but particularly residential buildings) based on thematic groupings.

The citywide survey by Folke Nyberg and Victor Steinbrueck, *A Visual Inventory of Buildings and Urban Design Resources for Seattle, Washington* (Seattle: Historic Seattle Preservation and Development Authority, 1975-77), remains the most comprehensive published inventory and analysis of Seattle's built fabric. More recent efforts tend to be more focused; an example is *Historic Survey and Planning Study of Fremont's Commercial Area,* prepared by Carol Tobin for the Fremont Neighborhood Council (under the auspices of the Office of Urban Conservation in the Department of Neighborhoods), which addresses the historic sigificance of the commercial vernacular at the neighborhood level.

In recent years, research by students in the University of Washington College of Architecture and Urban Planning, particularly in the Preservation Planning and Design Program, has begun to address the history of selected specific vernacular elements of Seattle's built environment. A selection of these research papers has been compiled in manuscript form by Gail Dubrow as "Preserving the Vernacular Built Environment: Working Papers from the Perservation Planning and Design Program at the University of Washington," available at the College of Architecture and Urban Planning.

Andrew Willatsen

Willatsen's surviving notebooks, papers, and a transcription of a personal ledger are in the Manuscripts and University Archives Division of the University of Washington Libraries. The library's Special Collections Division holds a collection of Willatsen's surviving drawings as well as photographs documenting many of his early buildings. Willatsen is mentioned in H. Allan Brooks, *The Prairie School* (Toronto: University of Toronto Press, 1972), and his apprenticeship at the Studio is cited in Grant Manson, *Frank Lloyd Wright to 1910* (New York: Reinhold, 1958). The only monograph on Willatsen's career to date is Sylvia L. Gillis, "Andrew C. P. Willatsen, Architect, A.I.A. (1876-1974)" (M.A. thesis, University of Washington, 1980); copies can be found in the Architecture and Urban Planning Library and in the Art Library at the University of Washington. While useful for Willatsen's Prairie Style projects, this thesis does not address his later career. In addition, the list of extant Willatsen buildings presented in the appendixes is incomplete. Some of Willatsen's work is documented in contemporary periodicals such as *Pacific Builder and Engineer, Pacific Coast Architect, Bungalow Magazine,* and *Architectural Record.* Early photographs of the Clarke and Kerry houses can be found in Frank Calvert, ed., *Homes and Gardens of the Pacific Coast, Volume 1: Seattle* (Beaux Arts Village, Lake Washington: Beaux Arts Society Publishers, 1913). Willatsen's obituary appeared in the *Seattle Post-Intelligencer,* July 26, 1974.

W. R. B. Willcox

The University of Oregon Library holds the major collection of Willcox's drawings, papers, and correspondence. Included there (as well as in the Special Collections Division of the University of Washington Libraries) is the carefully researched paper by

Elisabeth Walton Potter, "W. R. B. Willcox: A Note on the Seattle Years," from *Festschrift, a Collection of Essays on Architectural History* (Salem: Northern Pacific Coast Chapter, Society of Architectural Historians, 1978), pp. 76-79. Also available in both collections is Nancy K. Smith: "Annals of Oregon: W. R. B. Willcox," *The Call Number* 29 (Fall 1968): 18-24, which was republished in *ARCADE: Northwest Journal for Architecture and Design* 4 (April-May 1984): 10-12. The Architecture and Urban Planning Library at the University of Washington also has a copy of a research paper by Don Genasci and David Shelman, "W. R. B. Willcox: His Architectural and Educational Theory," Department of Architecture, School of Architecture and Allied Arts, University of Oregon (February 1980). Willcox's own statements on architecture were occasionally published; see, for example, the text of his talk to the AIA, "Modern Architecture and How Determined," in *Pacific Builder and Engineer* 14 (November 16, 1912): 397-98. Willcox & Sayward projects occasionally appeared in contemporary publications, including *Pacific Builder and Engineer, Pacific Coast Architect,* and *Architectural Record.* (In addition, Elisabeth Walton Potter, who now resides in Salem and has a collection of materials related to Willcox, provided information and photographs for the preparation of the essay included in this volume.)

Locations of Extant Buildings and Projects Presented in the Text

The following is a list of locations for most buildings and projects that still stand that have been identified in the essays on the various architects. This list is as complete as it has been possible to make it, but a few addresses are nonetheless missing. As noted in the essays, these buildings are only a limited selection of extant buildings by each architect. The individual lists for some architects are very short, as many buildings mentioned in the text have been destroyed.

Buildings are identified by original names. Current names are also usually provided in parentheses, although some buildings may have changed uses since this list was compiled, and for this reason there may be some inaccuracies. The addresses given are current addresses. In some cases these are not the same as the original addresses because street names and address numbering systems have changed over the years.

Since this list is intended to aid in locating buildings, it is organized alphabetically by architect. Under each architect, buildings in Seattle are listed first (in alphabetical order), buildings located elsewhere in Washington State (in alphabetical order by city or town) are listed second, and those found elsewhere in the United States are listed third. The few buildings outside the United States are listed last.

Addresses are provided so that travelers may use this book as a guide in finding the works identified in the text. Anyone using this book as a guide must respect the privacy of the owners of these buildings. The inclusion of addresses in no way implies the public's right of entry to any property.

Albertson, Wilson & Richardson

Children's Orthopedic Hospital (now Queen Anne Manor Retirement Community)
100 Crockett Street
Seattle, Washington 98109

Cobb Building
1305 Fourth Avenue
Seattle, Washington 98101

Cornish School
710 E. Roy Street
Seattle, Washington 98102

[New] Infirmary Building (now Hall Health Center)
University of Washington
Seattle, Washington 98195

Law Building (now Gowan Hall)
University of Washington
Seattle, Washington 98195

Medical and Dental Building (now Medical-Dental Building)
509 Olive Way
Seatttle, Washington 98101

Mount Baker Park Presbyterian Church
3201 Hunter Boulevard S.
Seattle, Washington 98144

Northern Life Tower (now Seattle Tower)
1218 Third Avenue
Seattle, Washington 98101

Saint John Catholic Church
7912 First Avenue N.W.
Seattle, Washington 98103

Saint Joseph Catholic Church
732 18th Avenue E.
Seattle, Washington 98112

Mrs. Grant Smith house
619 W. Comstock Street
Seattle, Washington 98119

Trinity Methodist Episcopal Church
6512 23rd Avenue N.W.
Seattle, Washington 98117

Women's University Club
1105 Sixth Avenue
Seattle, Washington 98104

YMCA–New Central Branch
909 Fourth Avenue
Seattle, Washington 98104

Becker Building
114 S. I Street
Aberdeen, Washington 98520

South Court Apartments
834 Seventh Street
Bremerton, Washington 98310

Municipal Building for the City of Everett
3002 Wetmore Avenue
Everett, Washington 98201

Security Bank Building
203 Fourth Avenue E.
Olympia, Washington 98501

First Presbyterian Church
9 S. Eighth Avenue
Yakima, Washington 98902

Royal Insurance Building (now Furth Building)
201 Sansome Street
San Francisco, California 94104

Frederick Anhalt

The Anhalt Company apartment building (now
    The Belmont)
710 Belmont Place E.
Seattle, Washington 98102

The Anhalt Company apartment building (now
    Oak Manor)
730 Belmont Avenue E.
Seattle, Washington 98102

The Anhalt Company apartment building (now
    Belmont Court)
750 Belmont Avenue E.
Seattle, Washington 98102

The Anhalt Company apartment building
1005 E. Roy Street
Seattle, Washington 98102

The Anhalt Company apartment building
1014 E. Roy Street
Seattle, Washington 98102

The Borchert Company apartment building
417 Harvard Avenue E.
Seattle, Washington 98102

The Borchert Company apartment building
1201 E. John Street
Seattle, Washington 98102

The Borchert Company apartment building
    (now Twin Gables)
1516 E. Republican Street
Seattle, Washington 98102

Cora M. Graham store building
3055-3065 Beacon Avenue S.
Seattle, Washington 98144

Edwin C. Kellogg house
4006 N.E. 38th Street
Seattle, Washington 98105

Saint Stephen Episcopal Church
4805 N.E. 45th Street
Seattle, Washington 98105

Western Building and Leasing Company
    apartment building
1710 E. Denny Way
Seattle, Washington 98122

Western Building and Leasing Company
    apartment building
1405 E. John Street
Seattle, Washington 98112

Western Building and Leasing Company
    bungalow apartments
1401-1407 S. Bayview Street
Seattle, Washington 98144

Kichio Allen Arai

Nichiren Buddhist Church
1042 S. Weller Street
Seattle, Washington 98104

Nichiren Buddhist Church addition
1042 S. Weller Street
Seattle, Washington 98104

Nichiren Buddhist Church garage
1042 S. Weller Street
Seattle, Washington 98114

Seattle Buddhist Church
1427 S. Main Street
Seattle, Washington 98144

Shinran Shonin 700th Anniversary Memorial
 Hall
1427 S. Main Street
Seattle, Washington 98144

White River Buddhist Temple
3625 Auburn Way N.
Auburn, Washington 98002

Yakima Buddhist Bussei Kaikan
202 W. Second Street
Wapato, Washington 98951

Idaho-Oregon Buddhist Temple
286 S.E. Fourth Street
Ontario, Oregon 97914

Elizabeth Ayer

Winston W. Chambers house
3033 E. Laurelhurst Drive N.E.
Seattle, Washington 98105

William E. Forland house
18939 Edgecliff Drive S.W.
Seattle, Washington 98166

Aubrey Naef house
834 Hillside Drive
Seattle, Washington 98112

Robert F. Linden house
12903 Manzanita Road N.E.
Bainbridge Island, Washington 98110

L. C. Henry house
The Highlands, Washington 98177

Lee Doud house
11419 Gravelley Lake Drive S.W.
Tacoma, Washington 98499

W. Hilding Lindberg house
46 Country Club Drive S.W.
Tacoma, Washington 98499

Albert Schafer Castle
8261 Highway 106
Union, Washington 98592

William J. Bain, Sr.

Bel Roy Apartments
703 Bellevue Avenue E.
Seattle, Washington 98102

Samuel J. Calderhead house
2110 Waverly Way E.
Seattle, Washington 98112

Consulate Apartments
1619 Belmont Avenue
Seattle, Washington 98122

Louis T. Dulien house
4210 55th Avenue N.E.
Seattle, Washington 98105

Envoy Apartments
821 Ninth Avenue
Seattle, Washington 98104

First Presbyterian Church
Seventh Avenue and Spring Street
Seattle, Washington 98104

Gamma Phi Beta Sorority
4529 17th Avenue N.E.
Seattle, Washington 98105

Pi Beta Phi Sorority
4548 17th Avenue N.E.
Seattle, Washington 98105

J. G. Pursley house
1330 Broadmoor Drive
Seattle, Washington 98112

Rainier Vista Elementary School (now
 a Head Start facility)
3100 S. Alaska Street
Seattle, Washington 98108

Herbert Schoenfeld house
1107 Federal Avenue E.
Seattle, Washington 98102

John L. Scott house
939 Federal Avenue E.
Seattle, Washington 98102

Scottish Rite Temple
1155 Broadway E.
Seattle, Washington 98102

Clarence Shaw house
1656 Interlaken Place
Seattle, Washington 98112

Shoremont Apartments (now north half Lake
    Court Apartments)
2020 43rd Avenue E.
Seattle, Washington 98112

George F. Vance house
1208 Shenandoah Drive E.
Seattle, Washington 98112

Viceroy Apartments
505 Boylston Avenue E.
Seattle, Washington 98102

Yesler Terrace Housing
903 E. Yesler Way
Seattle, Washington 98104

Albert Brygger house
Euclid Street N.E.
Port Madison, Bainbridge Island,
    Washington 98110

Bebb & Gould

Anderson Hall
University of Washington
Seattle, Washington 98195

Art Institute of Seattle (now Seattle Art
    Museum)
Volunteer Park
Seattle, Washington 98112

F. H. Brownell residence
1137 Harvard Avenue E.
Seattle, Washington 98102

Central campus plan
University of Washington
Seattle, Washington 98195

Central Library (now Suzzallo Library)
University of Washington
Seattle, Washington 98195

Thomas Dovey residence
1017 E. Blaine Street
Seattle, Washington 98102

Fisher Studio Building
1519 Second Avenue
Seattle, Washington 98101

Penthouse Theater
University of Washington
Seattle, Washington 98195

Times Square Building
414 Stewart Street
Seattle, Washington 98101

U.S. Government (Hiram M. Chittenden) Locks
3015 N.W. 54th Street
Seattle, Washington 98107

U.S. Marine Hospital (now Pacific Medical
    Center)
1200 12th Avenue S.
Seattle, Washington 98144

Carl F. Gould residence ("Topsfield")
2380 Upper Farms Road
Bainbridge Island, Washington 98110

Everett Public Library
2702 Hoyt Avenue
Everett, Washington 98201

Pacific Telephone and Telegraph (now U.S. West)
    Company
Longview Office
Mississippi Street and Vendercook Way
Longview, Washington 98632

U.S. Post Office
1603 Larch Street
Longview, Washington 98632

Bebb & Mendel

Diller Hotel
1220 First Avenue
Seattle, Washington 98101

Fire Station No. 18
5427 Russell Avenue N.W.
Seattle, Washington 98107

First Church of Christ Scientist
1519 E. Denny Way
Seattle, Washington 98122

Frye Hotel
215-225 Yesler Way
Seattle, Washington 98104

Hoge Building
705 Second Avenue
Seattle, Washington 98104

George W. Miller house
1204 22nd Avenue E.
Seattle, Washington 98112

Oriental Block
606-610 Second Avenue
Seattle, Washington 98104

Schwabacher Hardware Company warehouse
(now part of Merrill Place)
401 First Avenue S.
Seattle, Washington 98104

University Heights School
5031 University Way N.E.
Seattle, Washington 98105

William Walker house (also known as Walker-
Ames house)
808 36th Avenue E.
Seattle, Washington 98112

Everett Theater
2911 Colby Avenue
Everett, Washington 98201

Beezer Brothers

John B. and K. L. Beltinck apartment building
319 16th Avenue
Seattle, Washington 98122

Blessed Sacrament Catholic Church
5049 Ninth Avenue N.E.
Seattle, Washington 98105

Blessed Sacrament Catholic Church rectory
5041 Ninth Avenue N.E.
Seattle, Washington 98105

Broadway State Bank (now Quality Rentals)
building
1501 Broadway
Seattle, Washington 98122

Cathedral School
803 Terry Avenue
Seattle, Washington 98104

Oliver D. Fisher residence
1047 Belmont Place E.
Seattle, Washington 98102

Homer L. Hillman residence
1051 Summit Avenue E.
Seattle, Washington 98102

Immaculate Conception Catholic Church
rectory
820 18th Avenue
Seattle, Washington 98122

Immaculate Conception School
810 18th Avenue
Seattle, Washington 98122

Edward J. O'Dea High School
802 Terry Avenue
Seattle, Washington 98104

Our Lady of Mount Virgin Catholic Church
1531 Bradner Place S.
Seattle, Washington 98144

Saint Joseph Catholic Church rectory
730 18th Avenue E.
Seattle, Washington 98112

Saint Joseph School
720 18th Avenue E.
Seattle, Washington 98112

Baker-Boyer Bank Building
W. Main Street
Walla Walla, Washington 99362

First National Bank of Walla Walla Building
(now First Federal Savings Bank)
East Alder Street
Walla Walla, Washington 99362

Saint Anthony Hospital (now Christopher
House apartments)
100 S. Cleveland Avenue
Wenatchee, Washington 98801

Saint Dominic Catholic Church
2390 Bush Street
San Francisco, California 94115

Mary Ann Larrabee Memorial Presbyterian
Church
Deer Lodge, Montana 59722

Saint Joseph Hospital
Deer Lodge, Montana 59722

Henry W. Bittman

Henry and Jessie Bittman residence
4625 Eastern Avenue N.
Seattle, Washington 98103

Eagles Temple
1404 Seventh Avenue
Seattle, Washington 98101

King County Courthouse (upper floors)
516 Third Avenue
Seattle, Washington 98104

Mann Building
1401 Third Avenue
Seattle, Washington 98101

Seattle Post-Intelligencer Building (now Group
    Health)
521 Wall Street
Seattle, Washington 98121

Terminal Sales Building
1932 First Avenue
Seattle, Washington 98101

United Shopping Tower (Olympic Tower)
217 Pine Street
Seattle, Washington 98101

William Volker Building
1000 Lenora Street
Seattle, Washington 98101

Monte Cristo Hotel
Hoyt and Wall Streets
Everett, Washington 98201

William E. Boone

Marshall-Walker Block (Globe Hotel)
300-310 First Avenue S. and 105-109 S. Main
    Street
Seattle Washington 98104

Breitung & Buchinger

Academy of the Holy Names of Jesus and Mary
728 21st Avenue E.
Seattle, Washington 98112

Capital Brewing and Malting Company building
    (now Jackson Building)
322-324 First Avenue S.
Seattle, Washington 98104

House of the Good Shepherd (now Good
    Shepherd Center)
4649 Sunnyside Avenue N.
Seattle, Washington 98103

IOOF (Odd Fellows) Temple
915 E. Pine Street
Seattle, Washington 98122

Triangle Hotel
551 First Avenue S.
Seattle, Washiongton 98104

St. Charles Hotel
4714 Ballard Avenue N.W.
Seattle, Washington 98107

Saint Mary Catholic Church
611 20th Avenue S.
Seattle, Washington 98144

Édouard Frère Champney

New Richmond Hotel (now Downtowner
    Apartments)
308 Fourth Avenue S.
Seattle, Washington 98104

Young Women's Christian Association Building
1118 Fifth Avenue
Seattle, Washington 98101

Elks Temple
565 Broadway
Tacoma, Washington 98402

Rogers Building
Granville and Pender Streets
Vancouver, British Columbia, Canada

Kirtland Kelsey Cutter

T. J. Heffernan house (now Bush School)
408 Lake Washington Boulevard
Seattle, Washington 98122

L. B. Peeples house
948 Harvard Avenue E.
Seattle, Washington 98102

The Rainier Club
810 Fourth Avenue
Seattle, Washington 98104

C. J. Smith house
1147 Harvard Avenue E.
Seattle, Washington 98102

C. D. Stimson house (Stimson-Green house)
1204 Minor Avenue
Seattle, Washington 98101

C. D. Stimson house ("Norcliffe"; later Piggott
    house)
The Highlands, Washington 98177

Seattle Golf and Country Club
The Highlands, Washington 98177

Elmer Fisher

Bank of Commerce
95-99 Yesler Way
Seattle, Washington 98104

Austin A. Bell Building
2324-2326 First Avenue
Seattle, Washington 98101

Burke Building fragments
900 block Second Avenue and/100 block
    Marion Street
Seattle, Washington 98101

[Second] Korn Building
115-119 Yesler Way
Seattle, Washington 98104

Pioneer Building
600-610 First Avenue and 106-108 James Street
Seattle, Washington 98104

Schwabacher Building
105-107 First Avenue S. and 93 Yesler Way
Seattle, Washington 98104

State Building
300-312 Occidental Avenue S. and
    155-159 S. Main Street
Seattle, Washington 98104

Yesler Block (now Mutual Life Building)
603-607 First Avenue
Seattle, Washington 98104

Hastings Building
835-839 Water Street
Port Townsend, Washington 98368

N. D. Hill Building
635-639 Water Street
Port Townsend, Washington 98368

James and Hastings Building
938-94 Water Street
Port Townsend, Washington 98368

McCurdy Block
834-844 Water Street
Port Townsend, Washington 98368

Augustus Warren Gould

Arctic Building
700 Third Avenue
Seattle, Washington 98104

King County Courthouse (lower floors)
516 Third Avenue
Seattle, Washington 98104

Albert Rhodes house
1901 Tenth Avenue E.
Seattle, Washington 98102

Standard Furniture Company Building
    (now Broadacres Building)
1601 Second Avenue
Seattle, Washington 98101

John Graham, Jr.

Bank of California Building
900 Fourth Avenue
Seattle, Washington 98101

Edgewater Apartments
2411 42nd Avenue E.
Seattle, Washington 98112

Northgate Shopping Center
Northgate Way
Seattle, Washington 98125

Olympic Hotel parking garage
415 Seneca Street
Seattle, Washington 98101

Seattle Mason Clinic (now Virginia Mason
    Clinic)
1100 Ninth Avenue
Seattle, Washington 98101

Sheraton Hotel and Towers
1400 Sixth Avenue
Seattle, Washington 98101

Space Needle
219 Fourth Avenue N. (Seattle Center campus)
Seattle, Washington 98109

Washington Natural Gas headquarters
815 Mercer Street
Seattle, Washington 98109

Westin Hotel and Towers
1900 Fifth Avenue
Seattle, Washington 98101

1600 Bell Plaza (now U.S. West building)
1600 Seventh Avenue
Seattle, Washington 98101

Bellevue Athletic Club
11200 S.E. Sixth Street
Bellevue, Washington 98004

Naval Regional Medical Center
Boone Road
Bremerton, Washington 98312

Veterans Administration Hospital (now VA
    Medical Center)
N. 4815 Assembly Street
Spokane, Washington 99205

Madigan Army Medical Center
Tacoma, Washington 98421

State Office Building
333 Willoughby Avenue
Juneau, Alaska 99801

Wells Fargo Building (now 44 Montgomery
    Building)
44 Montgomery Street
San Francisco, California 94104

Ala Moana Center
1450 Ala Moana Boulevard
Honolulu, Hawaii 96814

Montgomery Mall
7101 Democracy Boulevard
Bethesda, Maryland 20817

NorthShore Mall
Routes 128 and 114
Peabody, Massachusetts 01960

Clackamas Town Center
12000 S.E. 82nd Avenue
Portland, Oregon 97266

Lloyd Center
N.E. Ninth Avenue at N.E. Multnomah Street
Portland, Oregon 97232

Gulfgate Mall
I-45 and I-610
Houston, Texas 77087

Capitol Court
5500 W. Capitol Drive
Milwaukee, Wisconsin 53216

Wellington Square (now expanded as Galleria
    London)
355 Wellington Street
London, Ontario N6A 3N7, Canada

John Graham, Sr.

Bank of California (now Key Bank branch)
815 Second Avenue
Seattle, Washington 98104

The Bon Marché
Third to Fourth avenues, Pine Street
    to Olive Way
Seattle, Washington 98101

Coca-Cola Bottling Plant (now U.S. West
    building)
1313 E. Columbia Street
Seattle, Washington 98122

Dexter Horton Building
710 Second Avenue
Seattle, Washington 98104

Exchange Building
821 Second Avenue
Seattle, Washington 98104

Pierre P. Ferry house
1531 Tenth Avenue E.
Seattle, Washington 98102

Ford Assembly Building (now Craftsman Press)
1155 Valley Street
Seattle, Washington 98109

Frederick & Nelson Department Store
506 Pine Street
Seattle, Washington 98101

Joshua Green Building
1425 Fourth Avenue
Seattle, Washington 98101

Guggenheim Hall
University of Washington
Seattle, Washington 98195

Johnson Hall
University of Washington
Seattle, Washington 98195

Physics Hall
University of Washington
Seattle, Washington 98195

Roosevelt Hotel
1531 Seventh Avenue
Seattle, Washington 98101

Seattle Yacht Club
1807 E. Hamlin Street
Seattle, Washington 98102

Trinity Episcopal Church
609 Eighth Avenue
Seattle, Washington 98104

Women's Dormitory (now Hansee Hall)
University of Washington
Seattle, Washington 98195

Olof Hanson

Snoqualmie School (now Snoqualmie Valley
    School District headquarters)
211 Silva
Snoqualmie, Washington 98065

Boys' Dormitory (Dawes House)
Gallaudet University campus
Washington, D.C. 20002

J. Lister Holmes

Catherine Blaine Junior High (now Elementary)
    School
2550 34th Avenue W.
Seattle, Washington 98199

Katherine Coulon house
433 E. Lake Washington Boulevard
Seattle, Washington 98112

O. W. Fisher, Jr., house
3414 Shore Drive E.
Seattle, Washington 98112

J. Lister Holmes house
615 36th Avenue E.
Seattle, Washington 98112

Case Jones house
118 37th Avenue E.
Seattle, Washington 98112

Harry Lawton house
3146 Lakewood S.
Seattle, Washington 98144

Rainier Vista Elementary School (now
    a Head Start facility)
3100 S. Alaska Street
Seattle, Washington 98108

Samuel Rubinstein house
6258 Lake Shore Drive S.
Seattle, Washington 98118

Seattle First National (now Seafirst) Bank,
    Industrial Branch
2754 First Avenue S.
Seattle, Washington 98134

Seattle Public Schools Administration Building
815 Fourth Avenue N.
Seattle, Washington 98109

United Parcel Service warehouse
Eighth Avenue N. and Thomas Street
Seattle, Washington 98109

Yesler Terrace Housing
903 E. Yesler Way
Seattle, Washington 98104

"Collinswood" (now the Bloedel Reserve)
Bainbridge Island, Washington 98110

J. N. Donovan house
15th Street and Ferry Avenue
Bellingham, Washington 98225

Arnold Dessau house
The Highlands, Washington 98177

Phil Polsky house
Wessinger Springs
Beaverton, Oregon

Edwin W. Houghton

Mrs. W. E. Gordon house
2474 38th Avenue W.
Seattle, Washington 98199

Grand Opera House (now Cherry Street garage)
213 Cherry Street
Seattle, Washington 98104

Lippy Building
104-106 First Avenue S.
Seattle, Washington 98104

Maud Building
309-311 First Avenue S.
Seattle, Washington 98104

Moore Theater and Hotel
1914-1940 Second Avenue
Seattle, Washington 98101

Charles A. Riddle house
153 Highland Drive
Seattle, Washington 98109

Terry-Denny Building
109-115 First Avenue S.
Seattle, Washington 98104

B. A. Zeran apartment building (now Carter Hall
    Apartments)
901-905 N.E. 43rd Street
Seattle, Washington 98105

Clemmer Theater (now The Met)
W. 901 Sprague Avenue
Spokane, Washington 99204

Liberty Theater
1 S. Mission Street
Wenatchee, Washington 98801

Heilig Theater (now Fox Theater)
833 S.W. Broadway
Portland, Oregon 97205

Colonial Theater
42-50 E. Third Street S.
Salt Lake City, Utah 84101

Daniel R. Huntington

A. P. Burwell house
656 W. Galer Street
Seattle, Washington 98119

Arctic Club (now Hotel Morrison)
509 Third Avenue
Seattle, Washington 98104

Delamar Apartments
115 W. Olympic Place
Seattle, Washington 98119

Fire Station No. 2
2334 Fourth Avenue
Seattle, Washington 98212

Fire Station No. 7 (now a retail shop)
402 15th Avenue E.
Seattle, Washington 98112

Fire Station No. 12 (now Madrona
    Sally Goldmark Library)
1134 33rd Avenue
Seattle, Washington 98122

Fire Station No. 16
6846 Oswego Place N.E.
Seattle, Washington 98115

Fire Station No. 33 (now a residence)
10235 62nd Avenue S.
Seattle, Washington 98178

Firland Sanatorium Administration Building
    (now Mike Martin Administration Building,
    CRISTA Ministries)
19303 Fremont Avenue N.
Seattle, Washington 98133

Firland Sanatorium Detweiler Building
    (now King's High School, CRISTA Ministries)
19303 Fremont Avenue N.
Seattle, Washington 98133

Firlands Sanatorium (now CRISTA Ministries)
    Power House
19303 Fremont Avenue N.
Seattle, Washington 98133

First Methodist Episcopal (now First United
    Methodist) Church
811 Fifth Avenue
Seattle, Washington 98104

Fremont Branch, Seattle Public Library
731 N. 35th Street
Seattle, Washington 98103

Daniel R. Huntington residence
1800 E. Shelby Street
Seattle, Washington 98112

Johnson and Hamilton Mortuary (now
    law offices)
1400 Broadway
Seattle, Washington 98122

Lake Union Water Power Auxiliary Plant
and Lake Union Auxiliary Steam Electric
Plant (now Zymogenetics)
1203 Eastlake Avenue E.
Seattle, Washington 98102

David Newbrand house
2431 West View Drive W.
Seattle, Washington 98119

Northcliffe Apartments
1119 Boren Avenue
Seattle, Washington 98101

Piedmont Apartments (now the Tuscany
Apartments)
1215 Seneca Street
Seattle, Washington 98101

Rainier Chapter House, Daughters of the
American Revolution
800 E. Roy Street
Seattle, Washington 98102

Wallingford Fire and Police Station
(now 45th Street Community Health Center)
4423 Densmore Avenue N.
Seattle, Washington 98103

Hoquiam City Hall
609 Eighth Street
Hoquiam, Washington 98550

Seventh Street Theater
313 Seventh Street
Hoquiam, Washington 98550

E. H. Shumway Mansion (originally at
528 Lake Street S.; relocated)
11410 99th Place N.E.
Kirkland, Washington 98033

Paul Hayden Kirk

C & K (now Lakeview Boulevard) Apartments
1551-1559 Lakeview Boulevard E.
Seattle, Washington 98102

Central Plaza parking garage
University of Washington
Seattle, Washington 98195

Columbia Ridge tract house (one of 200
speculative houses)
2047 S. Ferdinand Street
Seattle, Washington 98108

Crown Hill Medical-Dental Clinic (now
1422 Clinic)
1422 N.W. 85th Street
Seattle, Washington 98117

Exhibition Hall (Seattle Center campus)
225 Mercer Street
Seattle, Washington 98109

Japanese Presbyterian Church
1801 24th Avenue S.
Seattle, Washington 98144

Jefferson Terrace
800 Jefferson Street
Seattle, Washington 98104

Blair Kirk house
725 32nd Avenue S.
Seattle, Washington 98144

Lake City Clinic (now Wu Building)
3202 N.E. 125th Street
Seattle, Washington 98125

Lakewood Community Church
5005 S. Ferdinand Street
Seattle, Washington 98118

Magnolia Branch, Seattle Public Library
2801 34th Avenue W.
Seattle, Washington 98199

Edmond S. Meany Hall for the Performing Arts
University of Washington
Seattle, Washington 98195

Charles E. Odegaard Undergraduate Library
University of Washington
Seattle, Washington 98195

Resident Theater (now Intiman Theater)
205 Mercer Street (Seattle Center campus)
Seattle, Washington 98109

Seattle Center parking garage
300 Mercer Street
Seattle, Washington 98109

University Unitarian Church
6556 35th Avenue N.E.
Seattle, Washington 98115

Frank Gilbert house
The Highlands, Washington 98177

Blair Kirk residence
3065 70th Avenue S.E.
Mercer Island, Washington 98040

C. Clement French Administration Building
Washington State University
Pullman, Washington 99164

Physio-Control Corporation headquarters
11811 Willows Road N.E.
Redmond, Washington 98052

McNair-Price Clinic
801 E. Main Street
Medford, Oregon 97504

Arthur L. Loveless

Arboretum Gatehouse
University of Washington Arboretum
1101 Lake Washington Boulevard E.
Seattle, Washington 98112

William Bloch residence
1439 E. Prospect Street
Seattle, Washington 98112

W. T. Campbell Building
4557-4559 California Avenue S.W.
Seattle, Washington 98116

Colman Building
811 First Avenue
Seattle, Washington 98104

Colman Pool
8603 Fauntleroy Way S.W. (Lincoln Park)
Seattle, Washington 98136

Lawrence Colman residence
9343 Fauntleroy Way S.W.
Seattle, Washington 98136

Darrah Corbet residence
300 Maiden Lane E.
Seattle, Washington 98112

Delta Gamma Sorority
2012 N.E. 45th Street
Seattle, Washington 98105

Lucille Eckstrom residence
3718 E. High Lane
Seattle, Washington 98112

H. C. Field residence
6007 N.E. Windermere Road
Seattle, Washington 98105

William E. Grimshaw residence
3038 E. Laurelhurst Drive N.E.
Seattle, Washington 98105

H. B. Kennedy residence
1620 Sunset Avenue S.W.
Seattle, Washington 98116

Arthur L. Loveless residence ("Hollyhock
    House")
7126 55th Avenue S.
Seattle, Washington 98118

Joel McFee residence
2825 Magnolia Boulevard W.
Seattle, Washington 98199

Fritz Miller residence
5135 N.E. Latimer Place
Seattle, Washington 98105

Alexander Pantages residence
1117 36th Avenue E.
Seattle, Washington 98112

John A. Porter residence
2624 Mt. Adams Place S.
Seattle, Washington 98144

Public Safety Building (now 400 Yesler Building)
400 Yesler Way
Seattle, Washington 98104

Seattle Repertory Playhouse (now Playhouse
    Theater)
4045 University Way N.E.
Seattle, Washington 98105

Paul R. Smith residence
530 McGilvra Boulevard E.
Seattle, Washington 98112

J. M. Sparkman residence
620 W. Howe Street
Seattle, Washington 98119

Studio Building (now known as the Loveless
    Studio Building or Loveless Studio
    Apartments)
711 Broadway E.
Seattle, Washington 98102

Zeta Psi Fraternity
4703 21st Avenue N.E.
Seattle, Washington 98105

Donald MacKay

Saint James Catholic Cathedral (now Church)
204 W. 12th Street
Vancouver, Washington 98660

Benjamin F. McAdoo, Jr.

John P. and Ola Mae Browning house
 (Browning-Green house)
2919 E. Howell Street
Seattle, Washington 98122

Ethnic Cultural Center Unit I
University of Washington
Seattle, Washington 98195

Fire Station No. 29
2139 Ferry Avenue S.W.
Seattle, Washington 98116

Benjamin F. McAdoo, Jr., office and residence
1718 E. Olive Way
Seattle, Washington 98102

George H. Hage house
2648 S.W. 167th Place
Seattle, Washington 98166

William B. and Helen L. Moorhouse house
3707 37th Avenue W.
Seattle, Washington 98199

Kenneth Ota house
10240 61st Avenue S.
Seattle, Washington 98178

Queen Anne (Forward Thrust) Swimming Pool
1920 First Avenue W.
Seattle, Washington 98119

Seattle First National (now Seafirst) Rainier
 Beach Branch Bank
9019 Rainier Avenue S.
Seattle, Washington 98118

Seattle First National (now Seafirst) Wedgwood
 Branch Bank
8405 35th Avenue N.E.
Seattle, Washington 98115

Smith Hall renovation
University of Washington
Seattle, Washington 98195

Seattle First National (now Seafirst) Bank, Lake
 Hills Branch
15550 Lake Hills Boulevard S.E.
Bellevue, Washington 98007

Benjamin F., Jr., and Thelma McAdoo house
17803 28th Avenue S.E.
Bothell, Washington 98012

Donald H. and Joanne Hochberg house
4148 78th Avenue S.E.
Mercer Island, Washington 98040

Herbert Rivkin house
4107 83rd Avenue S.E.
Mercer Island, Washington 98040

Riverton Heights Post Office
15250 32nd Avenue S.
SeaTac, Washington 98168

King County Blood Bank Center, Southcenter
 Branch
130 Andover Park E.
Tukwila, Washington 98188

Mother Joseph of the Sacred Heart
 (Esther Pariseau)

House of Providence (now Providence Academy)
400 E. Evergreen Boulevard
Vancouver, Washington 98660

Floyd A. Naramore

Daniel Bagley Elementary School
7821 Stone Avenue N.
Seattle, Washington 98103

Bagley Hall
University of Washington
Seattle, Washington 98195

Bryant Elementary School
3311 N.E. 60th Street
Seattle, Washington 98115

Grover Cleveland High School
5511 15th Avenue S.
Seattle, Washington 98108

Columbia Elementary School (currently housing an alternative school)
3528 S. Ferdinand Street
Seattle, Washington 98118

Dunlap Elementary School
8621 46th Avenue S.
Seattle, Washington 98118

James Garfield High School
400 23rd Avenue
Seattle, Washington 98122

Alexander Hamilton Junior High School
1610 N. 41st Street
Seattle, Washington 98103

John Hay Elementary School
(1921 building; currently housing an
alternative school)
411 Boston Street
Seattle, Washington 98109

Highland Park Elementary School
1012 S.W. Trenton Street
Seattle, Washington 98106

E. C. Hughes Elementary School
7740 34th Avenue S.W.
Seattle, Washington 98126

Laurelhurst Elementary School
4530 46th Avenue N.E.
Seattle, Washington 98105

Loyal Heights Elementary School
2511 N.W. 80th Street
Seattle, Washington 98117

James Madison Junior High School
3429 34th Avenue S.W.
Seattle, Washington 98126

Magnolia Elementary School (currently housing an alternative school)
2418 28th Avenue W.
Seattle, Washington 98199

John Marshall Junior High School (currently housing an alternative school)
520 N.E. Ravenna Boulevard
Seattle, Washington 98115

T. T. Minor Elementary School
1701 E. Union Street
Seattle, Washington 98122

James Monroe Junior High School
(now Monroe Elementary Building, West
Woodland Elementary School)
1810 N.W. 65th Street
Seattle, Washington 98117

Montlake Elementary School
2409 22nd Avenue E.
Seattle, Washington 98112

Roosevelt High School
1410 N.E. 66th Street
Seattle, Washington 98115

Whittier Elementary School
7501 13th Avenue N.W.
Seattle, Washington 98117

Couch Elementary School (now Metropolitan
Learning Center)
2033 N.W. Glisan
Portland, Oregon 97209

John Parkinson

B. F. Day School
3921 Linden Avenue N.
Seattle, Washington 98103

Butler Block (now Butler Garage)
601-611 Second Avenue
Seattle, Washington 98104

Jesuit College and Church (now Garrand
Building)
Seattle University
Seattle, Washington 98122

Seattle National Bank Building (now Interurban
Building)
102-108 Occidental Avenue S. and 155-159
Yesler Way
Seattle, Washington 98104

Seattle Seminary Building (now Alexander Hall)
Seattle Pacific University
Seattle, Washington 98119

Lionel H. Pries

Bel Roy Apartments
703 Bellevue Avenue E.
Seattle, Washington 98102

Convalescent Home for Crippled Children
(now Magnolia Health Center)
4646 36th Avenue W.
Seattle, Washington 98199

Max A. Gurvich house
3006 Webster Point Road N.E.
Seattle, Washington 98105

Karl Kreuger house
14301 Third Avenue N.W.
Seattle, Washington 98177

Richard Lea house
230 40th Avenue E.
Seattle, Washington 98112

Lionel H. Pries house
3132 W. Laurelhurst Drive N.E.
Seattle, Washington 98105

George Youell house
550 36th Avenue E.
Seattle, Washington 98112

Crucifix
Faith Lutheran Church
2750 McLeod Road
Bellingham, Washington 98225

Col. Julian P. Willcox house (now The Willcox
House)
2390 Tekiu Road
Bremerton (Holly), Washington 98312

Richard Lea house
2200 Davis Bay Road
Lopez Island, Washington 98261

Robert W. Winskill house
50 Madrone Park Circle
Mill Valley, California 94941

Bothin Building
903-911 State Street
Santa Barbara, California 93101

McKay Building (now LaPlacita Building)
746 State Street
Santa Barbara, California 93101

Auto Show Rooms and Seaside Oil Company
Building
318-330 State Street
Santa Barbara, California 93101

B. Marcus Priteca

Bikur Cholim Synagogue (now Langston Hughes
Cultural Center)
104 17th Avenue S.
Seattle, Washington 98l22

Coliseum Theater (now a retail store)
Northeast corner Fifth Avenue and Pike Street
Seattle, Washington 98101

Hills of Eternity Mausoleum
Mount Pleasant Cemetery
700 W. Raye Street
Seattle, Washington 98119

Seattle Opera House
351 Mercer Street (Seattle Center campus)
Seattle, Washington 98109

Seattle Theater (now Paramount Theater)
901 Pine Street
Seattle, Washington 98101

Temple de Hirsch Sinai Synagogue
1511 E. Pike Street
Seattle, Washington 98122

Tacoma Pantages Theater (now Broadway Center
for the Performing Arts)
901 Broadway Plaza
Tacoma, Washington 98402

Hollywood Pantages Theater
6233 Hollywood Boulevard
Hollywood (Los Angeles), California 90028

Robert C. Reamer

1411 Fourth Avenue Building
1411 Fourth Avenue
Seattle, Washington 98101

Donald Graham house
1900 Shenandoah Drive E.
Seattle, Washington 98112

Great Northern Building
1404 Fourth Avenue
Seattle, Washington 98101

Edmond Meany Hotel (now Meany Tower
Hotel)
4507 Brooklyn Avenue N.E.
Seattle, Washington 98105

Seattle Times Building
1120 John Street
Seattle, Washington 98109

Skinner Building
1326 Fifth Avenue
Seattle, Washington 98101

Weyerhaeuser Experimental House
545 36th Avenue E.
Seattle, Washington 981112

Bellingham Hotel (now Bellingham Towers)
119 N. Commercial
Bellingham, Washington 98225

Mount Baker Theater
106 N. Commercial
Bellingham, Washington 98225

Lewis and Clark Hotel
117 W. Magnolia Street
Centralia, Washington 98531

Lake Quinault Lodge
South Shore Road
Quinault, Washington 98575

Fox Theater (now Act Three Fox Tri-Cinemas)
W. 1005 Sprague
Spokane, Washington 98204

Northern Pacific Railroad Station
Yellowstone National Park
Gardiner, Montana 59030

Lake Hotel
Yellowstone National Park
Wyoming 82190

Mammoth Hotel
Yellowstone National Park
Wyoming 82190

Old Faithful Inn
Yellowstone National Park
Wyoming 82190

Willis A. Ritchie

Thurston County Courthouse (now
    Superintendent of Public Instruction)
600 Washington Street
Olympia, Washington 98501

Jefferson County Courthouse
1800 Jefferson Street
Port Townsend, Washington 98368

Spokane County Courthouse
W. 1116 Broadway
Spokane, Washington 99201

Charles W. Saunders

Bailey Building (sometimes Broderick Building)
613-621 Second Avenue and 113-117 Cherry
    Street
Seattle, Washington 98104

Beacon Hill Elementary School (now El Centro
    de la Raza)
2524 16th Avenue S.
Seattle, Washington 98144

Main Building (now Denny Hall)
University of Washington
Seattle, Washington 98195

Maud Building
309-311 First Avenue S.
Seattle, Washington 98104

Masonic Temple (now Egyptian Theater)
805 E. Pine Street
Seattle, Washington 98122

Observatory
University of Washington
Seattle, Washington 98195

Terry-Denny Building
109-115 First Avenue S.
Seattle, Washington 98104

Walla Walla (now Horace Mann) Elementary
    School (currently housing an alternative
    school)
2410 E. Cherry Street
Seattle, Washington 98122

Women's Building, Alaska-Yukon-Pacific
    Exposition (now Cunningham Hall)
University of Washington
Seattle, Washington 98195

Schack, Young & Myers

Arctic Club (now Hotel Morrison)
509 Third Avenue
Seattle, Washington 98104

Roy P. Ballard residence
2844 Cascadia Avenue S.
Seattle, Washington 98144

Baroness Apartments
1001 Spring Street
Seattle, Washington 98104

W. A. Batley residence
819 W. Lee Street
Seattle, Washington 98119

Chinese Baptist Church (now Chinese Southern
   Baptist Mission)
925 S. Weller Street
Seattle, Washington 98104

Civic Arena
325 Mercer Street (Seattle Center campus)
Seattle, Washington 98109

Civic Auditorium (now Seattle Opera House)
305 Mercer Street (Seattle Center campus)
Seattle, Washington 98109

Eldridge Buick dealership (now a part of
   University Center)
4501 Roosevelt Way N.E.
Seattle, Washington 98105

First Methodist Episcopal (now First United
   Methodist) Church
811 Fifth Avenue
Seattle, Washington 98104

W. Logan Geary residence
2838 Cascadia Avenue S.
Seattle, Washington 98144

Japanese Baptist Church
900 E. Spruce Street
Seattle, Washington 98122

Kenney Presbyterian Home
7125 Fauntleroy Way S.W.
Seattle, Washington 98136

J. D. Lowman building addition
1411-1419 Broadway
Seattle, Washington 98122

Sunset Motor Car dealership/J. D. Lowman
   building
1401-1409 Broadway
Seattle, Washington 98122

Perry B. Truax residence
1014 E. Galer Street
Seattle, Washington 98102

University Baptist Church
4554 12th Avenue N.E.
Seattle, Washington 98105

Veterans' Hall
Seattle Center campus
Seattle, Washington 98109

Women's Dormitory (now Hansee Hall)
University of Washington
Seattle, Washington 98195

ABC Warehouse and Transfer warehouse
   building
1156-1164 12th Avenue
Longview, Washington 98632

Colonial [mercantile store] Building
1426-1432 Commerce Avenue
Longview, Washington 98632

Columbia River Mercantile department store
1331-1339 Commerce Street
Longview, Washington 98632

Hotel Monticello
1405 17th Avenue
Longview, Washington 98632

Long-Bell Lumber Company garage
802 Vandercook Way
Longview, Washington 98632

Longview Company apartment building
1302 21st Avenue
Longview, Washington 98632

Longview Company apartment building
1328 21st Avenue
Longview, Washington 98632

Longview Company office building (now
   Myklebust Building)
1256-1262 Commerce Street
Longview, Washington 98632

Saint Helens Inn dormitory (now Oregon Way
   Hotel)
421 Oregon Way
Longview, Washington 98632

Edward Otto Schwagerl

Hunter Boulevard S.
Seattle, Washington 98144

Kinnear Park
901 W. Prospect Street
Seattle, Washington 98119

Mount Baker Boulevard S.
Seattle, Washington 98144

Mount Baker Park
2311 Lake Park Drive S.
Seattle, Washington 98144

University Heights Addition
Seattle, Washington 98105

Point Defiance Park
5400 Park Way N.
Tacoma, Washington 98407

University Place subdivision
Tacoma, Washington 98466

Wright Park (partly extant)
S. Sixth Avenue and S. "I" Street
Tacoma, Washington 98405

Riverview Cemetery
8421 S.W. Macadam Avenue
Portland, Oregon 97219

Somervell & Coté

J. Edward Clark residence
1415 Interlaken Boulevard E.
Seattle, Washington 98112

Columbia Branch, Seattle Public Library
4721 Rainier Avenue S.
Seattle, Washington 98118

Clare E. Farnsworth residence
803 E. Prospect Street
Seattle, Washington 98102

Fire Station No. 25
1400 Harvard Avenue
Seattle, Washington 98122

Green Lake Branch, Seattle Public Library
7364 E. Green Lake Drive N.
Seattle, Washington 98115

Perry Apartments
1019 Madison Street
Seattle, Washington 98104

William Piggott residence
1162 22nd Avenue E.
Seattle, Washington 98112

Providence Hospital
500 17th Avenue
Seattle, Washington 98122

Queen Anne Branch, Seattle Public Library
400 W. Garfield Street
Seattle, Washington 98119

Roman Catholic Diocese of Seattle bishop's
    residence
804 Ninth Avenue
Seattle, Washington 98104

Saint James Catholic Cathedral
820 Ninth Avenue
Seattle, Washington 98104

C. A. Sundt (speculative) house
8318 18th Avenue N.W.
Seattle, Washington 98117

C. A. Sundt (speculative) house
8322 18th Avenue N.W.
Seattle, Washington 98117

Sunset Club
1021 University Street
Seattle, Washington 98101

University Branch, Seattle Public Library
5009 Roosevelt Way N.E.
Seattle, Washington 98105

West Seattle Branch, Seattle Public Library
2306 42nd Avenue S.W.
Seattle, Washington 98116

Henry L. Yesler Memorial Branch, Seattle Public
    Library (now Douglass-Truth Branch)
2310 E. Yesler Way
Seattle, Washington 98122

Yorkshire (now Seymour) Building
525 Seymour Street
Vancouver, British Columbia

Victor Steinbrueck

Earl L. Barrett residence
5530 N.E. 55th Street
Seattle, Washington 98105

Betty Bowen Viewpoint/Marshall Park
W. Highland Drive and 7th Avenue W.
Seattle, Washington 98119

Capitol Hill Viewpoint Park (now Louisa Boren
    Park)
15th Avenue E. and E. Garfield Street
Seattle, Washington 98112

Faculty Center Building (Faculty Club)
University of Washington
Seattle, Washington 98195

Market Park (now Victor Steinbrueck Park)
2001 Western Avenue
Seattle, Washington 98101

Alden Mason residence
2545 Boyer Avenue E.
Seattle, Washington 98112

Space Needle
219 Fourth Avenue N. (Seattle Center campus)
Seattle, Washington 98109

Victor Steinbrueck residence
1401 E. Spring Street
Seattle, Washington 98122

House for Steinbrueck, Inc.
1714 Lake Washington Boulevard S.
Seattle, Washington 98144

William T. Stellwagen residence
7200 29th Avenue N.E.
Seattle, Washington 98115

T. H. Terao residence
626 Randolph Place
Seattle, Washington 98122

Frederick Anderson residence
5402 S. 288th Street
Auburn, Washington 98001

James Stephen

Coe Elementary School
2433 Sixth Avenue W.
Seattle, Washington 98119

[Old] Colman School
1515 24th Avenue S.
Seattle, Washington 98144

Emerson Elementary School
9709 60th Avenue S.
Seattle, Washington 98178

Greenwood Elementary School
144 N.W. 80th Street
Seattle, Washington 98117

John Hay School (1905 building; currently
    housing an alternative school)
411 Boston Street
Seattle, Washington 98109

Interlake School (now Wallingford Center)
4416 Wallingford Avenue N.
Seattle, Washington 98103

Latona Elementary School
401 N.E. 42nd Street
Seattle, Washington 98105

Lincoln High School (currently leased)
4400 Interlake Avenue N.
Seattle, Washington 98103

Queen Anne High School (now The Queen Anne)
201 Galer Street
Seattle, Washington 98109

Seward School (currently housing an alternative
    school)
2515 Boylston Avenue E.
Seattle, Washington 98102

Summit School (now The Northwest School)
1415 Summit Avenue
Seattle, Washington 98101

YMCA Downtown Branch
Fourth Avenue and Madison Street
Seattle, Washington 98101

Everett High School
2416 Colby Avenue
Everett, Washington 98201

Administration Building (now Thompson Hall)
Washington State University
Pullman, Washington 99164

Ellsworth Storey

George B. Barclay house
138 Madrona Place E.
Seattle, Washington 98112

George A. Bruce house
1618 40th Avenue
Seattle, Washington 98122

James E. Dyer house
2704 34th Avenue S.
Seattle, Washington 98144

Episcopal Church of the Epiphany
E. Denny Way and 38th Avenue E.
Seattle, Washington 98122

Robert M. Evans house
2306 34th Avenue S.
Seattle, Washington 98118

Francis G. Frink house ("Gray Gables")
140 Lake Washington Boulevard E.
Seattle, Washington 98112

Albert Mayer house
1416 41st Avenue E.
Seattle, Washington 98112

Phiscator Estate dwelling (J. K. Gordon house)
3311 Cascadia Avenue S.
Seattle, Washington 98144

Rainier Golf and Country Club
1856 S. 112th Street
Seattle, Washington 98168

Sigma Nu Fraternity
1616 N.E. 47th Street
Seattle, Washington 98105

Storey cottages
1706-10 Lake Washington Boulevard S.
1800-16 36th Avenue S.
Seattle, Washington 98144

Henry C. and Ellsworth Storey houses
260-270 Dorffel Drive
Seattle, Washington 98112

Edward F. Tindolph house
1622 40th Avenue
Seattle, Washington 98122

George W. Trimble house
3814 E. John Street
Seattle, Washington 98112

Unitarian Church (now University Presbyterian
    Church Chapel)
N.E. 47th Street and 16th Avenue N.E.
Seattle, Washington 98105

Harry E. Woolley house
3103 Mount Rainier Drive S.
Seattle, Washington 98144

Lookout tower/Mount Constitution
Bathhouses, picnic shelter, ranger's house
Moran State Park
Orcas Island, Washington 98280

Butler Sturtevant

Anderson Hall grounds; Medicinal
    Herb Garden; Stevens Way, Rainier Vista,
    Drumheller Fountain
University of Washington
Seattle, Washington 98195

Ambrose and Viola Patterson garden
3927 N.E. Belvoir Place
Seattle, Washington 98105

Yesler Terrace Housing
903 E. Yesler Way
Seattle, Washington 98104

Arnold Dessau house and garden
The Highlands, Washington 98177

Paul Piggott residence (formerly "Norcliffe")
The Highlands, Washington 98177

Frederick Remington Green garden
The Highlands, Washington 98177

Principia College
1 Belltrees Road
Elsah, Illinois 62028

Principia School
13201 Clayton Road
St. Louis, Missouri 63131

Roland Terry

Bank of California offices
Bank of California Building
910 Fourth Avenue
Seattle, Washington 98104

William K. Blethen residence
1011 39th Avenue E.
Seattle, Washington 98112

Canlis' Charcoal Broiler
2576 Aurora Avenue N.
Seattle, Washington 98109

John H. Hauberg, Jr., residence
1101 McGilvra Boulevard E.
Seattle, Washington 98112

Nordstrom Department Store
1501 Fifth Avenue
Seattle, Washington 98101

Paul Roland Smith residence
4105 E. Highland Drive
Seattle, Washington 98112

Philip A. Stewart residence
1225 N.W. Elford Drive
Seattle, Washington 98177

Florence Beach Terry residence
9805 Bayard Avenue N.W.
Seattle, Washington 98117

Tucker, Shields & Terry office building (derelict)
914 Lakeview Boulevard
Seattle, Washington 98102

Washington Park Towers
1620 43rd Avenue E.
Seattle, Washington 98112

John H. Hauberg, Jr., residence
2080 Beans Bight N.E.
Bainbridge Island, Washington 98110

Episcopal Church of the Redeemer
6211 N.E. 182nd Street
Kenmore, Washington 98155

Roland Terry residence ("Baycourt")
2079 Vista Road
Lopez Island, Washington 98261

Lakewood Terrace Dining Room (now Terrace
   Restaurant)
6114 Motor Avenue S.W.
Tacoma, Washington 98499

Doubletree Inn
205 Strander Boulevard
Tukwila, Washington 98188

Wilson Bradley, Jr., residence
Carpinteria Valley
Santa Barbara County, California 93014

The Canlis Restaurant
360 Kalaimoku
Honolulu, Hawaii 96815

Halekulani Hotel
2199 Kalia Road
Honolulu, Hawaii 96815

Kahala Hilton Hotel
5000 Kahala Avenue
Honolulu, Hawaii 96815

The Canlis Restaurant (now Alexander's)
Hilton Hotel
921 S.W. Sixth Avenue
Portland, Oregon 97204

Lawrence B. Culter residence
6120 Glendalough Place
Vancouver, British Columbia

Paul Thiry

Coliseum
400 First Avenue N. (Seattle Center campus)
Seattle, Washington 98109

Frye Art Museum
704 Terry Avenue
Seattle, Washington 98104

Lakecrest Apartment Court (now south half
   Lake Court Apartments)
2012 43rd Avenue E.
Seattle, Washington 98112

Museum of History and Industry
2700 24th Avenue E.
Seattle, Washington 98102

Saint Demetrios Greek Orthodox Church
2100 Boyer Avenue E.
Seattle, Washington 98112

Paul Thiry house
330 35th Avenue E.
Seattle, Washington 98112

Paul Thiry vacation house
address not available
near Ellensburg, Washington

Mercer Island Presbyterian Church
3605 84th Avenue S.E.
Mercer Island, Washington 98040

Washington State Library
Washington State Capitol campus (west)
Olympia, Washington 98504

Libby Dam
17115 Highway 37N
Libby, Montana 59923

Residence
U.S. Embassy
Santiago, Chile

Harlan Thomas

Chelsea Hotel (now The Chelsea apartments)
620 W. Olympic Place
Seattle, Washington 98119

Columbia Branch, Seattle Public Library
4721 Rainier Avenue S.
Seattle, Washington 98118

Corner Market Building
Northwest corner First Avenue and Pike Street
Seattle, Washington 98l01

Delta Kappa Epsilon Fraternity (now Tau Kappa
    Epsilon)
4520 21st Avenue N.E.
Seattle, Washington 98l05

Harborview Hospital
325 Ninth Avenue
Seattle, Washington 98104

Kappa Kappa Gamma Sorority
4504 18th Avenue N.E
Seattle, Washington 98l05

Queen Anne Branch, Seattle Public Library
400 W. Garfield Street
Seattle, Washington 98119

Rhodes Department Store (now Arcade Plaza
    Building)
1321 Second Avenue
Seattle, Washington 98101

Sales and Service Building (now Pacific
    Building)
Northwest corner Westlake Avenue
    and Mercer Street
Seattle, Washington 98102

Seattle Chamber of Commerce Building (now
    TRA, architects)
215 Columbia Street
Seattle, Washington 98104

Sorrento Hotel
900 Madison Street
Seattle, Washington 98104

Harlan Thomas residence
1401 Eighth Avenue W.
Seattle, Washington 98119

Henry L. Yesler Memorial Branch, Seattle Public
    Library (now Douglass Truth Branch)
2310 E. Yesler Way
Seattle, Washington 98122

J. M. Weatherwax High School
414 N. I Street
Aberdeen, Washington 98520

Vernacular and Popular

Dick's Drive-In (Wallingford)
101-119 N.E. 45th Street
Seattle, Washington 98103

Durn Good Grocery (now Roadrunner
    Coffeehouse)
2123 N. 40th Street
Seattle, Washington 98103

Finnish Temperance Society (now Lafurno's
    Italian Restaurant)
2060 15th Avenue W.
Seattle, Washington 98119

Gee How Oak Tin Benevolent Society
513-519 Seventh Avenue S.
Seattle, Washington 98104

Twin Teepees Restaurant
7201 Aurora Avenue N.
Seattle, Washington 98103

Youngstown Improvement Club (Disabled
    American Veterans, Chapter 23)
2404 Delridge Way S.W.
Seattle, Washington 98106

Andrew Willatsen

George H. Bellman house
2021 E. Lynn Street
Seattle, Washington 98112

Joseph C. Black house
222 W. Highland Drive
Seattle, Washington 98119

Fred Burwell house
425 35th Avenue
Seattle, Washington 98122

John H. Carter house
1615 36th Avenue
Seattle, Washington 98122

Church and North Offices
3701 S.W. Alaska Street
Seattle, Washington 98126

Albert E. Felmley house
6975 47th Avenue S.W.
Seattle, Washington 98136

L. George Hager house
303 W. Prospect Street
Seattle, Washington 98119

Frederick W. Handschy house
2433 Ninth Avenue W.
Seattle, Washington 98119

Frederick W. Hurlbut house
1015 E. Prospect Street
Seattle, Washington 98122

Orrin L. Martin house
3727 E. Prospect Street
Seattle, Washington 98112

George Matzen house
320 Kinnear Place
Seattle, Washington 98119

Oscar Maurer house
2715 Belvidere Avenue S.W.
Seattle, Washington 98126

James T. McVay house
1025 Belmont Place E.
Seattle, Washington 98122

Jeremiah Neterer house
2702 Broadway E.
Seattle, Washington 98102

Gustave E. Rasmussen house
3111 Cascadia Avenue S.
Seattle, Washington 98144

William E. Robinson house
2011 Eleventh Avenue E.
Seattle, Washington 98102

Elmer E. Vogue house
1016 E. Lynn Street
Seattle, Washington 98122

Our Savior Lutheran Church (now Everett High
    School Performing Arts Center)
2331 Hoyt Avenue
Everett, Washington 98201

C. H. Clarke house
The Highlands, Washington 98177

Carleton Huiskamp house
The Highlands, Washington 98177

A. S. Kerry house
The Highlands, Washington 98177

Richard L. Desimone house
2605 S.W. 170th Street
Normandy Park, Washington 98166

W. R. B. Willcox

Crouley Building
410 Fourth Avenue
Seattle, Washington 98104

Hotel/apartment building (now Pacific Hotel,
    empty)
317 Marion Street
Seattle, Washington 98104

Queen Anne Boulevard Retaining Walls
8th Avenue W., between W. Highland Drive and
    W. Blaine Street, 7th Avenue W., between W.
    Howe Street and W. Crockett Street
Seattle, Washington 98119

J. Warren Richardson house
702 23rd Avenue E.
Seattle, Washington 98112

Viaduct and footbridge
University of Washington Arboretum
Seattle, Washington 98112

Leroy D. Lewis house
The Highlands, Washington 98177

Carnegie Library (now Fletcher Free Library)
235 College Street
Burlington, Vermont 05401

Additional Significant Seattle Architects

The following is a list of architects and other designers who are usually considered significant in the history of Seattle architecture but who are not covered by the essays in this book. This catalogue offers basic information about each of these individuals (in a few cases, partnerships). It is intended to highlight key aspects of their careers. As with the essays, selection was based on available information, the knowledge of the Editorial Board, and the suggestions of others. It is likely that some significant individuals have been omitted, but such omissions are unintentional. They simply reflect the lack of available information.

One specific selection criterion was established. Those in active practice in 1993 were almost entirely excluded. Judgments of relative significance among current practitioners were simply too difficult to make. However, at the request of AIA Seattle, any architect who has been awarded the AIA Seattle Medal, even if currently practicing, has been included. (Similarly, one active landscape architect, who has twice been awarded the President's Medal, the closest equivalent award in that field, has been included.)

It should be noted that this list was prepared using readily accessible sources. Substantial research to verify this information has not been carried out, and as a result there are likely to be some errors of fact.

The initials at the end of each entry indicate the primary compiler. These include Dennis A. Andersen [daa], Shirley L. Courtois [slc], Duane A. Dietz [dad], Norman J. Johnston [njj], Katheryn Hills Krafft [khk], Jeffrey Karl Ochsner [jko], David A. Rash [dar], and Thomas Veith [tv].

Following the catalogue of Seattle practitioners, a short list is also provided of architects and designers from outside Seattle who have been responsible for significant Seattle designs. Again, this list is incomplete and it reflects readily available information.

Note: Place names are in Washington State unless otherwise noted.

Alden, Charles Henry (September 27, 1867- ?). Born Hingham, Massachusetts; attended University of Minnesota; M.A. from MIT, 1890; employed by Shepley, Rutan & Coolidge, Boston (sent to West Coast as supervising architect, Stanford University); employed by Howard & Galloway, San Francisco (sent to work on Alaska-Yukon-Pacific Exposition, Seattle, 1907); practiced independently in Seattle; worked on Buildings and Grounds Commission for Pan Pacific International Exposition, San Francisco (1913-15; while practicing in Seattle); published articles on city planning; date and place of death presently unknown. [daa]

Aldrich, C. R. Practiced architecture in Seattle, 1910; designed Central Building, Seattle (1910); dates and places of birth and death and career unknown. [daa]

Alexander, Charles A. (ca. 1865- September 29, 1897). Born in Glasgow, Scotland; arrived in the United States in 1887; arrived in Seattle in 1889; in partnership Beulah & Alexander (with Frank E. Beulah), 1889-91; practiced architecture alone after 1891; designed First Presbyterian Church, Seattle (1889-90, destroyed); superintended Trinity Episcopal Church, Seattle (1889-91); died in Spokane. [dar]

Baeder, Louis (d. November 22, 1954). Born in Fond du Lac, Wisconsin; arrived in Seattle from Chicago in 1907; served as assistant director of the Alaska-Yukon-Pacific Exposition, 1909; designed Western Blower Company Building, Seattle (1913), Nazarene Church [Fremont], Seattle (1923), Chancellor Apartments, Seattle (1930), other apartment houses, warehouses, and single family residences; chaired Washington State Chapter AIA committee that secured passage of first architectural registration law in Washington, 1919; first chair, examining board for architects; retired, 1951; died in Seattle. [tv]

Bassetti, Fred (b. January 31, 1917). Born and raised in Seattle; B.Arch. University of Washington, 1942, M.Arch. Harvard University, 1946; apprenticed with Paul Thiry (see essay), Seattle, 1943; with Naramore, Bain, Brady & Johanson, Seattle, 1946; with Alvar Aalto, Cambridge, Massachusetts, 1946; partner in Bassetti & Morse, Seattle, 1947-62; in Fred Bassetti & Co., Seattle, 1962-85; in Bassetti, Norton, Metler, Rekevics, Seattle, 1985-92; designed College of Engineering Library, Administration and Classroom Building, University of Washington, Seattle (1964-68), Ridgeway Dormitories, Western Washington University, Bellingham (1963-70), Federal Office Building, Seattle (1965-71), U.S. Embassy, Lisbon, Portugal (1979-83), AT&T Gateway Tower, Seattle (1981-91); winner of local, regional, and national design awards, works published nationally and internationally; visiting faculty member Columbia University, Rice University, University of Washington; chairman, Action: Better City program, 1967-68; president Allied Arts of Seattle 1971-72; president AIA Seattle 1967-68; AIA Fellow, 1968; AIA Seattle Medal 1988; residing in Seattle, 1993. [jko]

Beardsley, Everett J. Date and place of birth unknown; arrived in Seattle, ca. 1909; prolific contractor of houses and apartment buildings; known for Mediterranean Revival apartment buildings designed and built for himself during 1920s, including 1025-29 Summit Avenue E., Seattle (1925; now Hacienda Court apartments), 348 W. Olympic Place, Seattle (1928), 4204 Eleventh Avenue N.E., Seattle (1930; now El Monterey Apartments), 608 E. Lynn Street, Seattle (1930-31; now El Cerrito Apartments); date and place of death unknown. [dar]

Bindon & Wright (1956-73). Leonard William Bindon (June 27, 1899-April 6, 1980) and John LeBaron Wright (b. June 18, 1916). Bindon was born in London; B.Arch. University of Washington, 1924; M.Arch. Columbia University, 1927; employed by R. C. Reamer (see essay), Seattle, 1925-26; Vorhees, Walker & Smith, New York, 1927-28; James Gamble Rogers, New York, 1928; Paul Thiry (see essay), Seattle, 1933-34; private practice in architecture Bellingham, 1934-40; service in the Army, 1940-45; employed by Bebb & Jones, Seattle, 1946-48; partnership with John Paul Jones, 1948-56 (see John Paul Jones entry for projects). Wright was born in Bismark, North Dakota; B.S. in architecture University of Illinois, 1914; employed by U.S. Army Corps of Engineers in South America, 1914-43; service in Marine Corps, 1943-46; employed by Freedman, Altshuler & Sincere, Chicago, 1946-47; arrived in Seattle 1947; employed by Jones & Bindon, 1947-56; became partner on Jones's retirement; Bindon & Wright designed Norton Building, Seattle (1956-59; with Skidmore Owings & Merrill, San Francisco), Downtown Seattle Public Library (1956-59) with Decker, Christiansen & Kitchin), Bethlehem Pacific Coast Steel Corporation Office Building, Seattle (1960); Fire Station #32, Seattle (1967), multiple schools for Seattle, Bellevue, and Ferndale districts; Bindon retired 1968, died in Seattle; firm reorganized as partnership Wright, Gildow, Hartman & Teegarden (WGHT; with partners Elton Gildow, George Hartman, Clark Teegarden), 1968; Wright retired 1986; residing in Redmond 1993. [dad]

Bird & Dornbach (1888-90). Thomas G. Bird and George W. Dornbach; partnership designed Washington State Reform School (complex of frame buildings), Chehalis (1889, destroyed), Holyoke Building, Seattle (1889-90), Safe Deposit Building, Seattle (1889-90, destroyed). Both Bird and Dornbach practiced architecture independently in Seattle after 1891; later identified as contractors in city directories; places and dates of birth and death presently unknown. [daa]

Blackwell, James Eustace (d. April 5, 1939). Born in Virginia; practiced in Washington, D.C., and Rochester, New York, in late 1880s; arrived in Tacoma in 1891; partnership with Robert L. Robertson in Tacoma, 1891-93; worked on Port Orchard Naval Dry Dock design and construction; floating city dock at Portland, Oregon (late 1890s); arrived in Seattle in 1897; partnership with Robert L. Robertson in Seattle, 1897-1904; partnership Blackwell & Baker, with Frank Lidstone Baker (University of Pennsylvania graduate), 1911-14, designed Grand Trunk Dock, Seattle (1910-11), James A. Kerr residence, Seattle (1910-11), Armory, Bellingham (1911-12); died in Seattle. [daa]

Blair, Edgar (1871-1924). Born in Des Moines, Iowa; attended Columbia University; employed by McKim, Mead & White, New York, Baldwin & Pennington, Baltimore, and Mayre & Wright, Washington, D.C., prior to 1904; private practice in Washington, D.C., 1904-6, designed Champlain Apartments, Washington (1905, destroyed); arrived in Seattle, February 1906; employed by James Stephen (see essay); Seattle Schools Architect, 1909-18, designed Franklin High School, Seattle (1910-11), Ravenna Elementary School,

Seattle (1911-12), Ballard High School, Seattle (1912), McGilvra Elementary School, Seattle (1912-13), West Seattle High School, Seattle (1916-17), and more than thirty other schools and school additions; independent practice after 1918, designed Floramar Apartments, Seattle (1923); died in Seattle. [daa/khk]

Bodley, Alfred (1872-?). Born in London, Ontario; worked as contractor in London, 1895-97; began practice of architecture in London, 1897-99; arrived in Seattle January 1, 1904; in partnership Graham & Bodley with John Graham, Sr., 1904 (see Graham, Sr., essay); practiced architecture alone after 1904; designed John and Eliza Leary mansion, Seattle (1904-7), George L. Holmes house, Seattle (1904-5; later James V. Paterson house), First United Presbyterian Church, Seattle (1906-7; now Progressive Missionary Baptist Church); began Leary Building, Seattle (1906-7, completed by Beezer Brothers; later Insurance Building; destroyed); date and place of death unknown. [dar]

Brady, Clifton (October 16, 1894-June 9, 1963). Born in Walker, Iowa; B.Arch. Iowa State College, 1917; service in U.S. Army, 1917-19; arrived in Seattle in 1927; employed as associate under Floyd Naramore (see essay), Seattle, 1927-33, 1938-41; served as Washington State examiner in charge of architectural licensing, 1933-38; in partnership Naramore & Brady, Seattle, 1941-43; in Naramore, Bain, Brady & Johanson after 1943; president, Washington State AIA Chapter, 1947-48; died in Seattle. [dad]

Brust, William George (August 28, 1882-January 26, 1969). Born in Columbus, Ohio; studied architecture at University of Pennsylvania; employed as draftsman for E.F. Champney, 1912-15 (see Champney essay); in partnership Stephen, Stephen & Brust with James Stephen, 1920-27 (see

Stephen essay); practiced alone after 1927; known as a designer of churches in 1930s and 1940s, designed Phinney Ridge Lutheran Church, Seattle (1929), Our Redeemer Lutheran Church, Seattle (1946-47), Hope Lutheran Church, Seattle (1948); died in Seattle. [daa]

Bumgardner, Albert O. (1923-July 10, 1987). Born in Chatham, Illinois; raised in Illinois; attended Illinois State University, 1941-43, City College of New York, 1943-44; B.S. (architecture) University of Illinois, 1949; employed in various Seattle offices, 1949-52; independent practice after January 1953; designed Thomas Graham house, Seattle (1952-54), A. O. Bumgardner house remodeling, Seattle (1958-63); practiced in partnership, A. O. Bumgardner & Partners, 1960-63; Bumgardner Partnership, 1967-80; directed design of South Campus Center, University of Washington, Seattle (1971-74), Market Place North, Seattle (1978-82), Waterfront Place (multibuilding project), Seattle (1979-84); Bumgardner Architects, after 1980; winner of local, regional, and national design awards; works published regionally and nationally; appointments to local and state commissions, councils, and committees; AIA Fellow, 1971; AIA Seattle Medal, 1987; died in Seattle. [jko]

Callison, Anthony (May 21, 1932-January 25, 1988). Born and raised in Seattle; attended Bowdoin College, Brunswick, Maine; B.Arch. University of Washington, 1956; partner in Van Slyck–Callison, Seattle, 1960-65; in Van Slyck–Callison–Nelson, Seattle, 1965-70; in Callison–Erickson–Hobble, Seattle, 1970-74; formed the Callison Partnership, Ltd., Seattle, 1974; managed firm; served as partner-in-charge for Park Place Office Building, Seattle (1972), Crowne Plaza Hotel, Seattle (1980), Stouffer-Madison Hotel, Seattle (1983), Microsoft World Headquarters, Kirkland (1984), Inn at Semiahmoo, Blaine (1986);

leader in application of computer technology to architectural design; died in Seattle; AIA Seattle Medal, 1988 (posthumous). [jko]

Carleton, William Hodder See Young, Richardson & Carleton

Carrigan, John (d. July 24, 1922). Arrived in Seattle in 1908 from Bay City, Michigan; private practice 1908-22, designed Elk's Temple, Seattle (1912); died on business trip in Bay City. [daa]

Carroll, Theodore Bynette See Smith & Carroll

Chamberlain, Samuel (October 28, 1895-January 10, 1975). Born Cresco, Iowa; studied at University of Washington (class of 1917), later at MIT and École des Beaux-Arts; well-known etcher, photographer, author; later lectured on graphic arts at MIT; practiced architecture in Seattle, 1922 (for Stearnes & Brophy); died in Marblehead, Massachusetts. [daa]

Chamberlin, Arthur Bishop (March 12, 1865-September 28, 1933). Born in Solon, Ohio; raised in Wisconsin and Minnesota; employed as draftsman in Minneapolis, 1884-89 (studied delineation with Harvey Ellis); arrived in Seattle in 1890; employed as draftsman and delineator by Saunders & Houghton, 1890-91 (see Saunders essay), by John Parkinson, 1891-93 (see Parkinson essay), by William Boone, 1893 (see Boone essay); in these years he was the delineator of majority of drawings of Seattle work published in the professional press; practiced as architect, 1893-94, designed Collins Block, Seattle (1893); in partnership Chamberlin & Siebrand (with Carl Siebrand), 1894-95, designed two-room Denny-Fuhrman School, Seattle (1894; altered; now part of Seward School complex); practiced alone, 1896; practiced in Minneapolis as Bertrand & Chamberlin,

1896-1931; died in Minneapolis. [jko]

Chinn, Sam Wing. Place and date of birth unknown; B.Arch. University of Washington, 1922 (first Asian-American graduate in architecture in Washington State); employed by Andrew Willatsen, 1922-26 (see Willatsen essay); employed by Thomas, Grainger & Thomas, 1928-34 (see Thomas essay); in partnership Bockerman & Chinn (with Frederick W. Bockerman), 1937-38; architectural practice alone, 1939-40; designed George E. Sheets house, Seattle (1939), G. Diafos house alterations, Seattle (1939, destroyed); employed by Federal Housing Administration in Seattle, 1940-63; date and place of death unknown. [dar]

Comstock & Troetsche (Nelson A. Comstock and Carl Troetsche). Significant architectural practice in San Diego during land boom of mid-1880s; major projects including Pierce-Morse Block, San Diego (1887-88, destroyed), Jesse Shepherd house, San Diego (1887-88); contact with Judge Thomas Burke led to Seattle office in early 1889; designed Squire-Latimer Block (now Grand Central Mercantile), Seattle (1889-90), J. H. Marshall Block (now J&M Cafe), Seattle (1889-90), business building for John Leary (at Third and Marion), Seattle (1889-90, destroyed); partnership dissolved late 1890 (Troetsche retained San Diego practice); later careers and places and dates of birth and death unknown. [daa]

Corner, James N. See Skillings & Corner

Creutzer, John (d. August 1929). First practiced in Minneapolis, then Spokane; arrived in Seattle in 1906; provided architectural work and construction supervision for Alexander Pearson, a Swedish-American contractor, and for Henderson Ryan, Seattle architect-contractor; designed Swedish Tabernacle, Seattle (1906), Medical and Dental Building, Seattle (1927; with A.

H. Albertson, consulting architect; see Albertson, Wilson & Richardson essay); died in Seattle. [daa]

DeNeuf & Heide (1901-6). Emil DeNeuf (d. 1915) and Augustus Heide (May 4, 1862- ?); DeNeuf's date and place of birth, professional training unknown; arrived in Seattle in 1889; employed as draftsman for Elmer Fisher, 1889-91; independent practice (initially as Fisher's successor), 1891-94, designed new First Avenue facade for fire-damaged Schwabacher Building, Seattle (1892), designed W. P. Boyd house, Seattle (1893); practiced architecture in Guatemala, 1894-1900; mayor of West Seattle 1900-1905. Heide was born in Alton, Illinois; arrived in Washington Territory in 1889; practiced architecture in Tacoma and Everett, early 1890s, designed Harstad Hall, Pacific Lutheran University, Tacoma (1892); practiced in Los Angeles, mid to late 1890s. DeNeuf & Heide partnership formed in Seattle in 1901; designed E. F. Blaine house, Seattle (1900-1901), Lowman Building, Seattle (1902-3), Erickson Building, Seattle (partially built, 1902-3), American National Bank Building, Everett (1903), Union Trust Company Buiilding, Everett (ca. 1903), Washington State Building, Louisiana Purchase Exposition, St. Louis (1904, destroyed). DeNeuf moved to San Francisco in 1912; died in San Francisco. Heide designed Washington State buildings at Pan Pacific International Exposition, San Francisco (1914, destroyed), and at San Diego Exposition (1914, destroyed); later life and career unknown. [daa]

Deprosse, Victor. Place and date of birth unknown; practiced in various West Coast cities in late 1880s and early 1890s; listed in Tacoma directories in 1890, Seattle directories in 1890-91; designed two terrace housing projects in Queen Anne style for James McNaught, Seattle (1890, destroyed; renderings appeared in Seattle Chamber of Commerce promotional brochure), frame

Queen Anne style building for James McNaught, Anacortes (1890, altered); subsequent architectural practice in various partnerships in San Francisco in 1890s; date and place of death unknown. [daa]

Detlie, John Stuart. Born in Sioux Falls, South Dakota; engineering degree, University of Alabama; M.Arch. University of Pennsylvania, 1933; art director for MGM Studios, Los Angeles, 1933-41; served in Army, assigned to Seattle's camouflage program, 1942; employed by Young & Richardson, Seattle, 1946-51; work included Gaffney's Lake Wilderness Lodge, near Renton (1949-50); partner in Young, Richardson, Carleton & Detlie, Seattle, 1952-56 (see Young, Richardson & Carleton entry); partnership with Raymond Peck, Seattle, 1957-60, was prolific given its brevity; significant work included Temple de Hirsch, Seattle (1959-60; with B. Marcus Priteca, see essay), Zeta Beta Tau Fraternity, Seattle (1960), Bellevue Christian Church, Bellevue (1960), and several Goodyear Tire stores in the Puget Sound area; founding member and first director of Allied Arts of Seattle; first chair of the Washington State Arts Council; president, Washington State AIA Chapter, 1953-54; moved to Los Angeles in July 1960, worked for Daniel Mann Johnson & Mendenhall (DMJM); subsequent career unknown. [dad]

Dietz, Robert H. (b. January 26, 1912). Born in Nebraska, but raised primarily in Seattle; B.Arch. University of Washington, 1941; M.Arch. Massachusetts Institute of Technology, 1944; Hon. D.Sc. University of Nebraska, 1967; worked on radiation laboratory construction at MIT, 1942-43; bomb analyst for Office of Scientific Research Development, Princeton, 1943-45; designer, Anderson & Beckwith Architects, Cambridge, Massachusetts, 1945-47; appointed instructor, School of Architecture, University of Washington, 1947; assistant professor, 1948; associate professor, 1953;

professor, 1958; chair of graduate program in architecture, 1960; dean of College of Architecture and Urban Planning, 1962-72; private architectural practice and consultant with J. Lister Holmes, 1947-52 (see Holmes essay); associate and then partner with Lawrence G. Waldron, Seattle, 1952-57; designer of educational, commercial, office, and residential work with miscellaneous design awards; national president, Association of Collegiate Schools of Architecture, 1953-57; AIA Fellow, 1965; appointments to local, state, and national commissions, councils, and committees; various publications on school planning; and architectural education; retired 1975; residing intermittently in Washington and California, 1993. [njj]

Dose, Charles C. (d. ca. 1925). Son of real estate developer Charles P. Dose; employed as designer with Charles P. Dose & Company, Seattle, 1902-7; in partnership Dose, West & Reinoehl (with Thomas L. West and Claude A. Reinoehl), 1908; partnership published *Architecture of Dose, West & Reinoehl* (Seattle, 1908); in private architectural practice as C. C. Dose & Company, 1909-17; designed numerous Craftsman style houses and some apartment buildings, designed Mount Baker Park Club House, Seattle (1914); died in Seattle. [dar]

Doyle, Arthur (1819-1899). Born in Ireland; came to Lexington, Kentucky, at young age; served two terms as mayor of Lexington; served as colonel in Confederate army; following Civil War moved to Mobile, Alabama, then Denver, Colorado; arrived in Seattle in 1871; designed Frauenthal Building, Seattle (1876, destroyed), Squire's Opera House, Seattle (1879-80, destroyed), Martin Van Buren Stacy house, Seattle (1883-84, destroyed); retired 1884; died in Seattle. [daa]

Dozier, Henry (b. 1855). Born in Mississippi; arrived in Denver in 1879; employed as draftsman by E. P. Brink, 1883; in partnership Dozier & Cazin (with Alexander Cazin), 1887-88; in partnership Dozier & Walters (with W. E. Walters), 1892-93; designed W. Ridley store building, Denver (1892); in private practice 1884-97; designed A. H. Weber house, Denver (1889-90), "The Ramona"/George Filbeck Building, Denver (1891); charter member of Colorado Chapter AIA, 1892; designed White Pass & Yukon Railroad depot, Skagway, Alaska (1900); arrived in Seattle ca. 1901; in private practice, 1901-9; designed Pacific Hospital building, Seattle (1904), H. H. Dearborn house and stable, Seattle (1904-5), Alfred C. Smith apartment building, Seattle (1905); date and place of death unknown. [dar]

Durham, Robert L. (b. April 28, 1912). Born in Seattle; raised in Tacoma; B.Arch. University of Washington, 1936; employed by B. Dudley Stuart as draftsman, Seattle, 1936-37; cost engineer for Federal Housing Authority, 1938-42; rejoined architect Stuart, 1942, to form Stuart & Durham partnership doing mostly war housing; after World War II practice range expanded, designed Waterfront Fire Station, Seattle (1944), Smith-Gandy Auto Agency, Seattle (1947); after Stuart retired, practice reorganized as Durham, Anderson & Freed, 1954-80; designed schools, banks, churches; prepared masterplans for the Evergreen State College, Olympia (and designed its library) (1971), and the U.S. Naval Base, Bangor (1978); designed AGC Building, Seattle (1965), Atmospheric Sciences Building, University of Washington (1970), Horizon House Retirement Home, Seattle (1971); AIA Fellow, 1959; national AIA president, 1967-68; chancellor, AIA College of Fellows, 1980; AIA Kemper Award, 1981; noted watercolorist; retired 1980; AIA Seattle Medal, 1985; residing in Seattle, 1993. [njj]

Everett, Julian. Place and date of birth unknown; studied at Massachusetts Institute of Technology; arrived in Seattle in 1904; independent practice 1904-22 (occasionally associated with W. R. B. Willcox—see Willcox essay), designed Pilgrim Congregational Church, Seattle (1905-6), Temple de Hirsch, Seattle (1906-8, destroyed), Pioneer Square Comfort Station and Pergola, Seattle (1908); place and date of death unknown. [daa]

Ford, Sherwood D. (1872-1948). Born in England; came to North America in mid-1890s; worked in Montreal, then for Hartwell, Richardson & Driver in Boston; arrived in Seattle in 1907; employed by John Graham, Sr. (see essay), 1907-14 (with James E. Webster, took over Graham's Northwest projects when Graham was in Detroit, 1914-16); independent practice of architecture after 1917, designed Cambridge Apartments, Seattle (1928-29), Mayflower (later Music Hall) Theater, Seattle (1927-28, destroyed), Marcus Whitman Hotel, Walla Walla (1927-28), Washington Athletic Club, Seattle (1929-30); died in Seattle. [daa]

Fox, Norman Edward (May 17, 1903- ?). Born in Dayton, Ohio; moved to Seattle to work for J. Lister Holmes (1925-38; see essay); worked for the U.S. Army Corps of Engineers, Seattle, 1940-43; returned to Holmes's office, 1943-44; practiced as independent architectural delineator, Seattle, 1944-52, executing renderings for various architectural offices in Seattle; date and place of death unknown. [dad]

Gowen, Lancelot E. (December 16, 1894-March 3, 1958). Born and raised in Seattle; B.A. in architecture University of California, Berkeley, 1916; infantry officer U.S. Army, 1917-19; M.A. in Architecture University of California, 1921; graduate study in architecture while working in office of John Galen Howard, 1922; study at École des Beaux-Arts, American Field Service Fellow, and European and Northern Africa travel 1922-24; appointed instructor, University of Washington Architecture Department, 1924; assistant professor, 1925; associate professor, 1929; professor, 1937; coast artillery officer, 1943-46; major at time of discharge; practicing architect since 1926, but primarily recognized for teaching; extensive travel Europe, North Africa, Mexico, Orient; died in Seattle. [njj]

Green, Elmer Ellsworth. Place and date of birth unknown; advertised the sale of house plans and specifications in Seattle in 1907; published *Practical Plan Book,* with floor plans and photographs for over sixty Seattle houses, ca. 1912; established Victoria, B.C., office in 1912; designed numerous residences in Victoria; credited with the design of over thirty Seattle residences (including William W. Felger residence, 1915), apartment houses (including Ben Lomond Apartment Hotel, Seattle, 1910), and sorority houses, between 1907-15; place and date of death unknown. [khk]

Haag, Richard (b. October 23, 1923). Born in Louisville, Kentucky; attended University of Illinois, Champaign; B.L.A. University of California-Berkeley, 1950; M.L.A. Harvard University, 1951; traveling fellowship Kyoto University, Kyoto, Japan, 1954; employed by Hideo Sasaki, 1950; by Dan Kiley, 1951; by Lawrence Halprin, 1956; independent practice of landscape architecture in San Francisco, 1957; moved to Seattle, 1958; designs include Seattle Center redevelopment plans, Seattle (1962-64, 1978), Gas Works Park, Seattle (1981), Battelle Research Institute, Seattle (1982), U.S. Embassy grounds, Lisbon, Portugal (1985), Bloedel Reserve, Bainbridge Island (1986); winner of local, regional, and national design awards; works published nationally and internationally; appointed assistant professor, Department of Architecture, University of Washington, 1958; associate

professor, 1960; professor, Departments of Architecture, Landscape Architecture, and Urban Design and Planning, 1980; Chair, Department of Landscape Architecture, 1964-70; Council of Educators of Landscape Architects' Teacher of the Year, 1993; twice winner of ASLA President's Medal; residing in Seattle, 1993. [dad]

Hancock, Otis E. (November 11, 1893-March 10, 1972). Born in Duluth, Minnesota; moved with family to Seattle in 1907; attended Carnegie Institute of Technology, Pittsburgh; served in U.S. Navy, 1917-19; employed by Arthur Loveless (see essay), Seattle, 1920-22; B. Marcus Priteca (see essay), Seattle, 1922-23; Frank Fowler, Seattle, 1923-24; independent architectural practice, Seattle, 1925-27; partnership with Frederick V. Lockman, Seattle, 1925-33; independent practice after 1933; retired, 1971; died in Seattle. [dad]

Hargreaves, Kenneth L. See Turner & Hargreaves

Haynes, Charles A. (d. June 1940). Place and date of birth unknown; may have come from Minnesota; established Seattle office of Haynes & Cantin, 1907; in practice with Charles E. Troutman, Aberdeen, ca. 1911; partnership with J. Merrill Brown, Seattle, November 1912; partnership with Clarence W. George, Aberdeen, ca. 1923; designed Butterworth Mortuary, Seattle (1923); designed many revival style houses (including Robert P. Greer residence, Seattle, 1910-11), apartment houses, and commercial projects, Seattle and Aberdeen, 1907-40; died in Seattle. [khk]

Heide, Augustus See DeNeuf & Heide

Herrman, Arthur P. (December 3, 1898-March 17, 1993). Born and raised in Milwaukee; B.A. in architecture Carnegie Institute of Technology, Pittsburgh, 1921; apprentice at Alden & Harlow, Pittsburgh,

1921-23; appointed instructor, University of Washington Department of Architecture, 1923; assistant professor, 1925; associate professor, 1929; professor, 1937; appointed director, University of Washington School of Architecture, 1937 (at retirement of Harlan Thomas); first dean, College of Architecture and Urban Planning, 1958-68; under his administration the program expanded to add urban planning, landscape architecture, and architecture at graduate level; retired 1968 (moved to California); died in LaVerne, California. [njj]

Hoggson, Noble (July 8, 1899-October 29, 1970). Born and raised in New York City; Bachelor of Business Administration, Yale University, 1922; M.L.A. Harvard University, 1927; partnership Spoon & Hoggson, White Plains, New York, 1928-30; moved to Seattle in 1930; employed by Butler Sturtevant (see essay), Seattle, 1930-31; independent practice as landscape architect after 1932; consultant to University of Washington Arboretum, 1932-33; landscape architect for Mount Rainier and Lassen national parks, 1933-36; designed landscape plans for the Seattle Art Museum, Volunteer Park (1933-34), Dorothy Dunn Bailey Garden (south of The Highlands) (1941), Sand Point Naval Housing Project, Seattle (1943, with E. Clair Heilman), Maurice Dunn Garden (south of The Highlands) (1949), design work for Bloedel Reserve, Bainbridge Island (1966-69); Claude Bekins garden, The Highlands (1966-69); died in Seattle. [dad]

Holmdahl, Otto E. (d. March 2, 1967). Born in Sweden; arrived in Seattle in 1919; designed parks in Bremerton, Ellensburg, Aberdeen, and others in Washington and Oregon; designed landscaped garden settings for many homes by Arthur L. Loveless (see essay); landscape architect under Paul Thiry (see essay) for World's Fair, Seattle (1962); designed the grounds for the Washington State Library, Olympia (1954-59);

Aberdeen Community Hospital, Aberdeen (1959); design work at the University of Washington Arboretum, Seattle (ca. 1960); died in Seattle. [dad]

Horrocks, Pierce A. Place and date of birth unknown; practiced in partnership McQuaker & Horrocks (with Andrew McQuaker), Seattle, 1919-22; designed Nels Hansen residence, Seattle (1919-20), Thomas Harris building, Renton (1920), R. C. Sherill residence, Seattle (1920-21); independent practice, 1922-31; designed Green Lake Baptist Church, Seattle (1922-23, now the Apostolic Faith Church), Woman's Century Club, Seattle (1925-26, now the Harvard Exit Theater), W. B. Morse residence, Seattle (1926); employed as project architect by B. Marcus Priteca, 1939-41 (see Priteca essay); supervised Seattle Buddhist Church (1940-41, with A. K. Arai—see Arai essay); date and place of death unknown. [dar]

Ivey, Edwin J. (1883-February 25, 1940). Born in Seattle; graduated in architecture from University of Pennsylvania, 1910; practiced in partnership Milner & Ivey (with Warren H. Milner), Seattle, 1911; draftsman for Joseph S. Coté (see Somervell & Coté essay), 1913; in private architectural practice, 1914-19; in partnership Ivey & Riley (with Howard H. Riley), 1919-22; in private practice, 1922-40; designed numerous speculative houses for H. E. Harold, Seattle (1917), Ira Hinckley factory building, Seattle (1920), high school building, LaConner (1920-21), R. B. Allen residence, Olympia (1921-32), Chester Thorne residence alterations, American Lake (1922-23), C. W. Stimson residence, The Highlands (1924-26), L. C. Henry residence, The Highlands (1927-28), Mansel P. Griffiths residence, Seattle (1928-29), Ferry Investment Co. Building, Seattle (1930, with J. L. Skoog); Winston W. Chambers residence, Seattle (1938-39); died in Mount Vernon, as a result of an automobile accident north of Everett. (See also Elizabeth Ayer essay.) [dar]

Johanson, Perry Bertil (May 9, 1910-June 15, 1981). Born in Greeley, Colorado; received B.Arch. University of Washington, 1934; employed by Smith & Carroll, Seattle, 1934-36; in partnership Smith, Carroll & Johanson, 1936-51; in partnership Naramore, Bain, Brady & Johanson, 1943-81; Naramore et al. directed design of additions to Harborview and Providence hospitals, University of Washington Medical School, and additions to the University of Washington Health Sciences Center; Washington State AIA Chapter president, 1950-51; died in Seattle. [dad]

Johnston, Norman J. (b. December 3, 1918). Born in Seattle; raised in Olympia; B.A. (art) University of Washington, 1942; B.Arch. University of Oregon, 1949; M.U.P., 1959, and Ph.D., 1964, University of Pennsylvania; apprenticed with Joseph H. Wohleb, Olympia, 1945-50; planner for City of Seattle Planning Commission, 1950-54; architect with Nelsen, Sabin & Varey, Seattle, 1954-56; appointed assistant professor, Department of Architecture, University of Oregon, 1956; associate professor, Department of Architecture, University of Washington, 1960-64; professor, Departments of Architecture, Landscape Architecture, and Urban Design and Planning, 1964-85; associate dean, College of Architecture and Urban Planning, 1966-84; chair, Department of Architecture, 1984-85; professor emeritus, since 1985 (but continued to teach until 1989); founding member Allied Arts of Seattle, Friends of Seattle Olmsted Parks, State of Washington Capitol Campus Advisory Committee; appointments to local, state, and national commissions, councils, and committees; author, *Cities in the Round* (1983), *Washington's Audacious State Capitol and Its Builders* (1988); AIA Fellow, 1982; AIA Seattle Medal, 1991; residing in Seattle, 1993. [jko]

Jones, John Paul (August 12, 1892- ?). Born in Maumee, Ohio; employed by architect George S. Mills, Toledo, Ohio, 1909-10; attended Denison University, Granville, Ohio, 1911-13; employed by Mills, Rhines, Bellman & Nordhoff, Toledo, 1913-14; B.Arch. University of Pennsylvania, 1916; employed by Spier & Gehrke, Detroit, 1916-17; came to Seattle ca. 1918; employed by Bebb & Gould (see essay), Seattle, 1919-39, became junior partner 1926, partner in Bebb & Jones, 1939-47; partnership Jones & Bindon (with Leonard Bindon), 1947-56; designed Bellingham City Hall, Bellingham (1939), Student Union Building, University of Washington, Seattle (1947-52); initial designs for Downtown Seattle Public Library (1956); date and place of death unknown. [dad]

Jones, Victor Noble Jarrett (April 21, 1900-December 14, 1969). Born in Exeter, Ontario; B.A. (architecture) University of Washington, 1924; M.Arch. University of Pennsylvania, 1926; employed by partnership of Wilson Eyre & John Gilbert McIlvaine, Philadelphia, 1912-26; employed by Charles Z. Klauder, Philadelphia, 1926-28; in partnership with McClelland & Pinneh, Seattle, 1930-32; partnership, McClelland & Jones, Seattle, 1933-46; Victor N. Jones & Associate, Seattle, 1946-55; Jones, Lovegren, Helms & Jones, Seattle, 1956-ca. 1965; first Medical School building, University of Washington, Seattle (ca. 1952; with Naramore, Bain, Brady & Johanson); Administration Building, University of Washington, Seattle (1947-49), Washington State Ferry Terminal on Seattle waterfront (1964-67); retired ca. 1965; died in Seattle. [dad]

Josenhans, Timotheus (1853-1929). Born in Wurttemberg, Germany; came as child to United States; raised and educated in Ann Arbor as engineer; employed briefly as draftsman by William LeBaron Jenney, then as railroad construction engineer, Chicago;

arrived in Oregon in 1880; employed as draftsman by Joseph Sherwin and Warren Williams, Portland; arrived in Seattle in 1888 as draftsman for Hermann Steinmann; designed powerhouses for Seattle's electric and cable railways (1888-89); partnership with James Stephen, 1894-97 (see Stephen essay); partnership Josenhans & Allan, 1899-1912 (with Norris Best Allan), designed Blethen house, Seattle (1901), Parrington Hall, University of Washington, Seattle (1903-4); died in Seattle. [daa]

Kimball, William D. (1855-1907). Born in Virginia; practiced architecture in Minneapolis and Milwaukee, 1880s (published renderings in *American Architect and Building News* mid to late 1880s); arrived in Seattle in late 1901; designed stations for Independent Telephone Company, Seattle (1902, demolished), James Moore house, Seattle (1902), Thomas Bordeaux house, Seattle (1904); died in Seattle. [daa]

Lawton & Moldenhour (1922-1928). George Willis Lawton (December 29, 1864-March 28, 1928) and Herman A. Moldenhour (1864-December 1976). Lawton was born in Wisconsin, came to Seattle in 1889; employed as draftsman by Saunders & Houghton, 1889-91; in partnership Saunders & Lawton, 1898-1914 (see Saunders essay); independent practice, 1915-22, responsible for design of Masonic Temple, Seattle (1914-16; begun by Saunders & Lawton). Moldenhour was born in Wisconsin; came to Seattle with his family, and worked as office boy with Saunders & Lawton; Lawton & Moldenhour designed many large apartment buildings, office buildings, institutional structures; designed Fourth and Pike Building, Seattle (1927). Lawton died in Seattle. Moldenhour practiced independently after Lawton's death, supervising architect for original Seattle-Tacoma Airport Administration Building (1948-49; altered); died in Seattle. [daa]

Leissler, Frederick W. (1904-November 28, 1989). Born in Lake Forest Park, Washington; attended Roosevelt High School, Seattle; landscape architecture degree Oregon State University, 1926; employed as landscape architect, Seattle Parks Department, 1927-35; designed planting for Seward and Lincoln parks, Seattle; appointed assistant director, College of Forestry, University of Washington, 1935-39 (supervised design and construction of the University of Washington Arboretum); National Park Service landscape architect and ranger, serving in Olympic National Park, 1946-56; landscape architect for U.S. Bureau of Public Roads, 1958-69 (serving with Lady Bird Johnson's "Keep America Beautiful" program); died in Genoa, Nevada. [dad]

Lovett, Wendell (b. April 2, 1922). Born and raised in Seattle; B.Arch. University of Washington, 1947; M.Arch. Massachusetts Institute of Technology, 1948; designer, then associate, with Bassetti & Morse, Seattle, 1948-51; independent practice after 1951, designed Lauren and Ann Studebaker house, Mercer Island (1969-71), Gerald and Jo Frey house, Bellevue (1971-72), Max and Carol Scofield house, Mercer Island (1974-76), Anne Gould Hauberg condominium, Seattle (1985-86, with Alan Liddle), Dr. Charles Simonyi house, Medina (1986-89); winner of local, regional, and national design awards; works published nationally and internationally; appointed instructor, Department of Architecture, University of Washington, 1948-51; assistant professor, 1951-60; associate professor, 1960-65; professor, 1965-84; professor emeritus since 1984; guest professor, Technical University, Stuttgart, Germany, 1959-60; AIA Fellow, 1978; AIA Seattle Medal, 1993; residing in Seattle, 1993. [jko]

Mahlum, Edward K. (b. November 13, 1909). Born in Seattle; raised in Norway, returning to U.S. in 1927; B.Sc. in Arch. North Dakota State College, 1934; employed by M. O. Foss Architects, Fergus Falls, Minnesota, 1934-38, designed David Park residence, Bemidji, Minnesota (1937); employed by C. H. Johnston, Architects, St. Paul, 1938-40, designed University of Minnesota Museum of Natural History (1938) and Student Union Building (1940); employed by Naramore & Brady, Architects (and later Naramore, Bain, Brady & Johanson), Seattle, 1940-48; service as officer, U.S. Army, 1942-45; independent practice as Edward K. Mahlum Architect, Seattle 1948-68, designed Norway Center (now Mountaineers Building), Seattle (1950), Norse Home Retirement Center, Seattle (1952), Hearthstone Retirement Center, Seattle (1960-66), North Seattle Community College (1966-70); partnership Mahlum & Mahlum Architects, 1968-75, designed Group Health Cooperative Eastside Hospital and Medical Center, Redmond (1970-75); partnership, Mahlum, Mahlum & Nordfors, 1975-79; winner of local and regional design awards; works published nationally; president, Puget Sound Chapter CSI, 1966-67; involved with federal legislation for mortgage guarantees for private facilities for the aged, 1950s; active in Seattle's Norwegian community; retired 1976; residing in Seattle, 1993. [jko]

Meany, Stephen J. Place and date of birth unknown (paternal cousin of historian Edmond S. Meany); arrived in Seattle in 1882 (from San Jose); employed as draftsman for W. E. Boone (see essay), 1882; practiced architecture in partnership Donovan & Meany (with James P. Donovan), 1882-83, designed North School (Denny School), Seattle (1883-84, destroyed), Grace Hospital, Seattle (1883, destroyed); in independent practice designed Poncin Block, Seattle (1883-84, destroyed), Kenney Block, Seattle (1883-84, destroyed); employed as draftsman by Arthur Doyle on M. V. B. Stacey house, Seattle (1883-84, destroyed); employed as draftsman by Donald MacKay (see MacKay

essay) on Occidental Hotel, Seattle (1882-84, destroyed); in independent practice, 1889-92, designed Occidental Hotel (Seattle Hotel), Seattle (1889-90, destroyed), Colman Building (first two floors only), Seattle (1889-90, altered), Newport Hotel, Seattle (1899-1900, destroyed); place and date of death unknown. [daa]

Mithun, Omer (June 10, 1918-March 22, 1983). Born in Marcus, Iowa; received certificate in industrial education, Hibbing Junior College, Hibbing, Minnesota, 1938; B.Arch. University of Minnesota, 1942; graduate degree in naval architecture, University of Michigan, 1945; directed construction and ship repair, Naval Shipyard, Bremerton, 1945-46; employed by Naramore, Bain, Brady & Johanson, Seattle, 1946-47; partnership, Wilson-Mithun Partners, Bellevue, 1949-52; partnership, Mithun & Nesland, Bellevue, 1952-55; designed Surrey Downs, Bellevue (1952-55); continued as Mithun & Associates, 1955-58, 1960-80; designed Bellevue Presbyterian Church, Bellevue (1954-58), Bellevue Medical Dental Center, Bellevue (1962-68), Tally Building, Bellevue (1969-70), Everwood Park, Bellevue (1973-76); partnership, Mithun, Ridenour & Cochran, 1958-60; incorporated as the Mithun Associates in 1980-84; winner of local, regional, and national design awards; works published nationally; part-time instructor, University of Washington School of Architecture, 1947; assistant professor, 1950; associate professor, 1960; professor, 1967; retired from university, 1982; chairman, Bellevue City Planning Commission, 1953-72; appointments to local and state commissions and committees; AIA Fellow, 1973; leader in energy conservation and solar energy applications in design; died in Bellevue. [jko]

Moldenhour, Herman A. See Lawton & Moldenhour

Morrison, Earle Wilson (d. 1955). Practiced in Spokane (with V. S. Stimson), 1919-26; came to Seattle in 1926; designed Olive Tower Apartments, Seattle (1928-29), Textile Tower, Seattle (1930-31); died in Seattle. [daa]

Nelsen, Ibsen (b. October 2, 1919). Born in Ruskin, Nebraska; learned carpentry and cabinetry from Julius Nelsen (Danish immigrant builder); Captain, U.S. Army, southwest Pacific, 1941-45; B.Arch. University of Oregon, 1951; employed by Naramore, Bain, Brady & Johanson, Seattle, 1951; by Morrison Knudsen Company, Seattle, 1951-52; independent architectural practice, Seattle, 1953; partnership, Nelsen & Sabin, 1954-60; partnership Nelsen, Sabin & Varey, 1961-67; designed Morris Graves house, Lolita, California (1965-67); independent practice after 1968; designed Inn at the Market (Pike Place Market), Seattle (1975-82), Stewart House (Pike Place Market), Seattle (1975-82), Museum of Flight, Seattle (1975-87), Merrill Court, Seattle (1981-86), Ibsen Nelsen house, Vashon Island (1986-90); winner of local, regional, and national design awards; works published nationally and internationally; assistant professor (part-time), University of Washington, 1957-65; chairman, Municipal Arts Commission, Seattle 1967-68; president, Allied Arts of Seattle 1969-70; vice-president, AIA Seattle, 1960-61; AIA Fellow, 1981; AIA Seattle Medal, 1989; residing on Vashon Island, 1993. [jko]

Nestor, John (1836-1912). Born in Ireland; came as child to United States; practiced architecture, San Francisco, mid-1860s; arrived in Portland in 1864; designed Ladd & Tilton Bank Building, Portland (1868, destroyed); arrived in Seattle in 1883; designed Frye Opera House, Seattle (1883-84, destroyed), T. T. Minor house, Seattle (1884, destroyed), Gordon Hardware Company Building, Seattle (1889-90, destroyed), Frye (Stevens) Hotel, Seattle (1889-90, destroyed), Hinckley Block, Seattle (1890-91, destroyed); died in Seattle. [daa]

Olson, Oliver William (January 9, 1914-March 28, 1993). Born in Seattle; studied at University of Washington; employed by Naramore, Bain, Brady & Johanson, Seattle 1945-46; in partnership Olsen & Olson (with Bjarne Olsen), Seattle, 1947-51; independent practice after 1951; designer of churches in Pacific Northwest, designed Trinity Lutheran Church, Seattle (1950-51), Chime Tower, Washelli Cemetery, Seattle (1950), Crown Lutheran Church, Seattle (1956-57), Gloria Dei Lutheran Church, Coos Bay, Oregon (1959-60); died in Seattle. [daa]

Osborne, Edward Thomas. Born in England; worked in New Zealand, California, British Columbia, and Alberta; arrived in Seattle ca. 1910; employed as draftsman by E. W. Houghton, John Graham, B. M. Priteca, Bebb & Gould (see essays); renowned delineator, especially for watercolor renderings, many of which were published; occasional independent practice, 1920-30, designed Trinity Episcopal Church, Everett (1920-21), Charlesgate Apartments, Seattle (1922), Lynnwood Apartments, Seattle (1922-23); co-designer (with McCarter & Nairn) Vancouver, B.C., Opera House (1921-22); date and place of death unknown. [daa]

Ozasa, Sabro. Born in Japan; arrived in United States ca. 1894; arrived in Seattle in 1909; first Asian-American to practice architecture in Seattle; designed Gaffney and Hyde apartment building, Seattle (1909-10, destroyed), Cascade Investment house, Seattle (1909-10), R. Malan house, Seattle (1910), Panama Hotel, Seattle (1910), Specie Bank of Seattle building, Seattle (1910-11, destroyed); date and place of death unknown. [dar]

Palmer, Isaac. Place and date of birth unknown; active in Seattle as architect-builder, 1870s-90s; designed First Baptist Church, Seattle (1872, destroyed), L. V. Wyckoff house, Seattle (1872, destroyed), King County Courthouse, Seattle (1877, destroyed), Central School, Seattle (1883, destroyed 1887); place and date of death unknown. [daa]

Patterson, Daniel J. Place and date of birth unknown; employed as draftsman in Seattle, Whatcom, and Spokane by Willis Ritchie in early 1890s (claimed to be principal designer of King County Courthouse and Spokane County Courthouse; see Ritchie essay); relocated to San Francisco after Seattle divorce scandal, 1893; architectural practice in San Francisco after 1893; published renderings in *California Architect and Building News,* designed several stations in Mission Revival style for Southern Pacific Railroad in Texas and California; designed Union Station, Seattle (1908-11); died in California. [daa]

Richardson, Stephen Hinley See Young, Richardson & Carleton

Ryan, Henderson (1878-?). Born in Alabama, educated at University of Kentucky; arrived in Seattle in 1898; contractor-builder, 1899-1900; independent practice as architect, 1900-1923; designed Roycroft Apartments, Seattle (1906-7), Swedish Baptist Church, Seattle (1904-6, destroyed), Ballard Public Library, Ballard (1903-4), Waldorf Hotel, Seattle (1906-7), Maryland Apartments, Seattle (1910-11), Liberty Theater, Seattle (1912, destroyed), Neptune Theater, Seattle (1921-22); died in California; date of death unknown. [daa]

Sandved, Peder. Born in Norway; studied for two years at Horticultural University, Copenhagen, Denmark; arrived in Lima, Ohio, 1904; arrived in Seattle in 1908; practiced landscape design, 1908-17; designed grounds of O. D. Fisher residence, Seattle (1908-9), grounds of J. A. Kerr estate, Seattle (1910-11; including first underground sprinkling system in city); grounds of Dr. Lewis Deckman sanitarium at Lake Crescent (1911-12); after 1917, proprietor of Sandved Nursery; date and place of death unknown. [dar]

Sexton, Frederick A. Born and educated in England; practiced architecture in Tacoma, 1887-91, designed Puget Sound University Main Building, Tacoma (1890, destroyed); practiced architecture in Everett, 1891-94; practiced architecture in Seattle after 1901, designed Bayview School, Ballard (1907, destroyed), designed many houses in Mission Revival style, Seattle; date and place of death unknown. [daa]

Siebrand, Carl (1866-1938). Born in Germany, training unknown; arrived in Seattle in 1889; employed as draftsman by Warren Skillings, 1893; practiced in partnership Chamberlin & Siebrand (with A. B. Chamberlin; see entry), 1894-95, designed two-room Denny-Fuhrman School, Seattle (1894; altered; now part of Seward School complex); practiced independently after 1896; designed Snohomish County Courthouse, Everett (189?), Horace C. Henry house, Seattle (1894), buildings at Bremerton Navy Yard (1895-97); known as brewery and cold-storage architect; designed some U.S. Navy buildings at Pearl Harbor, Hawaii; died in Seattle. [daa]

Shay, Alban Aurelius (February 17, 1899-1991?). Born in Columbus, Ohio; studied at University of Washington; University of Pennsylvania B.Arch., 1922 (member of Architectural Society; Second Medal in Beaux-Arts Design); employed by Warren & Wetmore, New York, then George B. Post & Sons, New York; joined Bebb & Gould (see essay), Seattle, 1924; independent practice, Seattle, 1927-35; in partnership Thiry & Shay (see Thiry essay), 1936-39; resumed independent practice, 1940-75; works include Van Waters & Rogers, Inc., Portland (1949, with S. Ivarsson, Engr.), Nat Rogers residence, Seattle (1950), Otteson residence, Seattle (1953?), Washington Chocolate Company Factory, Seattle (1953), Scientific Supplies Company, Seattle (1954); retired 1975; died in Seattle. [tv]

Skillings & Corner (1893-98). Warren Porter Skillings (May 11, 1860-August 1, 1939) and James N. Corner (1862- May 1, 1919). Skillings was born and raised in Portland, Maine; attended Bowdoin College, 1877-80; employed as draftsman in Boston ca. 1882-89; arrived in Seattle in 1890; designed Washington State Pavilion, World's Columbian Exhibition, Chicago (1893, destroyed); Corner was born and raised in Boston; co-author (with E. E. Soderholtz) of *Examples of Domestic Colonial Architecture in New England* (1891) and *Examples of Colonial Architecture in Maryland and Virginia* (1892) (both later reissued without Corner's name); participated in British Columbia Parliament Buildings competition, 1892; arrived in Seattle in 1893; Skillings & Corner designed Union Trust Block, Seattle (1893), Rialto Building, Seattle (1894, destroyed), [West] Queen Anne Elementary School, Seattle (1896); Skillings practiced architecture in Eureka, California, 1900-1910; in San Jose, 1910-30?; died in San Jose; Corner practiced architecture in partnership Boone & Corner, 1900-1905 (see Boone essay); alone 1906-19; died in Seattle. [daa/jko]

Smith & Carroll (1931-37); **Smith, Carroll & Johanson** (1937-51). Francis Marion Smith, Jr. (March 11, 1908- ?), Theodore Byrnette Carroll (October 23, 1903- ?). Smith was born and raised in Deer Lodge, Montana; arrived in Seattle in 1930; employed briefly by Seattle Home Merchandise; formed partnership Smith & Caroll; Carroll was born in Minneapolis, Minnesota; B.Arch. University of Washington,

1927; employed by Andrew Willatsen (see essay), Seattle, 1927-30; Perry Bertil Johanson (see Johanson entry) became partner, 1937-51; later lives and careers of Smith and Carroll unknown. [dad]

Sonnichsen, Sonke Englehart (1879-1961). Born in Laardal, Norway; educated in architecture and engineering at Norway's Technical Institute; came to United States in 1901; employed as draftsman and designer by Somervell & Coté, John Graham, Sr., and B. Marcus Priteca (see essays); designed Norway Hall, Seattle (1915); consulting architect to School Board of Vancouver, B.C., 1914-17; later practiced with B. Marcus Priteca (see essay) in Los Angeles; died in Seattle. [daa]

Spalding & Umbrecht (1908-11). A. Walter Spalding (August 5, 1859- ?) and Max Umbrecht. Spalding was born in Massachusetts; B.S. Boston University, 1881; practiced architecture in St. Louis, 1881-85; in Minneapolis, 1885-99; in Lewiston, Idaho 1899-1900; arrived in Seattle in 1901; designed Hofius house, Seattle (1902), Stimson Hotel, Seattle (1905-6, destroyed), University Congregational Church, Seattle (1905-6, destroyed), Robert Moran house (now Rosario Resort), Orcas Island (1906), Presbyterian Church, Snohomish (1907-8, destroyed). Umbrecht practiced architecture in Syracuse, New York, and New York City; sent to Seattle in 1900 by Smith family (of the later Smith Tower) and shared an office with Clise Investment Company; designed W. L. Smith Building, Seattle (1900), Colonial Block, Seattle (1901-2), John W. Clise house (now Marymoor Park), Redmond (1904); Spalding became a contractor in 1912; date and place of death unknown; Umbrecht's later life and career unknown. [daa]

Sproule, John R. (July 27, 1908-October 17, 1993). Born in Winnipeg, Canada, he soon came with his parents to Tacoma and then Seattle; B.Arch. University of Washington, 1934; apprenticed with J. Lister Holmes (see Holmes essay) and Paul Thiry (see Thiry essay); independent architectural practice, Seattle, 1936-44, designed Sproule house, Seattle (1936), Home Management House, University of Washington, Seattle (1942; destroyed), Holly Park Public Housing, Seattle (1943, with others); served in the Scientific Research and Development program in the mid-1940s at Princeton; returned to Seattle, 1948; instructor, University of Washington School of Architecture, 1948; assistant professor, 1951; associate professor, 1960; retired from University, 1978; died in Seattle. [njj]

Steinmann, Hermann (1860-April 14, 1905). Practiced architecture in St. Louis, 1883-87; arrived in Seattle, November 1887; designed Squire Building, Seattle (1888, demolished), Mechanics Fair Association Building, Portland, Oregon (1888, destroyed), Brew House for Bay View Brewery, Seattle (1889, destroyed), Terry-Kittinger Block, Seattle (1889-90), Brewery building, Victoria, B.C. (1890); subsequent practice in New York City as brewery architect; died by suicide in New York City. [daa]

Stoddard, George Wellington (1896-September 28, 1967). Born in Detroit; B.S. University of Illinois, 1917; practiced in partnership with father, Lewis M. Stoddard (d. 1929), 1920-29; designed Winthrop Hotel, Tacoma (1926-27); practiced alone, 1929-55; designed larger homes, clinics, banks, apartments houses; practiced as Stoddard, Huggard & Associates (with Francis Huggard), 1955-60; designed Memorial Stadium (now part of Seattle Center), Seattle (1947), University of Washington Stadium south stands, Seattle (1950), Green Lake Aqua Theater, Seattle (1950); died in Seattle. [slc]

Stuart, Bertram Dudley (1885-1977). Born in London; practiced in Edmonton, Alberta, and Vancouver, B.C.; arrived in Seattle in 1918; practiced in partnership, Stuart & Wheatley, with Arthur Wheatley, 1925-30; designed Exeter House Apartments, Seattle (1927), Bergonian Hotel (now Mayflower Hotel), Seattle (1926), Marlborough Apartments, Seattle (1926-27); practiced in partnership with Robert Durham, 1941-77; died in Seattle. [daa]

Thompson & Thompson (1899-ca. 1912?). Charles L. Thompson (July 7, 1842- ?) and his son, C. Bennett Thompson. Charles L. Thompson practiced architecture in New Jersey after 1865, in Kansas, in Salt Lake City, 1890-99; arrived in Seattle in 1899; Thompson & Thompson designed residences and commercial buildings in the International District, including Moses Building, Seattle (1900-1901, altered), Galbraith residence, Seattle (1902-4, destroyed), Low Building, Seattle (1908), Goon Dip Block, Seattle (1910-11), Bikur Cholim Synagogue, Seattle (1909-12, destroyed); places and dates of death unknown. [daa]

Tidemand, August (d. 1907). Born near Trondheim, Norway; practiced in Minneapolis, mid-1880s; came to Tacoma as draftsman, 1889; in architectural practice in Seattle after 1891, designed Colman Building annex, Seattle (1899-1900, destroyed), Colman Building addition, Seattle (1902-4); died in Seattle. [daa]

Towle & Wilcox. Arlen H. Towle and Frank N. Wilcox; partnership in Seattle 1889-91; Towle had previous practice in San Diego; Wilcox had been trained as civil engineer; Towle & Wilcox designed Cort's Theater (later Lyric Theater), Seattle (1889-90, destroyed), Palmer Building, Seattle (1889-90, destroyed), Kline and Rosenberg Building, Seattle (1889-90, altered), Leschi Casino (on Lake Washington), Seattle (1889, destroyed); Towle practiced subsequently in British Columbia; Wilcox practiced as architect and engineer in Seattle until 1894;

dates and places of birth and death unknown. [daa]

Turner & Hargreaves (1954-64). Edwin Thurlow Turner (June 13, 1905- ?) and Kenneth L. Hargreaves. Turner was born and raised in Great Bend, Kansas; B.Arch., University of Washington, 1929; employed by Harry T. Whittaker, Victoria, B.C., 1929-32; by George Stoddard, Seattle, 1935; by William J. Bain, Sr. (see essay), Seattle, 1935-42; independent architectural practice, 1946-53. Hargreaves received B.Arch., University of Washington, 1938; employed by store fixture and cabinet companies, Seattle and Los Angeles, 1938-51; employed by Metropolitian Building Company, Seattle, 1951-54; Hargreaves became a junior partner in DeLaney & Associates, Seattle, 1964; Turner was employed as architect by General Services Administration, Seattle, 1964; later careers unknown. [dad]

Umbrecht, Max See Spalding & Umbrecht

Van Siclen, William Doty (April 29, 1865–July 14, 1951). Born in Clearwater, Michigan; practiced architecture in San Jose, California, ca. 1895-1900 (published renderings in *California Architect and Building News,* 1893, 1895); arrived in Seattle in 1901; employed as draftsman by James Stephen, 1901 (see essay), Saunders & Lawton, 1901-2 (see essay); practiced as architect, 1902-12, designed Eitel Building, Seattle (1904-6), A. L. Palmer Building, Seattle (1906-7), Northern Bank & Trust Company Building (now Seaboard Building), Seattle (1906-9), San Remo apartment house, Seattle (1907); in partnership with Louis Macomber in Vancouver, B.C., 1911-13; moved to Edmonton, Alberta, 1912; moved to Brownsville, Texas, ca. 1925, projects in Tulsa and South Texas; died in Brownsville. [daa/jko]

Voorhees, Victor W. Place and date of birth unknown; established Fisher & Voorhees in

Ballard, August 1904; designed business and apartment buildings in Ballard, 1904; individually credited with the design of over 110 building projects, 1904-29, including cottages, residences, apartment buildings, commercial laundries and garages, industrial buildings and factories, fraternal halls, retail stores, banks, and hotels; designed Washington Hall, Seattle (1908), Vance Hotel, Seattle (ca. 1927), Vance Building, Seattle (ca. 1929); advertised the sale of house plans and a book of house, cottage, and bungalow plans, 1907; published *Western Home Builder* (by 1911 in 7th edition); supervising architect for Willeys-Overland Co., designing automobile showrooms and garages, Seattle and Spokane, after 1917; listed as an architect in Seattle city directories until 1957; place and date of death unknown. [khk]

White, William P. Practiced architecture in Seattle, 1902-22; designed Jefferson Apartments, Seattle (1905, destroyed), Kinnear Apartments, Seattle (1907-8), Astor Hotel, Seattle (1909), Calhoun Hotel, Seattle (1909-10), other apartment buildings and hotels; places and dates of birth and death unknown. [daa/khk]

Wickersham, Albert. Arrived in Seattle (from Portland), 1889; employed by New York architect A. B. Jennings as supervising architect for initial phases of Denny Hotel, Seattle (1889-1903, destroyed); independent architectural practice by 1893; designed Maynard Building, Seattle (1892-93), Seattle Hardware Company Building, Seattle (1904-5), multiple small commercial and remodeling projects; dates and places of birth and death unknown. [daa]

Wightman, Roberta (b. 1912). Born in Chicago, raised in Illinois, attended Oberlin and Middlebury colleges; degree in landscape architecture University of Illinois, 1938; involved in major public work for Springfield, Illinois; arrived Seattle in 1944; worked at University of Washington Arboretum and with Edwin Grohs; independent practice of landscape architecture after 1948; projects throughout Northwest including churches, schools, housing, hospitals, parks, industrial sites, residences; founder and first president, Washington Chapter, ASLA; retired, though continuing consulting work; residing in Seattle, 1993. (njj)

Wilcox, Frank N. See Towle & Wilcox

Willcox, William H. (May 26, 1832-February 1, 1929). Born and raised in Brooklyn; practiced architecture, in New York City, 1853-60; drew maps for the Union Army in the Civil War; employed briefly by Dankmar Adler, Chicago, 1871; practiced architecture in Chicago, 1872-79 (as Willcox & Miller, 1875-77); in Nebraska, 1879-81, designed Nebraska State Capitol Building, Lincoln (1879-82, destroyed); in St. Paul, 1882-91 (as Willcox & Johnston, 1886-90); arrived in Seattle in 1891; practiced in partnership Boone & Willcox, 1891-93 (see Boone essay); alone 1893-95; practiced in Los Angeles, 1895-98; in San Francisco, 1900-1906?; practiced as surveyor in San Francisco, 1907?-12; subsequent career unknown; died at Veterans Home in Yountville (near Napa), California. [jko/daa]

Wilson, Clayton D. May have arrived in Seattle from San Diego in 1900 or 1901; employed by Bebb & Mendel (see essay), Seattle, 1901; independent architectural practice after 1901 (briefly associated with William W. de Veaux, 1903); won competition for Temple de Hirsch, Seattle (1904, not built); designed Municipal Building, Seattle (1905-9; later Public Safety Building, now 400 Yesler Building), remodeled Pantages Theater, Seattle (1907, destroyed); extensive residential practice, western Washington; in partnership Wilson & Love-

less, with Arthur L. Loveless (see essay), Seattle, 1908-12; practiced independently, Seattle, 1912-39, designed West Seattle Congregational Church (1912). other commissions include small commercial and residential structures; date and place of death unknown. [tv]

Wolfe, Myer R. (July 15, 1918-June 25, 1989). Born in Malden, Massachusetts, raised in Haverhill; B.S. in Technology (architecture), University of New Hampshire, 1940; Master of Regional Planning, Cornell, 1947; Air Corps captain, China-Burma-India theater, 1943-46; assistant professor of architecture (teaching city planning), University of Kansas, 1948-49; assistant professor, School of Architecture, University of Washington, 1949; associate professor, 1954; professor, 1958; founder of Department of Urban Planning, 1962 (chair, 1962-67); dean of College of Architecture and Urban Planning, 1979-82; Fulbright grants to Denmark in 1959 and Italy in 1965 as well as many other teaching, guest lectureship, and consultancy appointments in this country and abroad; retired, 1983; died in Seattle. [njj]

Yoho, Jud. Place and date of birth unknown; owner of Craftsman Bungalow Company, located in Seattle, Los Angeles, and New York; published *Bungalow Magazine* (ca. 1909-18); associated with Edward L. Merritt; Yoho & Merritt designed Craftsman style bungalows in Wallingford, Ravenna, Green Lake, University District, and Northgate area, 1911-24; date and place of death unknown. [khk]

Young, Richardson & Carleton (1956-67). Continuation of the successor firm to Schack, Young & Myers (see essay); also Schack & Young (1929-33), A. M. Young (1933-41), Young & Richardson (1941-50), Young, Richardson, Carleton & Detlie (1950-56; see Detlie entry); later The Richardson Associates (1967-77); now

TRA. Arrigo M. Young (February 19, 1884-June 27, 1954; see Schack, Young & Myers essay). Stephen Hinley Richardson (July 15, 1910-October 22, 1984); born in Ogden, Utah; arrived in Seattle in 1928; attended University of Washington; M.Arch., MIT, 1935; first worked for Young, 1936; became partner, 1941; retired from firm, 1970; died in Seattle. William Hodder Carleton (1908-August 25, 1984); born in South Prairie, Washington; spent childhood in Nome, Alaska; arrived in Seattle in 1919; attended Stanford University; degree in architecture University of Washington; joined firm, 1946; became partner, 1950; retired from firm, 1974; died in Seattle. The firm designed Seattle Parks Department headquarters (1948-49), Gaffney's Lake Wilderness Lodge, near Renton (1949-50), Terry Hall/Lander Hall, University of Washington, Seattle (1950-57), sanctuary addition to Saint Stephen Episcopal Church, Seattle (1956-57); Cathedral House/Bloedel Hall addition to Saint Mark Episcopal Cathedral, Seattle (1957-59), Group Health Cooperative Hospital, Seattle (1958-60), National Bank of Commerce, Renton (1960-61), Cascade Center, Bellevue (1962-63), concourse additions to Seattle-Tacoma International Airport (1963-65), State Office Building No. 2, Olympia (1973-75). [dar]

Zema, Gene K. (b. September 2, 1926). Born and raised in Sacramento Valley, California; B.Arch. University of Washington, 1950; worked briefly for local practitioners; independent practice mid-1950s to 1976, designed Zema Office and Gallery, Seattle (1961), Zema house, Seattle (1965), Wells-Medina Nursery, Medina (1968), Stephens house, Seattle (1970); co-designer (with Daniel Streissguth and others) of Gould Hall, University of Washington, Seattle (1970-72); closed practice 1976, established Japanese antiquities gallery; residing in Seattle and on Whidbey Island, 1993. [njj]

List of Non-Seattle Architects and Designers Who Did Significant Seattle Designs before 1980

This list is a partial catalogue, based on readily available information, of firms from outside Seattle who did significant Seattle architectural projects. As this is a historical guide, no projects after 1980 are listed.

Adler & Sullivan, Chicago: Seattle Opera House project, 1890-91 (unbuilt).

Bakewell & Brown, San Francisco: Saint Mark Episcopal Cathedral, 1926-30 (see Champney essay).

Belluschi, Pietro, Portland, Oregon: Harry W. Myers house, 1940-41 (as principal of A. E. Doyle & Associates); Seattle First National Bank headquarters (now 1001 Fourth Avenue Plaza) (as consultant to Naramore, Bain, Brady & Johanson).

Bogue, Virgil G., New York: Plan for Seattle, 1910-12.

Bradlee, Winslow & Wetherell, Boston: Boston Block, 1887-88 (destroyed; with Boone & Meeker).

Clark & McInnes, Aberdeen, Washington: Church of the Immaculate Conception, 1904-5.

Crapsey & Lamb, Cincinnati: First Presbyterian Church, 1906-8 (destroyed).

Dunham, George Foote, Portland, Oregon: Fourth Church of Christ Scientist, 1914-22; Third Church of Christ Scientist, 1919-23.

Eames & Young, St. Louis: Alaska Building, 1903-4 (with Saunders & Lawton); New Washington Hotel (now Josephinum), 1906-8.

Erickson, Arthur, Vancouver, B.C.: Bagley Wright house, The Highlands, 1977-81; Harbor Steps, 1980-94(?) (with the Callison Partnership and David Hewitt).

Fulton, John C., Uniontown, Pennsylvania: First Methodist Protestant Church (now offices of Arai/Jaskson Architects & Planners), 1905-7.

Gaggin & Gaggin, Syracuse, New York: Smith Tower, 1910-14.

Halprin, Lawrence, San Francisco: Freeway Park, 1974-76 (with Sakuma James Peterson Landscape Architects).

Hamhill, Harold B., New York: Woolworth's store building, 1939-40.

Heath, Gove & Bell, Tacoma: William L. Rhodes house, 1906-8 (as Heath & Twitchell); A. V. Love Dry Goods & Loft Building, 1925; Thomson Hall, University of Washington, 1946-48; Communications Building, University of Washington, 1950-51, 1955-56.

Heins & LaFarge, New York: Saint James Catholic Cathedral, 1903-7 (see Somervell & Coté essay).

Hobart, Lewis, San Francisco: D. E. Fredericks house, The Highlands, 1931.

Hornblower & Marshall, Washington, D.C.: Samuel Hill house, 1908-9.

Howard & Galloway (John Galen Howard), San Francisco: Alaska-Yukon-Pacific Exposition, 1908-9 (destroyed) (supervising architects); Architecture Hall (Fine Arts Palace, AYP Exposition),

University of Washington, 1906-9; Meany Hall (Auditorium Building, AYP Exposition), University of Washington, 1906-9 (destroyed).

Howells & Stokes, New York: Metropolitan Tract plan, 1907-12; White-Henry-Stuart Building, 1907-15 (destroyed); Cobb Building, 1909-10; Metropolitan Theater, 1910-11 (destroyed).

Jennings, A. B., New York: Denny Hotel, 1889-93? (destroyed).

Kirby & Randall, Syracuse, New York: George Kinnear house, 1886-88 (destroyed, 1958).

Kleemer, Otto, Portland, Oregon: Addition to Occidental Hotel, 1887-88 (destroyed).

Lockwood-Greene Company, New York: Post-Intelligencer Building, 1947-48 (with Henry Bittman, see essay).

Matthews, Edgar, San Francisco: Chappel house, 1906.

McCammon, J. N., Associates, Dallas: Seattle Municipal Building, 1959-61 (with Damm, Daum & Associates).

Mellor & Meigs, Philadelphia: Phi Gamma Delta Sorority House, 1928-29 (with J. Lister Holmes, see essay).

Mies van der Rohe, Ludwig, Chicago: KING Broadcasting Company Building project (Portage Bay site), 1967 (unbuilt).

Mitchell/Guirgola Associates, Philadelphia: Condon Hall, University of Washington, 1971-74 (with Joyce, Copeland, Vaughn & Nordfors); Westlake Center project, 1976-78 (unbuilt).

Olmsted Brothers, Brookline, Massachusetts: Parks and boulevards plan, 1903; University of Washington plan, 1904; John and Eliza Leary estate, 1904-7; Alaska-Yukon-Pacific Exposition plan, 1906-9; The Highlands subdivision, 1908-9; Fort Lawton Improvement Report, 1910; perhaps as many as 100 additional projects (list available at UW Special Collections).

Orr, Robert H., Los Angeles: Westminster Presbyterian Church, 1920-23; First Christian Church, 1922-23.

Palliser & Palliser, New York: M. J. Carkeek house, 1885 (destroyed).

Platt, Charles, New York: R. D. Merrill house, 1908-9 (with Carl F. Gould); Thomas D. Stimson house, The Highlands, 1923-27.

Post, George B., & Sons, New York: Olympic Hotel, 1922-24 (with Bebb & Gould).

Rapp & Rapp, Chicago: Seattle (Paramount) Theater, 1926-28 (with Priteca & Peters; see Priteca essay).

Reed & Stem, St. Paul: King Street Station, 1904-6 (interior altered).

Roth, Emery & Sons, New York: Logan Building, 1957-59 (as consultants to Mandeville & Berge).

Simon, Louis A., Washington, D.C.: Federal Courthouse, 1939-40 (with Gilbert Stanley Underwood, Los Angeles).

Skidmore, Owings & Merrill (SOM), San Francisco: Norton Building, 1956-59 (with Bindon & Wright); Nordstrom Department Store, 1971-74 (with Roland Terry & Associates, see essay).

Sturgis, R. Clipson, Boston: F. H. Osgood house, 1903.

Taylor, James Knox, Washington, D.C.: Federal Building (old Post Office), 1903-8 (destroyed).

3-D International, Houston: Seafirst Fifth Avenue Plaza, 1978-81.

Van Norman, Charles B. K., Vancouver, B.C.: Tower 801 Apartments, 1969.

Walker & McGough, Spokane: Kane Hall, University of Washington, 1966-71.

Weber, Peter J., Chicago: Seattle Public Library, 1903-6 (destroyed).

Wetmore, James A., Washington, D.C.: Federal Office Building, 1931-33.

Whitehouse & Price, Spokane: Art Building, University of Washington, 1947-48; Music Building, University of Washington, 1947-50.

Williams, Warren H., Portland, Oregon: First Baptist Church, 1878 (destroyed); James McNaught house, 1883-84 (destroyed).

Wright, Frank Lloyd, Chicago/Spring Green/Scottsdale: Hotel project, 1894 (unbuilt); Jay E. Roberts house, 1955 (unbuilt); (three houses in the region outside Seattle)

Yamasaki, Minoru, & Associates, Troy, Michigan: U.S. Science Pavilion, Century 21 Exposition (Pacific Science Center), 1959-62(with Naramore, Bain, Brady & Johanson); IBM Building, 1962-64 (with Naramore, Bain, Brady & Johanson); Rainier Tower and Rainier Square, 1973-78 (with Naramore, Bain, Brady & Johanson).

Researching Seattle's Architectural Past

DAVID A. RASH

Research into the history of Seattle's architecture can be very rewarding, but it can also sometimes be tedious and time-consuming. Although the history of Euro-American settlement in Seattle began less than 150 years ago, and it would seem that information should be easily accessible, resources are often scattered and some kinds of information are not readily available.

Because there has been relatively limited research on Seattle's architectural history to date, a strong body of fundamental factual information has not been gathered and published and a coherent analytical framework has not yet emerged. The situation has been further confused because some published guidebooks and other popular accounts include information that is in error in matters of attribution or dating of architectural works. Others have apparently depended on a limited set of sources so that the resulting accounts have inadvertently repeated the biases inherent in those particular sources.

This discussion of architectural research in Seattle focuses on the available resources and how they may be accessed by those pursuing architectural research. As can be seen from the "Sources of Information" appendix in this book, a wide variety of sources are available for documenting architectural design in the Pacific Northwest in general and Seattle in particular. Some of the resources are useful to research the career of a specific practitioner; others are appropriate for research over selected periods; still others are more general in nature. Surprisingly, some resources may be found only outside this region, although most are available locally. While some nonlocal resources are discussed here as appropriate, it is impossible to include all such sources, or even to catalogue them.

Conceptually, historical sources can be divided into two broad categories—primary and secondary. As defined by Harry Ritter in *Dictionary of Concepts in History* (Westport, Conn., 1986), primary sources are generally those providing eyewitness testimony or based on eyewitness testimony; a simpler view is that a primary source is any evidence which is contemporary with the subject being investigated. Secondary sources are those derived from primary sources. They are usually not contemporary with the subject being investigated. Typical examples of secondary sources include articles in scholarly journals or other periodicals, monographs on particular architects or firms, studies of particular architectural styles, periods, geographic areas, or specific building types, and also biographies.

Because they are derivative, secondary sources are generally considered to be less reliable, and all historical investigations should be based, insofar as is possible, on primary sources. Nonetheless, one must also recognize that not all primary sources are equally reliable, as noted by John Tosh in *The Pursuit of History* (London, 1991). For this reason, the discussion in this appendix subdivides primary sources into the following subcategories: original primary sources, contemporary primary sources, noncontemporary primary sources, constructed (usually extant) buildings, and photographs. Original primary sources include those documents that were generated during the process of realizing an architectural design, whether or not it was actually constructed; these include architectural drawings, specifications, construction contracts, building permits, project correspondence and other office records, and even contemporary papers of designers or clients, as well as death certificates, census records, and other similar government records. Contemporary primary sources are typically published accounts that are contemporary with the design and/or construction of an architectural project or career; these include articles published in local newspapers and various trade journals, bid notices and similar "building intelligence," postconstruction reports, city and telephone directories, fire insurance maps, plat maps, and other similar documents. Noncontemporary primary sources are typically published accounts, but they are *not* contemporary with individual projects; these generally include autobiographies and obituaries. Constructed buildings and photographs are treated separately because they exist independent (in a sense) of any specific time reference. Secondary sources are not further subdivided in this appendix; however, differences among various types of secondary sources are recognized and discussed.

Primary Sources: Original

Original primary sources are generally considered the most reliable and objective source materials. But this still depends on the specific type of original primary source. Correspondence will generally reflect the writer's point of view, as will personal papers such as diaries. Architectural drawings do not always reflect the building as actually constructed. Building permits, while not subject to personal bias, may fail to represent the building as constructed or may omit or misstate pertinent facts (for example true street address, all relevant individuals and/or firms involved, actual costs, and so forth), or even if the building was actually constructed.

Architectural drawings are one of the most useful sources for documenting and understanding a building. But they are often not available, especially for buildings dating to the nineteenth century. Unfortunately, architectural drawings have frequently been deemed of little value once the building has been constructed (or, even more frequently, if it has been destroyed). Further, once an architect retired or died or a firm dissolved, drawings and other records have frequently been lost. Organizations (other than surviving firms or clients) that may have drawings relevant to Seattle architects and architecture include the Special Collections and Preservation Division of the University of Washington Libraries (hereafter UW Special Collections), the City of Seattle Department of Construction and Land Use (DCLU), the Museum of History and Industry in Seattle, and the Eastern Washington State Historical Museum in Spokane (primarily the K. K. Cutter Collection). In addition, the Seattle School District, a surviving public client, holds an extensive collection of drawings for Seattle schools. Of these repositories, DCLU and UW Special Collections have the most extensive collections and tend to be the most useful for the researcher.

As part of the Seattle city government, DCLU has drawings on microfiche pertinent only to those buildings for which building permits were sought. Drawings for residential construction, including some multifamily projects, were not retained until the 1980s. Drawings for nonresidential construction may also be missing from DCLU records prior to the 1930s. But some drawings do survive from the earlier periods, and a routine check for projects at DCLU should be a typical part of an architectural research project.

Architectural drawings at UW Special Collections are generally organized by individual architect or architectural firms and limited to those whose practices were in western Washington. Since many local practitioners had work outside Seattle, individual collections may contain drawings covering a wide area while concentrating on the Puget Sound region. Occasionally, the individual collections may include works by other architects, usually as a result of one architect altering or renovating the earlier work of another. Although indexes and inventory lists are usually available for the various collections, these indexes are sometimes incomplete. (Recently, however, efforts have been made to create an architectural records database at UW Special Collections. At present this database contains more than four thousand projects from more than forty architects and can be searched by building type, city, street address, client, architect, date, and a few other categories.)

The building permit process for the City of Seattle traces its history back to the fire of June 6, 1889. Theoretically, it should be possible to locate a permit for every building constructed since 1890; in practice this ideal is not achievable. Although the city has microfilmed all permits ever issued that are still extant, some microfilm has been lost over the years and the original permits can be viewed only by special permission. Another difficulty facing the researcher is that permits are issued in numerical sequence (as well as microfilmed in numerical sequence), and not all of them have been cross-referenced to street addresses. For nonresidential construction, some permits have been cross-referenced as early as the 1890s; cross-referencing is more complete after 1910. For residential construction, cross-referencing occurs with some regularity after World War II. The cross-referencing that does exist is based on the current legal street address, which is not always the current street address in use or the street address listed on the building permit when originally issued. This can be particularly confusing when street names have been changed over time. Nonetheless, while searching permit histories can be time-consuming, permits are usually one of the most accurate sources for both building attributions and dates of construction, and thus are an essential tool for the researcher.

As the permitting process has evolved, additional permits beyond the original building permit have become required. These include permits for electrical systems, mechanical systems including plumbing, and, most recently, land use. Until recently, these additional permits were rarely cross-referenced to street addresses. In addition, at some point the city's building inspectors began filing formal reports as to whether a building was being constructed in compliance with the permit and plans on file; these reports were generally not attached to the permit record until after World War I. (Curiously, stables for horses, and presumably cows as well, required a letter of certification from the city's Heath Department before a permit would be issued; similar structures for chickens and other animals required no such certification, at least while such structures were allowed within the city limits.)

Project correspondence can be an extremely valuable source for following a project from imagined possibility to constructed reality. Unfortunately, it rarely survives. Detailed project correspondence was most frequently generated when the architect or client lived in another city. Surviving firms or family members of either architects or their clients are the most likely private repositories for such correspondence. In the public domain, the Historical Society of Seattle at the Museum of History and Industry, the Manuscripts and Archives Division of the University of Washington, and the Washington State Historical Society in Tacoma are the most likely repositories containing material related to Seattle architecture. There may also be some materials in the Division of Manuscripts, Archives and Special Collections of the Washington State University Libraries in Pullman.

Death certificates are helpful in providing primary biographical information. In addition to giving a person's date and place of death, they usually also include date and place of birth, name of spouse or closest living kin, names of parents, occupation, and similar data. Although generally correct, such supplemental information is usually furnished by the closest surviving kin, and mistakes can occur. In Washington, death certificates previous to 1907 must be obtained from the individual county where the death occurred. After 1907, death certificates can be obtained from: Vital Records, Center for Health Statistics, P.O. Box 9709, Olympia WA 98507-9709. (Each request for a certificate requires the name of the person at the time of death, the approximate date of death, and the place of death by city or county. A fee for this service is required with each request.)

Also useful for biographical information are the U.S. census records. Profitable use is predicated on knowing the location of a given individual at the time of the decennial census. In Seattle, from 1890 on, the increasingly numerous local population does tend to make these records intimidating if one is tracing a single individual. One might consider consulting the Genealogical Department at the downtown Seattle Public Library for specific suggestions regarding specific individuals. (In addition, at the time this book was published, census records had been released only through 1920. Because census records are sealed for seventy-two years, the 1930 census will not be available until the year 2002.)

Primary Sources: Contemporary

In general, contemporary primary sources are less reliable than original primary sources, but they are more numerous and are more likely to have survived and be accessible to the researcher. The most common problem in contemporary primary sources is the potential for publication errors, including misspelled names, inaccurate attributions, and the lack of reportage

of subsequent progress or changes in a given project. One distinct advantage of contemporary primary sources is that they provide a contextual frame of reference that original primary sources alone rarely offer.

Nineteenth Century: For nineteenth-century architecture in Seattle, the most useful contemporary primary sources are the local newspapers. In that period, new construction was significant news and was frequently reported. The *Seattle Post-Intelligencer* and its predecessor, *The Weekly Intelligencer,* provide the earliest extant coverage, beginning in 1876; however, the newspaper's record copies of the period from December 4, 1880, to June 8, 1881, and from October 2, 1881, to April 4, 1882, were destroyed in the fire of June 6, 1889. Published copies of the *Seattle Times* are generally not available prior to 1889, while other newspapers such as the *Seattle Herald* or *Seattle Telegraph* have survived with only intermittent issues available. A similar difficulty faces the researcher seeking information about work by Seattle architects in cities and towns in the region outside Seattle: many small-town newspapers survive only in incomplete runs if at all. In Seattle, the Microforms and Newspapers Division of the University of Washington Libraries has the most complete available series of Seattle and regional newspapers on microfilm. The downtown Seattle Public Library has complete microfilm runs for only the *Seattle Post-Intelligencer* and the *Seattle Times.* Elsewhere, Holland Library of Washington State University in Pullman has an excellent collection of eastern Washington newspapers on microfilm, and the Washington State Library in Olympia has perhaps the most complete statewide collection of newspapers on microfilm.

Although illustrated professional architectural journals appeared in the United States after the Civil War, the relatively undeveloped state of the architectural profession in Washington during the nineteenth century meant that coverage of Seattle architecture was limited and sketchy. The first regularly appearing national professional journal, *American Architect and Building News,* based in Boston, began publication in 1876. Although it covered architecture nationally, in its early years it emphasized the work of eastern architects. Subsequently, other illustrated professional journals appeared, including *California Architect and Building News* (San Francisco, 1879); *Inland Architect and Building News*—later *Inland Architect and News Record* (Chicago, 1883); *Northwestern Architect and Improvement Record*—later *Northwestern Architect and Building Budget* (Minneapolis, 1883); and others based in Cincinnati, Denver, Milwaukee, St. Louis, and Atlanta. Publication of architectural journals in the nineteenth century was often a marginal proposition. They appeared and disappeared; some were bought and sold repeatedly, changed titles, or were merged out of existence. The depression that began in 1893 seems to have been particularly hard on architectural periodicals. Only a few that were available in 1890 were still being published after 1900. Some of the journals of this period have been indexed by the Avery Library of Columbia University in *The Avery Guide to Architectural Periodical Literature.* However, indexing prior to 1900 is incomplete and a search for illustrations should include a physical search of the journals themselves.

Seattle buildings began to appear as illustrations in architectural journals after 1889. *American Architect and Building News* carried illustrations of Seattle buildings in the 1890s. Copies are available at both the Architecture and Urban Planning Library at the University of Washington and the Art Department of the Seattle Public Library; the latter set is more complete. *Inland Architect, California Architect,* and *Northwestern Architect* all provided some coverage of Pacific Northwest architecture in the late

nineteenth century. Both *California Architect* and *Inland Architect* are available locally on microfilm at the Architecture and Urban Planning Library of the University of Washington. (Unfortunately the *Inland Architect* microfilms do not include a complete set of plates.) Minneapolis-based *Northwestern Architect* published a surprising number of illustrations of Seattle architecture and also occasionally carried Seattle "building intelligence" (reports of bid awards, construction, and the like). However, it is the most difficult of these journals to use, as it cannot now be found in the Pacific Northwest. A complete run does not survive in any library in the United States, nor do surviving partial runs make up a complete run. Partial runs can be found at the Minnesota Historical Society (St. Paul), the Art Institute of Chicago, and the Library of Congress.

Some of the local or regional magazines that provide useful information include *The West Shore* (1875-91), *Smalley's Magazine/The Northwest: Illustrated Monthly Magazine* (1883-1903), and *The Washington Magazine/The Pacific Magazine* (1889-92). These magazines tend to extol the virtues of the region to an extreme degree, while rarely mentioning less desirable aspects. The emphasis on the development potential of the region has provided one lasting benefit. Some of the illustrations in these magazine are the only available illustrative material for now lost structures, while others provide a useful means for dating available photography. Although UW Special Collections has copies of these magazines, both *The West Shore* and *Smalley's Magazine/The Northwest* are on microfilm at the University of Washington Libraries, and this is the preferred format for using these materials, due to their increasing fragility. The downtown Seattle Public Library also has microfilm copies of *The West Shore* and original copies of *The Washington Magazine/The Pacific Magazine.*

One very valuable resource for documenting changes to urban environments in the United States is the collection of fire insurance maps created by the Sanborn Map Company from the mid-nineteenth to the mid-twentieth century. These maps can provide significant information regarding the condition of a given building at the time the maps were drawn, as well as how the building has been altered over time. (An excellent overview of the usefulness of these maps can be found in Kim Keister, "Charts of Change," *Historic Preservation* 45 [May/June 1993]: 42-49, 91-92.) Locally, UW Special Collections has the 1888 Seattle volume and most of the 1916-19 five-volume set for Seattle; the Microforms and Newspapers Division of the University of Washington Libraries has the available microfilm collections for Washington, Oregon, and Idaho.

Although plat maps provide less detailed information than the Sanborn maps, they can be used to track the growth of a given city. They also allow one to identify the legal description of a property, which is sometimes essential in confirming the applicability of a particular building permit to a particular street address. The downtown Seattle Public Library has a current set of Kroll Map Company's plat maps for King County as part of its maps collection. UW Special Collections has a number of historical volumes of *Kroll's Atlas of Seattle, Washington,* dating to ca. 1912, as well as current volumes. The 1905, 1908, and 1912 editions of *Baist's Real Estate Atlas: Surveys of Seattle, Washington* (Philadelphia) can be found at UW Special Collections as well.

The annual editions of local city directories, as published by R. L. Polk and Company, for example, tend to be a useful source for tracking individuals on a yearly basis. Aside from providing addresses, city directories often have specific information regarding occupational status and, less frequently, spousal identification. Like many recent telephone directories, city directories have historically had two principal subdivi-

sions, the alphabetical "personal" listings (including businesses similar to the "white pages") and the classified business listings (similar to the "yellow pages"). City directories often also include a list of public buildings and a street guide; this may be helpful in identifying changed street names. Telephone directories can also be used to track individuals, but they generally provide less supplementary information. Both types of directories can be used for establishing an approximate date of completion for various architectural projects. UW Special Collections probably has the best regional collection of locally available city directories for the nineteenth century, while the downtown Seattle Public Library is better for the twentieth century; the Seattle Public Library's collection is limited to Washington State localities plus Portland, Oregon, but also includes some historical telephone directories. UW Special Collections also has a collection of regional telephone directories. (A list of architects and landscape architects in Seattle, extracted from the city directories through 1959 and compiled by Duane Dietz, is available at UW Special Collections.)

If an architect who is the subject of research happened to join the local chapter of the American Institute of Architects, then a perusal of the historical records of the chapter should be made. The local AIA chapter was founded as the Washington State Chapter in 1894. Initially it included members from the entire state. Later, as individual cities and regions established independent chapters, the "Washington State Chapter" came to focus primarily on Seattle. In 1961, its name was changed to Seattle Chapter AIA (and today the preferred name is AIA Seattle). Records of the Washington State Chapter are in the Manuscripts and Archives Division of the University of Washington Libraries. The membership application forms generally provide limited biographical information, educational background, and a brief professional resume. The *Monthly Bulletin* issued by the chapter can be found in UW Special Collections, and reflects the activities of the organization. (Since the chapter was founded in 1894, these materials are most useful for the twentieth century.)

Twentieth Century: For documenting twentieth-century architecture, the variety of locally available contemporary primary sources is greater than for the nineteenth century. In addition, twentieth-century contemporary primary sources are increasingly indexed, although rarely to the degree that the researcher of architectural history will desire. UW Special Collections maintains an extensive card catalogue, the Pacific Northwest Regional Newspaper and Periodical Index, which can provide citations for various subjects within its own collections, including its newspaper clipping files, Architects' Reference File, and its scrapbook collection, as well as selected periodicals. For buildings, these citations are frequently to more recent secondary sources, rather than contemporary primary sources. For individuals, these citations are usually to published biographical sketches or obituaries. The UW Special Collections also has a series of bound typewritten indexes to the *University of Washington Daily*, which can provide citations to major articles concerning campus buildings and events from about 1900 to World War II.

The Art Department of the Seattle Public Library also maintains card catalogues of interest, but of more limited scope. One catalogue can provide citations to significant articles on local buildings published in journals like *Pacific Builder and Engineer* (principally) or *Inland Architect* and *Western Architect* (occasionally). Another more extensive catalogue exists for the series of art scrapbooks that the Art Department has developed for both architects and buildings; these scrapbooks tend to be most useful for subjects after World War II and consist mostly of clippings from the *Seattle Post-Intelligencer* and *Seattle Times*. In addition to the scrapbooks, the Art Department has a series of folders, alphabetized by the last names of selected architects, in its Northwest Regional Vertical File, which is most useful for the post-World War II era.

While these indexes and catalogues can be useful in obtaining general information, the detailed information necessary to reconstruct the history of an architectural career or a specific building will almost always require a direct search of material not currently indexed. As with the nineteenth century, the most readily available and potentially useful materials for research are the contemporary newspapers and trade journals.

From the turn of the twentieth century to the present, the single best source for information regarding local construction is the *Seattle Daily Journal of Commerce.* This newspaper traces its roots back to 1893 as *The Daily Bulletin.* Then, as now, this newspaper published official city notices; however, it was not until the late 1890s that it consistently published city building permit intelligence or provided coverage concerning local construction news. This paper can be reviewed on microfilm at the Microforms and Newspapers Division of the University of Washington Libraries. (The years 1907 through 1910 are missing from the UW microfilm collection. However, the Microforms and Newspapers Division does have a partial run of the *Seattle Daily Record,* beginning with October 12, 1908, which contains much of the same factual information. The *Record* was eventually absorbed into the *Journal of Commerce.* In addition, Seattle Public Library does have microfilm of the these years of the *Bulletin/Journal of Commerce.*)

In the twentieth century, the local general daily newspapers, such as the *Seattle Post-Intelligencer, Seattle Times,* or the *Seattle Star,* can also provide some useful information. Architectural reporting, however, tended to be limited to the Sunday real estate pages and most often favored larger "news-worthy" projects, such as downtown office buildings, major institutional construction, and public works.

A number of regional architectural journals were published prior to World War II which can provide documentary and pictorial information. As in the nineteenth century, the publication of a regional journal has proved a sometimes difficult proposition, so such journals tend to have limited runs and to change names frequently. The Art Department of the Seattle Public Library has partial runs of *Architect and Engineer/Western Architect and Engineer, Architecture and Building Edition/Pacific Architect and Builder/Architecture West, Bungalow Magazine, The Northwest Architect, The Pacific Coast Architect/California Arts and Architecture, Washington State Architect,* and *Western Architect.* At the University of Washington, incomplete runs of *Pacific Coast Architect* (1911-13) can be found at UW Special Collections, and *Western Architect* (1905-31) can be found at the Architecture and Urban Planning Library. Each of these journals provided more coverage of Seattle work than national architectural journals, but each also focused primarily on the locality in which it was published.

The *Washington State Architect* was published in Seattle as the official organ of the former Washington State Society of Architects (a separate organization from the AIA), and, as such, tended to concern itself with the professional activities of the organization rather than individual practitioners. During the late 1920s, it did publish some building intelligence, as well as some illustration of work by members. Incomplete runs can be found at the Art Department of the downtown Seattle Public Library and at the Architecture Branch of the Washington State University Libraries in Pullman.

Although *Pacific Builder and Engineer* (originally *Pacific Record*) was, and continues to be, more of a construction trade journal than an architectural journal, its place of origin was, fortunately, Seattle. From its inception in 1903 until 1916, it provided the best *regional* summary of building intelligence available, not only for Seattle, but also for Portland, Tacoma, and, to a lesser degree, other areas in Washington, Oregon, Idaho, and British Columbia. In 1916, it discontinued its publication of building intelligence for six months in favor of more feature articles; when publication of building intelligence resumed in July 1916, the quality of reportage was markedly lower. Copies of this journal can be found at UW Special Collections or requested from the Newspapers, Magazines and Government Publications Desk of the downtown Seattle Public Library. (Insofar as the weekly building intelligence is concerned, the copies at UW Special Collections appear to be more complete from 1904 through 1907, while copies at Seattle Public Library are more complete from 1906 through 1915.)

Other local periodicals that may be useful, more for their pictorial information than their documentary information, include *Argus* (1894-1984), *Commonwealth* (1902-5), *Seattle Mail and Herald* (1896-1907), and *The Town Crier* (1910-37). UW Special Collections has limited runs of *Commonwealth* and *Seattle Mail and Herald,* as well as complete runs of *Argus* and *The Town Crier.* These periodicals (except *Commonwealth*) are also available on microfilm at the University of Washington Libraries.

Since 1900, national professional architectural journals have generally been more stable. For example, *Architectural Record* began publication in 1891 and continues today. *Progressive Architecture* began as *Pencil Points,* a journal for draftsmen, in 1920 (the name was changed in 1946). However, *American Architect and Building News*— later *American Architect*—did not survive the Depression, and *Architectural Forum,* which began publication in 1892 as *The Brickbuilder,* came to an end in 1974. These national journals featured Seattle architecture occasionally and can be useful for pictorial evidence and building descriptions. Accurate dating of buildings, however, is rarely possible from these journals. A search of such periodicals can begin using the *Avery Guide* and can proceed using the journals' own annual (or for some journals, semiannual) indexes, before one actually proceeds with a physical search of individual issues. Very occasionally, assessments of Pacific Northwest architectural achievement appeared in national journals. These can be useful as summaries of the current state of work in the region and can offer a contemporary context for more focused research. Two of the more frequently consulted assessments are: Herbert Croly, "The Building of Seattle: A City of Great Architectural Promise," *Architectural Record* 32 (July 1912): 1-21 (which offered a summary of Seattle's architectural progress as seen by an eastern critic); and "Architecture of the Northwest," *Architectural Record* 113 (April 1953): 134-46 (on the question of regionalism in Pacific Northwest architecture). (Because these general articles tend to be derivative, they probably should be considered secondary rather than primary sources.)

Primary Sources: Noncontemporary

The principal difference between contemporary primary and noncontemporary primary sources, as the nomenclature implies, is the passage of time. As stated near the beginning of this discussion, sources which recorded eyewitness testimony, or which were based on eyewitness testimony, have traditionally been considered primary sources, at least in a conceptual sense. In a pragmatic sense, with regard to accuracy and reliability, eyewitness testimony that is not contemporary with recorded events often has serious errors of fact. In architec-

tural history this seems particularly true with regard to project dates and attribution of designs. Certain facts and documents can become forgotten, lost, or destroyed long before their importance is recognized, even by an architect who has recognized that his or her career may be sufficiently meritorious to recommend an autobiographical record for posterity. Additionally, as noted with regard to sources such as project correspondence or personal diaries, an autobiographical record will invariably reflect the writer's point of view. Thus, noncontemporary sources that are still categorized as primary must nonetheless be used with special care.

In comparison to contemporary primary sources, or even original primary sources, there are relatively few noncontemporary primary sources available regarding Seattle architects or architecture aside from obituaries.

If one limits autobiographical writing to the traditional account of one's own lifestory, then there are few such works by local architects, except for those published in conjunction with various subscription histories that were popular prior to World War II. The subscription histories themselves are classified as secondary sources by most researchers, and, for the sake of convenience, are discussed in this appendix as such. One example of an autobiography of a Seattle architect is John Parkinson's *Incidents by the Way* (Los Angeles, 1935). Since this was prepared almost forty years after Parkinson left the region, apparently from personal recollections, the information on his Seattle career is lacking in detail and inexact in dating; much of it cannot be verified from other contemporary sources. Other autobiographical accounts may also suffer from similar difficulties.

The question of autobiographies has been complicated by the recent appearance of the "as told to" account. For example, Steve Lambert's *Built by Anhalt: A Biography* ([Seattle?], 1982) is Lambert's transcription of audio tapes recorded by Fred Anhalt, and is written as a first-person singular narrative; thus, although titled a biography, the account is in fact autobiographical. While the book is valuable for the picture it provides of Anhalt and his times, the factual information, such as dates, chronology, attributions, construction costs, and so forth, deviates significantly from information available in contemporary primary sources. Thus, although autobiographical accounts are primary sources, the many errors often found in them are not unexpected if the writer has relied principally upon his or her own memory as the sole record on which to base accounts of noncontemporary events.

If the category of autobiographical writing is broadened to include accounts that architects have written regarding their own personal interests, then the extent of available autobiographical writing by local architects is much wider. Specific citations can be gleaned from the "Sources of Information" appendix. Cautions similar to those regarding traditional biographical writing should be observed for these writings as well; these writings are most valuable in ascertaining design philosophies and objectives important to the particular architect author.

Some historians consider obituaries to be primary evidence, since many obituaries are written by someone acquainted with the deceased person, often the next of kin. This is most commonly true when the obituary appears in a newspaper published in the locality where the deceased lived. Even with this stricture, the obituary is rarely more accurate than a death certificate in regard to factual information, and it often contains discrepancies similar to those found in autobiographical writing, since the author of the obituary is necessarily once removed from the anecdotal information the obituary may contain. Outside of the local newspapers, obituaries are often far more prone to errors. A typical example

that exemplifies the problem is the Edward O. Schwagerl obituary in the March 1910 issue of *The Northwest Architect*, where the funeral date is given as the death date.

Primary Sources: Constructed Buildings

To a large extent, the study of architectural history is the study of constructed buildings. Therefore, constructed buildings are among the most significant primary sources available to the architectural historian. Nonetheless, a caveat does exist regarding their use as sources for understanding architects' designs: Buildings tend to be regarded by users more as utilitarian objects than inviolate artistic creations; consequently, changes are often made to buildings over time. It is these changes which can lead to historical error.

In this book, authors have tended to emphasize new design work, but some examples of altered work have been included and these can illustrate the complexity of the issues involved in research. For example, the present King County Courthouse was originally designed by A. W. Gould beginning in 1912 and completed in 1916 (see A. W. Gould essay). While the original design that was published in the Seattle papers had twenty-three stories, including a central block crowned with a tower, only six stories were constructed initially. The building was expanded vertically to twelve stories in height during 1929-30, but the architect was Henry Bittman in association with John L. McCauley, not Gould (see Bittman essay); the new design was complementary to Gould's constructed project, but was not a faithful continuation of Gould's original design. During 1968-69, the building experienced major interior and exterior alterations. Recently, King County adopted a long-term plan to restore the building to its 1930 appearance. These changes can be traced because they are known from other sources. Were the building the only source available, it would be much more difficult, if not impossible, to ascertain the exact design sequence, or to attribute correctly the various portions of the design. Nonetheless, regardless of the later changes, the present King County Courthouse is still a useful source regarding Gould's work. The present height and massing do provide a general sense of the scale intended by his original design. The extant fabric of the base stories provides evidence of Gould's architectural embellishment program for the building.

When buildings have been altered, it is sometimes possible to recreate the original design, either graphically or by reconstituting the building fabric, even when a graphic record does not exist. This is most easily accomplished when the alterations have been minor and have been only modifications that are evident in the extant structure—changes in window or door locations, resurfacing of the exterior or interior finishes, and the like. Depending upon the nature of the alterations, recreation of the original design can sometimes be accomplished principally by a careful examination of the building fabric. However, such a recreation should be confirmed, whenever possible, by consulting available documentary evidence. If the alterations have been major, then other written and visual documentary evidence may provide the only means to determine the original configuration of the building. Without such evidence, the original form of the building will likely remain a matter of conjecture.

Primary Sources: Photographs

Photography is the one medium which most closely resembles, in two-dimensional form, a three-dimensional object, like a building. Therefore, photographs are an invaluable resource for the researcher in conveying an accurate description of a given building. This is especially critical if the building has been altered or destroyed, but, as with constructed buildings, one must be aware of the possibility that alterations may have been made between the time the building was completed and the time the photograph was taken. In this regard, it is essential that the photograph be reliably dated (either specifically from records or approximately from visual evidence), so that a time reference to the design can be successfully established. If there is no reliable date available, the photograph can still be quite useful, but the researcher should keep in mind the potential for future revisions or clarifications if new documentary or visual evidence is discovered.

An example of the difficulties that may arise is suggested by the illustration of the first Seattle Buddhist Church in the Charles W. Saunders essay on page 39. Even though this photograph was taken within four years of the completion of the structure by Saunders & Lawton, it does not illustrate the building as it was originally designed and built. South Main Street, the street fronting the site, was regraded between the completion of the building and the photograph, requiring the creation of a new entrance directly into the basement and the addition of stairs to the front porch. This gives the building a much more vertical appearance than originally intended. Unfortunately, an earlier photograph of this significant, but now destroyed, building has yet to be found. Similarly, the photograph of the Perry Apartments building in the Somervell & Coté essay on page 122 was taken within five years of the completion of the original structure, but does not faithfully illustrate the original design. By the time of the photograph, the building had been altered by the construction of a one-story lobby addition by Joseph S. Coté, in the original open-air entrance courtyard. The photograph does faithfully illustrate Coté's design for the addition. (Accurate dating of the photograph is possible due to its use, in the year it was taken, in advertisements by various suppliers of materials used in construction of the building.)

Repositories that hold significant general collections of photographs related to Seattle architecture include UW Special Collections, the Museum of History and Industry in Seattle, the Art Department of the downtown Seattle Public Library, and the Washington State Historical Society in Tacoma. At many of these repositories, photographs are divided among several collections. This is usually related to the origin of the photographs and the frequent desire or requirement that photographs taken by a single photographer or a collection assembled by a particular collector be retained intact. For example, among the photograph collections at the Museum of History and Industry are the Seattle Historical Society Collection and the PEMCO Webster & Stevens Collection, which are filed completely separately. As a result, the researcher will need to consult with the curators at each repository concerning the particular structure of the collections at that repository. The Seattle School District has a large collection of photographs related to school buildings. (Like architectural records, photographic records at UW Special Collections can increasingly be found in their growing computerized database, making it easier to locate a photograph regardless of the collection with which it is stored.)

Another important repository of photographs of Seattle buildings is the King County Regional Archives. In 1938, King County made an inventory and took photographs of all structures then standing in the county. Copies of the inventory cards, which were updated until 1973, and of the photographs are available on request. Researchers seeking photographs of an individual building should write to King County Regional Archives, 1809 S. 140th Street, Seattle WA 98168. To find a photograph of a particular structure the archivist needs the legal description of the property (lot, block, and plat numbers) or tax account numbers of the property. A photocopy of the "property card" is available for a nominal fee; a 5 x 7 or 8 x 10 inch print of the photograph can also be ordered. (Fees must be prepaid and may change from time to time, so the researcher should call the Archives to confirm charges.) A researcher who wishes to consult more than two cards should call the Archives and arrange an appointment.

Surprisingly, the Oregon Historical Society in Portland also has a large number of Washington photographs, including some for Seattle. The Oregon Historical Society mantains a card index file to its collections which is categorized by location and subject, making it relatively easy to determine if a photograph of a particular building or site is held. Nominal fees are charged for the use of the reference library where the card files are maintained, as well as for the reproduction of photographs.

Another photographic archive in the care of a public agency which may be useful is maintained by the City of Seattle Department of Engineering. The photographs in this archive are organized by streets, and the views are of the streets rather than buildings; however, buildings often are shown incidentally. The Department of Engineering will make photographic copies for a fee.

Secondary Sources

Although secondary sources are the most readily available to the general public, they are also the most likely to contain significant factual errors. This is not intended to depreciate their value (this book is itself a secondary source), but reflects the problems that arise with the passage of time. As noted for noncontemporary primary sources, certain facts and documents may be forgotten, lost, or destroyed long before their importance is realized. While a diligent researcher will attempt to recover as much information as possible prior to publication, some sources will inevitably be missed.

The most useful early secondary sources tend to be the various subscription histories, primarily for their biographical information. Examples include Julian Hawthorne and Col. G. Dougles Brewerton, *History of Washington, the Evergreen State* (New York, 1893), two volumes; *A Volume of Memoirs and Genealogy of Representative Citizens of the City of Seattle and County of King, Washington* (New York and Chicago, 1903); Clarence B. Bagley, *History of Seattle* (Chicago, 1916), three volumes; or Clarence B. Bagley, *History of King County* (Chicago, 1929), four volumes. Although the biographical information contained within each was typically provided by the individual described, factual errors of some significance do occur (such as W. Marbury Somerville's claim to have graduated from Cornell University, in Bagley, *History of Seattle,* pp. 832-33—a claim which is not supported by the academic records available at Cornell).

Some of the early published booklets that are significant from the point of view of illustrative material include: *Seattle Illustrated* (Seattle, 1889); *Illustrated and Descriptive Book of Buildings by E. W. Houghton, Architect* (Seattle, 1902); M. Hume, *Seattle Architecturally* (Seattle, 1902); *The Work of Bebb and Mendel, Architects* (Seattle, 1906); *Seattle Architectural Club Yearbook* (Seattle, 1909, 1910); and Frank Calvert, ed., *Homes and Gardens of the Pacific Coast, Volume 1: Seattle* (Beaux Arts Village, Lake Washington, 1913). These can all be found at UW Special Collections, while *Seattle Illustrated* and *Homes and Gardens of the Pacific Coast, Volume I: Seattle* can also be found at the Seattle Public Library. (As recently as 1988, the latter was republished by the Queen Anne Historical Society, and copies may still be available.) In addition, the Portland (Oregon) Architectural Club also published a yearbook during the 1900s based on its annual exhibition begun in 1908, which usually included work by Seattle architects; however, the researcher will need to consult the Portland Public Library for available copies, although UW Special Collections does have copies of the 1908, 1909, and 1913 editions.

Seattle was also the site of publication of a number of plan books, especially for residential architecture, during the early twentieth century. These are discussed in detail in the essay in this volume titled "Pattern Books, Plan Books, Periodicals." The downtown Seattle Public Library is the best source for plan books, including the locally issued Victor W. Voorhees, *Western Home Builder* (Seattle, 1911), and E. Ellsworth Green, *Practical Plan Book* (Seattle, 1912). UW Special Collections has a more limited selection of plan books, as well as two periodicals, *The Coast* (1901-11) and *The Westerner* (1905-14), which frequently included plans and articles, often with home building advice. (UW Special Collections also has a collection of suppliers' catalogues once used by local architects for specifying elements like window frames, chimney caps, custom glass, and so forth, which may be of interest to some researchers.)

Among the earliest, and still most common, approaches to presenting Seattle architecture to the general public in a more or less comprehensive fashion have been guidebooks of varying degrees of completeness and reliability. These include: Victor Steinbrueck, *A Guide to Seattle Architecture, 1850-1953* (New York, 1953); Sally B. Woodbridge and Roger Montgomery, *A Guide to Architecture in Washington State: An Environmental Perspective* (Seattle, 1980); Bob Peterson and Earl D. Layman, *The Sights of Seattle, Downtown: A Photographic Tour* (Seattle, 1981); and Caroline Tobin with Mary Randlett, *Downtown Seattle Walking Tours* (Seattle, 1985). Virtually all of these include errors of dating and attribution; they are most useful as a way to begin to learn about Seattle architecture.

A pioneering attempt at documenting Seattle's architectural heritage was Folke Nyberg and Victor Steinbrueck, *A Visual Inventory of Buildings and Urban Design Resources for Seattle, Washington* (Seattle, 1975-77), which resulted in a published report and sixteen neighborhood maps identifying, in a consistent manner, significant local buildings. Like many pioneering efforts, the report and maps contain factual errors. Still, this is useful in establishing a general context for appreciating and understanding Seattle's architectural fabric.

Other works that are also useful in a contextual sense include: Victor Steinbrueck, *Seattle Cityscape* (Seattle, 1962), *Seattle Cityscape #2* (Seattle, 1973), and *Market Sketchbook* (Seattle, 1968); Thomas Vaughan, ed., *Space, Style and Structure: Building in Northwest America* (Portland, 1974), two volumes; and Lawrence Kreisman, *Historic Preservation in Seattle* (Seattle, 1985). (Of these works, *Historic Preservation in Seattle,* which is based on the historic landmarks nominations forms, tends to be the most reliable.)

In recent years, several published works have dealt with local architecture. A partial list includes: Jim Stevenson, *Seattle Firehouses of the Horse Drawn and Early Motor Age* (Seattle, 1972); Lawrence Kreisman and Victor Gardaya, *Art Deco Seattle* (Seattle, 1979); Lila Gault and Mary Randlett, *The House Next Door: Seattle's Neighborhood Architecture* (Seattle, 1981); Steve Lambert, *Built by Anhalt: A Biography* ([Seattle?], 1982); Lawrence Kreisman, *West Queen Anne School: Renaissance of a Landmark* (Seattle, 1984); Lydia S. Aldredge, ed., *Impressions of Imagination: Terra-Cotta Seattle* (Seattle, 1986); Casey Rosenberg, *Streetcar Suburb: Architectural Roots of a Seattle Neighborhood* (Seattle, 1989); and Lawrence Kreisman, *The Stimson Legacy: Architecture in the Urban West* (Seattle, 1992). These publications vary widely in content and reliability and should be used with some caution.

Historical journals, like *Pacific Northwest Quarterly* or *Columbia: The Magazine of Northwest History,* generally present the most recent efforts in research and scholarship regarding Seattle and Pacific Northwest architecture. As for Seattle architecture in particular, one can find a great deal published, although most of it has appeared since 1980. Articles on Seattle architecture have also occasionally appeared in the *Journal of the Society of Architectural Historians.* Aside from the informational value of such articles, those in *Pacific Northwest Quarterly* and *Journal of the Society of Architectural Historians* almost always include footnotes. While primarily a scholarly tool for citing documents that support the information in the article, footnotes can provide invaluable leads to obscure sources of related interest that can often be otherwise difficult to find. (Footnotes can also be used by the researcher to gauge the reliability of the information presented in the text of the articles in these journals.)

Although the irregularly appearing Seattle architectural tabloid publication, *ARCADE: Northwest Journal for Architecture and Design,* focuses on architecture in general, not architectural history, it has occasionally included historical articles of widely varying quality and content.

The presence of the University of Washington in Seattle has resulted in some scholarly works on Seattle architects and architecture presented as academic theses. These can be found in the Architecture and Urban Planning Library (or, occasionally, in the Art Library, depending on the graduate program involved—architecture, urban planning, or art history). Like the journal articles noted above, academic theses are usually footnoted. In addition, in 1987, the Department of Architecture at the University of Washington initiated *Column 5,* an annual architectural journal with articles by faculty and students; this, too, has occasionally carried historical articles.

Finally, in addition to published secondary sources, two public agencies in Washington State have been involved with documentation of architecture in Seattle in conjunction with specific buildings or geographic districts of some significance. The Office of Archaeology and Historic Preservation of the Washington State Department of Community Development is responsible for the nominations that are made for listing on the National Register of Historic Places. The Office of Urban Conservation of the City of Seattle Department of Neighborhoods is responsible for the nomination of city landmark buildings and historic districts. Listing on the National Register and the city landmarking process requires formal documentation recorded on nomination forms. Although of uneven quality, these nomination forms can provide leads to sources of information specific to the subject being nominated, and they can provide some insight as to the state of research on local architectural history at the time the nomination was completed. Copies of these forms are generally available through the agency involved; these agencies may require the payment of fees to cover reproduction costs. Somewhat out-of-date lists of individual landmarks are readily available. The City of Seattle's list (as of 1985) is available in the form of "Appendix B: City of Seattle Landmarks," in Lawrence

Kreisman's *Historic Preservation in Seattle* (Seattle, 1985). A similar, but considerably older, list of state landmarks was published in Washington State Parks and Recreation Commission, *Preserving Washington's History: A Bicentennial Report* (Olympia, 1977). The state list was, unfortunately, not updated as part of the Washington State Office of Archaeology and Historic Preservation publication, *Built in Washington: 12,000 Years of Pacific Northwest Archaeological Sites and Historic Buildings* (Pullman, 1989).

Conclusion

This essay offers only a general introduction to sources for architectural history research in Seattle. For particular architects, periods, or buildings and building types, it is possible that there will be more specialized resources available.

The extraordinary variety of resources for architectural research can seem overwhelming, but for the researcher with patience and perseverance, there is a wealth of material available. Accessing the material may seem confusing or difficult, but at all of these repositories there are librarians and curators who can provide an introduction to their collections and who will have ideas about particular resources that might be consulted.

Contributors

Dennis Alan Andersen is a Lutheran clergyman. He was formerly in charge of photographs and architectural drawings at the University of Washington Libraries Special Collections Division, and is currently a member of the Seattle Landmarks Preservation Board, serving as its vice president in 1993-94 and its president in 1994-95. He has also authored or co-authored several articles on aspects of Seattle architecture.

Alexa Berlow received her Master of Urban Planning degree from the University of Washington in 1994. She also received Certificates of Specialization in Preservation Planning and in Urban Design.

T. William Booth graduated from Harvard University Graduate School of Design and began his career as an International Style architect. His Seattle-based practice includes residential projects expressing the traditions of Seattle and the Pacific Northwest. Booth is co-author with William H. Wilson of *Carl F. Gould: A Life in Architecture and the Arts* (Seattle, 1994).

Meredith L. Clausen is a professor in both the School of Art and the Department of Architecture at the University of Washington, teaching architectural history. She is author of *Frantz Jourdain and the Samaritaine: Art Nouveau Theory and Criticism* (Leyden, 1987), *Spiritual Space: The Religious Architecture of Pietro Belluschi* (Seattle, 1992), and *Pietro Belluschi: Modern American Architect* (Cambridge, MA, and London, 1994), as well as numerous articles.

Duane A. Dietz, a graduate of the University of Washington (B.A., English, 1988; B. Landscape Architecture, 1990), is a registered landscape architect currently working for Jones & Jones, Architects and Landscape Architects. He is compiling a reference guide, "Seattle Architects and Landscape Architects 1869-1959," and is also continuing his research on the careers of J. Lister Holmes and Butler S. Sturtevant.

Gail Lee Dubrow is an associate professor in the Department of Urban Design & Planning at the University of Washington, teaching preservation planning, vernacular architecture, and related subjects. She is also director of the Preservation Planning and Design Program in the College of Architecture and Urban Planning. She is the co-author, with Gail Nomura, of *The Historic Context for the Protection of Asian/Pacific American Resources in Washington* (Olympia, 1993), and author of *Planning for the Preservation of American Women's History* (New York, forthcoming).

Thomas J. Estep is employed by Gregory J. Bader Architects in Seattle. He has been active with the Seattle Architectural Foundation VIEWPOINTS tours program. He is an associate member of the AIA, and has written several articles on architecture in Seattle.

Jess M. Geissel, a native of Puyallup, received a B.A. in history from Western Washington University in 1981. He is an independent designer and historian based in Seattle.

Grant Hildebrand is a professor in the Department of Architecture at the University of Washington, where he has taught design and history since 1964. He received the university's Distinguished Teaching Award in 1975. He is also a registered and practicing architect. He is the author of *Designing for Industry: The Architecture of Albert Kahn* (Cambridge, MA, 1974) and *The Wright Space: Pattern and Meaning in Frank Lloyd Wright's Houses* (Seattle, 1991).

Norman J. Johnston is professor emeritus in the departments of Architecture, Landscape Architecture, and Urban Design and Planning at the University of Washington and a Fellow of the American Institute of Architects. He is author of *Cities in the Round* (Seattle, 1983) and *Washington's Audacious State Capitol and Its Builders* (Seattle, 1988), as well as multiple articles on the architectural and urban history of Washington State.

Katheryn Hills Krafft is a cultural resource specialist and former staff member of the City of Seattle, Division of Urban Conservation. Her interest in James Stephen grew out of her work on the documentation and rehabilitation of Summit and Interlake schools. Her involvement with historic preservation projects includes research on historic military posts, fire lookouts, courthouses, and schools. She recently completed the field work and documentation phase for a study of dairy barn design in the Snoqualmie River Valley.

David L. Leavengood practices architecture in Seattle and Montana and is a member of the AIA. While teaching at the School of Architecture at Montana State University in the early 1970s, he began researching the work of Robert C. Reamer. In 1985 he undertook the restoration of the Roosevelt Arch, a Reamer-designed stone gateway at the north entrance to Yellowstone National Park. He is currently completing a monograph on Reamer's life and work.

Henry Matthews, a native of England, received his degree in architecture at Cambridge University. He is a professor in the Department of Architecture at Washington State University, teaching architectural history and historic preservation. He is currently completing a monograph on Kirtland Cutter.

Esther Hall Mumford is a writer whose works include *Seattle's Black Victorians, 1852-1901* (Seattle, 1980), *The Man Who Founded a Town* (Seattle, 1989), and *Calabash: A Guide to the History, Culture, and Art of African Americans in Seattle and King County* (Seattle, 1993). She edited *Seven Stars and Orion: Reflections of the Past* (Seattle, 1985), and she is also the author of numerous essays, including, "African Americans in Washington State" in *Peoples of Washington* (Pullman, 1989).

Jeffrey Karl Ochsner is an assistant professor in the Department of Architecture at the University of Washington, teaching design, preservation, and architectural history. He is the author of *H. H. Richardson: Complete Architectural Works* (Cambridge, MA, and London, 1982). His articles on Pacific Northwest architecture have appeared in *Journal of the Society of Architectural Historians, Pacific Northwest Quarterly, Column 5* (student journal of the Department of Architecture), and *ARCADE.* He is also a registered architect and a member of the AIA.

Caterina (Rina) Provost completed her Master of Architecture at the University of Washington in 1992. Her undergraduate education includes a B.S. in Civil Engineering at Case Western Reserve University, Cleveland, and a B.A. from Duquesne University, Pittsburgh. She lives in Seattle, where she works as an architectural intern and design consultant. Her publications include "A Theatre in Purgatory: Can the Music Hall Be Saved?" *ARCADE* 10 (1990), and essays on the history of trusses in *Construction History Journal* and *Proceedings of the Canadian Society for Civil Engineering.*

David A. Rash is a project manager for Pacific Rainier Roofing, Inc., of Seattle. From 1990 through 1993, he served on the Special Task Force for Architectural Tours of the Seattle Architectural Foundation and developed script material for several VIEWPOINTS tours. He has written numerous articles on architecture in New York and Washington. In addition, he was curator of the exhibition "The Changing Face of Carpenter Hall" for the rededication of that building for the School of Architecture at Washington State University in 1992.

S. Sian Roberts received her B.S. from Haverford College in Haverford, Pennsylvania, and her M.Arch. from the University of Washington in 1992. She is a registered architect currently employed by the Miller/Hull partnership in Seattle.

Drew Rocker is an architect working for Zimmer Gunsul Frasca in Portland, Oregon. He received his M.Arch. at the University of Washington in 1989. His interest in Lionel Pries began when he encountered Pries's watercolors as a student volunteer in the Special Collections Division of the University of Washington Libraries.

Mary E. Shaughnessy is an architectural intern in Vancouver, B.C. She received her B.A. from Simon Fraser University in Burnaby, B.C., and her M.Arch with a Certificate in Preservation Planning and Design from the University of Washington in 1992. She was a contributor to the architectural guidebook *Exploring Vancouver* (Vancouver, B.C., 1993)

Cheryl Sjoblom currently serves as Director of Public Relations for the Sisters of Providence Health System, based in Seattle. In the past she has been a communications consultant and an editor with a publishing firm.

Miriam Sutermeister holds a degree, with concentration in architectural history, from the University of Washington. She has worked with Allied Arts of Seattle, the Washington Trust, and Historic Seattle, and was instrumental in saving the Olympic Hotel (now the Four Seasons Olympic) from demolition in the mid-1970s. Her interest in B. Marcus Priteca dates back to her study of his career for Seattle's Jewish Historical Society in 1982.

Wayne Suttles was born in Seattle, grew up in the Puget Sound region, and was the first to receive a Ph.D. in anthropology at the University of Washington. He has done ethnographic and linguistic research on the Northwest Coast and on Okinawa, and has taught at the University of British Columbia, the University of Nevada, and Portland State University. He is author of *Coast Salish Essays* (Vancouver, B.C., 1987) and editor of the Northwest Coast volume of the *Handbook of North American Indians* (Washington, D.C., 1990).

Thomas Veith is a graduate of the University of Washington (B.A.E.D., 1975; M.Arch., 1991) who currently practices as a designer in Seattle. In 1990 he was managing editor of *Column 5* (the student journal of the Department of Architecture). His M.Arch. thesis addressed the work of Arthur Loveless, and he is continuing his research on Loveless and other Seattle architects of the early twentieth century.

William H. Wilson received a Ph.D. in American history from the University of Missouri. He is Regents Professor of History at the University of North Texas, Denton. His most recent book is *The City Beautiful Movement* (Baltimore, 1989) and he is a co-author with T. William Booth of *Carl F. Gould: A Life in Architecture and the Arts* (Seattle, 1994).

Index

In addition to the Publishing Partners listed on the copyright page, grateful acknowledgment is made to the following for their contributions to the publication fund for this book:

Patrons

Anonymous
Baylis Brand Wagner Architects
The Bumgardner Architects
The Callison Partnership, Ltd.
Carolyn D. Geise FAIA
Fletcher Wright Construction
Richard Haag FASLA
Integrus Architecture
Norman J. Johnston FAIA
Mahlum & Nordfors McKinley Gordon
Paul Schell
Barnett Schorr FAIA
Thiry Foundation, in memory of Paul A. Thiry Sr.

With thanks

Fred Bassetti FAIA
Tom Bosworth FAIA
George Hanson AIA
Anne Gould Hauberg
David N. James AIA
Jones & Jones
Kelbaugh Calthorpe & Associates
Paul Hayden Kirk FAIA
Garold Malcolm AIA
John Morse FAIA Architect
Ibsen Nelsen FAIA
Stuart Silk Architects
Richard Youel AIA